Pure Act

# Pure Act

## THE UNCOMMON LIFE OF ROBERT LAX

*Michael N. McGregor*

FORDHAM UNIVERSITY PRESS
New York  2015

**Catholic Practice in North America**

Angela Alaimo O'Donnell and John C. Seitz, series editors

Fordham University Press has no responsibility for the persistence or accuracy of URLs for external or third-party Internet websites referred to in this publication and does not guarantee that any content on such websites is, or will remain, accurate or appropriate.

Fordham University Press also publishes its books in a variety of electronic formats. Some content that appears in print may not be available in electronic books.

Visit us online at www.fordhampress.com.

Library of Congress Cataloging-in-Publication Data available online at catalog.loc.gov.

Printed in the United States of America

17  16  15      5  4  3  2  1

First edition

For Sylvia,
who is always there,
and in memory of Doris McGregor,
who always was

# Contents

Prologue: Going Back     1

1   A Mutual Wonder-field     9

2   Ends and Means     22

3   Portals to a Land of Dusk     41

4   The Cottage     60

5   *Lo, the sun walks forth!*     86

6   Suicide Notes     98

7   The Scream     115

8   Aquinas and the Circus Beckon     125

9   The Siren Call of Hollywood     138

10   On the Road with the Cristianis     146

11   Being a Presence in Postwar Marseilles     155

12   Entering the Lion's Mouth     174

13   Paris, *Jubilee*, and Kerouac     184

14   Inspiration in a Greek Diner     199

15   A New Poetics     212

16   "Original Child Bomb" and an Island Home     237

17   The Sorrow of the Sponge Diver     256

18   A Saint of the Avant-Garde     272

19   Alone in the World     285

20   A Galapagos of the Spirit     296

21   All Thoughts as They Come     309

22   The Flaw in the Ideal     317

23  Hell Hath No Fury                                      330

24  Finding a Common Language                              345

25  Pure Act Becomes Pure Love                             360

26  The Peacemaker's Handbook                              371

    Epilogue: The Singer and the Song                      389


    *Notes*                                                395

    *Bibliography*                                         425

    *Index*                                                431

    *Acknowledgments*                                      443

*Photographs follow page 198*

*I think it's a metaphysical concept*
*starting with Aristotle and flowering in St. Thomas*
*that God is pure act and that there is no* potentia *in Him.*
*. . . Almost everything else in the universe is* in potentia,
*it's on its way to being pure act,*
*on its way to unity with God.*

ROBERT LAX


*Depending upon the reader, it is all either baffling or beatific.*

American Library Association
*Booklist* review of *33 Poems,*
the first Lax book issued by
a major American publisher

# Prologue: Going Back

Years had passed since my last visit—since he was alive—and I had no idea how I'd feel. His niece had offered me his home, a humble whitewashed haven high above the island's harbor. I'd been in it countless times but only once or twice alone, while he was shopping for his cats or strolling by the sea. He'd leave the key out in the lock when he was gone, inviting anyone who happened by to enter. Poised there by the frosted glass, it said that he had nothing to hide. Nothing worth stealing. Nothing he would keep from anyone, even his time. He'd moved to Patmos, called the Holy Isle, in part because people on the island he loved most, Kalymnos, suspected him of hiding things. Of stealing secrets. Of being a spy. Nothing could have hurt him more or been further from the truth. He loved them more than they would know—the fishermen, the captains, the sponge divers. He had searched for them throughout his life—a society as pure and true as theirs—and they meant more to him than anyone, except perhaps his circus family or the man who'd been his closest friend, the monk and writer Thomas Merton.

It was Merton who had led me to him in the first place, painting such a vivid portrait of him in his autobiography that I wanted to meet him, not knowing he was living on the same Greek island I was as I read about him. Twenty years had passed since then, years of mentoring, of friendship, decline, then death. How would I feel, I wondered, when I saw the door without the key, the room without his bed, the walls without their quilt of postcards, quotes, and children's drawings? "Acquire the spirit of peace and a thousand souls shall be saved around you," one quote said. Had that spirit lingered there? Or had it died with him?

By the time I reached Kos, the nearest island with an airport, I'd been traveling for thirty hours from my home in Oregon. Nowhere had I felt the joy I always felt when I returned. Was it only that he wasn't there? Or that I'd stayed away too long? Or that my life had changed too much—that I was married now, a tenured professor, closer to his age the day we met than to my own back then? As I set my bags down on the hydrofoil's floor for the four-hour crossing to Patmos, I felt weary, wondering why

I'd traveled all that distance, what I hoped to find. I looked out at the stillness of the sea, the bright Greek light I knew from all those mornings all those years ago, and like a swell of sunlit waves, it all came back: the joy and peace of all those visits, all those talks, all those days I climbed those whitewashed stairs and knocked against that glass, waiting with the sightless cats to hear his tender "Yes?"

It felt like cheating then to take the shorter hydrofoil route, the easy flight from Athens. The ferry ride once seemed the only way to reach his island, a nine-hour journey from the modern world back into the stark simplicity of Patmos. I'd sit out on a hard-backed bench to feel the sun or press myself against a wall to keep the wind from whistling through me, and when the day had hardened into night, I'd stare into the black ahead until I saw the lights of Chora floating like the orbs of some celestial city, high above whatever cares I'd brought along.

Have I grown soft, I wondered as the engines thrummed, accepting comfort in a way he never did? Then the hydrofoil was shooting forward, shuddering on its slender shafts, and I was flying like a bird toward Patmos, winging toward that land we call the past. If only he could be there on the dock, I thought. If only we could climb the stairs together. If only I could go back to that day I read about him, unaware that he was living steps away.

———————

I'd gone to Europe that year, 1985, because I had questions. Huge questions. Seemingly unanswerable questions. They were questions about how to live in a world full of pain and violence and need. A world in which few people seemed to think about the way they lived and its effect on others. For the past three years I'd been writing about poverty, oppression, and illness in the world's poorest countries. I'd interviewed subsistence farmers in remote areas of Bangladesh, Khmer Rouge refugees on the borders of Cambodia, and children in Nepal and India crippled by diseases long eradicated from developed nations. In a camp surrounded by barb-wire, I'd listened to a beautiful Vietnamese refugee describe repeated rapes by Thai pirates. I didn't know what to do with her tears, or with the endless lines of homeless people on Calcutta's streets, or with the orphan girl who took my hand and squeezed it tightly in Thailand, as if a touch could make up for the sight she'd lost to disease.

From reading everything I could about the causes of entrenched poverty and how the Third World came to be, I'd learned that people weren't poor because disease or drought alone had devastated them or because they had too many children. They were poor because history had made them poor or kept them poor while others grew rich. They were poor because the world was arranged the way it was, with structures in place that kept the wealthy nations wealthy. America was part of the problem, but so was Europe. Most of the history I read, in fact, was a history of European occupation, European extraction of natural resources, European imposition of cash-crop farming and enslavement or virtual enslavement of native populations.

The main question that tortured me was this: What should I be doing? How should I be living? Just writing about misery and efforts to alleviate it didn't seem enough. I wanted to understand the problems and the history well enough to know exactly what to do, and I was young enough to hope to find a grand solution. So I quit my job, sold my car, and headed off to Europe, hoping I could find the answers there.

By the time I wandered down toward Athens, I'd been traveling for half a year, talking to people in a dozen countries, reading histories, and learning about cultures and attitudes, but the questions remained. I was ready to stop somewhere and spend time contemplating rather than moving, to see if I'd learned anything worthwhile. Among other things, I wanted to write a novel about my experiences. To do that, I thought, I needed to live somewhere quiet and remote—somewhere like a Greek isle. The problem was, I didn't know anything about the islands, so I decided that whenever I was ready to go I'd take the next boat out, wherever it was going.

I'd already identified my boat when I walked into an English-language bookstore in search of reading material for my time alone. Merton's autobiography was on my mind because I'd read about it in an Henri Nouwen book, but the last thing I expected was to see it there on the bookstore shelf, a copy from the 1950s, unread. The books around it were shelved spine out, but this one had its cover and its title, *The Seven Storey Mountain*, on display. I had little money, but it cost just 400 drachmas ($1.25), so I bought it.

The winds were strong that night, the seas high, as I sat out on the third-class deck finishing a book that ended with this admonition: Stay open to miracles. A Greek man I'd had lunch with in Athens had told me the first stop on the boat's itinerary, Patmos, was a beautiful island, so I planned to get off there. By the time we reached the small port town of Skala, it was after midnight and the only miracle I wanted was a fresh-made bed. I spied an unassuming sign for the one-star Rex hotel, and moments later, from my spartan room, I watched the ferry pull away, leaving me alone in winter on an island where I couldn't speak the language, thousands of miles from home. Two days later, having found a cheap apartment that was nothing but a chilly concrete box, I began writing my novel and, while pondering what book to read that night, felt drawn to Merton.

Merton's story appealed to me at once, of course—it's the story of a young, spiritually oriented writer trying to figure out how to live—but it was the wisdom offered by a friend of his that impressed me most, especially in one pivotal scene.

The scene is familiar to anyone who knows Merton's story: It's the spring of 1939, the year the world will go to war, and a twenty-four-year-old Merton is walking toward Greenwich Village with his closest friend, Robert Lax. They're talking about something related to Merton's future when Lax asks suddenly, "What do you want to be, anyway?" Merton writes:

> I could not say, "I want to be Thomas Merton the well-known writer of all those book reviews in the back pages of the *Times Book Review*," or "Thomas Merton the assistant instructor of Freshman-English at the New Life Social Institute for Progress and Culture," so I put the thing on the spiritual plane, where I knew it belonged and said:
> "I don't know; I guess what I want is to be a good Catholic."
> "What do you mean, you want to be a good Catholic?"
> The explanation I gave was lame enough, and expressed my confusion, and betrayed how little I had really thought about it all.
> Lax did not accept it.
> "What you should say"—he told me—"what you should say is that you want to be a saint."
> A saint! The thought struck me as a little weird. I said:

"How do you expect me to become a saint?"

"By wanting to," said Lax, simply.

When Merton countered that he couldn't be a saint, Lax, who'd grown up Jewish but was reading Catholic books along with Merton and, according to Merton, had an "inborn direction to the living God," responded, "All that is necessary to be a saint is to want to be one. Don't you believe that God will make you what He created you to be, if you will consent to do it? All you have to do is desire it."

That idea—that desire alone can lead us toward the things that we should do, the way that we should live—was antithetical to everything I'd learned in church as a child, and yet it seemed true. Sensible. I couldn't believe that anyone could be so wise so young and made a mental note to look for Lax in later Merton books back at home, not knowing he would enter my life much sooner than that.

That concrete box was colder than I thought a rented room could be, especially on an island in Greece, and one day, as the temperature dipped toward freezing, I'd finally had enough. Why not go to the mainland for a while, I thought, and check into a heated room until the weather warmed? The more I thought about it, the better this plan seemed, and so one night I headed to the harbor and huddled in a doorway waiting for the boat to come.

That night seemed the coldest yet, the kind of night on which the choppy seas might make the narrow Patmos harbor too dangerous for the ferry to stop. I waited for an hour, then another, shivering against the cold, and just when I was ready to return to my apartment, I heard a voice inside me say, *If you'll endure, God will bless you.* I wasn't used to hearing voices, but Patmos is the island of the Revelation and I'd had dreams while living there that seemed like prophecies, and so I listened. Moments later the boat's slow lights appeared.

As I boarded the ferry, I walked beside an Australian man who told me that he too had come to Patmos to write. Many writers had tried living there, he said, including a prominent American poet who lived there still—a man named Robert Lax.

I couldn't believe it. When I described the man I'd read about in Merton's book, the Australian said he was sure they were the same. At this point I was heading *away* from Patmos, but I felt certain that this man, this poet—*Robert Lax*—would be there when I returned.

The Australian told me the locals called Lax Petros for some reason, so when I was back on the island after my time away, I asked the woman at the grocery store if she'd ever met him. "Yes," she said, "he comes in every day." But when I checked the next day and the next, he hadn't shown. Finally, on the fourth day, she had news for me: I was to meet him at the post office at ten the next morning when he came down for his mail.

It was raining that next morning, and no one on Patmos went out in the rain, but I trudged down to the post office anyway. Sure enough, he wasn't there, so I left a note asking him to meet me at the taverna next door at six that evening. When I arrived at six, the rain had stopped, but the taverna was closed. Not knowing what to do, I was turning to go when I heard a gentle voice behind me say, "Hello?" As soon as I looked, I knew it was him—not just any Robert Lax but Merton's.

He stood an inch or two shorter than me, with bushy white hair that struggled out below a neat gray Irish cap. His face was long, with a long nose and sharply etched cheeks that ended in a white goatee. His skin and voice suggested a man half his sixty-nine years, and his eyes, though shadowed, shone with life. In his down jacket and desert boots, he looked surprisingly American, but I suspected that the things he had to tell me would be hard to find back home. We searched for a place to talk, and when we'd settled into a noisy restaurant, I ticked off the coincidences— the miracles—that had brought me to him. Then, with youthful pluck, I said, "God must have something for you to tell me, or me to tell you." He just smiled, as if used to that kind of thing.

———————

I could see his smile and hear his voice again as I gazed out from the hydrofoil at the town of Chora, clinging to the hill below the island's famous monastery. I had called Ritsa from Kos, and she was there at the dock to meet me. Since Lax's death, she and her husband, Nico, had taken care of his old house. She had a German couple with her who had decided to vacation on Patmos after seeing a museum installation called *Three Windows*, a video exploration of Lax's island life filmed just days before the last time I saw him. Would I mind, Ritsa asked, if they came with us to the house? Their eyes shone with the anticipation of seeing where this uncommon man had lived. There was a cruise ship in port and Skala was full of foreigners in leisure clothes. What a far cry from the winter night we met, I thought, when Lax had led me up the empty stairways to his home.

The house looked much as it had then, with its whitewashed walls and blue-shuttered windows, but even from the outside it seemed less alive. The half-blind cats that mewed and scattered from his porch were gone, the porch itself too scrubbed, too clean. The keyhole in the door was empty. Inside, the poster advertising Circus Roberto still hung in the entryway, but the circus had moved on. The main room where he slept and wrote was bare, with bookshelves standing where those drawings, quotes, and photographs had been. The back room, where he'd kept his books, held only some of Nico's paintings, two cheap chairs, an empty bed. The kitchen and the bathroom looked the same and yet too neat. Too lifeless.

When Ritsa and the Germans were gone, I felt alone in a way I never had before, even when he died. How could I ever write about him, I wondered. How would I know what to say? How could I conjure his spirit?

As I thought these thoughts, I scanned the books he'd left behind and found one I'd given him, with prewar pictures of the Jewish ghetto in Krakow, where his mother's family lived. Turning to the title page, I read what I had written over a decade earlier: "A 'postcard' from the past to remind us of what came before as we seek to create what will come after." Now, like the people in the photographs, he was part of what came before and I was alone in my attempts to create what would come after.

Sitting in a folding chair, I held the book between my knees and listened to the stillness in the room, the faint barking of a distant dog, the far-off sounds of town. This is the scene they'd open with if this were a movie, I thought, a lingering shot from behind my head with only ambient sound. An image to convey the loss, the sorrow. If only I knew how to start the book as well.

Looking at the shelves again, I spied a paperback of William Maxwell's *All the Days and Nights*, a collection of short stories by the legendary editor, one of Lax's lifelong friends. "For Roberto with love," Maxwell had written on the title page, followed by this quote from Conrad:

The task approached in tenderness
and faith is to hold up unquestioningly,
without choice and without fear, the
rescued fragment.

As soon as I read it, I knew where and how to begin.

# 1     A Mutual Wonder-field

Lax lived at the center of a labyrinth on Patmos, surrounded by jumbled houses and crisscrossing paths halfway up a high hill. Just beyond his simple house, the white block dwellings of the port town Skala gave way to a narrow, rocky peak the locals called Kastelli. The ancients built their outpost there, and you can still find shards of hand-worked terracotta sprinkled near the timeworn stones. When I lived on Patmos, I used to go up there to gaze out at the sea, seeing all the way to Turkey if the day was clear. It was the perfect place to contemplate the future or the present or the past, which seemed to blend on Patmos, as if the island had no fixed time.

Skala means *stairs* in Greek, and stairs were what you first encountered climbing up to Lax's place. That first night I just followed him, but later, when I had to find the way myself, I learned that you could ask any local "To Petros?" and he or she could point the way: around a corner to a concrete path, up a narrow passageway and out along a corridor. At the top, where you could see the harbor far below, you ducked beneath the neighbor's laundry and dodged the cats that scattered from his porch. The cats multiplied each year and were afflicted with ailments that made their eyes weep and some of them go blind, but he had names for all of them and wanted them to live as freely as possible. When someone suggested they be spayed, he replied, in a rare show of anger, "I didn't come to the holy island of Patmos to castrate cats." His only intrusion into the cats' lives was to feed them fish the fishermen gave him or, if no Greeks were bearing gifts that day, fish he purchased at the store. The cats' food often cost him more than his own.

Exactly why he had come all the way to the holy island of Patmos and lived in such simplicity on the fringe of a traditional and, some would say, outmoded society was a question that intrigued me, especially when I learned how promising his early life had been. But it took years to find a satisfying answer. I'm not sure he himself understood the many turns of fortune that had led him there, but he was where he wanted to be, doing what he wanted to be doing, and his contentment living simply, loving freely, and writing undisturbed so late in life lessened my anxiety about my own future.

In an interview I read much later, when the interviewer described Lax's life in Greece as "voluntary exile," Lax said he didn't feel at all like an exile. For anyone raised in the Western tradition, moving to Greece is like returning to your "cultural roots," he said. "The great ages of philosophy, and of drama, live here in a strange way, but very real. Where they live mostly, I think, is among the unlettered people in Greece—the farmers and fishermen who have inherited points of view and proverbs, popular maxims, whole ways of looking at things and of turning things over in their minds, from the great ages of Greek civilization. They keep these things in very pure, living form, so that when you're living in Greece, you're surrounded by good minds in a good state of health, and by inheritors of good, living traditions."

With little history of their own other than centuries of subjugation to the Turks, modern Greeks looked back to both ancient and biblical times for their inspiration and their pride. They didn't need to study the old ways, Lax believed, because those ways were in their blood, including the biblical injunction to be kind to strangers.

When William Maxwell mentioned Lax's preference for simple people in one of the many letters they exchanged when they were older, Lax gave credit to his father, Siggie, who immigrated to the United States from Austria when he was sixteen. Unlettered himself, Siggie, who never lost his accent, introduced his son to the types of people he would choose to spend his life among, including those who worked in the circus.

"He'd take me to a field early in the morning (or down to the railroad tracks) to see a circus pull into town," Lax wrote Maxwell. One day they saw a "funny little woman" walking in front of them and Siggie asked her if she was with the circus. Yes, she said, she was a dancer.

> We went to see the circus the next afternoon, but first stopped in at the side-show. And there on the platform was our friend wearing feathers and a beak near a sign that said Koko the Bird-Woman.
>
> He introduced me to gypsies too, and street sweepers and people who sold peanuts in the park (I remember most of their faces and certainly remember liking them). Maybe even feeling they were going to be my people.

Siggie sold clothes for a living and for a while peddled them door-to-door. When he came home from making his rounds one evening, Lax's mother asked him how he'd done.

"I didn't sell anything," he replied, "but I made some nice new friends."

––––––––––––––

I knew none of this the night I met Lax, of course. I knew only what Merton had written about him, including a description of him as a "combination of Hamlet and Elias. A potential prophet but without the rage. A king, but a Jew, too. A mind full of tremendous and subtle intuitions, and every day he found less and less to say about them."

In the forty years since that description was written, Lax had grown more comfortable with speaking his mind. Or maybe he had simply explored his "intuitions" fully enough to be able to verbalize them. That first night, in that noisy restaurant, we talked about everything: him, me, Merton, writing, faith, and life. He told me he had come to Greece for a brief visit twenty years before and decided to stay, after working as a professor at Connecticut College, a film critic for *Time* magazine, and a screenwriter in Hollywood.

"What films did you write?" I asked.

"Oh no," he said, the wry smile I'd seen earlier returning. "Maybe I'll tell you after I know you better. They were the worst movies of all time."

He had lived in Paris, Marseilles, and New York, but he couldn't live in New York anymore, he said. It wasn't the size of the city so much as the wayward interests and ambitions of the people there, the focus on materialism and "getting ahead." His poetry, he said, was usually about nature: "Simple things like sun, sun/moon, moon. I like to write in a way that can't be misunderstood, and when you write things like 'red, red,' or 'black, black' there aren't too many ways people can take them." I thought he was joking or oversimplifying but soon found out he was telling the truth. His approach to poetry had changed greatly over the years, along with his life, conforming more and more to what I came to call the wisdom of simplicity. He and Merton had made a vow when young to write simply, and Lax had taken it to a daring extreme.

I tried to steer him away from Merton because I wanted to know about his own life and thought, but it was clear that Merton was the subject he was most often asked about, and so we talked about their friendship, which began when they were classmates at Columbia University. I knew from Merton's book that Lax was an accomplished poet even then, which meant that he'd been writing poetry for fifty years—so long, he said, that it was just like breathing. The Swiss publisher Pendo Verlag had issued his most recent books and he'd become far better known in Europe than America. In fact a major European museum, the Staatsgalerie in Stuttgart, was about to host a retrospective look at his career.

It was the Stuttgart exhibition that started us down the road from chance meeting to friendship. When we were done eating and he had insisted on paying for my meal, claiming he had invited me out, he asked if I'd come up to his house the following evening to help him pack some things to be shipped to Germany. So I would know where to go, he walked me up those stairs and paths that zigzagged to his house. Everyone we passed, from children to old women in black, called out, "Yahsoo, Petros!," and every time he heard a motorbike, however distant, he pressed himself against a wall, as if afraid of anything that smacked so clearly of the modern world.

(He told me that night why the locals called him Petros: "When I first came here someone asked me my name and I said, 'Robertos.' 'Petros?' he said and I said, 'Yes, okay,' and I've been called that ever since." He said it with a shrug, as if resigned to his fate, but the smile on his lips suggested he enjoyed the nickname. I learned later that he had let the error stand because he didn't want the man to feel bad.)

I didn't know it then, but such a quick and easy invitation to his home meant he'd seen something in me he liked. He was always gentle and friendly with those he didn't know, but he took his time letting people in. I don't know if his approach was calculated or subconscious; maybe it was some of both. In the years ahead I'd read the letters he received from strangers and see the visitors who came in increasing numbers as he aged and more of his work made it into print. Some were Merton lovers. Some fanatics. Some had read a bit of Lax's poetry or come across his prose somewhere. Some had heard that there was some old wise man living as a hermit on the island. And some had simply ended up on Patmos for some other reason and learned that someone sage and interesting was living there. Some came looking for a guru or a saint and some to see an offbeat poet or a man who'd been close to Merton. Some, it seemed, came just to argue. And a few—a precious few—came wanting nothing more than conversation, settled in themselves already. Lax was too compassionate to turn anyone away, but he established barriers, agreeing to meet some in town, allowing others to his house, and limiting the times even those he felt closest to could visit. Only in his later years did he let his friends visit him at will.

I was fortunate to meet him in winter, when Patmos was mostly free of foreigners, and in the year I did, before the Staatsgalerie exhibition and the publication three years later of *33 Poems*, his first book of poetry issued by a major American publisher. Both brought increased attention and more visitors. There was something more than good timing in our friendship, though. From the first, there was a sympathy between us, an unspoken understanding—not the kind men share who have grown up together and lived through the same epoch but the kind that develops sometimes between an older person and a younger one, each contributing from his own age and perspective.

Lax was protean in his responses to others, able to make all kinds of people feel they had a special relationship with him. The content and even the style of his letters varied according to the interests and perspectives of their recipients. But there was something more between us, especially in the later years, when I had matured as a writer and a person. One year, when I already had a small collection of the slim brown volumes of his writing Pendo put out, I asked him to write a line or two in the latest one. In each of the others he'd written only my name and his or, after I married, my wife's name, mine, and his (or, when he knew her better, just *hers* and his), but this time I wanted more. He looked uneasy.

"What do you want me to write?" he asked. "There's not much difference between us."

"Write that then," I said, and he did.

But I'm getting ahead of myself. That first night, I'm sure, I was just a naïve boy who had washed up on his shores. He took his time climbing the hill, not because he was getting old but because he believed life was best lived slowly. (*slow boat / calm river / quiet landing* is etched on the stone that marks his grave.) When we reached his place, after speaking gently to his cats, he sat me on a sofa in the main room and went into the kitchen to fix us tea. Before he left the room, he thrust a newly published book into my hands: *Merton By Those Who Knew Him Best*. I found him listed first under "Merton the Friend," with a photograph of him looking exactly as he looked that night, Irish cap and all.

Whatever the book might have told me, I was far more interested in looking around the room I was in. It was maybe twelve feet square with a long low table covered by a cloth in front of me, a simple single bed in the far corner, and two other, slightly higher tables along the wall to my right. Every surface other than the bed and the long table, including the open floor along the walls, was covered with books, papers, pens, and other writing and drawing implements. (I learned later that a local man had made the low sofa table for him and he had promised he would keep its surface clear—a promise he kept.) The walls, where you could see them, were a monstrous sea-slime green, but you didn't look at them for long. The rest of the room was far too interesting. A large Japanese lantern covered the ceiling light above my head, and on the walls above the tables to my right (one a simple board, the other a folding table) he'd taped postcards, photographs, quotes, and drawings that had fused into an idiosyncratic mosaic. One uneven row included a photograph of Merton with the Dalai Lama. Through the glass French doors across the room, I could see a small second room with bookshelves full of books and more papers and boxes. In the midst of it all, near the edge of the folding table, sat a metal typewriter, waiting to be used. It was an old portable too big to move easily, an apt symbol of the life he'd lived.

When Lax returned with my tea, he sat down on a cheap wooden chair across from me and we continued our conversation. Among the people he mentioned who had been his friends were Jack Kerouac, Dylan Thomas, and Ernesto Cardenal, a man I knew only as the Nicaraguan Sandinistas' minister of culture and supposed enemy of the United States, not the novice he had once been under Merton or the poet who had done a Spanish translation of Lax's first and best-known book, *The Circus of the Sun*.

I knew from reading Merton that Lax had converted to Catholicism at about my age, and I asked if he missed having Catholic fellowship living in an Orthodox country.

"Being here is like living in a church," he said.

He told me his best friend on the island was an old man named Da-mianos Theodosiou, who used to be a seaman. During his years at sea Damianos became quite devout, and when he retired onto land, he and his wife built a church.

"They spend all their time now taking care of it," said Lax, "dusting off an icon here or there. I spend quite a bit of my time with them."

As he spoke, it occurred to me that you took only what you wanted or were prepared for from this man called Petros—no less, no more. He didn't force his views or wisdom on you but stated them plainly in the course of conversation, enthusiastic enough to want to offer a thought but patient and polite enough to wait his turn.

But these brief recollections, culled from journal entries I made at the time, make Lax sound far too serious. There's a line in an old Supremes song, "Remember me as the sound of laughter," and when I remember Lax, that's how I remember him. A conversation with him never ran for long without a joke or a funny story. Judy Emery, who edited two of his books, told me she remembered times "when he'd say something funny and you'd start laughing, then he'd start laughing because you were laughing, and he'd actually fall on the floor shaking with laughter." When something struck him as particularly funny, he'd pull his legs up under him and lean out over them in glee like a five-year-old. Wilfrid Sheed, who worked with Lax at *Jubilee* magazine in the 1950s, wrote in the *New York Times Book Review*, "An old friend says admiringly that Merton and Lax remained the most childish men he'd ever met, right to the day of Merton's death."

That was it, I think, the thing that struck you most about Lax when you first met him: he was childlike in many ways, and yet he was wise about the world's difficulties and sorrows. Merton wrote once that Lax meditated on "some incomprehensible woe." Mark Van Doren, a Colum-bia professor and Lax's friend, thought his only problem was that he couldn't "state his bliss." Perhaps it was a combination of these two—of woe and bliss—that formed his delightfully peculiar personality, prompt-ing Kerouac to call him a "laughing Buddha."

"Take it with you," Lax said about the Merton book when I got up to go. As he opened his door to the chilly night, I peeked into the kitchen where he'd made our tea. It wasn't a kitchen really, just a small room with a sink, a gas hotplate, and another flimsy table, this one filled with thrown-together kitchen items—plates, cups, crackers, cans—that in their randomness looked artistically composed. A lemon slice left out and drying epitomized the place—and Lax: a sign of simple, unpretentious daily life that didn't interrupt but was central to his process of creation.

*sun, sun/moon, moon.*

---

I suppose Lax urged me to take the Merton book that first night because it saved him breath. Most of the entries were straightforward reminiscences of Merton by people like Joan Baez, Lawrence Ferlinghetti, the Dalai Lama, and Thich Nhat Hanh, but Lax's entry was an interview that included the story of how he and Merton met. It was 1935. Both were in their first year at Columbia, Lax having entered one term ahead of Merton, and both were contributing to the university's humor magazine, *Jester.* When Lax told the editor, Herb Jacobson, that he admired Merton's short stories and would like to meet him, Jacobsen said that Merton had said the same about Lax's poetry. He walked Lax down from the fourth floor of John Jay Hall, where the *Jester* offices were located, to the dining room on the first floor, where Merton was sitting at a table.

"Merton looked up and shook hands," Lax said, "and it was really an amazing meeting right away. It was the friendliest look, the friendliest handshake I'd ever remembered. You know, there was no question in my mind that we were friends from that moment on."

Although I'd gained some sense of their college friendship from *The Seven Storey Mountain* and learned more from Lax's interview, I had no idea at that point how much these two men meant to each other throughout their lives. Years after Merton's accidental death in 1968, Lax carried three things with him all the time: a notebook for jotting thoughts for poems, a miniature version of the Psalms with print so small it hurt your eyes, and a photograph of Merton. He said once he never felt more himself than with Merton, and many have said that Merton was never more truly himself on the page than in his letters to Lax.

In the reams of writing about Merton's college and postcollege days, starting with his own autobiography, Lax is always around somewhere, sometimes as companion or interlocutor, sometimes as footnote. He plays a large enough role to be noticed by readers like me, but he often seems Zelig-like, appearing primarily at pivotal moments. Most who write about Merton's life credit Lax with inspiring him during those crucial early years, but few acknowledge, or even see, the impact he continued to have even after Merton entered the monastery. It wasn't until the publication in 1978 of *A Catch of Anti-letters*, a much-delayed collection of their humorously inventive yet often deeply personal correspondence, that Merton watchers knew how lively and extensive their friendship was. Even that book, which Merton edited before his death, covered only a short period, 1962–67. It took a more exhaustive collection edited by Arthur W. Biddle and published by the University Press of Kentucky in 2001 (one year after Lax's death) to reveal the true extent of their involvement in each other's lives. Published under the title *When Prophecy Still Had a Voice*, the letters in the Biddle collection begin in June 1938, about the time most biographers write Lax out of Merton's story, and run to the end of Merton's life. Playful as these letters appear on the surface, they contain some of deepest feelings either man ever expressed.

Actually I've used the word *reveal* too loosely. Even after the publication of Biddle's book, few understood how much these two friends communicated to and relied on each other because their letters were, in essence, written in a secret language. Any two people who have known each other long and well develop some kind of shorthand—neither needs an explanation of events experienced together or the full names of books and movies shared—but Lax and Merton's language was unusually complicated. It wasn't just that both were intelligent, inventive, and verbally acute but also, and even more, that they admired and were greatly influenced by the man both thought the greatest writer of the twentieth century, James Joyce, especially his difficult masterpiece, *Finnegans Wake*.

Among the obsessions they inherited from Joyce were a coining of macaronic words with parts from German, Latin, French, and other languages; a relentless punning on anything and everything, including the names of books they'd read, people they'd known, and movie stars they'd liked when younger; and a sly, slanting referencing of literature and history that gave otherwise ordinary-seeming expressions a double meaning. Like Joyce, they communicated a broad and serious perspective on the world through humor, letting themselves go in whatever direction they wanted without worrying that they'd seem frivolous or flip. Their many earnest discussions as young men—about faith and art and purpose—gave their correspondence a context that allowed the wackiest comment or wildest thought to be one more *yes* they were saying to one another.

Many of Merton's letters have been published, and some of them—to thinkers and writers such as Czeslaw Milosz, Boris Pasternak, and Dorothy Day—are finely composed essays, but nowhere is he more *alive* on the page than in his writing to Lax. The two of them are like the jazz musicians they once liked to watch jamming in the early hours of a Manhattan morning—blowing and riffing, soloing and chasing, establishing patterns and then heading off in new directions. Sometimes they fill single letters with riffs on a particular subject, and sometimes they return to the same subject over weeks or months, turning it into a recurring motif. Even playing counterpoint they are always supportive and affirming.

Both men changed greatly over the course of their lives, and both made friends easily—each had hundreds of correspondents—but in their letters to each other they remained the playful, earnest, intelligent, and often silly young men they were when they first met. They were touchstones and sounding boards for each other, their communication like that of twins, requiring no more than a word or gesture to be understood.

Although they tried at times to talk about each other, the depth of friendship these men shared could never be adequately expressed. The best description of how they were together comes from the poet Ron Seitz, who had the good fortune to go on a picnic with them the last time they saw each other, in the summer of 1968, when Lax visited Merton at his monastery months before his death. Their lifelong knowledge of each, Seitz wrote, "created a mutual wonder-field of eye contact, glints of recognition accompanied by continual bursts of laughter and headnods of glad agreement about most everything, which I began witnessing before the handshakes hello were completed. . . . Their conversation . . . wended its way in and out of various subjects, breaking off here and there to make handheld leaps to familiar territory without a pause or direct connection. I just let my ear follow along from this to that, picking up on bits that fit." This is as good a description as any of what it's like to read their letters.

---

The most intimate record of their early friendship I've found is a poem Lax wrote after Merton's death called "Remembering Merton and New York." Written in Lax's spare and vertical style, it evokes a time, a place and a relationship as much through what it doesn't say as what it does—a common characteristic of Lax's later poetry. ("I can understand that his poems did not click," Merton once wrote to Henry Miller, after sending him a volume of Lax's work. "I suppose you have to know what is in all the blank places.")

In his poem, Lax focuses on places, names, and characteristics still vivid to him decades later: books Merton introduced him to, like *Brighton Rock* and *The Dark Night of the Soul*; actors they both enjoyed, like Humphrey Bogart, Charlie Chaplin, and the Marx Brothers; and venues they frequented together, like Café Society, where they listened to Lena Horne and Billie Holiday, the Theater Palace, where they heard Duke Ellington and Judy Garland, and the Savoy in Harlem, where they saw Louis Armstrong. In the midst of listing Merton's favorite authors—Blake and Hopkins, Dante and Rabelais—and his "French" and "English" traits, Lax pinpoints what he and others appreciated most about their friend:

Maj
or
char
ac
ter
is
tic:
(gen
u
ine)
live
li
ness.

I didn't know Lax then, of course, but when I did, I would have said his major characteristic was the same. The only girlfriend he ever had, Nancy Flagg, who eventually married his college friend Robert Gibney, once said to him, "It's not fair. There should be a good acceptable name for the sort of talent you and Gibney have. Not for formal writing. Discipline, organization, all that stuff. But the wonderful talk and jokes and journals and letters to friends."

*Liveliness* is as good a name as any.

---

As close as Lax and Merton were, they were very different people and they ended up in very different places. It's been said that Merton never had a thought he didn't publish. As a result, his life has been well chronicled and celebrated, while Lax's life has stayed obscure and Lax himself quixotic. Over the years I knew him, I heard stories about things he'd done, like working at the *New Yorker*, traveling with a circus, and living in a flophouse-cum-whorehouse in Marseilles. I heard about days with Kerouac in Greenwich Village, editing work with *New-Story* magazine in Paris, and a year with banana farmers in the Canary Islands. I learned to understand and appreciate his poetry, his general philosophy, and his approach to faith. But no matter how much I heard and learned, I couldn't put it all together. I didn't know what had driven him through these various adventures or what it was he found on Kalymnos he hadn't found elsewhere.

Where, I wondered, did he leave the path his Ivy League education prepared him for and become, as one critic called him, the poet who fell off the map? I assumed that his friendship with Merton, whose autobiography was about a talented young man eschewing the American Dream, had something to do with it. But there had to be more. After all, he hadn't ended up in a monastery but on a remote Greek island, and while he and Merton agreed on many things, he had a distinctly different perspective on the world. When he died, I decided to write a book about him in part because he had lived such an unusual—and unusually inspiring—life but also because I wanted a good excuse to explore the reasons why.

---

I spent a week with Lax that first visit, climbing up to his house each night and packing the manuscripts and books he collected from the room's four corners. When I left to meet a friend in Egypt and eventually fly home, I asked if I could leave something with him: the portable typewriter I'd used to draft my novel. By then it was spring on Patmos; the highs were in the mid-70s and the rockroses and wildflowers were out. I'd met the travel writer Rick Steves before leaving for Europe, and he'd asked if I'd be interested in leading European tours for his then-fledgling company that summer. My plan was to go home for a couple of months, lead a string of tours, and head straight back to Patmos. My short time there hadn't answered my big questions, but the island had been a healing place. A cheap one too; my apartment cost $3 a day. Living and writing there, with Lax nearby, seemed the ideal life.

Lax didn't say no to my request, but he suggested in his gentle way that I might want to keep my typewriter with me. Having lived a peripatetic life when he was younger, he knew better than most how way leads on to way, and every material object in his possession was a psychological burden, especially if it belonged to someone else.

As it turned out, I didn't see him again for a year and a half. By then we'd exchanged several letters and I'd read more of Merton's writing, but rather than simplifying my life, I'd let it grow more complex. Once again I washed up on Patmos looking for answers.

It was just before midnight, two days before Thanksgiving in 1987, when I staggered off the ferry and went looking for Lax once more. The wind was bitterly cold that night and I was bone-weary after leading tours for four straight months. In the year and a half since I'd left Patmos, I'd accepted an offer from Rick Steves to be his business partner and split my time between office work and guiding. But the partnership was ending (in part because I'd learned, as Lax had learned before me, that I wasn't meant for commerce) and I was feeling lost.

Lax wasn't on the island when I landed—he'd gone north for a reading tour—but he'd sent a note saying he'd arrive on Thanksgiving night, so I contented myself with memories of the life I'd lived my first time there. I tried to replicate it by renting the same small apartment, but spring had been budding then, and now we were slipping into winter. Feeling sad at spending Thanksgiving alone, I remembered words I'd read in a Merton book on the ferry: "The man who fears to be alone will never be anything but lonely, no matter how much he may surround himself with people. But the man who learns, in solitude and recollection, to be at peace with his own loneliness, and to prefer its reality to the illusion of merely natural companionship, comes to know the invisible companionship of God."

Lax had learned that kind of peace, I knew.

As I made my way through the dark and the wind to meet his boat, the houses and restaurants I passed were silent, the air an unscented void where in spring I'd smelled the orange blossoms. The island was black, the sea blacker still, and the lights that lit the concrete quay were cold and sterile. This was the world Lax lived in alone for months each winter.

Thanksgiving wasn't a holiday on Patmos, of course, so there were few locals at the dock to meet the ferry. I stood in the shadows by myself and watched the boat draw near. When Lax appeared, he looked pale and nervous, as he always did around cars and busyness, but when he saw me his face lit up. Stepping far away from the disembarking vehicles, he hugged me awkwardly and insisted I come up to his house to share the meal he knew his neighbor Katina had left for him. As I followed him up those now-familiar stairs, our discussions began again—or, as was truer with Lax, simply continued, as if we'd been talking just the night before. We found right away that we'd been thinking along similar lines. We'd even clipped the same paragraph from the *International Herald Tribune*, a quote from the philosopher William James: "I have often thought that the best way to define a man's character would be to seek out the particular mental or moral attitude in which, when it came upon him, he felt himself most deeply and intensely active and alive. At such moments there is a voice inside which speaks and says: 'This is the real me!'"

Writing and solitude fostered that attitude in us, we agreed. Not commerce. Not busyness. He mentioned the title of a book he liked, *Alone for Others*, and I quoted his friend Merton, who said that choosing solitude for ourselves is also choosing it for others, for we cannot give ourselves fully to others if we are not fully there.

The next afternoon I climbed up Kastelli and sat for a long time watching the sun's rays move like spotlights over the water, feeling the deep relief of doing nothing. The air seemed still despite the breeze, and I had a feeling I often felt on Patmos, that I was both looking at art and part of the canvas. On my way back down, I stopped to visit Lax, feeling like the neighbor boy who comes to watch you work on your car. Although he usually wrote at that time of day, he ushered me in and fixed me tea and soon we were talking about our own and the world's need for peace.

"I'm hopeful," he said, his eyes solemn, "that the world's societies are caught up in an evolutionary moment, one that will bring us into the ideal city, where music will play and all will move to it. If you decide to put on all blue clothes and do cartwheels across the square, that will be fine and in time with the music."

When I asked how we get there, he said he didn't know, but he thought the first step was to be positive and hopeful. We must live our beliefs, he said, and if we believe that violence shouldn't be a part of life, then we should eliminate it from our own lives at least. He had done this long ago by limiting his dealings to people of a gentle nature.

"What about people who can't escape dealing with violent people?" I asked.

"They have to arrive at their own answers," he said, "but they can remain nonviolent if they are resolved to do it."

I wanted to argue with this idea, to call him naïve, but I granted him the perspective of his years. I wouldn't learn until after his death that his answer came from his own painful experience.

Coincidentally, the next morning I started reading Tolstoy's *The Kingdom of God Is within You*, the book that inspired Gandhi's use of nonviolent tactics. Tolstoy believed that nonviolence is an indispensable part of the Christian life, which he defined as neither a goal nor a set of standards for living but the process—the pursuit—of perfection. What should set the Christian apart, he wrote, is his attempt, in every moment, to conform as closely as possible to the life of Christ.

When I took these thoughts to Lax, he expressed a similar view, speaking less of the *Christian* life than life in general. "In every moment," he said, "we make decisions, both large and small. True life comes in understanding that these decisions are of ultimate importance."

---

I didn't know it then, but the importance of consciously making decisions moment by moment had been central to Lax's thinking since his college days with Merton, when one of their favorite things to do was watch jazz musicians jam. The 1930s were an amazing time to live in New York if you loved jazz, and as the list of places and musicians in Lax's poem about Merton makes clear, the two of them did. They loved it for its own sake—its rhythms, moods, and energy—but as with everything they shared, they found something deeper in it too. In a long discussion with Arthur Biddle, only part of which appears in the book Biddle edited, Lax talked about his and Merton's love not just for jazz in general but for jam sessions in particular and what he came to call "pure act."

"A real jam session is likely to start at three in the morning and get good by five," Lax said, "and by that time all the customers have left, it's only the musicians playing for each other, to each other, with each other, and they are just astonishing each other by these felicitous turns they find in the music. . . . They're talking and they're playing and it isn't a competitive thing except in the very best way."

What impressed Lax most was the musicians' ability to be so conscious in the present moment that each could improvise and yet remain in harmony with the others. One man playing his best, in fact, improved the playing of them all. Over time he came to believe that this ability or condition was essential to improving the quality of both individual and community life. He saw it at work in his relationships with Merton and their college friends. As each pursued his own activities, making conscious decisions about his own life, his decisions encouraged and inspired the others.

Later, when Merton had disappeared inside a monastery and their other friends had scattered, Lax found purer models of this kind of conscious living in circus performers and Greek islanders. Eventually he linked it to a view of life and God adapted from St. Thomas Aquinas. God, Aquinas wrote, is *pure love* and *pure act*, while all else in the universe languishes in *potentia*. When we act consciously and yet spontaneously, Lax thought, we become pure act ourselves—we become like God. If, that is, we act in love.

---

When Lax arrived at Columbia in the fall of 1934, he was a shy and gawky but confident boy who'd spent considerable time in Manhattan already. The only son of Jewish immigrants from Eastern Europe, he bore an immigrant family's hopes and ambitions, buoyed by a Jewish mother's love. (Although he'd done well in college, his mother was so concerned about him the last semester of his senior year that she sublet a professor's apartment on campus to make sure he was eating right. When he had trouble assembling his senior thesis, she spread the pages across her apartment floor and put them in order.) In the middle of his eighth-grade year, his family had moved from the upstate town of Olean to Elmhurst in Queens, in part because his mother wanted him to be exposed to the greater culture in the city. In high school he often rode the subway into Manhattan to attend the theater or poke through bookstores. The most important cultural figure in his life, however, was a boy three years ahead of him at Elmhurst's Newtown High School, Ad Reinhardt.

Then and later, all the way to the end of his life, Lax considered Reinhardt, who had been drawing since infancy and was already earning money from his art in high school, the consummate artist—a boy and then a man to emulate. It was Reinhardt's complete dedication to his art that impressed Lax, his understanding that *artist* was not a profession or a lifestyle but a definition of one's self that encompassed everything.

During Lax's freshman year at Columbia, Reinhardt was the editor in chief of *Jester* and transformed it from a run-of-the-mill college magazine printing stale adolescent jokes into a publication noted for its clever writing and first-class art. In addition to upgrading the publication's drawings and illustrations, he added more photographs and published longer, wittier stories and poems. One of the first things Lax did when he reached campus was send his old schoolmate some of his humorous poems and drawings, and when Reinhardt published several of them, the two became friends. In the coming months Reinhardt would introduce Lax to some of the young men who would become his closest friends, including Seymour (Sy) Freedgood, who would room with Lax his senior year, and John Slate, who would accompany him on his first trip to Europe the summer after his sophomore year.

As Lax would discover, *Jester* was more like a privileged club than a student group. Slate, for example, had already moved on to Columbia Law, but he continued to contribute to the magazine. Lax and Merton would do the same after they graduated, just because the editors liked them. When criticized for being obscure, *Jester* writers claimed to write for each other rather than the general student population.

Like Lax, most who wrote for *Jester* had worked for high school publications. They thought of themselves as writers and editors but only in the context of school. It was Reinhardt who helped them lift their sights, taking as their competition not the *Harvard Lampoon* but the *New Yorker*, which was still a humor magazine then. During Reinhardt's tenure and in subsequent years, *Jester* resembled the *New Yorker* in both content and design, mixing cartoons and reviews with stories and opinion pieces. The writers Lax and his friends admired were Robert Benchley, E. B. White, and James Thurber.

Although he kept a journal for a while in high school, Lax had abandoned the practice by the time he reached college, leaving no clear record of his thoughts during those crucial years. Later, when he started journaling again, he wrote that his high school entries had all been "associated with bilious attacks or dizzy spells from loneliness maybe." Loneliness wasn't a problem in college. In quick succession during his freshman year, he made friends not only with Merton, Reinhardt, Freed-good, and Slate but also two other Roberts—Gerdy and Gibney. These were the men he likened to those jamming jazz musicians. There was a harmony among them in almost all they did, a feeling of mutual support and encouragement. Lax recognized this harmony as a kind of love and spent much of his later life searching for a community that replicated it.

One of the things that distinguished these men beyond their wit and writing ability was their outsider status, whether chosen by them or imposed by others. Most of Columbia's student body in the mid-1930s was white, Protestant, and privileged. (The yearbook for Lax's senior year shows only one African American, Benjamin W. Johnson, "Captain of the Track Team, World Champion, 60 meter dash." Like almost everyone else in the book, Johnson is dressed in a dark suit and conservative tie.) Columbia's president at the time, Nicholas Murray Butler, was a tight-fisted autocrat and former Republican presidential candidate who had been running the university for over thirty years. (He would rule for forty-three years altogether.) Widely viewed as pompous and arrogant, Butler dismissed faculty members who disagreed with him, openly admired Mussolini during his early years in power, and pursued an anti-Semitic policy that severely limited the number of Jews enrolled at his university.

And it was *his* university. When a friend of Lax's named Robert Burke ("one-time Junior President of the Class of '38, and University boxing champion") led a demonstration against Butler's decision to send a representative to a celebration in Nazi Germany, Butler expelled him. Despite an uproar that reached beyond the Columbia campus and even a lawsuit, Butler refused to reinstate Burke and later barred him from campus. He refused to rescind an invitation for a Nazi ambassador to speak at Columbia too. An art history professor lost his job for opposing that decision. Butler received the Nobel Peace Prize in 1931 for his work as a "leader of the more establishment-oriented part of the American peace movement," but in his domain peace was imposed rather than negotiated.

In this "establishment-oriented" atmosphere, virtually everyone in Lax and Merton's circle was outside the mainstream. Reinhardt, for example, had grown up Lutheran but was already moving toward communism, which he would embrace more fully after graduating. Merton had been raised a Protestant, but outside the United States. He spoke with a slight British accent, and most of his attitudes and opinions were more European than American. Gibney, who had grown up Catholic, was by nature a rebel, quick to offer a clever but cynical comment on whatever subject was being discussed. (When Lax, a Jew, became a Catholic years later, Gibney said all he had to do was blacken his face and he'd be all three things southerners hate.) Of the remaining four, all but Slate, whose mother was an immigrant from Wales, were Jews.

While anti-Semitism is still a vexatious problem in the United States, it is hard to remember or appreciate in our post-Holocaust world how ubiquitous and almost commonplace it was before the war, not just in the South, where the Ku Klux Klan had more members than there were Jews in the country, but also in the North. Public figures like Henry Ford, Charles Lindbergh, and Father Charles Edward Coughlin spoke openly against Jews in newspapers and on radio. As late as 1938, public opinion polls showed that most Americans had a low opinion of Jews in general. During the two decades after World War I, an unpublished quota system severely reduced the number of Jewish students at many of the country's top universities—from 40 to 20 percent at Columbia, for example.

Anti-Semitism was at its peak in Europe during this time, of course. Hitler took power just one year before Lax entered Columbia and invaded Poland one year after he graduated. Among the America Firsters who battled to keep the United States out of the war, including Ford and Lindbergh, many spoke highly of Nazi policies. More indicative of the general atmosphere, perhaps, is how few in the country defended their fellow Americans.

But while others like Burke were pursuing principled public defiance, Lax, Merton, and their friends were gathering on the fourth floor of John Jay Hall, where the offices of most student groups and campus publications were located. Although it was a chaotic place, full of shouts and insults and running around, it was a refuge too, where intelligent and energetic young men could pursue their interests, their cleverness, and even their silliness without the heaviness the outside world imposed. Politicians were figures to be mocked, demonstrations follies to be ridiculed. It wasn't that serious discussion didn't take place or make its way onto some of the publications' pages, particularly those of the student newspaper, the *Spectator*, but simply that skepticism and scorn prevailed.

"It was the noisiest and most agitated part of the campus," Merton writes.

> It was not gay, exactly. And I hardly ever saw, anywhere, antipathies and contentions and jealousies at once so petty, so open, and so sharp. The whole floor was constantly seething with the exchange of insults from office to office. Constantly, all day long, from morning to night, people were writing articles and drawing cartoons calling each other Fascists. Or else they were calling one another up on the phone and assuring one another in the coarsest terms of their undying hatred. It was all intellectual and verbal, as vicious as it could be, but it never became concrete, never descended into physical rage. For this reason, I think that it was all more or less of a game which everybody played for purposes that were remotely esthetic.

The sharp edge of keen perception was always part of Lax's humor. Even so, it's hard to imagine him involved in this sort of rough play. Fifty years later, when I asked him to describe the worst thing he'd ever done, he remembered an incident from this time. His side had just triumphed in a dispute between *Jester*'s editorial and business teams. One of the business students bowed down in mock praise, and Lax, caught up in the moment, put his foot on the boy's neck. No one was offended, he said, but he had crossed some personal line, implying a hubris that frightened him.

The love of language Lax and his friends shared gave them impressive verbal acuity, but their hyperawareness of meanings and pseudo-meanings, connotations and denotations, could have a deadening effect on individual words and thoughts. Every term or concept was suspect, subject to the charge of being phony—even words such as *contemplation* and *mysticism* Lax and Merton would later embrace. (Their distrust of mysticism came out in a game they called Subway Mysticism. Standing in the middle of a subway car, they'd pretend the train's acceleration was taking them into a mystic trance.)

Professor Mark Van Doren wrote that in those days Lax was "so uncommunicative and so shy that even if I had tried I could have uncovered none of his secrets," but Lax's supposed inarticulateness might have come less from shyness than reluctance to mock things he took seriously. It's unlikely he was ever much of a mocker anyway. As the story about his foot on the boy's neck shows, it disturbed him deeply to ever do anything that degraded another person, even in jest.

Although Merton writes of arguments with Lax, it's doubtful Lax ever said anything that provoked an angry or violent response. It wasn't just that he was rail thin and gawky (with a face, he wrote, that people had described as looking like "a horse, Count Orgaz, any long-face Modigliani, John Carradine as the Devil of Shark's Island, Abraham Lincoln and Savonarola") but also that he had a gentle disposition. One reason he eventually left New York for good was that he didn't have the heart for competition, except of the friendliest kind. As Van Doren was to write years later, he had a great "love of the world and all things, all persons in it." Part of his particular existential search, especially when young, was for ways to love and reconcile everyone and everything. For him this wasn't some sentimental wish but rather the prime purpose of life. And it was inextricably bound with writing.

"Characteristically he conceived the function of those who knew how to write, and who had something to say, in terms of the salvation of society," Merton wrote in his autobiography in the late 1940s.

> Lax's picture of America, before which he has stood for twelve years with his hands hanging in helplessness at his sides—is the picture of a country full of people who want to be kind and pleasant and happy and love good things and serve God, but do not know how. And they do not know where to turn to find out. They are surrounded by all kinds of sources of information which only conspire to bewilder them more and more. And Lax's vision is a vision of the day when they will turn on the radio and somebody will start telling them what they have really been wanting to hear and needing to know. They will find somebody who is capable of telling them of the love of God in language that will no longer sound hackneyed or crazy, but with an authority and conviction: the conviction born of sanctity.

Merton was too limiting, I think. Lax saw more than just one country living in harmony. As his comments to me suggest, he saw a whole world moving to the same music. A world he loved in all its particulars already. Many who have written about him in his later years have called him a hermit or a solitary, but Lax never wanted to leave the world as Merton did; he wanted to embrace it. "The daily life is Bob's religion," wrote Alex Eliot, a critic and friend he worked with at *Time* magazine and stayed with the first time he went to Greece, "it is his form of prayer."

In a 1986 interview, Lax said:

> I think a writer should be immersed in life, and also to withdraw from it; at least enough to sit quietly and write. I think you can be immersed in the life of the community around you, and also be immersed in your own life, your own inner life, which can also be as thronged and active as the life of any community you might be living in. Immersed is a good word; it sounds to me like sinking to the bottom of the medium you're living in. But sinking in a way that allows you to breathe, and to see, and eventually to sum up or recapture what you've seen in writing. I think you can only *confidently* drop to the bottom of a medium you're living in if you love it.

One of the problems with biographies, especially autobiographies, is that they look back at earlier periods through filters: new perspectives, new theories, new ideologies and moods. This was especially true for Merton, who had become not only a Catholic between his college days with Lax and his writing of *The Seven Storey Mountain* but a Trappist monk and priest as well. During those twelve years he said Lax stood with his hands hanging helpless at his sides, wanting to save society—the twelve years since they first met—so much had changed for both of them that his picture of Lax (and of himself, for that matter) as a college student is inevitably skewed. Add to this that his book was heavily censored and that his own desire not to make his pre-Catholic and premonastic life sound like too much fun constrained him, and it's easy to imagine that Lax was a less spiritually focused and more physically immersed character in college than Merton suggests.

Start with this: The college antics and adventures Merton does include in his book *were* fun. Half the pleasure of reading it, as with reading St. Augustine's *Confessions*, is participating vicariously in them. And Lax was clearly there for many of them, fully engaged. He drank, sometimes to excess. He smoked, both cigarettes and, on at least one occasion, pot. (In 1970, while working on *The Man in the Sycamore Tree*, his irreverent biography of Merton, Columbia friend Ed Rice asked Lax in a letter if it would be okay to say that he was the first middle-class white guy he ever saw smoking pot. Lax told me that Billie Holiday once invited him back to her apartment in Harlem to listen to music and smoke dope; worried about his studies, he declined.) And he went out with, danced with, and probably slept with women, though he seems to have chosen abstinence early on.

Lax eventually gave up all of these activities, but it's important to note that he didn't go through life surrounded by a spiritual aura, as some who have written about him have suggested. He was a boy, a college student, a member of a group with a strong antiestablishment streak. He was more cautious than others perhaps, quicker to consider the consequences of things he did and learn from experience (his aunt said he was the only child who looked both ways before crossing a street in his baby carriage), but he lived a full social and physical life.

What Lax mostly was in college was what many bright students are: a young person trying to discover who he was or could be—reading new books, contemplating new ideas, trying out new thoughts and attitudes. He wasn't looking for a role to play, however; he was looking for an authentic self. *His* authentic self. One of the most notable things about him is how important he considered the search to be and how long he kept at it—long enough not only to see his authentic self emerge but to understand that it had been there all along.

"When I was in college," he wrote in a journal decades later, "I had a checking account, good for about 15 dollars a week. So every Friday I'd make out a check for 15 dollars, & sign it, each time, I thought, with a different flourish. At the end of the month the checks would come back cancelled from the bank and I'd look at them again. The signatures all turned out to look exactly alike."

One of the main differences between Merton and Lax was that Merton was a brilliant and tireless self-promoter, while Lax was often taciturn or tongue-tied in public, relying on his work to speak for him. Another was that Merton was vitally concerned—in college and later—with finding answers, while Lax seemed much more comfortable with questions. Decades down the line, while Merton shouted to the world what he'd discovered in the cave of solitude, Lax sat quietly within, offering an occasional smoke signal.

---

Throughout his early schooling Lax was an overachiever, and the same was true in college. Although he took no notes in class (he preferred to listen, he told me) and by his own admission spent his senior year in a fog, he achieved an A– average in classes that included an Important Books of the World colloquium; a three-year sequence on literature from Greek and Roman times through the nineteenth century; Mark Van Doren's renowned year-long course on Shakespeare; Jacques Barzun's Thought and Culture in the 19th Century; Philosophy of Art; and Mediaeval and Renaissance Latin. It was as a poet and editor, however, that he truly excelled. The year he served as editor in chief of *Jester*, 1936–37, the American Association of College Comics named it the country's funniest college humor magazine. In addition to editing, Lax wrote movie and theater reviews, added an occasional end piece, and contributed poems and playful articles. His humor is the kind you'd expect from an Ivy League humor magazine, and the striving to be urbane is palpable, but the writing is sharp even when a poem is silly or a story goes nowhere.

During his senior year Lax was an editor in chief again, this time for the *Columbia Review*, the university's literary magazine. He oversaw a radical redesign and put an illustration by Reinhardt, who had graduated two years before, on the cover. Merton had graduated too, but Lax slipped a portion of one of his novels into the journal's first issue and his review of Aldous Huxley's *Ends and Means*, a book Lax had suggested Merton read, into the second issue. That same year Lax won Gold and Silver Crowns from the King's Crown Board (a student affairs group), was selected to write the lyrics for the school's annual Varsity Show, and was voted "best writer" by his classmates (a distinction Merton had earned the year before). That spring Van Doren and Barzun chose several of his poems for their annual showcase of student work, and Lax appeared in the *Columbian*'s "Hall of Fame." Finally, the Boar's Head Society awarded him first prize for his poem "The Last Days of a City," which he read at a public event.

The Boar's Head Society was an adjunct to Columbia College's venerable poetry group, the Philolexian Society, which Lax and Merton both joined. Bored with the Society's stuffiness and focus on noncreative matters, they once formed an antisociety with fellow classmate John Berryman. The purpose of their new society was entirely creative: reading and commenting on each other's work. The first meeting went as planned, but at the second meeting Berryman read a long poem the others couldn't understand, then gave his own explication of it. They never met again.

---

Although he never wrote about it, one of the most important things Lax did during his college years was travel to Europe with John Slate in the early summer of 1937. Their itinerary took them to Paris, Marseilles, Cannes, Venice, Como, and back to Paris. In later years Lax referred to the trip only when telling two of his favorite stories, but the love he developed for Europe suggests it had a profound effect on him. I know from personal experience that traveling in Europe when young makes the books you've read and the history you've learned come alive. For a Columbia student in the late 1930s this must have been especially true. In those days before colonialism and post-colonialism became part of university studies, everything learned at a major liberal arts institution like Columbia—philosophy, literature, art, history, and language—came out of the European tradition. Beyond that, things were *happening* in Europe. The Spanish Civil War was raging (Guernica was bombed just weeks before Lax left the States) and, one year after the Berlin Olympics, Hitler was in the full flush of his early power. Having announced Germany's withdrawal from the Treaty of Versailles, he was cementing his alliance with Mussolini and making it clear he was ready for war. The World Exposition in Paris opened only days before Lax's arrival there. Although dedicated to peace and coexistence, it featured intimidating monumental architecture from Germany and the Soviet Union and, in the sleekly modern Spanish Pavilion, the summer's most talked-about work of art: Picasso's *Guernica*.

Despite events in Spain, it was still possible in the summer of 1937 to think that Europe could avoid all-out war—to believe, like Neville Chamberlain, who became Britain's prime minister just days before Lax landed on the Continent, that negotiation could lead to "peace in our time."

Lax never wrote about his travels with Slate or what he thought, as a Jew, being so close to Hitler's Germany. Of the two stories he told about the trip, one was lighthearted and the other was deeply personal, setting up his return to Europe fourteen years later.

In the first story, he and Slate were on a train passing through the Alps. Out of boredom or mere goofiness, they'd taken to barking whenever their train went through a tunnel. At one point they were having a high-minded discussion with a young German when a tunnel appeared. At the tunnel's end, the German said, "You know very well the method of barking."

(Slate became a traveling salesman, and for years he would call Lax from wherever he was and bark into the phone. Lax would bark back and Slate would hang up without ever speaking.)

The other story is just as brief. The two friends stepped off the train in Marseilles, intending to stay a day or two, but something about the city frightened Lax. When they went into a café near the port, it scared him even more and he rushed back to the station. He didn't know what it was that frightened him, but fourteen years later, fired by a desire to live by faith alone, he remembered his fear and returned to Marseilles to face it.

The trip with Slate was only one of several events that made an impact on Lax that year. He attended several sessions of Bob Gerdy's class on Scholastic philosophy and came away with an intense interest in St. Thomas Aquinas that would last throughout his life. Bob Gibney was interested in Scholastic philosophy too, and that spring the three of them talked about becoming Catholics. In doing so Gibney would be returning to his origins, but Gerdy and Lax would be moving from Judaism to Christianity. None of them acted on the impulse.

Aquinas was just one of many writers drawing Lax toward Christianity in those years. Another was T. S. Eliot, who had joined the Anglican Church a few years before. Lax in fact credited Eliot with prompting his thoughts of conversion. I don't know what of Eliot's he was reading, but *Essays Ancient and Modern* had appeared the year before. In it Eliot wrote, "All one's views and theories, of course, have some ultimate relation to the kind of man one is. But only the Catholic, in practice, is under the manifest obligation to find out what sort of man he is—because he is under the obligation to improve that man according to definite ideals and standards." Although Eliot capitalized the word *catholic*, he was using it in a broader sense to mean a member of the universal Christian church. Given the other things Lax was reading that year, including Huxley's *Ends and Means*, and the views he later expressed about all of mankind coming together under God, it's easy to see how such a passage might have affected him.

————

It should come as no surprise that although they had met two years before, 1937 was the year Lax and Merton became close friends. Merton was making his own move toward Christianity that year, and as they traded books, their thoughts began to overlap until it was impossible to say which of them initiated any particular thought or belief. In his autobiography Merton concentrates primarily on his own development, but he suggests more than once that his exchange of ideas with Lax deepened the thinking of both of them. Over the next three years, in fact—the three years in which they spent the most time in each other's company—they read the books and developed the ideas that would guide them along their future paths. One of those books was *Ends and Means*, which Lax read first and gave to Merton in November 1937.

Written as a kind of guidebook for making moral decisions on both a global and a personal level, *Ends and Means* was also an announcement of Huxley's conversion to belief in a kind of mysticism. Merton's description of his reaction to the book might easily have come from Lax:

> Huxley was too sharp and intelligent and had too much sense of humor to take any of the missteps that usually make such conversions look ridiculous and oafish. . . .
>
> On the contrary, he had read widely and deeply and intelligently in all kinds of Christian and Oriental mystical literature, and had come out with the astonishing truth that all this, far from being a mixture of dreams and magic and charlatanism, was very real and very serious.
>
> Not only was there such a thing as a supernatural order, but as a matter of concrete experience, it was accessible, very close at hand, an extremely near, an immediate and most necessary source of moral vitality, and one which could be reached most simply, most readily by prayer, faith, detachment, love.

Huxley advocates freeing oneself from the perverted idea that ends justify means, arguing that it is the use of evil means—war, violence, and so on—that makes good impossible. By renouncing these more animalistic impulses, we can free our mind and will. "Not only that," Merton writes, "once the spirit was freed, and returned to its own element, it was not alone there: it could find the absolute and perfect Spirit, God. It could enter into union with Him: and what is more, this union was not something vague and metaphorical, but it was a matter of real experience."

Huxley drew from a combination of Western and Eastern religious traditions, sending Merton on a search for Eastern texts he didn't know. These texts took tangible form a few months later, when Lax's roommate, Freedgood, brought a man into their dorm room who influenced Lax's and Merton's thinking about living in union with God more than anything they'd read.

---

While Lax and Merton were developing spiritually, they were developing as writers too, learning to think of themselves as artists while gaining a deeper understanding of what it meant to make art. Reinhardt was influential in this area, as were teachers like Meyer Shapiro and Lionel Trilling, but the man who had the greatest influence on their awareness and appreciation of the written arts in particular was the professor and poet Mark Van Doren.

In his autobiography Merton describes stumbling into Van Doren's year-long Shakespeare class by accident and, seeing Lax and others from the fourth floor of John Jay Hall in the room, deciding to stay. This was in the fall of 1936, when Van Doren was the film critic for the *Nation*, having served as the magazine's literary editor for four years in the 1920s. He was beginning his sixteenth of thirty-nine years at Columbia and had already published most of the poems that would win him a Pulitzer Prize for his *Collected Poems, 1922–1938* four years later. He had established a reputation as one of the university's best teachers too, an accomplishment Columbia students would celebrate after his retirement by naming their yearly teaching award the Mark Van Doren Award.

Van Doren's particular gift as a teacher is hard to pin down, perhaps because it was so multifaceted, drawing from all he was as a poet, critic, mentor, and man. Several years after Lax had graduated, he struggled to convey what made Van Doren's teaching so extraordinary. In an unpublished poem, he compares Van Doren to trees giving shade, praises his laugh, and wonders at the depth not of his knowledge but of his love—for the world, his students, and especially his subjects.

There was something more, though, something ethereal, maybe ineffable:

he was a musician
and a sly musician, too:
his classes sang
although he scarcely seemed
to breathe

upon the strings;

a psalmist too:
he was the creator
reflected in every stone
and leaf and vine

he stood before the vision
wondering,
until we saw it too

Shakespeare was the perfect subject for Van Doren because he could find the whole human world in it. "All that year," Merton writes, "we were, in fact, talking about the deepest springs of human desire and hope and fear; we were considering all the most important realities, not indeed in terms of something alien to Shakespeare and to poetry, but precisely in his own terms, with occasional intuitions of another order." In other words, he was teaching them about life.

The importance Van Doren attached to mindful precision in poetry, teaching, and daily life comes through in his response to hearing Lax misquote a Shakespeare line one day. "If you're going to quote," he said, "get it right."

---

It's important to remember that although Lax and Merton were serious about sorting out what they believed and digging deeper into spiritual matters, their budding ideologies and theologies were mainly theoretical, grounded only in what they'd read and their own limited experience. Then, in the last month of Lax's senior year, a tiny man wearing a white cloak, a yellow turban, and blue sneakers walked into his dorm room, proving the truth of the Zen saying *When the student is ready the teacher will appear.*

Lax's roommate, Sy Freedgood, had invited the strange-looking man to stay with them for a few days as they were packing to leave school. Freedgood's future wife had met him while studying philosophy at the University of Chicago, and he had stayed with Freedgood's family on Long Island for a while, where Freedgood's ancient grandmother stayed far away from him, thinking he was the hereditary enemy of the Jewish people. In reality he was a Hindu monk named Mahanambrata Brahmachari.

According to Merton, Brahmachari came from an ashram called Sri Angan (the Playground) on the outskirts of Calcutta led by a Hindu messiah whose mission was to foster universal peace and brotherhood. In 1932 the ashram received an invitation to send a representative to something called the World Congress of Religions at the Chicago World's Fair, and the young Brahmachari, who had never been out of India, was chosen to go. He was given enough money to buy a ticket for "a little more than half the distance," says Merton, after which he'd have to rely on heaven for his needs. Heaven was more than up to the task. By the time he landed in Lax's dorm room, Brahmachari had been in the United States for at least five years, had earned a doctorate at the University of Chicago, and had lectured on subjects such as Hindu Gods in Everyday Living to civic groups and colleges like Smith and Vassar. He doesn't seem to have been paid for any of these lectures. Whenever he needed something, someone gave it to him. When he was out of funds, he'd leave an open purse on a table. When he wanted to go somewhere, he simply walked down to the train station.

Although Brahmachari told both Lax and Merton things that influenced their decisions then and later—including the advice to look deeper into their own traditions rather than adopting some Eastern religion they would never understand as well—it was his presence and demeanor that made the greatest impression on them. He was, Lax said later, the first true "holy man" they'd ever met.

"I feel sure," Lax said, "that what held me about him was not so much his ideas . . . but his personality, and the kind of civilization—the kind of planet—he came from . . . as though I had always felt there must be that kind of planet somewhere and I was glad to see a representative of it come our way at last."

The superiority of where he came from to where Lax and his friends were living wasn't something Brahmachari ever had to speak about because they could feel it when they were with him. "It was easy for him to let us see through his eyes," Lax said, "because he was always living in the present moment and seeing through his own eyes and you could practically see what he was seeing, how he was seeing things. We once offered him a cup of coffee and his refusal was polite and quiet, but it was obvious that it wasn't the sort of thing that he would drink; it would be an assault on his body and his organism to drink a thing like that."

The monks at Brahmachari's ashram were vegetarians and wore only robes and turbans, not shoes. Even in his Keds (which someone had given him), Brahmachari's walk was as light as a cat's, Lax said, and his approach to everything was gentle. "He didn't make a fuss about not eating meat, he just didn't eat it. . . . There was never the slightest thing heavy about him or his company."

Lax came from a Reform family that didn't follow Jewish dietary laws, but Brahmachari's advice and especially his manner made such a strong impression on him that he began to study the Jewish scriptures and attempted to keep kosher while continuing to read Catholic writers with Merton. He began to write a "novel" about Brahmachari's life as well, with Brahmachari's blessing. One day, after Brahmachari had returned to India, Lax saw his face in a dream and woke up realizing he hadn't worked on the book for a long time. A short time later he received a letter from Brahmachari. "How's the 'book'?" he wrote. "Or did I say something to you about it in a dream?"

The influence of Brahmachari's words and way of being was so pivotal and long-lasting that Merton mentioned him in his last letter to Lax, days before he died. By then, based in part on decisions Brahmachari had led him to, Lax was living in a manner much like that of the guru in blue sneakers.

———————

When he was older Lax never drank anything stronger than tea, but just before I left the island that year I coaxed him out for one small glass of wine to celebrate his seventy-second birthday. We sat and talked for hours. He seemed to want to help me decide the next steps in my life, not knowing his mere presence had helped me already. Don't be too impetuous, he cautioned. Above all, observe. And learn. And *write*.

# 3    Portals to a Land of Dusk

When you meet a man in his sixty-ninth year and he seems at peace with himself and the world, it's tempting to think his road has been smooth, his decisions easy. And Lax portrayed his life that way. Instead of discussing his doubts and despair, his years of wandering and wondering what he should do, he spoke of times when things were good, like his days with Merton or his childhood. Although his parents were both immigrants and Jews at a time of widespread anti-immigrant and anti-Semitic feeling, he grew up in a place of tolerance and relative prosperity, and so his early years as the long-awaited son in a family and culture that venerated boys brought him mostly joy. He was a happy, smart, precocious boy in a family of strong women who doted on him and told stories meant to show his specialness.

There was the time, for example, when he was crawling along the floor at his grandparents' house and bumped a table insert. The insert shifted and tottered, as if about to fall on him and then, while the adults held their breath, settled back against the wall.

And the time his sister Gladys (called Gladio), who was eleven years older and a second mother to him, asked if he knew why everyone in the family liked him. "Because you like us so much," she said.

And the many times he heard a complicated joke and was able to repeat it verbatim—evidence, obviously, of his intelligence and good humor.

A photograph taken when Lax was just a few weeks old shows him in his mother's arms with everyone in his family looking down at him except his sister Sal, who stares somewhat skeptically at the camera. It's tempting to view the photograph as a foretaste of the family's various roles in his life. A balding Siggie stands gently in a suit and tie in the shadows in back. Lax's mother, Betty, dominates the scene physically, her body larger than the others and the look on her face one of competent concern. Gladio stands slightly apart, almost angelic in a light dress, her hands behind her back and her face adoring, as if waiting patiently for the day she'll assume responsibility for her brother's well-being.

They all knew he was going to do something uncommon with his life. Something extraordinary. Especially his mother, who did everything within her power to make her hopes for him come true.

———————

The photographs are sepia, the color of the lost and mourned: sad-faced men in hoary beards and skullcaps reading the Talmud or the Torah, a smiling woman in a fine full dress with lace across the chest, vendors' shops with living quarters up above, and panoramas of the district's squares, including a two-page spread of an enormous crowded market. Most touching are the mundane moments: a small boy showing off a shoe to a girl carrying water bottles, a woman holding up a goose while talking to a shopkeeper, a fish above a market scale, its mouth dripping water.

The book is dedicated to "all Polish Jews, after whom weep the deserted cities, towns [and] villages, whose traces are disappearing or have already disappeared"—and that's the way things looked the day I found it in a bookshop in Kazimierz, Krakow's old Jewish quarter: the streets deserted, the squares empty. You could almost hear the weeping for the disappeared, including Lax's mother's family. Lax had asked me to send him a postcard from this place where his ancestors lived, but here was something better, I thought: a wormhole to the world they lived in. A book so accurate and comprehensive, Stephen Spielberg used it to evoke the times and place in *Schindler's List*.

It wasn't until I opened the book again after Lax had died that I noticed how many of the white-bearded men in those old photographs had the same look in their eyes I'd seen in his in contemplative moments. It was a far-gazing look that conveyed an almost painful awareness of life in its many dimensions and the profound significance of each moment lived. "Every moment is a gift and so is the flow through which the moments go," he said once, "and so you let the moments come, you let the moments go."

But in each moment, as he'd said to me, we make decisions, large and small, and if his mother's family had decided to stay in Krakow, he might have been one of those whose lives Spielberg depicted—saved, perhaps, but probably lost.

After purchasing the book, I visited the Rumah Synagogue, the only synagogue still left in Kazimierz, and a cemetery behind it with a wall made entirely of old gravestone fragments full of Hebrew letters. I wondered if any of those fragments came from graves that held Lax's ancestors and if his feeling of being at home with the less fortunate came in part from his connection to this humble place where his mother was born. A place—a moment in history—his family escaped.

————————

According to the 1910 census, Rebecca (Betty) Hotchner entered the United States in 1881 when she was three years old. Like many young men at the time, her father was fleeing Austro-Hungarian Emperor Franz Josef II's recently instituted draft, knowing that Jews were harshly treated in the emperor's army. Why the family settled in Elmira, New York, is unclear, but there was no Ellis Island at the time and immigrant ships often sailed far up the Hudson before discharging their passengers. Betty's family wasn't prominent, but it was said her grandfather had made trappings for the emperor's carriages. The family wasn't wealthy, but they had enough to avoid the stigma of traveling in steerage.

At the time her family emigrated, Betty had only one brother, Henry, who was one year old. A second brother, Maurice, would be born in 1884, and two sisters, Celia and Rosamund (called Roz), would come later, when Betty was already a teenager. Maurice was a sickly baby, and at some point when Betty was still young, her mother, Hedwig (who might have married her husband, Saul, in the Rumah Synagogue I visited), took him back to Europe to be treated by a peasant woman with a reputation for working miracles with ailing children. She took Betty and Henry with her too, and they stayed for three years in a place Betty, in a paper she wrote later in her life, called simply "Austria." Whether or not this was Krakow no one knows, but it seems likely. What is clear from Betty's paper is that it was far from Vienna and that she remembered her sojourn there, even years later, as idyllic. She describes a spring evening with "gaily uniformed soldiers escorting beautiful women" and a summer night with the far-off sound "of an accordion singing bright Viennese waltzes." She writes of summer days of play with local children and of "tremulous evenings" when the adults had gone away and the "children would sit near the huge white kitchen stove to hear the peasant house-maid telling stories of war, always war."

The housemaid she writes about, Yagga, was probably the miracle-working peasant who bathed Maurice daily in a bath of boiled pork skin and bones until he was, as one member of the Hotchner family put it, "plump and rosy." Betty writes just enough about Yagga and her world to make a reader long for a fuller description. A whole book. Although she was never a writer per se, her writing is fluid and filled with both telling details and a sense of story, as shown in this paragraph about preparing for the emperor's passage through the city:

> To celebrate the event there were to be fireworks and illuminations. The caretaker of our house called for volunteers to help him make mud candle-holders, glorified mud-pies. Childish fingers worked de-lightedly all afternoon. In the evening lighted candles were placed on the windowsills, balustrades and all conceivable vantage points. We children were permitted to keep eyes shining an extra hour. How could we know when the Emperor's train steamed by in the distance? We couldn't. Eyelids drooped, candles flickered, shutters closed. Dark-ness. The next day we were told the Emperor had passed through the city at three o'clock in the morning.

The childish delight and sense of belonging in this passage are fol-lowed almost immediately by a description of leaving the idyll behind: "Finally the farewell to grandparents, aunts, uncles and the faithful Yagga who had been in the family since Mother was a child. The ocean trip back to America." She goes on to say that she couldn't understand her American playmates because she had forgotten the English she knew. She relearned the language by reading picture books, understanding only "a word here and there" and making up her own plot. She attended school, of course, and did so well in it her teachers hoped she'd go to col-lege. When the subject was raised with her father, however, he said there was only enough money for his sons. As was too often the case for bright girls in those turn-of-the-century days, Betty's best option was to go to a business school, where she learned to type and take dictation. She worked for a while in New York City, where her family had moved, but she longed for a different life—the life in the country she had lived for those few glorious years as a child. Then Siggie came along and moved her upstate.

---

Sigmund (Siggie) Lax made his way across the Atlantic alone in 1893 when he was sixteen, probably from Vienna. His destination was Coudersport, Pennsylvania, where his uncle Saul Deiches owned a clothing business. Saul was from his mother's side, some of whose forebears had been rabbinical scholars. The forebears on his father's side were Sephardic Jews, which means they came originally from the Mediterranean region, not far from where Lax lived the last part of his life. There were Laxes in Spain and even in Turkey, he told me once. He seemed to like that he was surrounded by people connected, however distantly, to his father.

Siggie lived with his uncle and aunt and worked in his uncle's clothing store while going to high school. Most of the store's clients were lumbermen who brought their pay to town to drink and fight on Saturday nights. Siggie was in town to see it all because the stores stayed open until midnight on those Saturdays to address the loggers' more prosaic needs. According to Gladio, Saul wanted him to study law when he finished high school, but Siggie was a "reluctant scholar," so Saul made him manager of his men's store in Olean.

Betty writes in her autobiography of longing to live in the country and the coming of a "sweetheart" who turned that longing into reality. That sweetheart was Siggie, who moved to New York City with his uncle before going to Olean and met Betty when Saul Hotchner invited his fellow clothing merchant to dinner. When the two were married and had settled in Olean, Siggie brought his parents, Naftali and Regina Lax, and his younger brother, Joseph, across from Austria. All three Lax men worked for Saul Deiches in his store, one of several he owned in the greater Pennsylvania–southwestern New York area, until, in 1908, they bought it from him. Rechristening it Lax and Lax, they moved the store from 170 N. Union to a larger space a few doors away, where they sold men's personal accessories, shoes, and hats in addition to tailored clothes.

By the time Lax was born on November 30, 1915, Olean had been riding a mostly rising economic tide for over forty years, ever since the Olean Petroleum Company completed a pipeline from the Pennsylvania state line to the Olean railroad yards in 1874. The first commercial oil well in the United States was drilled at Titusville, Pennsylvania, in 1859, but it was the discovery of oil five years later in the nearby town of Bradford, a stone's throw from Olean, that initiated America's first oil boom. Although petroleum consumption in those pre-automobile days was modest, the output from what came to be called the Bradford Oil Field, an 84,000-acre pool that spills across the Pennsylvania–New York border, was impressive. In 1881 the Bradford field provided 83 percent of the oil consumed in the United States and 77 percent of the oil produced in the entire world.

In *A Pocket of Peace: A History of Bradford 1879–1979*, Mary Ann Johnston reports that Bradford's first settlers were loggers who hoped to find coal in the area's hills, not knowing a rich ocean of oil ran beneath them. She credits a man named Lewis Emery Jr. with beginning the Bradford rush when he struck oil in 1875 and the value of his land rose from 6¼ cents to $1,000 an acre. The news brought throngs from everywhere who sank wells wherever there was land. The height of the rush came in 1882, when 11,800 wells were drilled in a single year. A photograph in Johnston's book shows small wooden shacks on a bare hillside with wooden derricks all around. The burning of the natural gas that came up from the wells (considered useless in those days) sent flames ten feet into the air, turning night into day, and fires were a regular occurrence.

Wing, Wilbur & Company opened Olean's first refinery in 1877, and in 1880 the Acme Oil Refinery moved there. As the town boomed, fortune seekers poured in, including a twenty-four-year-old from Mobile, Alabama, named Harris Wolfe Marcus. While visiting the area on his honeymoon, Marcus noticed on a walk through Olean that all of the storefronts were full. Thinking the town's future would be bright, he convinced his wife's brother, a Bradford oilman, to help him buy a grocery store, and the young couple moved up from the South to run it. Within a few years Marcus had bought out his brother-in-law and turned the little shop into the H. W. Marcus Department Store, the flagship of the H. W. Marcus Company, with investments in a number of enterprises, including oil.

Over time Marcus became one of the area's richest landowners and an Olean town leader. After meeting Alexander Graham Bell on a trip out west, he installed the town's first telephone, and he served on the Chamber of Commerce for many years. He is best remembered, however, as the organizer and then leader of the town's Jewish community, the man most responsible for fostering the tolerant environment Lax was raised in.

By the end of his first year in Olean, Marcus had drawn together a group that called itself the Olean Social Club, with sixteen local Jews as charter members. The club grew rapidly, becoming a congregation that met in a variety of buildings before breaking ground on its first synagogue in 1928. Marcus would serve as leader of the Olean Jewish community for sixty years, fifty of them as congregation president. He would eventually buy the Olean House Hotel, a landmark in the town and in Lax's childhood. And he would sire five children, the oldest of whom, Benjamin (called Benji), would one day marry Gladio, putting Lax's modest family in proximity to wealth.

---

North Union Street, where Siggie and his family had their shop, was one of the two most important streets in Olean. It was lined with restaurants, cafés, and stores of every sort: groceries and hardware stores, at least one jewelry store and bookseller, cigar stores that rolled their own, and the Italo-American Fruit Company, which sold not only fruit but ice cream and an assortment of candies made on the premises. The Western Union office was there, the First National Bank (the first bank in Cattaraugus County), and, of course, the Marcus store.

The other important street, State Street, was just a block away from the Lax shop, beyond the 225-room Olean House Hotel, whose accommodations, one writer claimed, were equal to those available in any of the larger East Coast cities. Early twentieth-century photographs show an ornate iron canopy out front and a spacious lobby with fluted columns, chandeliers with glass shades shaped like flowers, and a delicately painted, inordinately high ceiling. The hotel was popular with East Coast residents who came by train to spend time in the beautiful countryside around the Allegany River.

From the late 1800s until 1927, a regional trolley system carried passengers (and freight) from Olean along a triangular route with Salamanca, New York, and Bradford, Pennsylvania, at the other corners. Along the way, they passed through some of the most beautiful countryside in the two states, crossing and recrossing the river and rising up through wooded hills. In later years, after the trolley system fell victim to the automobile, Lax's brother-in-law Benji Marcus would build a cottage in those hills and Lax would spend two summers there with Merton and their college friends, living in a manner some have said influenced the Beats.

---

While Siggie built his clothing business, Betty busied herself raising their three children—Gladio, Sylvia (called Sally or just Sal), and their much younger brother, Bobby. But Betty had city energy and child rearing wasn't enough to use it up. In her spare time she helped found the local YMCA and the town's swimming pool, where she taught swimming. She raised funds for the Jewish Congregation's first synagogue, taking responsibility for its signature feature, an elaborate rose window. And she took classes at St. Bonaventure College. After studying voice, she even started singing in the local Methodist and Presbyterian church choirs.

Betty often took Bobby along on her various outings, giving him his first taste of Christianity and the friars who ran St. Bonaventure, both of which would be important sources of spiritual succor and peace when he was older. St. Bonaventure is a large, modern school today, with a variety of attractive, mostly brick buildings, including a state-of-the-art library annex where Lax's papers are kept. In those days, however, it was a small, rural Catholic college with mostly wooden buildings. The college's first building, built in 1856 and housing the monastery, was still standing then, as was an 1888 structure in the shape of a church, where the library was. Both are long gone, as are the music hall that held the Franciscan Institute and the barn out back where the college's pigs and cows were kept.

Betty and Bobby probably traveled on one of the trolleys that ran to the college along a spur line from the Olean Railway until 1928. Once they arrived they might have seen a man driving a team of horses around the campus. Francis Griffin—or "Griff," as he was known—would become a legend at St. Bonaventure, a maintenance man who "had a kind of mysticism," according to one professor. Among the things Griff was known for was driving his workhorses across the campus each day, to the delight of students and the chagrin of administrators, who thought the horses undignified. Every spring he'd say he was training his horses for the Kentucky Derby, and every winter, when the first snow fell, he'd greet everyone he passed by shouting, "Welcome to Miami Beach!" (When Lax spent time on campus again in the late 1950s he came to know Griff and often wrote to him while traveling.)

As involved as Betty became in the Olean community, some vital part of her still yearned for the greater intellectual and artistic stimulation of New York City. She tried to satisfy it with summer stays at Chautauqua, the famous lecture center just west of Olean, but Chautauqua was only a seasonal fix and it lacked the other big draw of New York, her family, so when she could, she took her children to the City.

Whereas Lax's father was, as one relative put it, "a sweet but not terribly effective person," everyone remembered his mother as a formidable combination of assertiveness, strength, intelligence, and caring attention. Liveliness and curiosity too. Lax never wrote about her, but he told his niece she was "sweet and helpful, smart and wonderful." She knew the words to every opera, he said, and would sing them around the house. She was clearly the solid center around which the family revolved.

The best description of Betty I've found comes not from Lax or his siblings but from her own sister, Celia, who was thirteen years younger and felt "adopted" by her:

> All that impressed her of beauty, tenderness, of interest, really, she passed on to me. She told me stories, sang to me, and was my shelter in any childish distress. Every night I fell asleep to the music of Chopin . . . and she would sing songs, accompanying herself. Her voice was warm & sweet. . . . She was my solace and joy in all the distresses of a child trying to adjust to, or even revolting against all the strange *right* ways to do things. She was patient, loving, kind and approving. She tried to give me confidence in my poor ability to cope with the gigantic problems of childhood.

Betty would tell her a story every morning to help her begin a "good day," Celia writes, and she always looked and smelled good.

When you opened her dresser drawer a gently sweet fragrance, like herself, would be there to greet you. She was dainty and delicious at all times, and most especially she was so blessed good to me. On weekends when her "crowd" of friends went out, she would take me, too, if they were going swimming or picnicking. She taught me to swim and gain confidence in all the ways that she could. And this has helped me all through my life, and her memory has been a benign and blessed influence on anything good that I may have done. I was a quick and impatient child—always in a hurry. She tried to teach me better, and whatever I may have of tolerance and patience I can trace to her.

Except for the impatient part, Lax might have written this passage.

Throughout his early childhood, Lax's family lived on Sullivan Street in a large, two-story Victorian with a roomy porch. The street was wide and lined with houses of similar size and style. It was just five blocks from the school Lax would attend and even closer to the downtown core. Many days Betty walked her son three blocks to Second Street, then two blocks to State, where they stopped at Dimitri's pastry shop, one of several Greek-owned businesses Lax thought predisposed him to all things Greek. No doubt they'd often stop at Siggie's clothing store too, which was close enough for Siggie to walk home for lunch.

Lax's memories of those early days were few and hazy, but one thing he remembered clearly was waking from a nap when he was three. He sat up in bed and looked around the room. "So this is Paris," he thought. Of course he'd never been to Paris and certainly had no idea what the city looked like. He'd probably heard the line somewhere—maybe from one of the Broadway tunes his mother liked to sing.

The most significant event of Lax's early life happened when he was five. Betty received what she called a "dull, blinding" letter saying her father was gravely ill, and the family made a hasty trip to New York City to see him one last time. He died soon after, on July 20, 1921. "There was searching into philosophy, psychology, Theosophy, Unitarianism—anything that would offer consolation," Betty writes. What helped most was time and a decision she and Siggie made to move back to New York. You can feel her excitement at living in the City again in her description of a moment on what might have been their first day there: "A bright, cool morning. New York. 34th Street. A young boy trudging beside his mother. 'Do you realize this is our home now? That we're not just down for a visit?'" Although they stayed only a short time before returning to Olean, Lax had had his first taste of city life.

———————

It's always dangerous to speak too confidently about what is inherited in a person or his work, but one of the distinguishing characteristics in Lax's writing, as well as his life, seems to come straight from his mother: an almost equal attraction to urban energy and rural peace. For years after graduating from Columbia, he migrated between Olean and New York City, where he moved again with his mother when he was thirteen and stayed until he finished college. Decades later the city-like energy of Kalymnos attracted him as much as or more than the peace and quiet of Patmos, the mostly rural island he'd eventually live on. On busy Kalymnos the people seemed more alive to him, the atmosphere more dynamic.

Olean and New York. Country and city. The yin and yang of Lax's early world. In many ways he spent his life trying to draw the virtues of these poles together—to reconcile the gentle idyll he was born into with the more dynamic possibility he found in what he sometimes called the "holy" or "celestial" city.

This is why the *hermit* mantle never settled easily on Lax's shoulders, even when he was living alone in Greece in his later years. In the book many have declared his greatest achievement, the poem cycle called *The Circus of the Sun*, he evoked both the beauty of the circus as a whole and the beauty of the individual performers. As Jeannine Mizingou writes in her analysis of it for the *Encyclopedia of Catholic Literature*, his "depiction of human relations refutes the modern notion of the self as isolated and autonomous, encouraging a selfhood that is realized in giving to others, in becoming part of grace by both experiencing and transmitting it."

That element of grace may have been an inheritance too, this one from Siggie. By all accounts he was an extremely gentle and peaceful man who built his Olean business less by industriousness than friendliness. The family's collective memory of him is that he "loved every footstep," as Lax's niece Connie Brothers has said. If a fly landed on him, he would leave it alone, reluctant to disturb it. An early photograph of him shows a wide-faced young man with close-cropped hair in a bow tie, blazer, and polished boots. He sits in a wooden rocker on a simple porch with his aunt and uncle, his hands in his pockets—content, it seems, to sit and chat and watch the world go by.

When Lax talked about his father, he usually emphasized two characteristics he had himself: his gentle nature and his enjoyment of people, especially those on society's fringes. As a Jew in an area with few Jews and an immigrant with a noticeable accent, it's doubtful Siggie ever forgot his own outsider status. Whatever the reasons, his preference for people like Koko the Bird-Woman implanted a love for simple people in his son. The only photograph I've seen of them alone together shows Siggie in a three-piece suit and round-brimmed hat with a chubby-faced boy of maybe three in a thick coat clinging to his fingers. They seem to be ambling somewhere. Seeing Siggie's casual pose, it's easy to imagine them on their way to a park where gypsies have camped or returning from a predawn trip to watch the circus arrive.

———————

The importance and impact of the circus, especially in the rural areas of America, is largely forgotten now, but at the end of the nineteenth century and beginning of the twentieth, before movies and radio became the main sources of entertainment and information, circuses brought the outside world to those in small towns and isolated areas. P. T. Barnum could call his circus "The Greatest Show on Earth" because in most areas there was nothing to rival it. The first circuses performed on wooden platforms, the expense of which could be justified only in major cities, but in 1825 Joshuah Purdy Brown held a performance under a large canvas tent and the circus took to the road. When train travel came along a few decades later, circuses were free to go everywhere, and they did. At the turn of the century, one hundred circuses and "menageries" were touring the country, among them the Ringling Brothers Circus, which took up sixty-five railroad cars and required a dozen acres for all of its equipment and personnel. The arrival of the circus—with its parade from train to staging ground, its elaborate setup and colorful characters, its reenactment of world events and outsized spectacle—was so important that in 1901 the Board of Education in Bridgeport, Connecticut, closed schools on circus day.

In 1927, the last year Lax lived in Olean, the Ringling Brothers and Barnum & Bailey show was so large it came down from Elmira in one hundred double-length railroad cars carrying "1009 zoological rarities; 350 trained horses, 90 zebras, camels and horses performing at one time; 800 men and women arenic stars from every country," as well as a "congress of strange people combined in one side-show." The main tent, with its five rings and six stages, seated fifteen thousand people. Among the main attractions were "Pawah, the sacred white elephant of Burma," a "hundred funny clowns," and Miss May Wirth, "the greatest bareback rider in the world."

The circus was in its last decade of small-town prominence—before "The Jazz Singer" appeared in 1927 and entertainment audiences turned more completely toward the movies—when Siggie took his son on those predawn walks. Lax fell in love with the movies too, but he never forgot the joy of watching the circus pull into town or going to a performance with his father. Throughout his life, if a circus was nearby, he did his best to attend a performance, and of course his first book was about the circus. In it he writes:

> They are with me now, the golden people; their limbs
> are intertwined in golden light, moving in a heavy sea
> of memory: they come, the beautiful ones, with evening
> smiles: heavy-lidded people, dark of hair and gentle
> of aspect, whose eyes are portals to a land of dusk.
> Their melancholy holds me now; sadness of princes, and
> the sons of princes: the melancholy gaze of those I
> have not seen since childhood.

Later in life Lax said his happiest days were those he spent traveling through western Canada with the Cristiani Brothers Circus in 1949, the trip that inspired *The Circus of the Sun*. The journey began just weeks after Siggie died. The connection between the circus and Lax's earliest memories of his father certainly made the experience more profound.

———————

At some point in Lax's early childhood, probably after the family's first attempt at living in New York City, his grandfather retired from the family's clothing store and his uncle Joseph left to open his own ladies' ready-to-wear store, called The Fashion, in the family's original retail space at 170 N. Union. It may have been Joseph's return from World War I in 1918 that freed Lax's parents to try living in New York and their decision two years later to return to Olean, perhaps with the intention of making enough money to try big city living again, that pushed him out on his own. Whatever the reasons, after about 1920 Siggie had the business to himself. At Betty's suggestion, he renamed it Sigmund Lax, the Progressive Clothier. No doubt the name was an attempt to distinguish it from the other, supposedly less progressive men's stores that had opened in booming Olean, including one just a block away. It may have been a reminder too, if only to themselves, that their vision of the world and its possibilities was bigger than that of others in Olean.

Lax's parents sold the Sullivan Street house before moving to New York, and when they returned they rented the lower floor of a large two-family house by the railroad tracks at 307 N. Clinton. They stayed there for the next eight years, until 1929, when they tried New York again.

---

In early photographs Bobby Lax was pudgy and round with a frightened look until he grew into a tall, thin boy with an easy smile. He was smart, creative, inquisitive, humorous, and physically awkward—traits that would stay consistent throughout his life. His good nature mirrored that of his mother and Gladio, with whom he spent the bulk of his time. He liked to spend time alone, though, too, a tendency that became more pronounced in later life. He started writing poetry when he was eight, influenced no doubt by his mother's interest in artistic endeavors. Even before he wrote anything you could call a poem, he liked to put marks on rocks and leave them where people would find them—inchoate attempts to send messages to the world.

Lax's first attempts at writing (stories as well as poems) coincided with Gladio's departure for college, suggesting that writing comforted him and helped him make sense of the world. His first publication came in 1927, when he was eleven, an encomium about Charles Lindbergh's solo flight across the Atlantic. Shortly after it appeared in the *Olean Herald*, the St. Louis Chamber of Commerce sent a letter telling him it had been included in a collection of tributes to be given to Lindbergh by the business community that had bankrolled his flight. Even in his eighties Lax could remember every word:

It happened on a fair May night
When Lindbergh made his nonstop flight
From New York to Paris he was to roam
Over land of trees and sea of foam
With nothing to eat but sandwiches five
How could he ever get there alive?
Straight to Le Bourget Field he flew
And everyone cheered for the Red, White and Blue
In my moral this truth you'll find
Keep faith and bravery first in your mind.

Around this same time, Betty wrote Polonius's advice to Hamlet in her son's autograph book: *To thine own self be true*. By all accounts he was. Inspired by shows he saw with his mother in Manhattan, he took an early interest in theater and built elaborate miniature sets, some with working lights and at least one big enough for him to climb inside. With his friends he put on circuses, although his complete lack of coordination kept him from performing.

By the time he entered the eighth grade, Lax was taking clarinet lessons and, inspired perhaps by Betty's public singing, decided to form a band. Taking Fred Waring's Pennsylvanians as their model, he and his three fellow musicians called themselves Lax's Oleanders. Whatever bandleader dreams he had, however, didn't last long. The group had rehearsed only a handful of times when, in the middle of that eighth-grade year, Lax's family moved to Queens. Lax would continue to visit Olean over the years and spend parts of several summers there, but except for two brief stretches after college, he'd never live there again.

———

Little is known about the Lax family's move to Jackson Heights, even the timing. Late in her life Gladio told an Olean historian that her father leased his business to the Richards Company in 1928 and eventually sold it to them. The following New Year's Day she married Benji Marcus at the Waldorf-Astoria in New York City, and the newlyweds settled in Scarsdale. With one daughter away at school (Sally was at Elmira College) and the other living near her family in the city, Betty's desire to return to New York must have been stronger than ever. In a 1939 journal entry, Lax writes that he moved to Queens on September 25, 1929, but also that he spent only half of his eighth-grade school year there. Given that he graduated from Newtown High School in Elmhurst, Queens, in 1934, his eighth-grade year would have been 1929–30. If we assume that the last half of a school year would begin after a winter break, Lax would have begun school in Queens in January 1930. A late 1929 or early 1930 move seems most probable for many reasons, including the dedication of Olean's B'nai Israel Synagogue on September 29, 1929, which Betty wouldn't have missed.

In any case, the 1930 census shows Lax and his parents residing at 291 Britton Avenue in Jackson Heights. They are paying $150 rent and have a "radioset." Although Siggie was only fifty at the time, in the column for his occupation it says "Retired." These were the early days of the Great Depression, just months after Black Friday. It may have been that he couldn't find a job or, if he did indeed sell his business before the stock market crashed, that he had enough in the bank to go without work for a while.

In Olean, Betty had been involved with the Conservative Jewish congregation because it was the only Jewish group in town, but Lax's family seldom went to temple except on high holidays. There is no clear record of their religious activities while living in New York, but with her family around her, Betty seems to have returned to her Reform roots. Not that her family was solidly Reform or even solidly Jewish. While some relatives remained part of the Reform tradition, others converted to Christianity or chose to have no connection to any religion. When Lax tried reading the Old Testament in high school, his mother discouraged him, telling him the important thing was to love God and his neighbor.

The most intriguing non-Jewish religious influence in Lax's early life came from Betty's older brother, Henry, who became a dedicated Theosophist before Lax was born. By the time Lax's family moved to Queens, Henry had become the actor John Barrymore's business manager. According to Barrymore's biographer Gene Fowler, Henry (who spelled the family name Hotchener) "served as secretary to Daniel Guggenheim, President of the American Smelting and Refining Company, and head of the vast Guggenheim family enterprises," then as "general manager of a realty enterprise of Maximilian Morgenthau," the uncle of Franklin Roosevelt's secretary of the treasury, Henry Morgenthau Jr., before becoming "deeply interested in after-death phenomena and oriental philosophy."

In pursuit of these new interests, Henry made a 1912 trip to India, where he met the Theosophical Society leaders Annie Besant and C. W. Leadbeater, as well as a young woman named Marie Rusak, who moved to California with him in 1916 and became his wife. Marie, the daughter of a California pioneer, Judge Allyn M. Barnard, and a graduate of Mills College, had given up an impressive singing career—including touring with John Philip Sousa's band, soloing with the Boston Symphony Orchestra, and singing opera in several European countries—to devote herself to the study of Theosophy. After meeting Besant in India, Marie became her deputy, traveling with her around the world to spread Theosophy's good news, before Marie became a celebrated lecturer in her own right.

Lax and his sisters had only limited contact with their famous uncle and aunt, but a photograph of Henry hung in the family's home and they were surrounded by Theosophical ideas. Lax seems to have read some of the movement's literature as well, including an early book by the movement's protégé, J. Krishnamurti, where he saw a poem in the vertical style he would one day make his own.

---

At about the time Lax's family moved to New York, his aunt Roz, a short story writer, gave him a subscription to the *New Yorker*, which was fairly new then. While continuing to write poetry, he started writing plays too, and when he thought about his future, he dreamed of three possibilities: becoming the next Harold Ross, the next Noel Coward, or the next e. e. cummings. He knew—or his mother convinced him—that all of these dreams required a seriousness of purpose as well as a good education and social skills. He would have to work hard to succeed. To stand out from the crowd.

And stand out he did. With eight thousand students spread over four grades, Newtown High School was much larger than Lax's school in Olean, but during his four years there he joined the Literary Club, the

Virgil Club, the Latin Club, and the Dramatic Club, serving as vice president of the last two. He was admitted to Arista, the scholastic honor society too, and was chosen to be editor in chief of Newtown's literary magazine, the *Newtown Lantern*. In addition to contributing poems and stories to the *Lantern*, he wrote a column for the school newspaper, the *X-Ray*, called "Man about the Annex" as well as feature articles, including an interview piece on Noel Coward called "Read, See Plays, Then Write Them Is Noel Coward's Advice to Newtownites." Much of his writing seems written with a smile.

While penning his own plays (one of which, *Subway to Camelot*, won an honorable mention in a local contest), Lax tried his hand at acting and succeeded even there. When the Dramatic Club presented a scene from *The Merchant of Venice* at a school assembly, an effusive *X-Ray* critic wrote, "Robert Lax played the role of Shylock, the Jew, so well that sufficient praise cannot be given him."

Lax's greatest successes, however, came in the areas of writing and scholarship. At the time, all of his poems rhymed and his writing was mostly conventional, but one poem, "Invitation," took second place in a regional contest; a short story, "Two Thieves and the Master of Krove," was published in *Scholastic* magazine; and a sonnet, "The Poppy," won the Inter-High School Poetry Contest of New York City, earning him a seat in a poetry course taught by the Columbia professor and future U.S. poet laureate Joseph Auslander. (He declined the opportunity, Lax told an interviewer decades later, because he didn't like the idea of studying poetry. A touch of youthful hubris, perhaps.)

As a scholar Lax had no equal. In his senior year he won his school's Chemical Club medal, Biology Club medal, and Roosevelt medal for general scholarship. Unsurprisingly he was named the class's valedictorian. For his commencement speech he wrote a poem with only one or two words to a line, his first in the vertical style he would become known for.

---

In a long, unsent letter written in his early twenties, Lax reflected on his high school writing—why he wrote and what he learned from writing. He did it first, he said, because it was fun and because he had discovered that fooling around with words could make a sentence much better or much worse. He compared it to fooling around with paint and coming out with something he had done himself that reflected what he knew and understood, something that was like the stories other people wrote. "You wondered how they did it," he wrote, "and now in a sense you knew. You knew that your stories weren't written as well as the stories you had read but you could believe that with some more practice, just writing more stories, they could get to be."

The experience of seeing his work published in the school magazine, he wrote, "gave me among the people who read it an assurance that playing good baseball or doing high jumps gives some guys, and when you're fourteen you'll grab onto any kind of assurance you can get." His desire for assurance, he admits, led him to write poems primarily to win prizes, although he still wrote many just for fun, such as this one published in the *Lantern*:

### WAGES OF CONVALESCENCE

I took my pills and tonic,
I gargled, swabbed, and sprayed,
I let the doctor gag me,
And what is worse, I paid.

I drank my milk with butter,
I sipped my soup with pain,
I'm well and—well, what have I?
I'm just myself again.

Only gradually did he perceive that poetry improved when the author wasn't merely good at manipulating words but also had something worthwhile to say.

———————

Lax's high school success earned him the ultimate American educational prize: a scholarship to an Ivy League university. When he moved from Queens to Manhattan, he took along a suitcase filled with his writings—carrying his dreams, as his parents and his grandparents had, into a new land.

# 4   The Cottage

My formal inquiry into Lax's life began in September 2001, when I flew to Buffalo and drove a rented car through the reds and yellows of early autumn down to Olean. The sky, a crisp cerulean blue, reminded me of summer skies on Patmos, but the nights were already cold. Lax's niece Marcia Kelly had graciously invited me to stay in her family's comfortable, two-story house—where Benji and Gladio had raised her and her sister, where Lax and Merton had stayed in their postcollege days, where Siggie had lived his final years and Lax his final weeks. A year had passed since his death but his medications and vitamins were still in the bathroom off the garden room downstairs. The wooden walking stick he used on Patmos and the broad straw hat he wore during daily walks along the quay were perched in a corner. On a later visit I would sleep in his last bed, but this time I stayed in a smaller room upstairs.

I'd come to Olean primarily to access Lax's archives in the Friedsam Library at St. Bonaventure University. The archives were new, successors to an earlier set at Columbia, and housed in a tiny room above the library's main hall, safe from disturbance and noise. The librarian in charge, Paul Spaeth, gave me a table and a chair and I spent my days in that windowless room, reading letters and journal entries, studying the various editions of Lax's poetry, and looking at old photographs of people and places, known and unknown. In the evening I took a box or two of my finds to the reading room downstairs to explore more fully, staying until the library closed. Then I drove the main street toward downtown, past the Walmart and the Applebee's, before turning onto Union, slowing as I passed the storefront where Siggie had his shop and the still imposing Olean House Hotel. I was always late to bed and the dusty house bothered my allergies, so when Tuesday the 11th came around, I decided to sleep in.

In addition to going through Lax's papers, I wanted to see the places he spent time when young, and I'd arranged a visit for that

Tuesday afternoon to the cottage where he and Merton and their friends spent parts of three postcollege summers. It was there they lived the communal life one critic called "a complete dry run of the Beat movement" and there, between his graduation from Columbia in June 1938 and his return to New York City in December 1940, that Lax worked out his most important early ideas, including the pacifism that put him at odds with Benji and the coming draft. A few years after those summers, Benji sold the cottage to the owner of a local radio station, who erected a giant transmission tower next to it. Although that had happened sixty years before my visit, the building was still standing, still inhabitable—still imbued with Lax's spirit, I hoped.

I had just awakened that Tuesday morning and was still debating whether to go to the archives before visiting the cottage when the telephone rang.

"Turn the television on," my wife said.

---

That morning's events in lower Manhattan and Washington, DC, affected my view of everything, including the cottage. As Mark, the radio station employee who lived there, showed me around, I kept thinking of Lax on that hill, in that building, knowing then as I knew now that war would soon begin. Pursuing peace was one of his lifelong obsessions, the word more sacred to him than any other word, except *love*. He called the little broadsheet of poetry he distributed in the 1950s and early 1960s *Pax*, Latin for *peace*, and the last book he published before his death was titled *The Peacemaker's Handbook*. I was glad he hadn't lived to see what I was sure would be a long, hard time of violence and drumbeating but not that I would have to live it without him.

The cottage was larger than I expected, the central room maybe thirty-by-thirty and the verandah, which in Lax's time had offered a commanding view of Olean and the hills and valleys around it, close to fifty feet long. The roof was pitched, with exposed beams a dozen feet above my head. A huge stone fireplace dominated the main room but gave out little heat. In most ways the cottage looked as it had in Lax's day, but

Mark or the radio station had installed a large television near a wall across from the door and as I stood there talking to him, a strange thing happened: the images of fire and collapse I'd seen too many times already were replaced by a giant graphic showing the flight paths of the two planes hijacked out of Boston. Each was identified by its flight number, its departure time, and the abbreviations for its departure and destination cities. One had been heading to Los Angeles, and from across the room the big block letters identifying it seemed to spell out BOB-LAX, as if ensuring that his spirit was with me even in this.

---

The first time Lax and Merton went up to the cottage, they were alone and stayed only a few days. Lax had just graduated, his final college weeks a flurry of activity, with Brahmachari perched on books in his dorm room, his mother feeding him health food, and Merton and other friends penning sections of his final project in a novel-writing class.

"The last year of school I ran around a lot and didn't go to classes and [was] generally so weak and jittery I could hardly walk," he wrote about those days, "but just the same I had the old high school formulas down so pat that at the end of the year I wrote another poem that won two prizes and graduated with honors in English." The poem, "The Last Days of a City," included these lines, which display verbal skill but also a sing-song conventionality Lax came to loathe:

> In pastoral song a city dies,
> Its face averted country-wise
> With gilded smile and perfumed breath
> It makes a pattern of its death.
> With dying ear attentive yet
> To tightened string and flageolet
> It skims in barge of silver sound
> The tides of voices underground.

The imagery suggests that Lax was ready to move from city pole to country pole. The barge metaphor might have come from plans he and Merton were hatching, with Benji's help, to travel up the Hudson River and along the Erie Canal by oil barge, then down to Olean from Buffalo.

Merton was in graduate school, but he had the summer off and had never been to Lax's hometown. In fact he'd never been anywhere west of New York City.

The barge plan fell through, so they took a train up the Delaware Valley instead. It wasn't the grand adventure they had planned, but the land was beautiful—"Those deep valleys," Merton wrote, "and miles and miles of high, rolling, wooded hills: the broad fields, the big red barns, the white farm houses and the peaceful towns: all this looked more and more impressive and fine in the long slanting rays of the sinking sun after we had passed Elmira"—and for these thoughtful, playful men, being with each other was adventure enough.

As the train clicked along, they talked about all kinds of things, including Brahmachari and Hinduism, Huxley's ideas on mysticism, and Buddhism. In the midst of their discussions, Lax mentioned his interest in Aquinas, but Merton refused to listen. It was the first time Lax had known him to say he was uninterested in anything, and it made Lax think that something was happening to his friend. That something turned out to be a movement toward the Catholic Church so strong that Merton was baptized five months later. During those months Merton became friends with the professor who had taught the Scholastic philosophy class in which Lax had started reading Aquinas. It was this kind of experience that prompted Merton to call Lax "one of the voices through which the insistent Spirit of God was determined to teach me the way I had to travel."

When they reached Olean, in addition to visiting the cottage, they stayed at the Olean House Hotel, went swimming in Cuba Lake, and drank and danced across the state line in Bradford. One day, on a drive to see a nearby Indian reservation, they stopped at St. Bonaventure so Lax could show Merton the library. Merton, though, wanted nothing to do with the place.

"I don't know what was the matter," he writes in *The Seven Storey Mountain*. "Perhaps I was scared of the thought of nuns and priests being all around me—the elemental fear of the citizen of hell, in the presence of anything that savors of the religious life, religious vows, official dedication to God through Christ. Too many crosses. Too many holy statues. Too much quiet and cheerfulness. Too much pious optimism. It made me uncomfortable. I had to flee."

The words sound humorous given what Merton went on to do—including teaching at that very school—but Lax's desire to show his friend a spiritual place and Merton's reaction to it throw the differences between them into sharp relief.

I've already said that Merton was a man who needed answers, while Lax was content with questions. These traits were connected to decisive action in one and contentment to let life flow where it will in the other. Lax told me once that whenever the two of them went to a new place, Merton would set off immediately to explore and get his bearings, while Lax would find a coffee shop and contemplate the place from there. Merton was physical and impetuous; Lax was awkward and slow to act. Where the two met was in their thirst for understanding, their desire to do good, their intelligence, and their humor. Even here, though, they differed. Lax's tendency toward the simple complemented and sometimes clashed with Merton's complicated thinking. When Lax told Merton later that all he had to do to become a saint was want to be one, everything in Merton said no—things couldn't be that easy. Nothing ever had been for him.

So when Merton saw all of those crosses and icons, those nuns and priests scurrying around, his vision of the place was very different from Lax's. Where he saw strict demands that made his will bridle, Lax saw spirituality and peace, ignoring the religious trappings. Whereas Merton saw a distinct difference between "holiness" and the more common living he was doing, Lax saw life as one big ocean, with spirituality an organic part of everything. And while Merton made his progress in leaps, by decisive acts, Lax's spiritual maturing was a natural growth.

In his biography of Merton, Michael Mott highlights this difference in a passage describing an argument they had about mortification while living together the following summer, months after Merton's baptism: "Merton saw the need [for mortification], Lax saw none and disliked the word. With Robert Lax, mortification, or rather a disciplined control, was the most natural thing in the world. You didn't set up a program, you lived a life in which such things happened spontaneously and without thought or planning. For Merton, it remained difficult to understand when Lax said simply, 'Nothing should be hard.' It took Merton several years to perceive that this simply represented a fundamental difference in their characters: it was no subject for a debate."

It's important to point out here that many things were hard for Lax—his struggle to find his place in life took years and was filled with fears, doubts, and mental anguish—but when difficulties arose, he slowed down. He waited. He believed deeply in the adage that all things come to those who wait. Merton forged ahead.

This difference between them can be seen in their attitudes toward writing, perhaps the most important and personal activity in either of their lives. Here's how Merton describes the difference as it stood in early 1939:

> The more I failed [to get work published], the more convinced I was that it was important for me to have my work printed in magazines like the *Southern Review* or *Partisan Review* or the *New Yorker*. My chief concern was now to see myself in print. It was as if I could not be quite satisfied that I was real until I could feed my ambition with these trivial glories, and my ancient selfishness was now matured and concentrated in this desire to see myself externalized in a public and printed and official self which I could admire at my ease. This was what I really believed in: reputation, success. I wanted to live in the eyes and the mouths and the minds of men. I was not so crude that I wanted to be known and admired by the whole world: there was a certain naive satisfaction in the idea of being only appreciated by a particular minority, which gave a special fascination to this urge within me. But when my mind was absorbed in all that, how could I lead a supernatural life, the life to which I was called? How could I love God, when everything I did was done not for Him but for myself, and not trusting in His aid, but relying on my own wisdom and talents?
>
> Lax rebuked me for all this. His whole attitude about writing was purified of such stupidity, and was steeped in holiness, in charity, in disinterestedness.

Lax told me more than once that the best thing to do was to write for yourself or maybe one other person. If others had a chance to read what you wrote, they were fortunate. Not that he didn't try to publish what he wrote—he wanted his work to be read as much as any other writer—but he didn't care about fame or even rejection. "The only criterion for how and what to write if you're sincere about writing so other people can read it and be happy, is to write just exactly what you please the way you want to," he wrote in 1939. "If you're writing for any other purpose there are all sorts of elaborate rules, most of which add up to: Write as though you were writing what you want to the way you want to."

―――――――

It's worth stopping here—freezing the frame, so to speak—and contemplating the friendship between these two men at this point in their lives. The rest of that summer they would communicate solely through letters, the beginning of thirty years of correspondence, but in the fall, when Lax moved back to New York, their college relationship would deepen significantly, culminating in a defining summer together on the cusp of war in 1939. After that their paths would diverge more and more as they saw each other less and less, until Merton's entry into the monastery one day after Pearl Harbor limited them to friendship by letter. Between December 1941 and Merton's death in 1968, they would see each other only six times, but the bond they forged that year, 1938–39, would help them make important decisions, endure the grief of death and despair, and support each other in countless ways while living continents apart.

―――――――

Merton's return to Manhattan after only one week left Lax unsure what to do. While Merton wrote about publishing a review in the *Nation*, his first national publication, Lax reported that he'd seen a movie staring Rudy Vallée and was reading Webster and Hopkins. When Merton asked Lax in late July why he hadn't written lately, Lax gave a semihumorous list of reasons, including "torpor, stupor, mama coming home, slate and freedgood coming and not coming, letter to n. flagg (who didn't write) and . . . tying my shoes." *Torpor* is a word he'd use in future letters to indicate a listlessness that came more from anxiety and Weltschmerz than actual depression.

After joking about a number of young women Merton seems to have met while he was there, Lax mentions a new one in town from Tulsa:

> Three times in one night I kept from asking her hey why didn't she marry me—which would have been silly. She says lots of people in Tulsa keep asking her that all the time. To the face she is not so pretty. It is her feet I like and the small of her back and all of that; and I did dance with her in a small blue bathing suit (hers) and her in bare feet

and to do this again I would offer venus twelve homing pigeons with suitable message and a General Sherman's Anniversary Edition of Bullfinch's Mythology.

This may be the right place to address more fully Lax's attitudes toward women and sex. I've mentioned already that he had only one girlfriend in his life, Nancy Flagg, and seems to have chosen abstinence quite young. Because he never married and he avoided intimacy with women after those early postcollege days, some have speculated that Lax was secretly gay. Some have even suggested that his relationship with Merton, while never sexual, was more intimate than has been known. I've found no basis for such speculation. Lax's decision to deny himself intimacy with women was conscious, practical, caring, and, at heart, spiritual. Considering who he was and what he wanted to do in his life (which was writing, but not writing that would probably ever make money), he felt he would never be able to support a wife. If he couldn't support a wife and maybe children, he felt it would be wrong to marry. If he wasn't going to marry, he thought it deceptive to date. At the same time, he saw a spiritual benefit not only in celibacy but in avoiding all relations with women beyond simple friendship. At the end of his life in Greece, he avoided all physical contact with women in public so there would never be even the appearance of anything improper.

It may have been that summer that Lax first felt the struggle between sociability and desire for solitude that would long define him. At the end of the letter in which he mentions his "torpor" and the young woman from Tulsa, he writes, "I stay up at the cottage alone lots of the time." Benji and his family weren't using the cottage that summer because a work crew building a state road over the hills had rendered the drive impassable. Lax, who never felt comfortable driving a car anyway, was content to access the cottage by foot. There was nowhere he had to go in a hurry, and he seems to have liked the peace being there alone gave him.

It's hard to say how long Lax stayed at the cottage that summer or what he did while there. He certainly read and may have drawn pictures. No doubt he went for walks in the hills. His most significant activity was starting the journal he would keep for the rest of his life. Like Thoreau and a handful of other prominent writers, he found the intimacy of journaling, with its freedom from scrutiny and yet quasi-public nature, more conducive than other kinds of writing to the working out of his values, dilemmas, and ideas. Eventually sections of his journals would make their way into print, a development he contemplated from the start. In his last years his journaling and poetry would come together, his daily entries rendered in long vertical lines.

The first lines of his first entry, made on August 4, 1938, are "I know that the things you put in a journal, incidents or comments, get to be more stale and hateful than any other kind of writing. I am not going to try to prevent this by any sort of rigid criterion of what to include or how to write it. This is about the fourth journal I've started simply because there's nothing else to do."

One intriguing early entry hints at how he had begun to see himself in relationship to his writing:

> The spider's innermost dream is his web: he has no position until he finds his own position at the center of his web. His web is appropriate to him and he is appropriate to his web. He knows the web's design before he spins it and yet he does not know it until he has seen it, un-till [sic] he has shaken it with his own weight. . . . The web is a part of the spider, it is neither greater nor less than he[,] as a mind or a heart is neither greater nor less than a man. Breaking the web does not maim the spider: for he still has it, not only the plan but the material, not only the material but the plan.

Whatever plans Lax might have been spinning, he had no money and eventually would have to find a job. Not that he was particularly worried about it. After all, he was an Ivy League graduate at a time when only 4 percent of Americans had a college degree, and he had watched earlier *Jester* editors go on to jobs at prominent publications. In time his college friends would cover the gamut, from the *Nation* to the *National Review*, *Time* and *Newsweek* to *Fortune* and *Vogue*. He himself would eventually join the staff of the *New Yorker*, but in those immediate postcollege months he was already having doubts about magazine editing. What he really wanted to do was write, and he feared that taking an editing position might interfere with the kind of writing he wanted to do, so he inquired about teaching English courses at St. Bonaventure. Nothing came of that, but in late September John Slate came to visit and persuaded him to seek his fortune in New York, where his friends were.

A fortune he didn't find. He couldn't even find a job, until he remembered a woman the Columbia employment office had put him in touch with just before his trip to Europe two years before, a Mrs. Lewis, whose husband was the manager of the Taft Hotel. At that point she'd been looking for someone to accompany the family to Westport, Connecticut, for the summer and teach her sons to box. Lax had no idea how to teach boxing, but a job was a job, so he asked a friend who was a Golden Gloves champion for advice. "Get a short haircut," the friend said, "and lead with your left." Lax didn't know what it meant to lead with your left, but he took the haircut advice and went to see Mrs. Lewis.

In *Hotel Kid*, his amusing memoir of growing up in the hotel his father managed for thirty-three years, Stephen Lewis describes his mother as "strong-featured rather than pretty," with "a large nose, long teeth, and wiry hair that turned gray late." She was a woman of leisure, he says, who rarely went anywhere, treated the hotel staff imperiously, and liked to sleep late. When she wanted clothes, she picked up the phone and described what she thought she'd like to a saleswoman at Saks Fifth Avenue, who sent possibilities to the hotel to be kept or returned. Everything else she needed, the hotel provided, from meals and alcohol to cigarettes and magazines. Most days she put on lipstick and rouge just before noon and dressed in a nightgown and robe to entertain friends for lunch. Most afternoons she played cards or hosted small parties and drank Scotch.

Unfortunately for Lax—or maybe fortunately, given his lack of boxing knowledge—a doctor told him he was too anemic to go anywhere but home to Olean that summer of 1937. Two years later his health was no better but his need for a job was more acute, so he contacted Mrs. Lewis again about caring for her sons. According to Lax, she said yes, then no, then yes again, and he moved from the YMCA into one of Manhattan's finest hotels. "The first Saturday night she was out," he wrote, "Merton and Me and O'Keefe got drunk in her livingroom and made so much noise the tenants complained, but no one dared call the managers [sic] apartment to stop his noise."

In his book Stephen Lewis gives a different version. He says his mother was looking for a young man to be a role model for her two young sons, someone "who would stay in the apartment on weeknights, help us with our homework, teach us to play ball, improve our posture, and bring us into mainstream America." He describes the young man Columbia sent as "a ball-playing student named Joe [who] came for his interview wearing a college sweater with blue piping." When Joe's plans changed, he recommended his friend Robert Lax.

Whatever the events that landed him there, Lax, who had spent little time with children, worked from the fall of 1938 through the spring of 1939 tutoring eight-year-old Stephen and his seven-year-old brother Peter (whose name Lax would appropriate later as a playful nom de plume).

"Mother never fully registered the difference between Bob and Joe," Stephen writes. "Bob was a lanky poet, half waif, half wraith." In the boys' bedroom,

> Bob, legs jackknifed to his chin in an easy chair he had dragged in, drank milk by the quart and talked. Tom [Merton], on the floor, and Peter and I, on our beds, listened to Bob on books, spiritual rebirth, the small town where he was born. His descriptions of Olean, New York, were so vivid we walked its streets in our heads. Bob and Tom both tried to explain eternity to us. "What happens after eternity?" we asked. "More," said Tom. "What after more?" "A hundred times more than everything since time began," said Bob, adding, "And that's just the first minute." Peter looked as if he were going to cry; Merton looked a little upset himself.
>
> The only walks we took with Bob were to the Roxy. We never played ball in the park. Bob tried to take me to a football game at Columbia, but he had never been to the stadium and we got lost on the subway. Still, Mother was very fond of him. She would come into our bedroom, stand near the door, and listen to him with a distant smile on her face. Though she rarely gave up control of a conversation, Bob was one of the few people she did not interrupt.

When the weather was nice, Lax would take his typewriter up to the hotel roof, where he could look out at the Chrysler Building, Radio City Music Hall, and the Empire State Building. A journal entry he wrote up there gives a humorous glimpse of his self-consciousness in those early days of being a writer on his own terms:

I walked around from part to part of the highest roof looking for a place where it didn't smell so bad [from the garbage incinerator]. Way up in a roof window at the hotel victoria was two guys in overalls watching me, just leaning out of the window and watching from the time I first came up. I always feel like a king on the highest roof and felt like Reginald Denny in the millionaire playboy when I took off my shirt and put on my sunglasses and took the lid offen [sic] my type-writer, and I couldn't tell if they thought it was an enviable thing to be doing or a foolhardy one, because on the one hand I could see they were used to working on rooves [sic] and knew all about the wind and the smell, and even how little joy there is potential or kinetic in sitting in the sun on a roof, and how elaborately I was prepared for it in fairy blue pants and sunglasses like it was cannes and a typewriter to write my thoughts with, or how maybe on the other hand they worked on rooves all day but never got a chance to sit out in the sun with their shirts off.

Whether he was writing on the roof or down in the apartment with the children yelling in the background, that October he started to compose a writing guide. His intention was probably twofold: to tell himself what he knew about writing and, if the opportunity should arise, to publish something for others. Most of what he would write from this time on, right through to the end of his life, would have this twofold purpose.

His writing advice includes the following: "Don't say excrement if you mean shit. . . . Don't say shit if you mean excrement either. If it's true about you it's true about everybody even if you're two headed and went over the falls in a barrel. Maybe not true but truable [sic]. . . . For this is the joy of all readers of all books, to say 'Yes, yes that's true.'" A few pages later he writes, "This part concerns the first twenty-seven pages of Henry Miller's *Tropic of Cancer*, a good first twenty seven pages. So far it's all I've read. It's written the way this is written, you sit down and you write fast and you don't rewrite. The idea is to communicate and not to have anyone say my what a pretty sentence."

He never finished his guidebook, but the few attempts he made say much about his approach to writing. Finding exactly the right word would become an obsession for him, and he never stopped believing that what was true for him would be—or at least could be—true for all people. He never forgot the lesson he learned from Henry Miller either: to write fast and trust your instincts. First thought, best thought. Merton believed the same thing. Later, when Lax came to know Jack Kerouac, what he liked best about Kerouac's writing was his devotion to what Kerouac called "spontaneous prose."

Starting perhaps with his time alone in the cottage, Lax had begun to see the value of examining himself and his thinking on paper, taking what he'd learned at Columbia and weighing it against his own experience. But that winter something happened that turned him even more introspective. When his mother visited him at Christmas, he noted in his journal afterward that whereas she had once guided him across streets, he now guided her. Less than a month later a blood clot ended her life at sixty.

A mother's death is difficult for anyone, and it was especially hard for Lax. He was still young and unsettled, and she had always been his inspiration and support. More than that, she had been the practical one who kept his impracticality from being an obstacle. In the days ahead, his journaling would become even more important to him, as would his friendship with Merton and his relationship with Gladio, who would fill the practical role in his life for almost sixty years.

Shortly after Lax's mother died, Merton moved from West 114th Street near Columbia to Perry Street in the West Village, where he was much closer to the Taft Hotel. Over the next several months, as Lax mourned his loss and Merton moved from becoming a Catholic to deciding to become a priest, they spent more hours together than at any other time in their lives. They talked on the telephone every day, went for long walks along the West Side docks, and planned a summer of writing in the Marcus cottage when Merton was done with his graduate studies and Lax had enough money to quit his job. That summer would be the culmination of their too brief time together, a period of writing, reading, and conversation without interruption or responsibility before they went their separate ways and the world plunged into war.

New York City was the undisputed center of the United States in 1939, an inspiration and seduction to people across the nation and around the globe, especially the young and ambitious. It had the six tallest buildings in the country, three Major League Baseball teams, and eight newspapers, including the *Daily News*, with a circulation twice that of any other U.S. paper. Broadway, which included Tin Pan Alley, was the center for not only theater but also popular music, and Times Square was called the center of the world. Despite the rumblings of war in Europe, optimism ruled. And nothing expressed that optimism more lavishly than the New York World's Fair, opened on April 30 by President Franklin Roosevelt and dedicated to the twin themes of Peace and Prosperity. Lax and Merton—smart and creative, talented and Ivy League–educated— had the world at their feet. But the bright moment of pure possibility— for the city and these two young men—was fleeting, as such moments always are.

"The brilliance of New York at the decade's close was a temporary thing and people knew it," David Gelernter writes in *1939: The Lost World of the Fair*, "as if the whole city had bustled momentarily into a shaft of sunlight on the floor of Penn Station's monumental waiting room and knew implicitly that it would be bustling right back out again soon. Ephemerality may have intensified the era's beauty, as it does autumn's."

Lax and Merton played in that shaft of sunlight together, not knowing how ephemeral their time together would be. In addition to their phone talks and walks, they met at least once that May at the World's Fair, where Merton introduced Lax to his latest obsession: the flamenco dancers at the Cuban Village. Dancing, jazz, and movies were all part of their routine, as were women (especially for Merton) and alcohol.

But as the world slipped toward war, they stayed aware of events in Europe and thought more and more about what they should be doing with their lives. Both were convinced that writing was central to who they were and what they were meant to do, but while Merton fretted about being recognized as a writer, Lax was content to write in his journal and compose his poems without undue worry about whether anyone else would read them.

"That spring we sat on the chicken dock [a pier on the Hudson River Merton found especially conducive to contemplation] in the bright sun," Lax wrote a year later, "believing we were writers and talking about others who wrote. We watched material, people, motions, words as though they were things for which if the proper metaphor could be found, a truth would be known. We started (that spring most articulately) with a belief which had come as a gradual and not a sudden revelation in a unity behind the many phenomena, and a tendency on the part of that which ruled events (the variable and the apparently invariable) to respond to love."

Because they spent so much time together and Merton destroyed all of the journals he kept before May 1939, we have only a few lines in *The Seven Storey Mountain* and Lax's often enigmatic writings to suggest what other enthusiasms the two shared during those months. Poetry was high on the list, no doubt, as was Merton's planned dissertation on Hopkins. Among the books they read and discussed, none impressed them more than *Finnegans Wake*. Merton cites its publication by Viking Press on May 4, 1939, as one of the two most important news items Lax conveyed to him by telephone that spring (the other was the election of Pope Pius XII), and one of Lax's few descriptions of their times together is of a gathering at Merton's apartment at which they drank "Rhein wine" while Merton read parts of the book out loud—a practice they would continue that summer.

Lax was slower than Merton to read Joyce's *Ulysses* and his collection of short stories, *Dubliners*, but the impression these stories left on him was so great that decades later, when the director John Huston made a faithful film version of *The Dead*, Lax couldn't enjoy it because some of Joyce's words had been altered. When I asked Lax at age eighty-one what writers had influenced him the most, Joyce still topped the list.

But as much as Lax and Merton appreciated everything Joyce wrote, the book they loved above all was *Finnegans Wake*. They loved the challenge of it and the audacity. They loved that it was surprisingly new and yet encompassed all the past and present too. They loved the variety of styles and references—the historical, cultural, philosophical, literary, and personal allusions—and they loved the sheer intellectuality of it. They also loved that it could be all these other things and still be autobiographical. It was the book *they* wanted to write. It elevated their thinking of what writing could do. It showed them that a modern writer could follow in the footsteps of Homer and Dante, presenting an entire worldview while simultaneously creating a new language to express it. It could be argued that Merton's later writings, taken together, present a similarly comprehensive view of life, while Lax's later works reveal an obsessive concern with fitting language precisely to experience.

When Lax and Merton moved to the Marcus cottage that June to concentrate exclusively on writing, *Finnegans Wake* had such an influence on their thought and work that Lax set down a guide to reading it that fall. (The guide was never published.) Whatever the effect on Lax's later poetry, Joyce's language certainly exerted a direct influence on the language he and Merton used in correspondence with each other. It is hard to find a page in their collected letters that doesn't show a Joycean influence.

------

Throughout that spring of 1939, while Merton focused on getting published—writing book reviews for the *New York Times* and the *New York Herald Tribune* and penning novels publishers rejected—Lax concentrated primarily on writing in his journal, putting his thoughts down as truthfully as he could. He continued to write poems and even tried his hand at love songs, but the journal was his main preoccupation. In it he set down his observations of the world, his thoughts about writing and living, his memories, and his views of himself. At times, like Merton, he made lists (an idea they seem to have taken from Rabelais, whom they discovered through Joyce)—of all the names he'd ever known, for example, or all the games he'd played as a child or all the sensations he felt when first waking up ("Dull pain in side, dull pain in right arch, slight clicks, awful taste in mouth . . . slight itchiness of scalp"). At other times he chose a subject raised by something that had happened to him, such as "reasons to cry," and wrote until he had exhausted his thoughts on the matter, ending in this case not with what had driven him to tears but an assertion that he wanted to be a good man.

> All this, to say that every time I say or imply that I think I'm a good guy that is what I mean: that instead of wanting to be all the things I used to want to be and that plenty of people still want to be: a rich man, a fireman, a good actor, an advertising executive, a writer, a poet, a hero, a suicide, a happy little fellow on an island paradise, what I want to be is a good man, and if you ask me what I mean by a good man I would say that the goodness I want to partake of is infinite and

that that infiniteness cannot by definition be defined, and that what an individual life has of that goodness is defined only by the whole of that life considered from all possible aspects and that it cannot be defined by the mind of the person living it at any point or points during the course of it, that all attempted word definitions are only the tiniest parts of definitions, but that maybe none of them are on the other hand completely false.

His idea of how a good person acts comes across most clearly in his contemplation of a dinner invitation on April 23, the only journal entry I've found that mentions his mother's recent death:

I go to Minette's because she asked me and she was my mother's friend. She asked me because she is good and kind and in the manner of a good woman, curious. The goodness is in having the kind impulse and in the curiosity. The kind impulse is to have the son of her friend who has died to dinner because he is alone in the city. The curiosity is as to how he will look and talk and seem, his mother having died and he being alone in the city. From these things she will draw half conclusions about him and his mother and from these half conclusions to further notions of friends and friends' sons and about, eventually, the nature of the universe. Knowing this and feeling that it is important for all men to have faith in the goodness of the universe and that good men encourage each other in this faith by some show of goodness, it is important not merely that I act and talk well, but that I look well and that the healthy look come from what I think to be a true physical means of physical health, the sun: not so much from vitamin pills or the sun-ray lamps at the St. George pool.

One day later he wrote the following, again about writing but applying equally to what became his approach to living: "I used to think it would be nice if you could put down that one word Irtnog to mean all you wanted to say, and now I think it would be good if I could put down ten million words all at once to mean all I wanted to say. But you just put one word after another and it is a very long time getting anything said except that each one says something."

On May 3, one month before he would leave New York to return to Olean again, Lax gave all of the writing he had been doing to his old teacher Mark Van Doren. He encouraged Van Doren to read only what was clear to him, then gave as succinct a description of how he approached journaling (both then and later) as I've been able to find in his writings:

> The book [i.e., the journal] is as talky as this letter, but that very fact is one of the things that the book is about, and I can't apologize for it properly without rewriting the book into the letter. What the book is is a lot of writing which I hope will shape itself into something more formal as I get to know more about it. I write what I feel like whenever I have time. One of the things you can say about writing is that it's something to look at the world through, and I'd like it to be a clearer and clearer window, without any lace curtains, or shades or mud on the pane, or shutters or window boxes to get in the way. The way it is now it has all of these things, but another important thing which, as long as I have it, makes their position a little less secure: my desire to get rid of them.

The letter ends with an unintentionally humorous summary of how other friends he has shown it to have reacted: "Gibney and I like it best and not all of it and not always. Merton likes it next best, and there's plenty of it he doesn't like. [John] Berryman liked one sentence and one poem but told me to hock my typewriter for a year, there was too much writing going on. Freedgood liked some of the first, but now doesn't like any of it and won't talk to me. His reaction is the only one I don't like."

---

In an article titled "The Beat Movement, Concluded," published in the February 13, 1972, issue of the *New York Times Book Review*, Wilfrid Sheed, who worked with Lax and his college friend Ed Rice at *Jubilee* magazine in the 1950s, wrote this:

> Much of the Beat lifestyle, or at least notes toward it, existed among a small group at Columbia University as early as 1939 and only needed missionaries to take it on the road and blend it. . . . According to Ed Rice's excellent little book on Merton, "The Man in the Sycamore Tree," Merton and his group proceeded to stage a complete dry-run of the Beat movement. Up at the poet Bob Lax's place in Olean they held novel-writing contests, watching each other narrowly to see who was going fastest. . . . They grew beards and shaved their heads, and by

1940 the place had swelled to a regular commune, with people cooking, chopping, writing and listening to Bix Beiderbecke around the clock. They even built a couple of tree houses to emphasize their position on adulthood, responsibility, politics.

This, of course, was written decades after those summers at the cottage, and while there may be some truth to what Sheed writes (Kerouac entered Columbia University in 1940, when Rice had just graduated, and the exploits of Merton and Lax and their friends were certainly known among the would-be writers and artists at the school), he takes great advantage of hindsight in making his connection. Rice himself, although working from memory and journals he kept during the two summers, seems to have conflated or embellished events to make them correspond more closely to the ethos embodied by Kerouac's seminal novel *On the Road*.

What is most remarkable about those summers—especially the first one—is just how much freedom and free exchange of thought Lax and Merton allowed themselves while avoiding the pit of self-indulgence. We tend now to think of the Beats and the hippies who followed them as pursuers of a licentious freedom that came to be centered on sex and drugs. While they talked about mysticism and enlightenment and read Eastern texts, most of them had a hard time following an ecstatic vision beyond its sensual sensations. (As we'll see in a later chapter, when Lax and Kerouac became friends in the 1950s, Kerouac felt a strong attraction to Lax's spirituality and talked about joining him at a Catholic retreat center on the outskirts of Paris, but those were the days just after the great success of *On the Road*, when fame, alcohol, and easy seduction were drawing Kerouac toward the slough of despond that would eventually kill him.) Lax and Merton weren't pursuing just a feeling but rather a sense of truth and of God and of themselves free from the expectations and trappings of the culture surrounding them. Although both came to be interested in Eastern spirituality (and had been exposed to it already in Brahmachari and their reading), their interest in 1939 was in finding something more akin to Plato's Good. More simply than even that, they wanted the freedom to write and read without thoughts of a career or even a need to make money.

Somewhat ironically, the idea of retreating to the cottage for a full summer came from an encounter Lax had while looking for what might be called a real job. Tiring perhaps of being a glorified babysitter at the Taft Hotel, he spent part of that spring looking for something more substantive. He was open to anything that involved writing, but he seems to have been most attracted to freelance work in radio or advertising, where his facility with words would stand him in good stead. As he told the story years later, it was a contact his brother-in-law had made for him, with a man named Bill Griffin, that helped him to see what he really wanted to do.

Griffin, who represented an agency responsible for scripts and commercials for a radio show, sent Lax home with some sample scripts and asked him to write one of his own along with a commercial or two. The show was sponsored by Lucky Strike cigarettes, so Lax, who smoked occasionally, took a pack of that brand along with him when he returned and tried to impress Griffin by smoking them.

"Well, I think you can write alright," Griffin said. "I just don't know if you can write this commercial stuff." Then he asked Lax what he really wanted to do.

"What I really want to do," Lax replied, "is go up to Olean and work at serious writing." He told Griffin about the Brahmachari book he was working on.

"So why don't you do it?" Griffin asked. Then he offered Lax $100 to help him get back to the cottage.

That was all the encouragement Lax needed. He talked to Merton, and Merton agreed to go with him. The only other person they invited along was Ed Rice, who was still at Columbia and would be the *Jester* editor the next school year. They didn't know him well, but they thought he had the right spirit. Merton's growing interest in Catholicism may have influenced the decision too; although Rice was far from devout, he was a lifelong Catholic who went regularly to Mass. In any case, Rice's deep interest in writing, his editorship, and his ability to take the summer off made him seem a good third companion.

As Sheed's article suggests, Rice's idiosyncratic and refreshingly candid biography of Merton, *The Man in the Sycamore Tree*, is one of the best sources for what went on at the Marcus cottage that summer. A second is *The Seven Storey Mountain* and a third is Mott's book. Lax answered questions about it in later years but spoke carefully, downplaying the less wholesome aspects that Rice and even Merton addressed more fully.

Built in 1926, the cottage had three smaller bedrooms and a kitchen in addition to the high-ceilinged main room and stone fireplace. A hand-made model sailing ship was set into the wall above the fireplace, and the furnishings were mostly antiques. For music there was a wind-up phonograph and a set of bongo drums Merton liked to play on a knoll across the drive. Outside, on the wide verandah, which ran the length of the building, the three friends set up a modest trapeze. Trees obscure the view from the cottage now, but in those days they could see Olean and, with a telescope they set up outside, even identify individuals on the golf course near Benji and Gladio's house.

"Mornings, though (memorably in August & September)," Lax wrote to Mott, "the town & valley were frequently covered with a meringue of white mist till ten or ten-thirty when it cleared. It was always exhilarating to wake up early and find yourself above the clouds. . . . There was a view of ranges of wooded hills to the east, too, sometimes with mist spilling over them: the whole thing a Himalayan kindergarten."

Having heard that William Saroyan had written a novel in five days, they decided to have a novel-writing contest, seeing what they could write in the same amount of time. The ultimate goal, Lax wrote on day three, was to "have three novels to send around to publishers with all the crazy parts and all the dirty words left in so they can see the way it really was in five days and maybe pay the three crazy guys to go on writing novels and growing beards . . . or maybe esquire will offer us a movie column which we won't take because we want to write books and get paid for writing them."

At first they worked on the kitchen table among the remains of half-eaten meals, "glowering at each other," according to Rice, "and trying to estimate the number of pages the other fellows are turning out." Then, when the rain and the cold subsided, they scattered: Lax typing on a card table in the garage and Rice setting up outside, while Merton stayed in the living room. To show their contempt for society and its conventions, they refused to read newspapers or listen to the radio, and they all grew beards (enduring insults from clean-cut locals whenever they went to town). They read banned books Benji Marcus had brought back from Europe too—Henry Miller's *Tropic of Cancer* (which Lax had been reading that spring) and D. H. Lawrence's *Lady Chatterley's Lover* among them. At night, if they didn't hitchhike to a movie in town or go to a local bar, they drank and smoked and played jazz records: Bix Beiderbecke, Bessie Smith, Louis Armstrong.

True to their image of themselves as literary bohemians, they paid little attention to things like eating and cleanliness, forgetting sometimes to bring food back from trips into town and subsisting on whatever was lying about. Rice records eating waffles for breakfast and lunch and Merton soaking hamburgers in Scotch for some reason (rendering them inedible). They mixed grapefruit juice with gin and dined repeatedly on cornflakes or shredded wheat. Merton did little cooking, concentrating instead on shopping and washing dishes until, he told Lax, he was having a dishwasher's dreams of being taken to a dance and made to feel ashamed of his hands. Despite his attentions, dishes piled up in a sink filled with awful smells until Lax's sister sent a cleaning woman.

What mattered to the three friends was their writing, the books they read, the people they knew, and the thoughts they had about all these things. The books ranged from those already mentioned to works by Rabelais, William Blake, Graham Greene, St. John of the Cross, and St. Augustine, most of which they got from St. Bonaventure, where the kindly librarian, Father Irenaeus, let them check out whatever they wanted for as long as they wanted to keep it. They had *Finnegans Wake* as well, of course, and one of their favorite things to do was read it out loud to one another.

The importance of that summer in deepening the three men's literary ambitions and convictions can't be overemphasized. The actual writing of their books was less important than writing them together—sharing the difficulties of the process, discussing ideas and theories, and learning together what writing a book really takes. Equally important was feeling the joy of writing whatever they wanted to write, not for a class or a prize or even necessarily for publication (although they had high hopes) but for each other and for themselves.

Although he started slowly, Rice finished his book the fastest, taking just ten days to write a 150-page humorous novel about a race around the world called "The Blue Horse." Merton started faster but his book, which he called at first "The Night Before the Battle" and eventually gave three different names, kept growing longer and longer, coming in finally at around five hundred pages. Lax had joined the novel-writing race, but he wasn't a racer by nature and his journal entry for June 12, the day the race began, shows that he wasn't even sure he would write a novel. Committing himself only to "five days of fast, maybe disorganized writing," he considers just writing in his journal or making lists or only making an "index of possible lists," which is what he does at first:

Trains I've been in
Towns I've been to
Suits I've Owned
Maids we've had
People I know who have had abortions
People I know who died
People I knew who committed suicide

The list of possible lists goes on for five pages.

Sometime later that day he began to write a scene, but instead of setting it up as fiction, he made it a movie scenario, giving lighting and camera directions. His descriptions of New York, though written quickly and without concern for grammar or punctuation, reveal acute observations and a happily wandering soul—characteristics that would remain part of Lax his whole life. What they don't show is any clear story. At one point—inspired perhaps by Van Doren having told him that Pearl Buck once translated a Chinese novel with 208 major characters and 155 minor ones—he made a list of characters drawn from people he had known or heard about that ran into the hundreds.

At his fastest, he could write only thirty pages a day but despite his fear that nothing he wrote would be as good as it might be, he continued plugging away, ending with two unfinished novels called "The Plague Full Swift Goes By" and "The Spangled Palace," the second a series of sketches about a traveling nightclub whose patrons follow it from town to town.

When Merton and Rice returned to Manhattan for several weeks in midsummer, Lax stayed on at the cottage alone. His attempts to write a book had led him beyond thinking about how to write to thinking about what he should be writing about. On July 17 he settled on Divine Love.

References to love for God appear in earlier journal entries, but the July 17 entry may be the first in which Lax gives full expression to his views on what it means to love and be loved by God. He writes of love in an active sense, stating unequivocally that any action coming from love is better than an action coming from fear or avoidance of pain, no matter how things may appear. To illustrate what he believes, he writes of a man who goes to pay the mortgage on his grandmother's house when he would rather go fishing. If that man acts out of fear rather than out of love for his grandmother, Lax declares, it would be better for him to go fishing: "Doing it is no worse than not doing it unless he understands why, unless his action to his old grandmother is based on love and hope and faith, not on a feeling of duty born of fear and superstition."

Next Lax expresses a belief that would guide his actions and even his approach to writing throughout the rest of his life—a belief that Merton marveled at and was deeply influenced by. The desire for God, he writes, is the one great desire everyone has; all smaller desires, even those that seem to lead us astray, are subsumed by it. In other words, if we can only see that what we truly desire is God, the smaller desires and fears that hinder our progress toward God will fall away.

This belief was at the heart of an argument Merton reports having had with Lax that summer. Merton was reading St. John of the Cross, which Lax would read after him. One of the aids toward deeper faith St. John recommends is mortification of the flesh. Given his love for sensual living, Merton could see why self-denial and punishment of one's body would be helpful, but the idea was abhorrent to Lax. "Desires can not be killed," he wrote in his journal, "but they can be educated, not by any hocus pocus of mere words but by an actual appeal to the understanding." Once a person understands what he really desires, that understanding will begin to guide his choices.

This is never truer than in writing, Lax thought. Writing he did out of love rather than fear or any other motive was more pleasant and sounded better to him when finished, its tone alone conveying hope rather than fear, preparing a reader for the day when he might be impelled to write his own confession.

Although Lax wrote many different things during his long life, a desire to discover and express Divine Love lay at the heart of his writing from that day on, and the fear that had held him back just the week before disappeared. It would return periodically, most notably two years later, when it would bring him close to a breakdown, but he understood already that love was its antidote.

Lax's writings about God's love at this point in his life can be misread as those of a Christian, but Lax was still a Jew. His understanding of God influenced Merton and he felt a kinship with Christian authors such as Augustine and Aquinas, but he would not be baptized into the Catholic Church for another four years. In fact there are indications that during this time Lax was doing his best to live according to the tenets of Judaism—not the Reform Judaism he had grown up with but a more Orthodox version. If the faith is true, he felt, you shouldn't water it down but live it as it was revealed. One reason he grew a beard that summer and later, while living in New York City, was to honor the Torah's prohibition against taking a blade to the hairs of one's face.

At some point—probably that summer, when he and Merton were having regular discussions about how to live and love God—Lax began reading the Bible. He started with the Old Testament, reading a few pages a day, and read right through the New. Along the way he began to believe that Judaism and Christianity were not contradictory but complementary.

Merton and Rice returned to the cottage for only a brief period before leaving for good in late August. Other college friends came for shorter visits, but by the end of October Lax was alone again. He seems to have liked the idea of living on his own—he now had a car to drive, records to listen to, and all the books he wanted to read—but the change of seasons brought cold weather and the need for money for heat and food. As he described the situation, he was "weak with hunger, crawling across the cottage floor toward a burning hamburger" he had tried to cook in the fireplace when his sister arrived to announce that the owner of the radio station wanted to give him a job.

When they met, the radio station manager, "a young man with slicked black hair and a deep voice like Orson Welles, pale skin and square rimless glasses, a little like death," said he'd heard Lax had worked for Lucky Strike, and Lax, equivocating, said yes. That was enough to earn him a job writing commercials. He worked half-days six days a week for $15.

Lax's attitude toward doing commercial work just because he needed money is apparent in his description of his first day:

Sitting in the office late the first afternoon I watched John Bradford [another commercial writer] writing with great facility ads for the

Cabin Bar and Grill—come out and join the fun—and for Ostermoor mattresses—lie down in luxury. I wasn't getting anywhere. It was hot and chalky and dry in the room, the steamy radiators hissed and misted the window. Outside, beyond the town, the hills were quiet and covered with snow, just visible in the winter night. I wanted to be up in the hill, sitting at the cottage, even snowshoeing. I didn't want to be at the Cabin Bar and Grill or telling people to go there.

These feelings would grow more intense—with graver consequences—when he landed a more prestigious but still commercial writing job on the *New Yorker* one year later.

---

It would be easy to overlook this period in Lax's life since little seemed to be happening, but those days at the cottage by himself may have influenced his decisions and direction more than any others. For the first time he was able to be alone whenever he wanted, to come and go as he pleased, and to write whatever he wanted to write whenever he wanted to write it. He always intended to show his writing to his friends and even send it out to publications, but there was no one looking over his shoulder or expecting anything from him, so the writing he did was natural and honest. The need to make a living would lead him out of his solitude into other pursuits, but the freedom he found in those cottage weeks would stick with him, calling to him in the midst of everything he did, until eventually he found a way to live the simpler life he wanted most. It has been said that real education is not learning but unlearning, stripping away all the wrong things we've been taught. What Lax would do over the next several years, sometimes consciously and sometimes unconsciously, would slowly free him from conventional thinking and ambition. By simplifying his desires, he simplified his needs and freed more time for creative contemplation. Without separating himself from the world he loved, he found ways to make his time his own.

More than the need to earn a living was about to intrude on his solitude, however. On September 1, just days after Rice and Merton left, Germany invaded Poland. Lax had no more doubt than anybody else that the United States would be dragged into the war and soon the draft board would come calling.

## 5    *Lo, the sun walks forth!*

On September 17, 1939, after seeing a movie in town and feeling sickened by the audience's applause for newsreel images of World War I and the American flag, Lax went to see his sister in the house I stayed in on that first visit to Olean. They probably sat in the comfortably furnished living room with its wall of books and windows to the street, where, on later visits, they mostly laughed. There was no laughter this time. When Lax said he was done with viewing newsreels because they were jingoistic, Gladio told him Benji didn't think he had the right to rail against war when he didn't read newspapers or listen to the radio. "He says you don't know what's going on," she said.

"I do know what's going on," Lax replied, "but no one else seems to. Men are killing each other and if Americans aren't careful they will soon be killing men too. I don't want to kill men." Perhaps to soften what had become a hard moment between them, he tried a joke: "Why should I kill strangers when I have been so shy and polite about not killing unpleasant acquaintances?"

The discussion continued, however, and what he recorded in his journal reveals both his fear of personal involvement and the impractical philosophizing that amazed and at times exasperated his friends.

"People who don't go to war lack sympathy for those who do," he said. Gladio didn't object to this, but she took exception to what he said next: that people should simply follow the Christian command to love your enemy and turn the other cheek. "If it is a good world," he said, "there is a way to lead a good life in it without becoming a murderer, and I believe it is a good world because there have been men like Jesus."

It must have disturbed Gladio to hear the younger brother she felt so close to express a worldview based solidly on Christian teachings, even if her own tendency was to believe in the efficacy of love. What he said next, though, must have troubled her even more. When she cited Hitler's cruelty to Jews as a humanitarian reason for going to war, he replied, "They're Jews in nose only: their belief is as pagan as Hitler's."

When she countered this by saying that the Jews are a people and a minority and one cannot let them be harmed, he answered, "I do not understand this humanitarianism that will send us off to kill others and be killed in order that a minority may not be harmed."

His words are still astonishing to read, especially after the Holocaust. He seems insensitive at best. What is truly astonishing, though, given how he went on to live his life, is the dedication they reveal to an absolute view—and absolute faith in that view—of what a person who loves God should and shouldn't do in this world.

"I drove home sad," he writes at the end of this journal entry, "because I wonder if anyone will ever understand why you shouldn't kill people, or even consider it as an alternative action in the cause of virtue, at any cost at all."

Naïveté, one might say. Impracticality. These charges were lobbed at Lax his whole life. What is remarkable here, though, is that he knew the practical thing to say and do and chose instead to believe, without dilution or emendation, what he read in the Bible, what Jesus taught: that in all circumstances, without exception, we are called to live a life of total love. For this man who still considered himself a Jew, Jesus was already his touchstone.

One day after his difficult discussion with Gladio, Lax wrote a "Speech to draft officers":

I do not want to go to war. I don't believe in killing. Am I a conscientious objector? Extremely. But I am not a member of an organization. No organization that I know, formed with the idea of peace at any price has stayed organized. But I am not a quaker. I do not belong to an organized religion. Neither did Christ, yet he was able to love his neighbors as himself, to forgive his enemies, to render unto Caesar the things that are Caesar's and unto God the things that are God's, and I hope that I may also be able to do these things. But Christ was Christ. But I am unwilling to add to my present sins by the sin of killing.

Will I do some charitable work? If I am needed for it and competent to do it. But I am most competent as a writer, I have practiced longest at it. My charity consists in attempting to write the truth as clearly as I can at a time when many others write intentional distortions.

You think I'm a coward. I think it takes more courage to refuse than to go. You think I have no sense of humor. I do not think it is funny to kill innocent men.

Three prayers for if they go to shoot me.

Hear, O Israel,

Twenty Third Psalm

The Lord's Prayer

What was still theoretical at this point would become concrete the following year.

---

The deepening of Lax's spiritual belief and his drift toward Christianity continued throughout that fall and winter. Over the summer, in addition to Joyce and large sections of the Bible, he'd read Dante, Hopkins, Eliot, Blake, Donne, St. Augustine, and *The Ascent of Mt. Carmel* by St. John of the Cross. That fall he was still reading Joyce and Blake while moving on to St. John of the Cross's *The Dark Night of the Soul*, Aristotle's *Delta Metaphysics*, and Jean Cocteau's *Les Enfants Terribles* and *Opium*. While the last of these might not seem spiritual, it was a passage in *Opium* that led to Lax's comment to Merton about wanting to be a saint. In *The Seven Storey Mountain*, Merton places this event in the spring of 1939, but his journal says it took place on Lax's birthday, November 30. This makes more sense since by then Lax would have read Cocteau and copied down this passage: "It is difficult to live without opium after having known it, because it is difficult to take the earth seriously after having known opium. And, unless one is a saint, it is difficult to live without taking the earth seriously." Below it, Lax wrote, "Dear Mr. C: How do you know you aren't or wouldn't be or couldn't be a saint? In the absence of this sure knowledge which no saint probably has ever had concerning himself, to attempt to live like a saint, according to Love, Faith, Hope and Charity, is not presumptuous. The Saints are examples of attainable human virtue, not a show of divine freaks." This is, in essence, what he said that made such a strong impression on Merton and, later, me.

An entire book—or at least a long article—could be written on how Lax's and Merton's reading that summer influenced their future thinking. I've already discussed Joyce's effect on them, and the influence of St. Augustine's *Confessions* on Merton's autobiography is obvious. The writer who may have made the deepest and longest-lasting impact, however, is St. John of the Cross. His "dark night of the soul" is often misrepresented as a time of depression and doubt, but in both *The Ascent of Mt. Carmel* and *The Dark Night of the Soul*, he presents it as an emptying of oneself, a putting aside of all sensory input and visions that leaves the advanced seeker after God dependent on pure faith alone. No crutches, no charismatic signs, nothing to rely on but a blind, humble, moment-to-moment faith in the living I AM. *New Seeds of Contemplation* and other later Merton books are full of images and thoughts from St. John's writings—images and thoughts Merton found reflected in Eastern religions. Lax, in essence, became John's seeker, shedding more and more of what we think are necessities as he aged, until he lived like the birds of the air and the grass of the field. That fall he copied down this passage from book 1, chapter 14 of *The Ascent of Mt. Carmel*:

> In order to arrive at having pleasure in everything,
> Desire to have pleasure in nothing,
> In order to arrive at possessing everything,
> Desire to possess nothing.
> In order to arrive at being everything,
> Desire to be nothing.

Around this same time, no doubt with the coming war and draft on his mind, he wrote to Rabbi David Lefkowitz in Dallas asking how someone like himself could find his place doing God's work in the world. Lefkowitz sympathized with his struggles and assured him that creative work could be a kind of ministry. A few weeks after receiving Lefkowitz's reply, Lax wrote in his journal, "I really believe that the spark in art is a part of an eternal and infinite mystery, like and part of the mystery of creation and of love."

The new year started quietly, with Lax writing, reading, working at the radio station, and skating on free afternoons, but it didn't stay that way for long. In early January he sent a collection of his poems, plays, and drawings to the *New Yorker* writer E. B. White, who was living in Maine at the time with his wife, the influential *New Yorker* editor Katherine White. He also sent three radio scripts to Norman Corwin, whose poetry-focused CBS radio show, *Words Without Music*, had been a surprise success the year before. Lax had never met either man, but he thought there was a chance his work was similar enough to theirs for them to like it. Not only did both write back in early February, but both applauded his writing.

Corwin called Lax's scripts "brilliant" and praised him in particular for his wit, irony, and spare style, but Corwin had moved on to a new show and the one Lax's work would have been perfect for, *Words Without Music*, was no longer on the air. Corwin's letter disappointed Lax, of course, but by the time it arrived, he'd already heard from White, who offered much better news. In a letter dated February 5, White wrote:

> I didn't like the looks of your book (I get an awful lot of junk sent me by terrible people) so I let it get bogged down under a lot of stuff; but today I pulled it out as a last stand against doing any work myself, and I got a lot of pleasure out of it. So did my wife, which is more to the point as she is never mistaken about anything, whereas I can sometimes be taken. In short, why don't you let us submit this to the New Yorker and see if they don't want it. I appreciate sharing a book with your girl in Northampton, but I am willing to share it with the western world if you have any desire for publication and I have never seen a graduate of Columbia, 24, who didn't, nor do I want to particularly.

*E. B. White* was writing this. *E. B. White*, the best-known writer of personal essays in the country. *E. B. White*, the favorite writer of Harold Ross, who edited the magazine Lax had dreamed of working for since he was thirteen. *E. B. White*, the only writer in America who seemed interested in the same things he was.

White was true to his word. On March 10, having moved into Benji and Gladio's house for the winter, Lax was sick in bed and reading Robert Burton's *The Anatomy of Melancholy* when Benji handed him a *New Yorker* envelope. Lax expected a polite rejection but instead found an enthusiastic letter from Gus Lobrano, the fiction and casuals editor. What the editors liked most was one of Lax's radio scripts—almost surely one of the three Corwin had rejected—a sardonic, two-part, multivoice poem that is half-satire and half-encomium with a commercial for a product called

Opium in the middle. ("Do you ever wake up feeling awful? Does the day settle on you like a great straw hat? . . . Is your husband or wife the last person in the world you want to see? Then what you need is Opium.") Lobrano wanted to edit it slightly but otherwise print it in its entirety.

Lax, of course, said yes.

Lax had written the poem-script "A Radio Masque for My Girl Coming Down from Northampton" in a single night and morning months before while anticipating a visit from Nancy Flagg, who is represented most specifically by a reference to her red hair and the name of the town where she was living. The acceptance is significant because it was Lax's first from a national magazine and the magazine was the one he admired most. Also, even in those days, being in the *New Yorker* brought the kind of exposure that could launch a career. But having this particular piece accepted must have been especially significant for Lax because he'd written it for himself and his friends and it was full of who he was—his interests, his wit, the work he'd done, and even his love.

Although Lax was sometimes inattentive to his studies as he neared the end of college, he had been by and large a dutiful student, an overachiever who knew how to succeed by following the rules. This carried over into his poetry, where he knew how to write to win prizes. He used a measured meter, chose subjects judges would consider fitting for poetry, and mixed the serious with the humorous just so. Yes, he wrote playful verse too, but even here he stayed within the generally accepted styles and boundaries.

The "Radio Masque" was something different. It incorporated his love of theater and writing scripts, his composing of commercials and knowledge of radio, even the kind of faux erudition he must have heard quite often at Columbia (which the *New Yorker*'s editors surely loved to see mocked). His reading of Cocteau shows up in his mention of opium, his dislike of war in a repeated newsboy shout—"War in China! War in China!"—and his interest in religion in a "pontifical" voice that speaks of the Church's "dove-gray lip." His knowledge of Corwin's work shines through in his use not only of an announcer but also a "second voice"—a Corwin innovation. Lax goes Corwin one better (maybe mocking him gently) by adding a third "deep, interpretive voice."

What Lax had come to desire deeply since moving to Olean a year and a half before was to write only what he wanted to write and see its value recognized by others. Nothing could have told him more clearly than the *New Yorker*'s acceptance of this particular poem that he was on the right track. His journals in the days to follow reveal a new resolve to write only in this way.

Less than a month after accepting "Radio Masque" the *New Yorker* accepted a second Lax poem, "Greeting to Spring (Not Without Trepidation)", which was actually published first on May 4, 1940, shortly before the German invasion of France. It begins in a light tone with warm images:

> Over the back of the Florida basker,
> Over the froth of the Firth of Forth,
> Up from Tahiti and Madagascar
> *Lo, the sun walks north!*

Halfway through, however, come the prescient lines:

> *At an outside table where the sun's bright glare is,*
> *We will speak of darkened Paris.*

In the last stanza the sun is transformed from a welcome warmth into a resolutely greater force high above our small designs:

> Over the plans of the parties at strife,
> Over the planes in the waiting north,
> Over the average man and his wife,
> *Lo, the sun walks forth!*

On May 5 Lax recorded his reaction: "Poem came out in New Yorker yesterday, and looked ok, read better than I thought would, only the first minute I seen it I felt naked or exposed or like I was a fifteen year old who had just heard his own voice among a lot of bass community singing." The publication earned him $26.

A few weeks later Lax traveled to Manhattan, where he had lunch with Lobrano, who took several more of his poems, including a "fable" called "The Man With the Big General Notions" Lax had written the previous year. (It wouldn't appear until October 10, 1942, when, like the "Radio Masque," it would take up a full page.) In a June 6 letter accompanying the check for the poem, Lobrano told Lax he had spent considerable time since their lunch envying the simplicity of his life. In a postscript he invited Lax to send something for the "Notes and Comments" section of the magazine's "Talk of the Town" if that kind of thing interested him. Although Lax doesn't seem to have taken Lobrano up on this offer, the magazine continued to publish his poems. The whimsical "Poem of Gratuitous Invective Against New Jersey" appeared on July 6 and a short poem called "The Last Syllable" on November 23.

Although the publications brought Lax little money, they boosted his confidence in his writing and the rightness of how he wanted to live. In his journal that winter and spring he expressed increased belief that writing what you want to write is the only way to really write. Perhaps because he was reading *Finnegans Wake* (which he finished in mid-February), he began to think of writing one unified "big book" that would tell the world everything he had to say.

Since the "big book" he envisioned would be centered on his journal, Lax began to think more carefully about the way the journal should be written, including what he should leave out. In theory, he thought, nothing should be left out, but he knew himself well enough to know that many factors might cause him to avoid writing some things—among them, embarrassment, superstition, and reluctance to bring others' foibles to light. He justified leaving things out by telling himself that the whole journal should be available to anyone interested in it. For better or worse, in the years ahead this approach led to journals that read more like letters than private musings. Only close reading and careful interpolation can reveal his true heights and depths. "I'm not trying to give an accurate record of a guy thinking . . . but an accurate impression, like a work of art," he wrote. "You might get a feeling of the rhythm and structure of one guy's thought and some little idea of its extension in time and written space even if some of the particular data was false, forged or overlooked."

The thinking he wanted to capture was less a monologue than a dialogue between a voice from the bottom of his head that made the "quick unaffected judgments and easy childlike decisions" of a six-year-old and a voice from the top of his head that sometimes sounded like "the crabbed voice of experience, not treating the six-year-old with the proper gentleness or respect," and at other times blended harmoniously with it.

While his *New Yorker* success seemed a big boost to his journal writing, it had a less salutary effect on his poetry. "Keep wanting as I have all winter to write a poem," he wrote on April 15, "big and long maybe or a lot of little ones. Keep getting scared about it." Writing a poem meant going into "a trance," but going into a trance didn't necessarily mean he would end up with a poem:

> What if I go into a trance and don't write no poem, and don't do no work and starve and worry my family and friends, and they either feed me or call doctors or send me off to a crazy house with money they could use for other things, normal important ones. . . . And for what, for a poem, to satisfy what, vanity maybe.
>
> But to say all this and to fear all this is to lack faith; the faith that when you are doing your best, even if your best is only a motionless trance, you'll be doing good, and when you are doing your best, you'll be watched out for, and those who watch out for you will gain, not lose by it.

Nothing he wrote in those days was more revealing—or more frighteningly prescient—than this.

---

After his lunch with Lobrano in Manhattan in early June, Lax ignored his boss's advice and quit his radio station job to spend the summer writing full time. He was already living at the cottage again when several of his college friends joined him, including Merton, Rice, Gibney, and Freedgood. Before the summer was over, others had come and gone, including Reinhardt and Flagg. With so many people around, the atmosphere was different from the year before, less like an isolated retreat than a summer camp or commune.

Lax and Merton were different too. In some ways they'd switched places. Lax's success at placing his poetry in the *New Yorker* and the pleasure he took from writing his journal had increased his desire to concentrate on his own writing rather than working for pay. At the same time, the need to earn a living and the possibility of commercial success made him think more consciously about writing things editors would like and even of being an editor himself. Merton, on the other hand, had been living a quieter, more spiritual life since the summer before and had plans to enter a Franciscan monastery in New Jersey in August. While his friends wrote and talked about novels or short stories and publication, he often sat by himself looking across the valley and saying the rosary. Feeling himself being drawn into temptations he had avoided successfully for months, he went down to St. Bonaventure College after a couple of weeks to live in a dormitory there, returning to the cottage only briefly several times before beginning to teach at St. Bonaventure in September.

Because so much has been written about Merton, it is natural to see him as the center of this group of friends, but during that summer at least Lax was the one who drew everyone together. Not only did the cottage belong to his brother-in-law, but Olean was his hometown and the idea of retreating to the hills to live a creative life was mostly his too. His friends were all more practically minded. More intent on building their careers. What was extraordinary about that summer was less that the lifestyle at the cottage presaged the more generally communal life of the later Beats or hippies than that so many talented, ambitious young people made time to enjoy being free—and freely creative—together.

Lax may also have been the one who most enjoyed it all. Much as he liked solitude, he liked being with his friends more. The scene at the cottage approximated his vision of the ideal life: a group of creative friends all creating in harmony with one another. On June 16 he wrote:

> Everywhere is the happy tick tick of the . . . typewriters in all parts of the room. Who is writing? Jim Knight is writing an account of his boyhood in the south. Peggy [Wells] is writing an account of her girlhood on riverside drive. Rice just stopped writing about an imaginary swing musician and is now trying to do a Herald Tribune crossword puzzle. [Bob] Mack is studying German. Gibney is drawing pictures. Freedgood and Merton are probably climbing five miles up the hill now at 11 at night when the movie has let out. I am typing because I like to hear the sound of my typewriter among the others.

Although Lax and several others tried to start another novel-writing contest, there were too many distractions for anyone to get much work done. Jazz was always coming from the record player, and alcohol flowed freely. Despite a lack of cars, people were always coming and going—taking taxis into town to see movies, walking down the road to drink at a bar, or hitchhiking somewhere. The sink was always full of dishes, the

garbage overflowed, and there were cockroaches and bits of paper every-
where, even outside, where wads of abandoned prose filled a
wheelbarrow.

People kept arriving and departing throughout the summer, but the
apex of activity seems to have come in early July, when Flagg was there.
She stayed for only a week but made a distinct impression on everyone,
including Merton, who, years later, remembered her sitting in the sun
combing out her long, red-gold hair. The day after she left, Merton left
too. Lax's journal for that day, July 19, includes the lines:

> Merton left today, for Virginia, maybe won't be back before he goes to
> monastery.
>
> N[ancy] left yesterday. Maybe return.
>
> Hot, sultry. A bird tried to sing.

A few days later Lax tried to capture what it had been like with so
many intelligent and creative friends gathered together:

> cottage conversation with 11 people: matters of taste, food jokes, recol-
> lection of childhood theories, pleasures, victories, defeats, theories of
> business and art with the tone of cosmological emphasis, exchange of
> compliments, discovery and report of new pastimes, light hearted
> evaluation of absent friends, cozy disgust at the progress of national
> and world affairs in art business and politics. pleasure at seeing old
> favorites: ellington chaplin marx brothers fields joyce picasso. doing
> new things, having the old ones revived or getting new recognition.
> theories of art, philosophy, intuitions concerning Life, art, business,
> people, animals, nature, the machine.

Only a handful of friends were left at the cottage after that, but in
August things picked up again, with Merton and others returning. By
then a Selective Service bill was working its way through Congress, and
around the fireplace at night, against a backdrop of World War I posters
they had pinned to the wall ("Blood or Bread" and "Remember the
Bond") they discussed their attitudes toward war. Although they all had
reservations about going to war, Lax was the only declared pacifist.
While Merton and Gibney said that they would go to war if drafted and
try to serve as noncombatants, Lax was against serving in the armed
forces in any capacity. The thought that he might be forced to become a

participant began to haunt him even more after September 16, when the first peacetime draft in U.S. history became law.

People continued to come and go throughout August, but by the 25th the group had dwindled to the college core—Lax, Merton, Reinhardt, Freedgood, Gibney, and Rice—plus Reinhardt's future wife and a woman who unsettled everyone by drawing a life-size nude of Walt Whitman on the wall. The weather was cold enough to turn the heat on, and the day was fast approaching when Lax would have to go back to work. One morning he gazed consciously around the living room, noting the coffee and the toast, the marmalade and the cat. Everyone was writing or drawing or talking softly. In his journal he wrote:

> Last night it was pretty: summer done: reinhardt dancing like at school: wine, spaghetti, salad (everybody here (but slate and flagg): grown, knew where we were and where else we might have been. I wanted to cry like flagg done when she left.
>
> Or maybe I just wanted to cry. But we certainly look as grown up as some grown up people I've seen.
>
> Not reading this, Rice just looked around the room at everybody busy, says, "Just like kindergarten."

As Lax seemed to know, things would never be that way again.

# 6    Suicide Notes

Violence and nonviolence were on my mind when I returned to Patmos in 1989, the year of Tiananmen Square and the fall of the Berlin Wall. I visited Lax twice that year—in April, when we celebrated the Greek Orthodox Easter together, and again in October, when I stayed for three weeks. The promise of peace was everywhere those days. While I was on Patmos the second time, Merton's old friend the Dalai Lama even won the Nobel Peace Prize. I came across an appropriate quote from Dwight Eisenhower and copied it into my journal: "People want peace so badly that one day governments are going to have to step out of the way and let them have it."

But governments aren't prone to stepping out of the way or letting people have peace. At almost the same time the Dalai Lama received the Peace Prize, those in power in East Germany selected a hardliner as their new leader and George H. W. Bush "redefined" Jimmy Carter's ban on assassinations. Of course the peaceful demonstrations in Tiananmen Square that fired the imagination of peace-loving people everywhere ended in a nauseating orgy of violence.

When I arrived on Patmos the second time, I'd been traveling for over five months. I'd given up the partnership with Rick Steves but continued to lead tours for him and I'd started my own small tour company, because, like Lax in his early days, I had to earn a living. Worn out from so much travel, I spent my time on Patmos sleeping, reading, and trying to write. Visiting Lax as well, of course. One night while walking to his house with a young Swiss woman who was also visiting him, we came across what looked like a pool of blood. Without thinking, I bent down and put my finger in it to make sure. She reacted with shock and alarm. "Never touch blood," she told me, but when I asked why not, she didn't know. "I've always been told not to," she said. I tried to laugh it off, but the thought of that blood on my finger stayed with me throughout the evening.

That night I dreamed I saw a large man with a beard like mine limping across a street. As I tried to help him, I put my hand on his back and felt something I thought was blood that turned out to be feces. Although I wanted to run from the smell, I dragged him to a tent and laid him down. He seemed to be drunk and there was a suggestion of violence about him, but I stayed the night with him, and when I woke up I found him dressed in fresh clothes, repairing an electrical outlet. He called me over to watch and learn, telling me the wiring in my house was badly in need of repair. Was the figure Christ, I wondered when I woke, or some version of me? Was it a dream of responsibility or vulnerability, guilt or innocence?

---

In *The Seven Storey Mountain*, Merton writes that he felt a shared responsibility for the European war because he was a sinner. If the biblical maxim is correct, he reasoned, that the actions of a righteous man have great power in their effect, then the flip side is equally true: that every unrighteous act or thought exerts power in the opposite direction. That late summer and early fall of 1940, Lax was feeling the heavy responsibility of his decisions, words, and actions too. On August 29, after noting that the Senate had passed the draft bill, he wrote, "Now what you say is important because you might get killed or sent off to war. Times, things are coming to a head; everyone is thrown into a dramatic context."

In a different era with a different young man, these might seem the melodramatic musings of self-creation, even self-importance, but Lax was worried about more than being subject to a draft. A young poet who had immersed himself in spiritual texts, he felt that what he did and said had wider, even eternal implications. He ended his entry with a manifesto of sorts, a provisional articulation of principles that would guide him throughout his life:

> These are serious times and what have you done, what are you doing? For the ages, for the present people, even for yourself? You sit here playing games, or in bed you think of old times, times you didn't have as much fun as you could have. Sometimes you make up speeches to draft officers—"I do not believe in killing. I will not kill." Should I be doing more? Games are good. The world is, or seems to be (except for disease, unfortunate accidents, hostile beasts, poison

plants, murderous theivish, blaspheming, idolatrous, lying, adulterous scandalous man) for joy. Youth a time of pleasure, for singing songs, and prayers. What if we leave nothing for the ages. Only saying the world is for joy and life a time of prayers and happiness. That has been written in the commandments, the psalms and the words of the prophets. We can perfect ourselves in the belief of it and in the actions, graceful, that come from the belief. And those things in the parentheses, according to the prophets and the psalmists (of all religions that share this belief) will disappear. The lion will lie down with the (fox, sheep) swords beat into (pruning hooks, plowshares). And I believe this. That the world will be good when men cease from evil, that other men cease from evil faster when you do, and that you can be good more and more easily by wanting to: by "loving the Lord, thy God, with all thy heart, and with all they soul, and with all thy might."

As his friends departed and war seemed more and more imminent, Lax fretted about what he should do. His money was running low and he hadn't done the writing he'd hoped to do. He felt increasingly that he had to choose how he was going to live and what he was going to write rather than just floating along as he'd done so far. Was he going to build on his commercial success by writing things he thought he could sell, or was he going to write what he felt like writing and trust that the best would find an audience in time? He tried to believe that the two could go hand-in-hand, but he couldn't quite. As most of his friends returned to New York City, his choice seemed to be between staying at the cottage and moving back to the City himself. It was the old tug-of-war between solitude and society. For a while, with his friends at the cottage, the two had seemed reconcilable. Now he was back to making a choice, and his future seemed to depend on his decision.

The sun shone for most of September, and while it did Lax put off his gloomier thoughts. His days consisted of writing, reading, walking, sleeping, and talking with Gibney, the only friend who'd stayed. When he heard that his sister had had a baby, he wrote that he spent most of his time feeling happy. But there was a snake in his Eden. Ever since the war had begun, he and Benji had argued about it. Benji believed in the need for war and supported America's entrance, while Lax insisted that it was always wrong to kill and talked about being a conscientious objector.

Their positions had put them at odds, and Benji, who had become an important man in Olean, seems to have worried that Lax's position would become known. By this time Olean, like most American communities, was strongly pro-war. Benji finally gave him an ultimatum: If he was going to register as a conscientious objector, he had to do it somewhere else.

Despite Benji's wishes, when Lax and Gibney registered for the draft on October 16, they were still in Olean. But there was snow on the hills already and the cottage was cold. On October 23 the boiler for the steam heat burst. Lax added a second sweater and typed in the kitchen, next to the open oven, but New York was looking more attractive. By the end of November he and Gibney were packed and ready to go. True to his nature, Lax recorded only the books he was taking along: the Bible, Shakespeare, Rabelais, Dante, three Joyce works, various classics and grammars, and St. John of the Cross. Driving through a snowstorm the entire way, they arrived in New York on December 3, and Lax headed straight to Morningside Heights to stay with Benji's nephew, Bob Mack, who was in graduate school at Columbia. Mack had been one of those staying up at the cottage over the summer and the two had become good friends. He would help Lax out of more than one rough period in the years ahead.

---

During his June lunch with Gus Lobrano, Lax had raised the possibility of working for the *New Yorker*, but Lobrano had told him there was nothing available. In a follow-up letter, however, Lobrano had asked if Lax was interested in writing for the magazine's "Notes and Comments" section. It's unclear whether Lax took him up on the offer but probably not. He tended to view summers the way a child does: as a time to do what you want rather than what someone else might want you to do. Once he was back in New York, though, Lax went straight to Lobrano to see if anything had opened up. This time Lobrano told him there might be a job for him. He seems to have been vague about what Lax would be doing or when the job might start, but whatever he said was enough for Lax to feel hopeful. He walked around New York with a smile, thrilled to think he might work for the *New Yorker*.

It wasn't just the promise of a *New Yorker* job that made him glad; it was everything about being in New York again. The day after he talked to Lobrano, he saw his favorite band leader, Duke Ellington, at the Apollo in Harlem, and soon he was making the rounds, visiting all of his friends. The day after Christmas he went to Virginia with Gibney and Merton's old girlfriend Ginny Burton. They stayed through New Year's, dancing and going to parties and playing poker. Back in New York, the three of them went to Kelly's Stables to see Coleman Hawkins and Billie Holiday.

Once the holidays were over, however, and the *New Yorker* still hadn't called, Lax felt frustrated. On January 7 he expressed his frustration in a letter to Merton and, one line before finishing it, picked up the phone to call Lobrano. Lobrano told him to come in and see the *New Yorker*'s managing editor, Ik Shuman, about "a bread and butter job" that seemed to be open. Writing in his journal that night, Lax indulged in rare self-pity:

> Having to see one more guy, about a job that was still indefinite and could be described as bread and butter, I finished Merton's letter, looked at my quickly saddening face in the mirror, turned out the light and lay on the bed, feeling sorry, not for myself, see, because I knew somewhere right below the surface that it was all going to be all right, that nothing they could do to me would do me any real harm, but that such a brave plucky little fellow, apparently so alone in the city, should be so carelessly treated, that they should think of so mistreating him, to imply that he would soon have a man-sized job, to keep him waiting not three weeks but four for an answer, then by a subtle polite graduation suggest one day that the job would be boring, the next that it would not pay well, all this time the brave plucky young man has less and less money and will soon, by cause of poverty take any job they offer him.

Earlier that morning Lax had cashed a check for $5, hoping he had $7 in the bank, and his landlady had knocked on his door after sending two notes asking for his rent. The rent was only $4 a week, but he was five weeks behind and he owed her for phone calls too. Having promised to pay her by the end of the week, he went to see Shuman that afternoon and was offered a job working just two hours a day for $20 a week. Despite what he had written in his journal, Lax said okay, and Shuman told him he'd have a definite answer for him the following week.

When the formal offer finally came on January 13, the pay had been bumped to $25. "It isn't handsome," Lobrano said, but it sounded fine to Lax. He was glad to have a job at last. The long delay, however, had left him less enthusiastic about working for the *New Yorker*. More fretful too, about whether they would like the work he did. Over the next year this combination would grow toxic.

———————

Later in Lax's life, some who wrote about him gave him retrospective titles, such as assistant poetry editor, but his job was nowhere near as lofty as that. His main task was answering letters to the editor. He was encouraged to write pieces for "Notes and Comments," for which he would be paid extra, but in the eleven months he worked at the magazine he wrote only two that made it into print, and only one of them appeared while he still worked there.

Lax announced his new job to his family and friends, but right from the start it brought him more anxiety than pleasure or pride. On January 18, when he'd been working at the magazine less than a week, he was already fretting about his performance. "The letters i write sound as though i resented having to write them," he wrote in his journal. "the jokes [Lobrano] asked me to do i didn't want to do; i didn't want to take a chance at making a bad one, one that stank like the letters to the editor stink of all kinds of inner perturbation and sadness. . . . i guess i'm closer to liking myself and being some things i wanted to be than i ever have been, but there ain't no spring in my step, no humor in what i write or draw."

What he seemed to be discovering was that he couldn't write on command—not anything that seemed good, anyway. He had always relied on what he called "trumpet attacks," sudden inspirations that even as a child had given him "such raptures that my poor adolescent body couldn't support them."

Sadness was seeping into Lax's soul. He hoped he could write it away, but it came from needing to make a choice he couldn't make: between pursuing a worldly idea of success and going his own way. "sometimes i think if i write a lot of this stuff straightening out little inner sadnesses then as a reward i'll find myself dancing around and writing some good happy poem," he wrote. "other times i think writing all this stuff acts like a lightning rod, dissipating the power of any (million dollar, or good poem) inspirations that might hit me. other times i think it's confusing million dollars with good poem that ties me up. but i don't know, i'll bet a good poem with the words i know would have an audience among the people now alive, maybe not a million dollars but an audience."

On January 19 he laid out the crux of his dilemma: "now that i've got the job on the New Yorker i'm scared of losing it or of not getting advanced: i.e. i let people who say boy you'd better work, or you'd better stop saying no when they ask you to do something scare me." The entry includes this seemingly hopeful but ultimately sobering line: "Sometimes i think this is a fine journal and that i just can't wait to die and get it published."

---

Reading Lax's entries over the course of 1941 is like watching an animal slowly dying. The ailing beast in Lax's case was one of several images he'd long held of himself: that of a writer and editor praised and rewarded for his work. The prizes he'd won for his poetry in school, the popularity of *Jester* when he was its editor, and the ease with which he'd placed several poems at the *New Yorker* had all fed the image. But over the past two years, since his graduation from college, he had been changing along with Merton. He had begun to understand at some level that life demanded a choice from the artist: write for the market or write for yourself.

Yes, a few people wrote for themselves and found the market liked what they'd written. When E. B. White, Mark Van Doren, and friends whose opinions he valued all liked his journal, Lax imagined himself one of them. His days at the *New Yorker*, however, made him suspect that things would not be so easy for him, a feeling reinforced on January 25, when Lobrano told him they wouldn't be running a poem Lax called "The Groundhog Poem." Lobrano assured him that he liked it but the issue it might have run in was already full. They couldn't use two fables he'd written either, because James Thurber did fables, and Lobrano didn't like a piece Lax called "The Prologue," which Lax had thought was one of his best.

The same day Lobrano rejected these works, Lax met E. B. White for the first time. Katherine White and Thurber too. The Whites had come down from their place in Maine for the day. After the meeting, which was brief and perfunctory, Lax described White in his journal: "Short, serious, good eyes, ruddy skin, thick face, tweed-like coat of a guy who has left the city and gone to Maine, confused, preoccupied about some things, more certain than me about others. Both of us kept looking down to our respective right (direction), no hearty Well, well, well."

In the days ahead Lax continued to write his letters for the magazine, worry about the war, and fret at night because he wasn't writing stories or poems. He began to think about quitting his job too but didn't know what to do instead.

Everything in Lax's life in those days seemed to require bewildering choices, and he saw approval or disapproval everywhere. Arriving late at work elicits a giggle he thinks is really an accusation of some kind, and choosing a vegetarian lunch earns him the waitress's admiration. He tells himself he should get out more, then stay in more, that he should laugh more, that he should be more serious. When he walks alone through the city, he remembers places he went with Merton and longs to return to the days they spent together. All the while he feels the pressure at work increasing.

On February 18 Shuman tells him to go easier with his answers to letter writers: "They seem a little tight, a little as though we wanted to get rid of them. When somebody goes to the trouble of writing us a clever letter we should go to a little trouble too and answer them back cleverly." Lax gives a snide reply, but only in his head and his journal: "I know, I know, that's my trouble, can't relax. I didn't think that letter was clever and I didn't think they'd think mine was. Besides, when I relax you take out the casual words. You must love people to be able to answer them so well. Maybe I don't like them or I'm scared."

That same day Lobrano says, "What I think you ought to keep in mind is that if you are writing for the Comments page, then when Mr. Ross comes back from Miami—did you know he was there?—when he comes back and tries to appraise your worth to the magazine he'll be more likely to try and find something good for you, some job, even the job you have, to keep you going at a modest salary, with any Comments you do as an addition to that."

Lax's fear is clear in the journal lines that follow his recording of Lobrano's words: "I don't know if I can write comments, sometimes I think

I can. I wouldn't like to get fired. I made such a family celebration about getting the job, I guess I'd be embarrassed to lose it after a month or two." He goes on:

> Buffaloed is baby. Can't seem to write notes and comments. Tell myself it is because I don't want to write it any way. Just want to sing and dance and play all day. And when I say it like that it seems like a good idea. Somebody ought to be singing and dancing.
>
> But isn't it hard, uncs, to think of the dancing when yr stomach is thinking of tomorrow's lunch.
>
> Sometimes it is.

---

The need for an income was the only thing standing between Lax and the life he wanted—that and a deeply American idea implanted in him in childhood and amplified at Columbia: that public recognition of one's success is tantamount to being successful. In the coming days his thinking on both would undergo a sometimes painful but ultimately freeing change. He would come to see that the alternative to increasing income is decreasing need and that success is interpreted differently if one's primary audience is God. In this, as in so many other important matters, his model was Brahmachari. It is better to have faith that what you need will come to you than the assurance of money in the bank, he wrote in his journal just days after the entry above. The thought was still theoretical, though—he hadn't tested it himself—and he hadn't yet shaken a vision of himself as someone people admired.

It wasn't just his job or the more commercial aspects of the *New Yorker* Lax disliked but all that was part of working in downtown Manhattan. What he wants to say in his comments, he writes in one entry, is "move the buildings further apart so some light can get into them, give the poor people more money, give the musicians a chance to play without starving and without turning into glenn miller, and do the same for the playwrights and poets, do something about the glass walls and glass suspenders at jay walter thompson and the church doors of the offices, and the same fast way they all walk, and do something about the fluorescent light in restaurants that makes the coffee and the coffee cake leer wickedly with their unnatural color."

He ends the page on which these visions are written with another vision, that of the Holy City, which he contrasts to the "doomed" city he sees around him. The Holy City, he writes, "is the end of a good civilization. In it city dwellers, farmers and even animals and plants are at their fullest and happiest: it is the city whose walls are Salvation and whose gates Praise. From it in a constantly varied rhythm and form, praise would vibrate and to it Love would flow."

The disconnect between his vision for the world and the reality of the world he lived in, between his desire for a peaceful place where he could write freely and his fear of failure at a magazine he had long dreamed of writing for, eventually became too much for him. He needed to make a choice he couldn't make, and so his mind and body, in their way, made it for him.

---

Lax wasn't the only one changing that year, a year that would end with America's entry into the war. The *New Yorker* itself was changing. It had always been viewed as a humor magazine, even by its editor in chief, Harold Ross, but the news from overseas was having a sobering effect. In *About Town: The* New Yorker *and the World It Made*, Ben Yagoda writes, "In any number of ways the Second World War was a turning point for the *New Yorker*. The war thrust it, not necessarily willingly, onto a wider stage, forever removed from it the label of 'humor magazine,' robbed it (as even the Depression had not) of the comfortable luxury of noncommittal politics."

As early as Germany's invasion of Austria in 1938, *New Yorker* writers and editors such as James Thurber, William Shawn, and Frank Sullivan had supported American intervention. Ross remained staunchly opposed "to beating any drums," as Yagoda puts it, but grim reports from Europe by A. J. Liebling and others were already darkening the magazine's pages when Lax worked there. No doubt they contributed to his sadness, as did the inescapable thought that American involvement would mean not only a draft but actual deployment, guns in hand.

---

A long entry from March 18, 1941, gives a fuller view of all the different factors in Lax's life at this time, the different ways he felt pulled internally. In the morning, after walking and going out for breakfast, he couldn't focus on writing letters or reading newsbreaks at work. Instead he wrote out the first line of a poem on a piece of yellow paper—"City of the Lord is long in building"—then walked around the office "in conspicuous meditation of the project." He seems to have done this until joining friends for lunch at a French restaurant, where he overheard people talking about how nice it is to not have a job. That afternoon he tried to write a comment for "Talk of the Town," rewriting it four or five times and still finding it "repetitious, ungrammatical, pointless." At four he went downstairs to eat a sandwich and found himself thinking about all the things that worried him. Back in the office he tried to write a story about a character like himself but found that it wandered, so he took the subway home and, closing his eyes, felt he was in a crowded zoo. "What would make the difference?" he asked himself. "Some kind of glance." When he reached home he found a letter telling him his Grandma Lax had died.

At this point Lax hadn't written anything for a month. He tried to think of his lack of writing as a kind of fast but couldn't quite. "After a number of years of asking What is life?," he wrote, "the answer come back, It is what it is." He went on to describe watching people on the sidewalk as he rode the bus to work, thinking that all they were doing was trying to keep themselves and maybe their families alive and have some fun on the side. They went about it all wrong, though, because they let themselves charge each other too much for things and spent too much time doing "unsatisfactory things" for fun. Satisfactory things were those that made all creation happier, done "for the greater glory of the Lord."

What followed was another of the visions that would eventually guide his own life (the italics are mine):

If for His sake they would build a holy city, which means a good city, not a superstitious one, then the prophets say and it is easy to believe that the Lord would delight in the world as a bridegroom over a bride. To say that all the bad in the world comes from intended malice of people may be true, but a lot of it seems to come from their not knowing what to do and the people who think they know either not bothering or daring to tell them. To think of a good life as a successful struggle against evil is dramatic and may have some truth in it too. *But maybe a good life can be lived quietly, maybe a guy with a good idea doesn't have to be particularly brave about presenting it. He can develop it and show it quietly to those whom he knows will like it, not in a rush—cast pearls before swine—[but] maybe work on it quietly all his life and live it for a heritage. If it's a practical good idea it may take its time about coming around to be understood and used, but right answers to problems are hard to overlook forever; it's likely to be noticed after a while and used.*

In this section he lays out what his life became, or at least how he came to see it in his later years. The section that follows describes his later life too, but from a different direction: "The essence of religion . . . is to love the Lord with all your heart and all your soul and with all your mind or might, and to love your neighbor as yourself. In both the new and old testaments, these two things are closely related and all other rules of ethics and mystical dogmas seem to be subsidiary to them."

During this time Lax had repeated visions of writing a "big important book." The visions were so constant they interfered with his work, and he went back and forth between thinking he should ignore them and thinking they were "admonitions" he should pay attention to. One night he wrote:

If I have an inner argument about whether to do something or not I usually threaten myself with something awful if I do it, then do it, then worry for days or months, no matter how peaceful the outcome of doing it was, that I shouldn't have done it; saying that the mere fact that there was an inner argument and I know I feel hopelessly uneasy if I defy an inner admonition is enough reason not to do it. The only reason, on the other hand, I defy them is (a) I want to do the thing I have advised myself against (b) I don't want the inner admonitions which can lead to actions which seem silly unnecessarily inhibiting, restricting, and superstitious, to become tyrannical. As tips the inner admonitions are fine, as rules with horrible threats attached they're closer to torture.

The torture he felt both inside and out—the seemingly irresolvable yet persistent questions about how he should live in the face of physical need, artistic desire, and commitment to love over violence—would soon have frightening consequences.

———————

One bright light in the dark night of Lax's time at the *New Yorker* was William Maxwell, who would eventually become a legendary editor but was only four years into his tenure at the magazine then. Maxwell is famous for his friendships with writers, especially those he edited. His friendship with Lax was something else. They shared a physical frailty and abhorrence of war, but it was more than that. Maxwell, who was seven years older than Lax, seems to have seen that Lax needed protecting in some way. Years later, in a letter to Leonard Robinson, who had worked with Maxwell at the *New Yorker*, Lax wrote about being at a party with him in Yorktown, where Maxwell had a house: "I'd have felt like a fish out of water except for Maxwell. We talked & he's been a gentle guardian angel in my life ever since." Maxwell seems to be the only person at the *New Yorker* Lax trusted enough to speak freely.

While Lax was struggling to find his way forward, Merton was teaching a summer class at St. Bonaventure College, where the crosses and icons had once frightened him. On campus one day he happened upon a lecture that would send both his and Lax's thoughts in new directions. The speaker was a Russian baroness named Catherine de Hueck who had founded a Catholic charity in Harlem called Friendship House. When Merton arrived, she was telling an assortment of religious figures and privileged college students that communism would make little headway in America if Catholics did their job. "For, she said, if Catholics were able to see Harlem, as they ought to see it, with the eyes of faith, they would not be able to stay away from such a place," Merton recalled later. "Hundreds of priests and lay-people would give up everything to go there and try to do something to relieve the tremendous misery, the poverty, sickness, degradation, and dereliction of a race that was being crushed and perverted, morally and physically, under the burden of a colossal economic injustice."

Impressed by her words and dedication, Merton asked if he could join her in Harlem. "Of course," she said, and two weeks later he did.

By that time, mid-August, Merton had had several phone calls, at least two meetings, and one physical with the local draft board. Originally awarded the desired 4E classification, meaning his petition for conscientious objector status had been temporarily accepted, he had been reclassified 1B. The only thing keeping him from being 1A was a mouthful of bad teeth. Meanwhile Gibney, who had filed for conscientious objector status alongside Lax, had been not only drafted but inducted. He was doing basic training at Ft. Bragg, where, he wrote to Merton, there were three suicides in three weeks.

Like Gibney, Lax never received conscientious objector status, but he was never drafted. The reasons and the timing are unclear, but at some point he was classified 4F—unfit for service. In the summer of 1942 he wrote that he'd been declared a "luny," which suggests a mental or behavioral component, but many people, including Merton and Lax himself, used this word for anyone labeled 4F. It's quite possible that Lax's extreme gauntness or the sacroiliac problems he sometimes complained of in his journals were the cause, but it's equally possible that his deepening depression over the war, his lack of writing at work, and his desire for a freer life played a part.

Merton stayed at Friendship House just two weeks, but that was long enough for Lax to join him there. They did little more than sort and maybe hand out clothes, but just being in Harlem and interacting with those who lacked not only resources but many basic human rights, including safety and hope, affected both of them deeply, as did the dedication of the others working there.

Merton was already planning to join a monastery, but his exposure to Harlem's poor made him wonder if he could serve God better doing charity work. When he returned to St. Bonaventure to teach that fall, three things dominated his thinking: joining a monastery, serving the poor, and pursuing peace in a time of war. If he had returned to Friendship House, I have little doubt that Lax would have joined him. But he didn't return. A few months later he entered the Trappist order. Except for six brief visits in later years, those hot summer days in Harlem were the last extended time Lax and Merton would ever spend together.

———————

Long before the summer began, Lax had written that everything he did at work had a sadness to it. As that sadness deepened, he retreated more and more into himself. At some point that summer he was moved from an open room on the nineteenth floor into an office of his own on the fourteenth, perhaps because he convinced someone that solitude would be better for his writing. The room was small and Lax spent much of his time looking out one window at the nearby roofs or out another "at a bank of offices where people at their phones were ordering piping & sheet-rock from someplace in Indianapolis." Although he seems to have typed constantly, he never finished anything.

"All the world is wasting my time," he wrote that fall. "I know there are only a couple of things worth doing. Things like feeding the poor. Everybody has always known that, everybody: Moses, Isaiah, Jesus, St. Francis, Dante, Saroyan. Here I sit in an office doing nothing."

Lax's world grew darker and more isolated still when S. J. Perelman returned to New York that fall from Hollywood, where, among other things, he had written screenplays for Lax's beloved Marx Brothers. When he was in New York, Perelman usually wrote in a rented room on Sixth Avenue, but that fall, still recovering from the death of his brother-in-law, Nathaniel West, and the Broadway flop of a musical he'd written with his wife, Laura, he wanted to try writing at the magazine's headquarters. To make room for him, the editors asked if Lax wouldn't mind moving to a larger but windowless room next door. Lax obliged.

The first thing Perelman did when he moved into Lax's old space was pull down the shade on the window that looked out on the bank of offices. Then he closed the door and got down to work. Or so Lax assumed, and the assumption increased his anxiety. In his new office next door, he rolled a sheet of paper into his typewriter, typed a line or two at the top, then pulled it out and started again. Over and over. When he wasn't doing this, he sat with his head in his hands in what he started calling his "cell." Anxiety and isolation were destroying him.

What happened next depends on who you believe retained the best memory of events. Thirty years later, as she was about to go to bed, one of Lax's cousins caught the end of a radio show celebrating the New Yorker's fiftieth anniversary in which Perelman was talking about his days at the magazine. She was about to fall asleep when she realized the story he was telling was about Lax.

According to Perelman, he sat for weeks fretting over not being able to write while someone in the next office typed constantly. Then one day a thin young man knocked at his door. Would he be willing to comment on something the young man had written, he was asked. Perelman expected a huge pile of papers, but the young man handed him only a single sheet with a few poetic lines on it. Perelman wasn't sure he understood the poem, or whatever it was, and offered only an evasive reply. After that the typing next door stopped. When Perelman asked Lobrano who the young man was, Lobrano said he was someone they'd been trying out who had written poetry for them but the arrangement wasn't working. Four months later Perelman read in a newspaper that an "unemployed salesman" with the young man's name had committed suicide. That seemed the end of the story until four years after that, when Perelman was on an ocean liner headed to Europe and saw the young man again. He wasn't dead at all, it seemed, just on his way to Greece to write poetry.

Perelman definitely has the timing of that shipboard meeting wrong since Lax didn't visit Greece for the first time until the 1960s, but there's no reason to disbelieve the rest of his story. The version Lax told in his reply to his cousin's letter was slightly more upbeat, as might be expected from a man looking back at one of the darkest times of his life, but it agreed with Perelman's on many points. He and Perelman talked more than once, he wrote, when Perelman came over to sit in his office and Lax asked about his days in Hollywood. He didn't remember showing Perelman a poem, but he did remember meeting on the crossing to Europe. Perelman invited him for cocktails and they talked about their New York days. When they parted, Lax said, Perelman gave him "a captain spaulding valediction: 'this has been a most fortunate encounter.'"

The papers in Lax's archives from this period reveal a scattered and perhaps disintegrating mind. Many pages have only a single line at the top: a random thought, a story opening, a line of poetry. Some are scribbled in thick pencil at an angle across the page. Lax is clearly scared to write anything the editors might reject, which means anything at all, and just as clearly he longs to be somewhere else, doing something more purposeful for the world. When he sees people walking down the street in the sun, he wants to be out there with them, outside what he calls "this dead building." His alternating views of New York and his ongoing Bible reading are reflected in his references to "Babylon" at some points and a "holy city" at others. The story beginnings are almost always focused on one solitary reflective person.

Two years later, when he looked back on his *New Yorker* job, he described it this way: "Sitting in a dark, no window office on the fourteenth floor, away from almost everyone. My hands folded across the top of the typewriter, my head on my hands. Duration: One Year. It ended 7 days before Pearl Harbor."

Seven days before Pearl Harbor would have been November 30, his twenty-sixth birthday. Lax told people later that he had quit, but his journals suggest that he was fired. In either case, it's clear from his writings that he was going to be fired. In an undated entry from the time, he describes dodging his landlords who are asking for his rent and going to his uncle's office to ask for $30 to pay it. His uncle shows him a list of other relatives he sends money to. Lax goes to the *New Yorker* offices next and sees Lobrano, who says to him, "What I think is maybe for your own good . . . leave."

A week after Lax's departure from the *New Yorker*—his failure, as he viewed it then—America entered the war he dreaded. Three days after that, Merton entered the Trappist monastery of Gethsemani. Lax spent his post–*New Yorker* days wandering in a melancholy daze. With his dreams of worldly success shattered, his best friend irretrievably gone, he felt, for the first time, utterly lost and alone.

# 7    The Scream

In September 2007, days before I returned to teaching after my first sabbatical, I spent a week in Lax's archives at Columbia University. By then I had attended Columbia myself, earning an MFA in creative writing, and I was a tenured professor of nonfiction writing at Portland State University. I'd been researching my book on Lax for six years and was hoping this would be the last of too many weeks inside the clean, cloistered confines of Columbia's Special Collections room. It was Friday afternoon, less than an hour before the Collections would close and I would head home, when I happened upon a jumble of journal entries that made the confusing pieces of Lax's story finally come together. My heart quickened as I scanned the pages, trying to read as many as possible before I had to leave. Here was my Rosetta stone, the key to understanding the hieroglyphic decisions Lax had made. It wasn't what was written on them so much as how it was written that showed me how deeply that awful year of 1941 affected the rest of his life.

Of all the journal entries Lax made over sixty years, the hardest to read is the one he set down on Thursday, December 11, 1941, one day after Merton entered the monastery. Riddled with incomplete sentences and abbreviations in place of words, it lists his activities—"Day went to Harlem. Clothes" and "Afternoon stood. Qondering [sic] where sleep where still could write"—as well as heavier thoughts—"last Sunday, war" and "Merton to trappists."

The entry ends this way:

One tthinks [sic] of the world heal
Shangr
O
xxxx
O

Lax had experimented with vertical poetry before, but we may be looking at the visceral source of his later attachment to the form. His thoughts on that day were so primal, so simply profound, they didn't require sentences or, at times, even words. Turned loose by the *New Yorker*, he had no home and no way to pay for an apartment, so he stayed with his friend Bob Mack and went to Harlem to hand out clothes to the desperately poor, the one activity besides writing that seemed to have meaning, however small, in a world shaken to its foundations—a world he gazed at without ideas or resources, a one-word plea on his lips: *heal.*

Here, in stark black type, is the death of his dreams for happiness and peace. Before the beautiful "Shangri-la" is complete, the line and the word itself disintegrate. The ground falls away, dropping the consciousness down the abyss, where the only possible sound is the sound that comes from the mouth in Munch's *The Scream.* Here, in his inarticulateness, Lax expresses the fear in the face of war of all who love peace.

———————

Merton's description of Lax as seeming to meditate on some incomprehensible woe was never truer than in those days when his hopes, his loves, and his beliefs had all been taken away. The entries I found in the archives that day are mostly undated, so it's unclear which came before and which after he left the *New Yorker*, but together they make it painfully clear he felt out of step with the world.

"This is how it feels to be a poet-suicide," he wrote. He was afraid he had killed the poet inside himself, the person he was meant to be, by seeking status and maybe fame in an alien land, and he didn't know what to do about it. "You have acted ungratefully to your Maker," he chastised himself. "Will you ask his pardon by secretness, carefully selected charity, neglect of everyday pursuit, flight to the mountains or the seeking out of counselors? Will you keep the wound secret until it is healed? . . . Will you destroy yourself quietly lest you come in full consciousness to shame?"

What Lax didn't realize, not yet, was that the self he had killed was only his public self. The self that longed for identity in the world. The feeling of being lost and alone went to the center of his being, but he was only twenty-six and deep in his heart he still believed two things: that there is a God whose essence is love and that it is possible to live a life of simple truth. In another entry filled with ellipses, these four lines reveal a bedrock resolve:

I am sick of all arguments
I want to do something simple and ok
Nobody can tell me this is not possible
Lots of people do it all the time.

He would spend the years ahead looking for that simple something, moving from place to place without a permanent residence or job. He would search and ponder life and love, faith and peace, until the wandering and wondering became his life.

---

Love and fear are normally at odds, but sometimes they come together to change a person. The change Lax went through in early 1942 was the most difficult and important of his life, and love and fear both played parts. Someone for whom worldly success means everything might say the change ruined him, and Lax too might have thought so at first. He had been programmed for success, even if his chosen field was poetry, so perhaps the despair he felt was inevitable. So much of what he had learned he had to unlearn before he could follow a truer path.

Troubled as his mind might have been, however, he saw his despair less as a permanent condition than a sickness for which he needed a cure. "Singing a good song will not mean that you are cured and won't cure you," he wrote in one of those undated entries. "Penitence, prayer and charity will." Penitence meant turning away from the desires that had caused the despair. Prayer meant communion with God but also living a disciplined life, including eating both kosher and vegetarian. Charity meant mostly one thing: working with the poor.

And so he moved into a tenement room at 207 W. 144th Street and spent his mornings writing as usual, his afternoons among the five storefronts of Friendship House on 135th, staffing the library or visiting shut-ins or handing out clothes to those in need. His room had two windows and hot running water, a rarity in the neighborhood, and the landlady served him fruit and hot cereal for breakfast, but he ate his other meals among his fellow workers, meals made from whatever food had been donated. If meat was included, he skipped the meal and ate at the Jewish Theological Seminary near Columbia, if he ate at all. (He spent his Saturdays—the Sabbath—at the Seminary too.) His diet often left him tired or ill, but those internal "admonitions" were torturing him still.

Beyond his desire to serve the poor as expiation for how he had let himself live, Lax might have moved to Harlem because it was the last place he'd been with Merton. During past separations they'd always called or written to each other, but he hadn't heard from Merton since his departure. He didn't know yet that Gethsemani's Trappists were allowed to send and receive mail only four times a year—at Easter, Assumption Day, All Saints Day, and Christmas.

In the evening Lax wrote letters for those in the neighborhood who couldn't write and went for walks despite the violence he saw on the streets. He had an almost visceral need to be in physical contact with those who were poor—to be, as he wrote in his journal, "a hand to administer charity, not a heart that gave." His need was spiritual but also practical and emotional. Being among the poor served God's call to make the world a holy place, but it also kept him from worrying about appearances or seeking success as others defined it.

Years later, when he had become a Catholic and was living near the sanctuary of Notre Dame de la Salette in the French Alps, he wrote a long contemplation of poverty, starting with the first of Jesus's Beatitudes: Blessed are the poor. "He is one of the Persons of the Blessed Trinity and at the same time a child born into poverty," he writes. "The Kingdom is meant for those who resemble Him."

The paper seems to be a first draft of something meant for publication, but I've found no evidence that the ideas were ever published, at least not in essay form. As in many of his poems, the parentheses in the following excerpts reveal alternative word choices he contemplated:

> He promises us (joy) happiness. More exactly, he reveals to us the conditions of happiness. More precisely still, he describes it to us, he tells us what it is, concretely: in what dispositions of spirit it consists, what

kind of life assures it, what sort of person has a chance to possess it . . . *the poor.*

. . . *Blessed are the poor, for theirs is the kingdom of heaven:* only poverty brings us close to that openness, that limpidity of the divine Persons. Our familiarity with them, and our happiness will be the measure of our (transparency), our dispossession.

. . . One must have entered deeply into the first beatitude to be capable of Beatitude itself.

. . . Blessedness/happiness and poverty are thus from the beginning, from the first word, indissolubly allied.

. . . Thus poverty inaugurates His message. It occupies a primordial place there. This is not to say, however, that it is the highest value or the most essential. The essential is love.

During those difficult days in Harlem, he began to see that poverty—of many kinds—was the necessary ground on which to build the life he envisioned.

Forbidding as some Harlem streets might be, Lax loved his nighttime strolls among the kind of people he wanted to spend his life around. After one walk he wrote, "One walks up the hill, one walks across 8th Avenue, down this street where the people are, they stand in the doorways, they dance outside the stationery stores, talk back and forth in front of the fluorescent light of the white-walled store, they stand in the doorway, they talk to one another as they pass on the street. Everywhere they tell one another the kind of individual each is."

Given his clumsiness and the toll the past year had taken on him, Lax's main contribution during the five months he spent at Friendship House may have been his peaceful, loving presence. In her autobiography, Baroness de Hueck describes him as a dreamer who didn't know which end of the mop to use, but she was fond of him and they stayed in touch for many years. Lax describes his main work as sitting on a bench in the back of the library with "one hand at one corner, one foot at the other corner, my head lolled slightly to one side, the troubles of a tumbling world resting foggily on my shoulders."

It may have been during his time in Harlem that he received his 4F classification. No doubt the draft board's decision pleased him, but he knew from Merton's experience that he could be reclassified at any time.

One of his last entries from Harlem has only these words: "tomorrow goes gerdy to war."

The fragmented references to heartache and gloom in the early pages of Lax's Harlem journal gradually give way to mentions of swimming or going to a show. When he can maintain a longer meditation, he contemplates the question of what it means to exist, not from a philosopher's perspective but a musician's. A philosopher talks about existence as if he himself didn't exist, Lax says, while a musician "grants that you and all about you exist." The meaning of this existence lies in what you produce—flowers if you're a farm, blues if you're a band, happiness or maybe woe if you're a soul. Ultimately, he concludes, "the answer is always: to exist is to exist. What are you going to do? He who asks with the most love (true) gets the best answer. He who courts the land, gets (if there be no tornado) the best vegetables, who courts the violin or typewriter gets the best music or writing, who courts the All and in courting the All courts whatever part he is in it, gets the good thing about life (which this time I will not call this life, just life)."

*Just life*—a simple loving of existence and one's own part in it.

Instead of recording his daily activities, Lax begins to let his writing float free, becoming a kind of pure poetry without being broken into poetic lines. The poetry comes from observation and feeling, contemplation and the freedom of an untethered mind. On April 20, for example, he begins by describing "the light of the sun, coming through the blue sky" and a feeling he had as a boy on this kind of day. Soon he is contemplating second chances, and then, as his contemplation becomes too easy, too airy, he cautions himself: "Careful, he said, lest you come to a perfect fugal end before the piece in its harmony is really started."

He doesn't know what is coming in his life, but he knows he needs to move at a measured pace so the healing can happen, the new life begin. He is not yet a Catholic, but he has read St. John of the Cross and he recognizes the dark night of the soul. "If those in whom this occurs know how to remain quiet, without care or solicitude about any interior or exterior work," St. John wrote, "they will soon in that unconcern and idleness delicately experience the interior nourishment."

Two days later, contemplating the war that has caused him so much agony, Lax notes that, except where the war has done damage, the world is the same, with spring coming on and young people dancing: "There is no more or less hope for the people in the war, only the assurance that at a certain time the wind blows and chaff is blown from the wheat. And no man will stop the wind from blowing."

What follows is a remarkably astute, unpublished poem:

Who is wise in the ways of war?
Only the Chinese philosopher under his tree
Only the Hindu mystic outside his wattle hut
Only the rabbi walking with his beard
Only the monk in his chapel
And are they wise about the war?

Who is wise about the war?
Only the child playing with his ball
Only the mystic working in his field
Only the charity lady carrying her basket
And are these wise about the war?

Who is wise about the war?
Only the wife waking in the morning
Only the mother waking with her child
Only the man who hurries to work
reading his newspaper on the train
And are these wise about the war?

Who hath wisdom in the world?
Only the innocent going to school
Only the aged sitting in the chair
Only the flowers and the silent animals
And have these wisdom of the world?

They who know the routines of their day
Who wake and go through them no matter
what winds blow
The workers in hospitals
The peaceful workers who stay away from the debris
or walk over it
Who do not close their eyes but in shame
for the wreckage

Who walk calmly about the city doing the business
they hope is good
These, are they wise?

He goes on to describe his vision of a community coming together, with one brooding dreamer observing it and telling the world what a wonder a true community is—an apt description of what he would find on the island of Kalymnos two decades later and the role he himself would play.

He ends his April 22 entry by admonishing the "sad writers of the world" to be "busy about the business of relieving the suffering of the poor and making plants grow, children happy, poets to sing," before, in an almost ecstatic, run-on style reminiscent of Joyce, he expresses the spirit and vision that motivate him: the welling of love that makes him want to dance as David danced before the Lord, a dance that starts in private, in purity, and soon becomes a dance of public inspiration, a pied-piper dance of love that will become the center and symbol of his future writing.

I don't mean to leave the impression that he had worked everything out or even that he knew exactly what he was expressing in a passage like this. It is full of misspelled words and was probably set down in the white heat of inspiration, maybe even mania. He was recovering, beginning to see more clearly, but he wasn't fully healed. A truer way of living was coming to him in visions, but he would need years to understand it fully and longer than that to actually live it.

---

Friendship House, with its particular mission and people, was probably the best place Lax could have gone in the state he was in. The staff and clients loved and accepted him right from the start, and he felt great affection and admiration for them. By Easter, when he received his first letter from Merton, he was recruiting workers for the baroness at the Jewish seminary, where he was studying Hebrew. In a letter to Merton sent on May 15, Van Doren wrote that his former student was happier at Friendship House than he had ever seen him. Lax may have put on his best face for his old teacher, but Harlem certainly helped him see that he *could* be happy again.

"Whatever work it is all feels the same because it is all prayer," he wrote around that time. "Being with people who understand this as well as [the Friendship House workers do] makes me see how far we were from it any of the time we thought we were close."

---

In mid-June 1942, encouraged by a doctor concerned about his poor diet and fragile health, Lax moved back to Olean to live in Benji and Gladio's house, where his father was already staying. He had lost a frightening amount of weight and his head hurt much of the time, but swimming and sailing with family and friends helped him ignore the voice inside him demanding continual penance for how he had spent his year at the *New Yorker*. Much of the summer he sat in the yard or a room in the attic contemplating his situation while trying to live not in the past or the future but the present. "here i am folks, amateur writer," he wrote one day, "watching a bee land on a clover and wondering if there is anything i do as neat."

By August he was feeling far away from the world, but he was writing and drawing pictures every day and thinking again of sending poems to the *New Yorker*, which had just published one by Merton. The war was still on his mind, but the draft was no longer a concern. "Gibney has just been discharged from Fort Bragg," he wrote in his journal that month, "and my draft board assures me that I won't be called until after the last old lady has showed her metals [sic]. We are both manic depressives and could, if business warrants, synchronize our phases."

Although his journal entries and letters to Merton over the years hint occasionally at depression—the *torpor* he had mentioned before—I've found no other reference to its opposite, mania. Was Lax being flippant? Or had he been diagnosed with this condition? Although it is more common in artists than in the general population and Lax's references to "bilious attacks" and "trumpet attacks" that sent him into raptures could be evidence of manic phases, it seems more plausible that whatever symptoms he displayed were limited to that difficult, chaotic fall and winter at the *New Yorker* and Friendship House.

---

By early fall Lax had returned to the life he'd been living before his move to New York, staying occasionally at the cottage and working at the radio station. By January 1943 he seemed to be his old self again. He spent most of his time reading and writing, walking and thinking, trying to focus on the moments he was living. "The people who say more or less to keep your eye on the present," he wrote, "are Jesus, St. Paul, Walt Whitman, Rabelais, Sha[kespeare], Dante, Blake—it must be a good idea."

When he did reflect on his *New Yorker* year, he was more charitable toward it than he'd been before. What he disliked most, he thought, was having wasted his time doing something he never should have been doing. But only by going through that experience could he understand it wasn't the life he wanted. The death of one way of living was necessary for the birth—or rebirth—of another.

Education, some people say, requires ridding oneself of false notions as much as seeking knowledge or truth. Over two tumultuous years Lax had rid himself of one false notion after another, including the idea, encouraged at Columbia, that living a good life meant chasing a socially determined idea of success. Having questioned everything he knew or believed, he had come to rely on his own present perspective as the measure of all things—a perspective shaped by a growing faith in a loving God and the writings of authors whose words rang true.

"He would look for example at a river," he wrote, "and he would have to remove, like stereopticon slides, a hundred pictures of the river which he had held before. Then he would come to the picture of the river as it really was. . . . The river might be much sadder, the whole image less vivid, less full of hope . . . but it would be the real river, as it was now, seen by the real person, as he was now."

The agony he'd gone through in his attachment to mainstream society and the balm he'd found in Harlem had shown him that there was more to the world and people than he had imagined. If people would only love each other here and now, they'd find more "sweetness and depth and wonder and drama" than they thought possible, even in themselves. The key, as Socrates had discerned, was to know and develop yourself first—to listen and pray and encourage whatever seemed unique and loving in you. It wasn't a particular habit or virtue, Lax decided, that made you you. It was something more like a color that seemed to be yours—something simple, indelible, given, and true.

# 8    Aquinas and the Circus Beckon

The night I met Lax he spoke of his "circus poem," telling me that Ernesto Cardenal had translated it into Spanish. The next night he told me he'd once arranged a circus performance for Pope Pius XII. I don't remember him saying he had traveled with a circus himself, but he must have mentioned it because most of his circus stories came from firsthand experience. In one, for example, he told a roustabout he was concerned for the safety of a cage boy named Billy who had been asked to fill in for a sick lion tamer. "You've seen Billy around here," the roustabout replied. "He's a pretty nice guy and people like him, right? Don't you think those lions have eyes?"

Before I left him that second night, he handed me what I would learn later was an original copy of his "circus poem." It was a series of poems, actually, bound in a tall, narrow book. *The Circus of the Sun / Robert Lax*, the title page read. In small, humble type, the first poem said:

Sometimes we go on a search
and do not know what we are looking for,
until we come again to our beginning

The beginning for Lax—of those poems, that book, even the truer life he found in Greece decades later—was a meeting that happened in mid-May 1943, when, feeling physically and emotionally stronger, he returned to Manhattan. The meeting took him back to an even earlier beginning: those childhood mornings when his father woke him before dawn to watch the circus come to town. "I knew right away," he told me fifty years later, "that a *big* thing had happened. I've never gotten over it."

Lax was in Manhattan to look for work and visit friends, and that May day he happened to run into Leonard Robinson, a Columbia friend he'd helped get a job on the *New Yorker*. Robinson was on his way to interview a circus family, the Cristianis, for the magazine's "Talk of the Town," the commentary section that had caused Lax such grief, and he invited Lax along. At that point the Cristianis were the most famous bareback riders in the world. They had performed in New York many times, usually with Ringling Brothers, but this time they were in town to appear in a Broadway show. Based roughly on their own adventures, the play would follow an Italian circus family fleeing the Nazi invasion. Vivienne Segal was set to star, with the family's most popular rider, Chita, taking over during the riding scenes. An actor had been hired to play the male lead as well, but he turned out to be allergic to horses, so Chita's brother Lucio was slated to take over. The rest of the family would play themselves.

The Cristianis had rented an apartment on W. 72nd Street near Riverside Drive, and when Robinson knocked on the door, a tiny woman curtseyed and let them in. Lax never got her name but she was probably Madame Sondrini, a dwarf and friend of the family who, like other circus friends in town, felt free to drop by anytime. A reporter who visited around the same time remembers the apartment being like a circus itself, with another dwarf, Count Bagonghi, making a business call; the black cook the Cristianis called Miss Five by Five in the kitchen; and many of Papa and Mama Cristiani's eleven children present:

> Around the table swirl the brothers and sisters already married who have stopped by to say hello. Someone mentions Mussolini and Papa Cristiani says sternly: "No politics, remember the digestion." And afterwards he brings out Fifi, the little Eskimo Spitz, to walk on her back legs or turn flip-flops in the parlor. Uncle Pietro, who now looks exactly like Victor Emmanuel of Italy, just sits and dreams and the family adores him. . . . Ordinarily Uncle Pietro is quite happy with a glass of wine and a cigarette burned to the fingers. But if he is teased long enough he will get mad and turn two somersaults in rapid succession to prove that at sixty-eight one can still be an acrobat.

Being an acrobat was the most important thing in the world if you were a Cristiani, more important even than the family's noble lineage, which, according to family lore, stretched back to biblical times. The family's first acrobat was Papa Ernesto's grandfather, Emilio, a powerful man who, while working as blacksmith to Italy's first king, spent his free time lifting weights and doing handstands. Wise to the ways of royalty, he took the king's young son, Victor Emmanuel III, with him to circuses that came to town, and the two of them learned every trick they could from the traveling performers. When Emilio had a son of his own, Pilades, he asked him one year what he wanted for his birthday and Pilades replied, "A circus." So Emilio gave him a one-ring show with a trapeze, a horse, and a monkey. It was Pilades who first began touring as a performer, taking his family with him, including his son Ernesto, who, when he met a beautiful trapeze artist named Emma Victoria, ran away with her to start a circus of his own.

Right from the start the Cristiani circus was a family affair. Papa himself trained the family's seven boys—Oscar, Daviso, Lucio, Benito (forced by injury to retire early), Belmonte, Paul (Mogador), and Pete (Parieto)—and four girls: Chita, Cosetta, Ortans, and Corky (Corcaita). They did some clowning but mainly they were acrobats, and although they performed tricks like bouncing from a teeterboard onto a chair held by a totem pole of brothers, what they were known for—what they lived for, what they did better than anyone else—was perform on horses.

Footage of the Cristianis is rare, but on YouTube you can find a blurry eight-minute clip made by Pete Smith, a journalist, in 1936. Financed by MGM and shown at theaters between feature-length movies, the short documentary has a cheeky and often painfully corny voice-over but it gives a glimpse of how amazing the Cristianis were. In one section, eight performers jump one after another onto a single moving horse. In another, three brothers do backflips through hoops from one horse to another, in unison. The film gives some idea how skilled and charming the Cristiani brothers were, but unfortunately it doesn't show Chita who, according to many sources, was like a ballerina on horseback.

Robinson's *New Yorker* piece, which ran on June 5, 1943, under the title "Waiting for Lucio," captures little of the family's charm and dynamism, which had such a transformative effect on Lax. Focused primarily on a conversation with the family's designated spokesman, seventeen-year-old Mogador, the article has that wry and knowing tone Lax wrote so easily once but came to distrust during his days at the magazine. Much as he liked Robinson, Lax must have cringed when he read it, especially the final line about Mogador's sister Ortans, who was sixteen at the time. As the title suggests, the conversation took place while waiting for Lucio, the family's star and leader. After weaving in some of the Cristianis' history and way of life, Robinson ends with these two lines: "At that point, Lucio called up to say that he wouldn't be home for dinner after all. We took one final look at Ortans, who is quite a dish, and wandered off."

When the Cristianis read the article, this last sentence made them seethe. Lax knew their reaction because, by then, he'd started visiting them at their practice facilities near Central Park. His months of fretting about what to do with his life had crystallized into a specific purpose the moment he met Mogador. Something about the way this handsome young man looked or moved or spoke made Lax want to spend time with him—and write about him.

---

Years would pass before the writing actually happened and even more before any of it was published—as individual poems in magazines and then as Lax's first book, *The Circus of the Sun*. The last of it wouldn't appear until Pendo Verlag published *Mogador's Book* in 1992, almost fifty years after Lax met the man in the title. By then Mogador's performances were far behind him, but Lax still remembered vividly the moment they met.

From that first moment, he said, he loved everything about the whole family, especially that they could have "such warm, alive—fulfilled, if you like—personalities and seem so familiar at the same time." He found these traits to be most pronounced in Mogador, whose name alone he thought beautiful, in part because it was so simple: "He was named Mogador because he was born in Mogador in Morocco. And one of the horses was named Kansas for a similar reason."

*Mogador's Book* ends with a letter to Mogador that includes these lines:

I still haven't gotten to say the thing
I want to say about you and the whole
family. It is that, to a greater degree than
almost anyone I know, you are what you
are. You are an acrobat in a family of
acrobats. And you have arrived at that
generation in the family which is most to be

desired, the time of ripeness, the moment
of fullest awareness of function and respon-
sibility of producing beauty, songs of
praise.

Lax had found the simple approach to living—the purpose and the model—he'd been searching for. Six years would pass before he traveled with the Cristianis and started writing his book—years of trying his hand at different professions in different places—but wherever he went, whatever he did, the Cristianis remained his vision of how to live in the world as individuals and as a community.

---

Lax stayed in New York into summer, living with Gibney and Slate while looking for work. He applied to be copy boy for a printer, but when the printer saw that he'd worked for the *New Yorker* he sent him to a former literary agent who was looking for an editor for a small magazine called *Clay*. Lax was there only a week before Mack, who had taken a job teaching philosophy at the University of North Carolina, invited him down.

Although Lax always called Mack his cousin, he was really Benji Marcus's nephew and in most ways he and Lax were as different as could be. While Lax was thin and physically challenged, Mack, a former water polo player, was strong and robust. While Lax was timid and obsessively nonviolent, Mack was good with his fists and often ended nights at bars in fights. While Lax was sometimes shy in pubic, Mack was brimming with self-confidence, in part because he was attractive to women. Both men were highly intelligent, however, and despite their differences they felt a strong affinity for one another. If Mack wanted Lax to join him, he didn't have to ask twice.

The two years Lax spent at the University of North Carolina were unusually pleasant years during which his *New Yorker* wounds finally healed. As soon as he arrived, he asked the English Department about teaching jobs and, thanks in part to his *New Yorker* work, was given two sections of freshman composition. Soon he and Mack had moved into a rooming house near campus and his life had settled into a comfortable routine.

In many ways university life suited him. His light teaching duties left plenty of time for other activities, and he had daily access to other intelligent people. In addition to taking graduate classes in medieval drama, Augustine, and Aquinas, he submitted poems and parodies to the student magazine, *Carolina*, and became friends with the editors. The only activity that brought him grief was teaching—not the teaching itself but the aftermath.

More interested in art than grammar, Lax turned his composition classes into creative writing workshops, having students write poetry or radio scripts and record their dreams. To teach rhythm in writing, he played jazz records. At the end of the term he felt they'd done their best so he gave them all A's. His approach didn't please the administration.

"I guess I've been fired," he wrote to Van Doren when the school year ended, "but so gently that I've hardly felt it." The department chair told him he had hoped to offer him classes for the next year, but none were available. When Lax asked if he'd done anything wrong, the answer was no. "I hope that's true," he wrote, "because I've done a lot of things I wanted to, and whatever it's been for the English Dept., it's been a happy year for me."

Some of that happiness came from studying Aquinas's *Summa Theologica* in Latin with the philosopher Helmut Kuhn. Kuhn told Lax he thought he could get a philosophy fellowship to write a book on charity and social action, so Lax applied and was awarded a Kenan Fellowship, renewable on a yearly basis while he worked toward a PhD. It included a yearly stipend of $700. Without giving up his desire to write about the Cristianis, Lax made plans to write a dissertation not on charity but on "the Cardinal Virtues and St. Thomas answering Aristotle." The dissertation was never written, but his study of Aquinas's theology bore fruit in other ways, giving him a name—*pure act*—and a theological underpinning for his evolving philosophy toward life. It also helped him make a decision he'd been contemplating for years: to be baptized a Catholic.

---

By the fall of 1943 Lax had been moving toward the Catholic Church for at least six years, since he and Gerdy considered converting in 1937. You might say he'd been moving in that direction even longer, since his mother took him to St. Bonaventure College as a boy. It was Merton's commitment to Catholicism, however, that drew him fully into the Church's orbit. He had attended Merton's baptism and participated in countless discussions with Merton and others about the writings of Augustine, Aquinas, Francis, Paul, John of the Cross, Thomas à Kempis, Blake, Dante, Maritain, Hopkins, and, of course, Joyce, whose work is full of Catholicism. He had worked for six months at a Catholic charity in Harlem, and even while trying to live by the tenets of Orthodox Judaism had found himself moving closer to the Catholic faith. So that December, when Rice told him in a letter to come to New York and get baptized, he did.

"I guess you could say he was born a Catholic and he finally got baptized," Rice told an interviewer, contrasting the ease of Lax's experience to that of Merton, who, Rice said, "really had to struggle with it."

The baptism took place on December 19 at St. Ignatius of Loyola Church on Park Avenue, with Rice, who had been Merton's godfather, playing that role again. When the Jesuit who was to baptize him questioned whether he knew enough about the Catholic Church, Lax told him what he'd been reading and the priest was satisfied. Before the ceremony took place, however, Lax had a question of his own: Could he be baptized and remain a Jew too? The priest gave an indignant no. Lax went ahead with the baptism anyway, but in his heart he always honored both faiths.

It was after Lax's baptism that Gibney suggested in jest he blacken his face so he'd be all three things southerners hate most. His words must have seemed particularly provocative to Lax at that moment, when he was experiencing southern life for the first time. He never wrote about the bigotry he witnessed in Chapel Hill, but in his journal that November he wrote, "Man who first said I'm a nigger & proud of it must have been a Jew."

In trying to explain his conversion near the end of his life, Lax spoke of the long Catholic tradition, passed down from generation to generation, which he thought made the Church wise and knowledgeable. His sister Gladio thought he felt drawn to the Church's intellectual tradition, a common reason for conversions among intellectuals in the middle of the twentieth century. While Gladio thought his conversion might have bothered their mother if she'd been alive, her own response was this: "I think you can pray just as well on your knees as with your hat on."

One of the most moving items in all of Lax's papers is a handwritten letter his father sent on January 8, 1944. In imperfect English and misspelled words, Siggie tells his son he adds his best wishes to those of the priest who baptized him, praying for him to be a good, healthy, prosperous man. "I am glad that you have found peace on earth," he writes before asking one favor: "Don't try to convert any Jewish person no mater how sincere you are about your faith because I would not like have you breack any mothers and fathers hearth."

Lax's reply is equally touching:

Dear Dad,

Thank you for your letter, the best I've ever gotten. I read it to Bob Mack and he said: "You don't know how lucky you are." Really no one could have written a more welcome letter or have said more right things in it. I've had the feeling all my life that you'd be with me as long as I was doing the best I could, and now I know it.

I believe what you say about not disturbing Jewish people. I believe if they follow the religion that was taught them as well as possible, they'll lead good lives. It's only if, like me, they feel somewhere between the two religions that they are likely to feel they have to make up their minds. I don't think you convert people by preaching at them. I think if you live well yourself they may ask you what you believe, and then you can tell them.

For me, it wasn't that I thought the Jewish Religion was wrong; it's that I think it is right, but that joining the Church was the best way for me to be a good Jew. That's hard to explain, but it's really what I mean.

Thanks again, Dad, for that wonderful letter. It's the best thing you could have sent me.

Love, Bob

Pleased as Lax was with his baptism, his joy wouldn't be complete until he shared it with Merton, so as soon as the ceremony was over, he caught the train to Indianapolis and hitchhiked the rest of the way to Bardstown, Kentucky, the nearest town to Gethsemani. A Bardstown priest arranged for him to ride to the monastery with a man going there for midnight Mass. The man's girlfriend was in his car, and before he dropped her at her house the two of them gossiped about someone they said didn't fit in in Bardstown. When the girlfriend was gone, the man told Lax the person they disliked came from New York, as if that explained the problem. When Lax said he was from New York, the driver said it wasn't being a New Yorker that made the person an outcast but being a Jew. Despite his dislike of confrontation, Lax managed to say that many of his friends and all of his relatives were Jews.

"Oh," the man said, "well this one was Orthodox."

They rode the rest of the way in silence.

When Lax reached the monastery, he was led down a grim hallway past a sign that said *No Women* and across a courtyard into the "graceful-looking" church Mass. It was Christmas Eve and the church was full, with monks behind their four-foot hymnals filling the choir stalls and others standing along the sides. Lax thought he saw Merton everywhere until he saw the man himself in a procession approaching the altar. "Of all the monks," he wrote to Gladio, "he looked the most pious, but like he sounds in his poems, really religious, not deceived or acting."

In *The Seven Storey Mountain* Merton remembers the moment he saw Lax too. He was turning with the rest of the monks in the middle of the service, he writes, when he found himself "looking straight into the face of Bob Lax." His first thought was that Lax would get baptized now, and after dinner that night, while telling the abbot who Lax was, he expressed this thought to him:

> "Isn't he a Catholic?" said Reverend Father.
>
> "No, Reverend Father, not yet."
>
> "Well, in that case, why was he taking Communion last night at the midnight Mass?"

The next day Lax was called into the abbot's office, where the two sat chatting nervously for a while. "Then a bell rings," Lax told Gladio, "he pushes a button and Merton comes dancing into the room. He has a white habit, pile of books under his arm. We shout back and forth while the abbot treats him like his favorite kid."

Although they had only a short time together, it was enough for Lax to see that his old friend had never been "happier, healthier or better situated."

Upon entering the monastery, Merton had given most of his writings to Van Doren, who had mentioned his poetry to the founder of New Directions press, James Laughlin. Laughlin's interest had prompted Van Doren to send a selection along with Lax for Merton to choose from.

With Lax's help, Merton picked what he thought were his best poems. A year later Laughlin published *Thirty Poems*, Merton's first book.

---

Inspired by his baptism and his time with Merton, Lax began to write more openly about Christian ideas while trying to avoid what he now felt were vain pursuits. In a February 1944 journal entry, he listed the following under the title "Get thee behind me": *Hollywood, song writing, best sellers, funny book, popular play, cartoons, funny poems, serious poems, journal.* He contemplated writing a novel based on his experiences at Friendship House, where the tenets he thought central to the Gospel were being lived out, but he wasn't sure that even this was what he should be doing with his life.

"Probably an apostle of a religion of love ought to go around being full of love," he wrote. But he hadn't yet learned to see being full of love as a vocation. As the year wore on and he continued his teaching, then his studies, he grew increasingly restless. He began to regret that he'd stopped writing regularly in his journal, and, inspired perhaps by seeing two more of his poems published in the *New Yorker*, he returned to writing poetry. Still, he wanted to do more.

"I want to write a book of praise, but not use the religious words," he wrote on October 30.

> That is because they should not be used lightly, and all the words I will be using for a while must be used lightly, set down tentatively.
>
> The holy words hold terror for some, are not respected by others. I will try to talk in little words that people respect and do not fear. They respect them like hammers, they fear them no more than they fear doors or windows.

Decades later he would come to be known as a poet of little words, common words he used in such a way that they became hammers of understanding, the rhythm of their blows resounding.

Concerned for Lax's spiritual life, Merton encouraged him to get confirmed, attend communion every day, and find a spiritual director. He encouraged him to visit Gethsemani again that Christmas too, bringing "everybody." Lax took this to include Robert Lowell, who had converted to Catholicism and written a mostly positive review of *Thirty Poems*. Although he tried to interest Lowell and others, in the end he went alone.

Lax's indecision about the work he should be doing and the resulting restlessness increased as 1945 dawned. Mack had moved on to a new position at Connecticut College, leaving Lax with less enthusiasm for staying in Chapel Hill. Although he felt fairly certain now that he should concentrate on writing, every time he worked on something he wondered if he should be doing something else. Among the things he thought at one time or another were more important than whatever he was doing were writing proverbs; writing letters or the "book on charity" he had contemplated; writing his journal; writing plays, movies, *New Yorker* articles, or "cole porter songs"; traveling the country singing spirituals and preaching the Gospel; or just sleeping and eating.

In addition to attending Mass each day, he started taking long walks to a black neighborhood in the nearby town of Carrboro. He enjoyed the easier approach to life he found there, which no doubt reminded him of Harlem. Although he wasn't sure what direction to take with his life, the quotes from friends and philosophers he copied in his journal, most of them Catholics, show him growing more comfortable with the idea of spending his life in writing and quiet contemplation, the activities that made him happiest.

The end of classes that May gave him an excuse to drift north for a while. He spent the summer between Olean and New York City, where he took photographs and wrote short sketches of people and situations he came across. His random observations include a note that he has taken pictures of some cats (cats crop up again and again in his life and writings) and the following musings: "I got no idea if it is right to kill flies" and "I've been scared since I was born." On August 4 he wrote the following to his UNC friend Mike Beam: "The newspapers say consolingly that the atom machine will make ice-cubes faster than anything we now have, that it will make a plane which will take us to the tundras faster than anything but an atomic bomb. That the secret is in the hearts of four scientific men of reliability, uniformity, purity, and efficacy. But I can't stop crying."

Three nights later he wrote in his journal, "This is the day after the first bombing of Japan by an atomic bomb. . . . The best guarantee against its misuse by the unscrupulous is to get rid of the unscrupulous, not by bombing them out but by teaching them how to live. We can't teach them until we know and until we live that way."

Lax didn't return to Chapel Hill that fall. Ed Rice told him *Life* magazine was looking for someone to write captions for photographs, so he went to the Time-Life headquarters at 9 Rockefeller Plaza and spoke to a man named Jim Crider. No, they didn't need a caption writer, Crider told him, but they did need help with book and film reviews. He gave Lax a couple of books to review, and the resulting reviews were well received, but Lax didn't want to spend so much time reading, so they made him an understudy to the great film critic James Agee.

For four months Lax sat in a dark room watching four movies a day for four days a week. *Time's* approach in those days was to send a researcher and a senior editor to screenings with its reviewer. The researcher would write down lines the reviewer reacted to and the editor would add final touches to the reviewer's review. In Lax's case, that seems to have meant giving a stronger sense of whether or not he liked the film. By the time the fourth movie came around each day, his eyes were hurting so much he disliked it automatically. Eventually he went to an eye doctor, who told him to quit. At least that's what Lax told an interviewer years later. *Time* art critic Alex Eliot, a cousin of T. S. Eliot, who became friends with Lax during this time, said he was dismissed because the editor could never figure out if he liked a film or not.

Eliot's story seems more in keeping with Lax's hesitancy to render public judgment on anyone or anything, but in the one published review I've been able to ascertain with some certainty was his, tone alone gives a good idea of what he thought of the picture.

————————

According to Lax, no one at Time-Life ever left without being fired, so when he told the editors he wanted to quit, they tried to find him something else. Nothing interested him, however, and he moved on. This was in February 1946. By then his old friend Leonard Robinson had moved from the *New Yorker* to the Sunday insert magazine *Parade*. A pictorial magazine printed on newsprint stock, *Parade* was just five years old in 1946 but had a circulation of two million. Robinson had already hired

Lax's old Columbia roommate, Bob Gibney, and Lax ended up working with him in a department called "Truth Is Stranger Than Fiction."

"We were just making up the contributions," Lax said later, "week after week. Some man had an alarm clock that he kept in the pouch of a kangaroo. When it went off the kangaroo would come over and tap him on the shoulder to let him know that morning had come. That kind of thing."

Although Lax's stay at *Time* was brief, it was long enough to establish a lasting friendship with Alex Eliot. Although their lifestyles were different, they had a similar sense of humor and both took great delight in daily life. Their conversations about movies segued into talk about making a 16-millimeter film together. Lax, who had been thinking about light and dark since his days in North Carolina, suggested they make it in Harlem, where, according to Eliot, he knew a "crimelord" who controlled a street they could shoot on. When they arrived, the man hugged Lax with "tears of joy" and insisted on buying them "ice-cold, powder-dry martinis."

"*Black & White*, we called our film" writes Eliot, "& it was in black & white. Mostly shadows of black families, kid-gangs, ballplayers, ice-wagons, garbage cans, on the hot bright pavement."

Lax would return to the theme of black and white, light and shadow, many times. And he was about to take his love of moviemaking to another level.

# 9   The Siren Call of Hollywood

During the first few years I knew him, Lax would occasionally talk about his days in Hollywood—seeing Groucho Marx riding along in a long black limousine, introducing the Cristianis to Gene Kelly, or spending time with his Theosophist uncle, who was John Barrymore's business manager. But he wouldn't tell me the name of the one movie he helped write—it was too awful, he said—or say much about his personal experience. I learned later that Merton tried to warn him away from Hollywood, urging him to pray for a vocation to the priesthood instead, and in most ways Hollywood seems an odd place for someone like Lax. But he had always loved the movies, had even made occasional attempts at writing screenplays on his own, and his months of watching a depressing parade of studio dreck had left him thinking he could write better scripts. So when his friend Mike Beam said he'd been offered a writing job at one of studios and asked if Lax would like to go along, he jumped at the chance.

In his later years Lax joked that anytime anyone opened a car door, he got in, which was certainly true most of his life, but this time he had several good reasons to go, beyond just wanting to try his hand at screenwriting. He had tired again of New York City, and a month's vacation in Bermuda with Gibney and Nancy Flagg (who was dating Gibney now) had reignited his love for travel. He had never been to the West Coast—had never seen much of the country at all—and he and Beam would be leaving the day after Labor Day, cruising the pre-interstate highways at the best time of year in a Plymouth convertible. An old Columbia friend, Pat Laughlin, whom Lax hadn't seen since before the war, was already in Hollywood. And then there was his Uncle Henry, the family's star, whose Hollywood tales and gift of an autographed picture of Charlie Chaplin when Lax was five had kindled an early desire.

(Prominent as Henry was, his wife, Marie, always outshone him, even in Hollywood. She was perhaps the first "psychic to the stars," and, although she had no training in architecture, she designed several Hollywood houses, including an eclectic, pseudo-Moorish mansion called Moorcrest that Chaplin lived in before it was sold to the parents of Mary Astor. It still exists in an area of the Hollywood Hills just west of Beachwood Canyon where the Theosophists' Krotona Colony was once located. By the time Lax made his way west, Marie had died, but Henry still lived in their house near Moorcrest.)

Impractical as he could be, Lax was not entirely without prospects in Hollywood. One of the other North Carolina students he and Beam had been friends with was Arthur Ripley Jr., whose father was a major movie director. Lax had met Ripley Sr. when he visited his son at school, and the younger Ripley had asked his father by letter to help Lax break into the movies. On the chance that nothing came from this connection, Lax had asked *Parade*'s editor Arthur Reef to make him the magazine's official "West Coast representative," thinking the title might open studio doors. In a pinch he might actually write something for the magazine too.

When Lax and Beam arrived in Hollywood, they stayed in a hotel for five days, then a depressing rooming house for two weeks, before moving into a one-bedroom apartment in a huge complex at the foot of the Hollywood Hills called Castle Argyle. It was a stone's throw from the RCA Tower and Hollywood Boulevard, a cheap place inhabited by actors and writers who'd come to make their fortune but hadn't struck it rich. (Laughlin lived one floor below.) The landlord, according to Lax, was a Russian general who was "nosey, tight-fisted and a religious fanatic." Lax had plenty of time to study the general's ways because he spent his first two months there unemployed. He worked on his own screenplays and went to studio interviews arranged by his agent, the former editor and publisher Donald Friede, but no one bought his scripts or hired him.

Finally, sometime in late November, Ripley Sr. called to hire him as a researcher on a new movie to be called *Atlantis* (renamed *Siren of Atlantis*) and star Maria Montez and Jean-Pierre Aumont. Lax was hoping to be a writer, of course, but Ripley convinced him that even though he would make the minimum for a researcher of $125 a week, he could stay on longer than if he were hired at the slightly higher wage paid to writers, which turned out to be true. Lax stayed involved with the film from the story conferences in November to the final cutting in June. His main work was researching the ancient stories about the lost continent of Atlantis and learning about the Tuaregs, the fierce nomads of the Hoggar Mountains in Algeria who figure significantly in Pierre Benoit's *L'Atlantide*, the novel on which the screenplay would be based.

Although Lax's wish had come true—he was contributing to the making of a major motion picture—he couldn't have landed on a worse project. Benoit's 1919 novel won the French Academy's Grand Prize, but *Siren of Atlantis*, the third of at least eight movies to be based on his book, was far less fortunate. If ever a film was ill-starred, in fact, it was this one. According to its entry in the American Film Institute's online catalogue, when the original script was submitted to the Production Code Administration in early 1947, the PCA chief Joseph I. Breen rendered it unacceptable "by reason of the improper treatment of illicit sex, the use of hasheesh, and other details." Nonetheless Ripley started filming that spring. When Breen asked to see the revised script, he was told that it was being rewritten during filming, using his suggestions as guidelines, and that he would receive a copy of the full script when it was done. When the PCA finally saw a cut of the film in December 1948, it granted a provisional certificate "with the understanding that the fade out on Aumont and Montez on the couch has been omitted, that the two dagger thrusts have been omitted in the killing of Aumont's friend, and that the last shot of Montez in the white dress has been trimmed one third."

But the movie's travails were far from over. In January 1949 the *New York Times* reported that "[German producer] Seymour Nebenzal's picture *Siren of Atlantis*, completed some eighteen months ago at a cost of $1,300,000 is about to see the light of day after extensive revisions which have added another $250,000 to the production bill. A trial engagement in Las Vegas, Nev., convinced Nebenzal that audiences could not understand the Pierre Benoit story because it was 'too philosophical.' So last summer the producer raised additional capital to recoup the original investment and sent the picture back to the cameras for two weeks with John Brahm directing."

According to the AFI, "Neither Brahm nor Ripley . . . was willing to take credit for the final version, and so film editor Gregg Tallas, who synthesized their efforts, was billed as the director of the picture. A modern source adds that United Artists rejected Nebenzal's rough cut and insisted on additional shooting and retakes. The situation was further complicated . . . by the fact that Maria Montez initially refused to appear in the necessary retakes until she was paid deferred salary due to her."

The strain of her participation in this star-crossed project must have been too much for Montez. She never made another movie, and, two years after its January 1949 release, she died of a heart attack at thirty-one.

So what was the movie about?

Two soldiers from a group of French legionnaires searching the Sahara for a lost archaeological expedition are captured by Tuaregs, desert nomads associated with an ancient civilization high up in the Hoggar Mountains that turns out to be the lost civilization of Atlantis. (Yes, since Plato first proposed it, Atlantis has been thought to be below the sea, but this is Hollywood after all.) The two captured soldiers, Andre St. Avit and Jean Morhange, are taken to the queen, Antinea (Montez, of course), who is irresistible and has a nasty habit of encasing her discarded lovers in metal. St. Avit falls under her spell, but Morhange manages to resist her long enough to attempt an escape with a female court dancer named Tarit Zerga. After their escape fails, Zerga kills herself and Morhange ends up in front of the queen. When he shouts insults at her, she vows to destroy him and locks him in a room beside hers. Meanwhile a character named Blades convinces St. Avit that Antinea has turned her amorous attentions to Morhange, and an enraged St. Avit stabs his friend to death. Feeling immediate remorse for his actions, St. Avit flees Atlantis. Three months later other legionnaires find him wandering the desert. When he tells them the incredible tale of his adventure, including his murder of Morhange, they don't believe him. He begins to doubt his own story, thinking it a dream, until one of Antinea's bodyguards is captured. The prisoner hands St. Avit the queen's amulet, the symbol of her desire, and St. Avit heads off into the desert on his camel to find her. When his corpse is discovered, the amulet is still in his hand.

The few comments the *New York Times* reviewer Alexander Wolcott made beyond a sardonic description of the plot and identification of the principal actors came mostly in the following paragraph:

But despite the fact that a couple of young, handsome officers of the French Foreign Legion arrive on the scene to be won, and then tragically cast aside by this royal temptress, the goings-on at Atlantis are far from exciting. Dull is the word for their adventures, which include some static, romantic mooning between Queen Antinea and one of the love-sick legionnaires; an attempted escape from the palace[;] and the slaying of one officer by the other in a jealous, drunken rage. And when lovers are not being dispatched—these luckless gents are preserved as golden mummies by the court embalmer, a discarded swain who has been rendered mute by this tireless dame—the cast is engaged in endless palaver, none of which could be described as exhilarating.

That was the beginning and almost the end of Lax's Hollywood career. When his work on the movie ended in June 1947, he hung around, jobless, hoping Ripley would hire him again, but nothing developed. His first movie had been "terrible," he wrote to Merton, and others on the producer's list looked "impossible." One, called "Johnny Macbeth," was about "a gangster who got to be head of a mob by killing Big Duncan, at his wife's [Lily Macbeth's] instigation. The ghost Banky shows up at their dinner party."

Unsure what to do or where to go, Lax spent his days wandering and taking photographs, living off what he called "gifts" and hoping for some kind of work to pay off a loan from his sister. After not journaling for several months, he started recording his observations again. Among them was a poetic meditation on shadows that hearkened back to the film he made with Alex Eliot and foreshadowed his later interest in simple contrasts in his poetry, especially his 1966 poem "Black & White" and his 1976 work "Light Dark, Dark Light."

Merton, who was on the verge of publishing *The Seven Storey Mountain* and rising to an uneasy fame, continued to encourage Lax to pray for a vocation, which he did, but no clear guidance came. On September 1, 1947, after months of idleness and one day after seeing Duke Ellington perform from the cheap seats at the Hollywood Bowl, Lax set down a long journal entry that suggests he was beginning to think his natural inclinations might be a kind of vocation themselves:

He was still absorbing his education. Still, at 31, he was watching, trying to make comparisons between what he saw & what he had read, what he believed must be true & what others seemed to believe. He became a part of the life around him only to a very limited degree. But he watched it; tried to make sense of it at all times. And by trying to make sense he realized he meant that he tried to make comparisons, classical comparisons drawn from the opinions of those around him.

The reasons even for his semi-detachment were hard for him to understand. There was a temperamental reason which seemed to be interior & perhaps habitual. An unwillingness to be attached. Perhaps a simple dislike for the risks inherent in attachment. Perhaps a more positive love of peace which left him unwilling to forgo the pleasures of his habit and to achieve the dubious rewards of those who went out to achieve the specific ends of attachment. There were others he almost believed to be providential,

The Lord is my shepherd,
I shall not want,
He makes me lie down in green pastures.
He leads me beside the still waters.

He would watch life from the detachment of his green pasture.

There was another aspect of this which seemed less noble: his willingness to accept gifts to prolong his periods of unemployment. To seek, in a leisurely manner, a suitable employment. Along with this was a willingness to leave a job when it seemed vain to him. To wander from a desk when a fair day called to him.

In 1947 America was still recovering from the Second World War and the challenge to its values and assumptions that war brought. While the postwar decades have traditionally been characterized as a conformist period, there was another side to that time, a restless searching for some kind of experience, especially among the young, that Kerouac would portray in his 1957 novel, On the Road. Lax was writing ten years earlier, but his observations about himself and those around him at this point capture the attitude and mood:

He knew he was not alone in this feeling for meditative indolence, this willingness to be carried by the stream of benefits, even to seek out the givers of gifts. He did not know if his own way of life had led him into the company of those of his kind, or if his whole generation in the land had (providentially or accidentally) been turned to meditative wanderers. He felt that there was a little truth in both theories. But he had met few who were as thoroughly committed as himself, as generally reconciled to this way of life.

He thought of the ant and the grasshopper and could not but feel that he & most of his friends were grasshoppers except that, like him, most of them seldom even fiddled. The streets on a saturday evening were full of grasshoppers without fiddles; Young men without a real purpose on the prowl for drink and women possibly, but mainly for sights and sounds & intervals of comfort, occasions for mild laughter, experiences that would serve on later nights for anecdote. They were young men seeing life and as they looked, it departed from them, line by line, hair by hair. They were young men with blank faces which time would slowly write on.

But there was another side of Lax too, a side that tired of the idleness around him and longed for more from life. He expressed it beautifully in a poetic entry three weeks later that reveals why he eventually moved on:

He ran the stream of faces as they passed
Through fingers in his mind like many coins,
Weighing their value to his private soul,
Appraising them as for the coming world,
His mind unbalanced, weighed them and found loss.
This was the city all of them had built,
This was the city none of them had wanted,
This was the town built upon private dreams.
And now it glowed, a furnace in the night,
Full of crackles, full of bright surprise—
Not full of wonder, never full of peace.
This was the city he had come to see;
And having seen it, would he turn to salt?

Lax lingered in Hollywood through the following spring, visiting with friends, talking with his uncle, and occasionally meeting stars. From January through the beginning of April 1948 he worked for $200 a week on a picture "called variously Monte Carlo, The Masquerader and the Bandit of Sherwood Forest," but nothing more came after that. The highlight of his last months in California may have been a chance meeting on a bus with his old hero Aldous Huxley. He gave Huxley a copy of

Merton's third book of poetry, *Figures for an Apocalypse*—a not inappropriate title for his own observations.

Lax might never have escaped his indolence and indecision if Bob Mack hadn't rescued him again, this time with a solid teaching offer: a one-year replacement for an ill professor in the Connecticut College English Department. No doubt Lax was glad to be heading back to where he came from, but there were aspects of California he would miss, the sun and wind among them. He expressed his feelings toward them most beautifully in a portion of a poem set down on November 12, 1947, just before the coming of the winter rains:

> The light of afternoon is on the houses
>     the white houses
>         wedged in the hill
>             set in the hillside like slabs of stone
>                 like flats of canvas
>                 like stiff paper.
> Only the palm leaves toss and rattle.
> Only the palm leaves nod & whisper
>     in the cool breeze of the afternoon,
> And the movement of the palms is like a dance
>                     is like nothing but a
>                     dance
>                         & the laughing speech
>                         of high born ladies.
> The palms are feminine.
> They are as beautiful as ancient dancers caught upon a vase.
> And they sing the song of the afternoon
> of the beauty of the sunlight and the wind.

He wouldn't live with sun and wind in the same way again until he settled in the Greek islands fifteen years later. But the song he sang that day—of his soul's delight in beauty—would receive its fullest expression, in rhythms echoing the rhythms here, in a series of poems he'd begin the following year, the poems that became *The Circus of the Sun*.

One year when I was in graduate school, I visited Lax on spring break and recorded a long interview with him, not because I expected to write a book about him but because I'd long wanted to record his thoughts and even his voice, and the assignment in one of my classes was to profile an artist. At the start of the interview, sitting in his small main room on a cold March day, he began talking about Cezanne. "Cezanne was only trying to paint woods as objectively as he could," he said. "As he saw them. But in his paintings they appeared unique because Cezanne saw them only as Cezanne. This is why a writer should try to get things down exactly as he perceives them. What results will not be some non-personal 'objective' piece but a piece imbued with all that he is—how he truly perceives the world. When we see a Cezanne, we see what he saw in the landscape, and that opens up the possibility of his sensitivity to the world being awakened in us."

When Lax moved to Connecticut in the late summer of 1948, more than five years had passed since the day he met Mogador and the other Cristianis, but they stood in front of him as vividly as they had on that first afternoon, and his desire to write about them remained as strong as ever. It's tempting to see his move to Connecticut College as a second attempt at education as a possible career, but I think he took the job for other reasons. First of all, he owed people money and he had no prospects in L.A. Second, it brought him back to the East Coast, where he felt more comfortable. Third, it reunited him with one of his favorite people, Bob Mack. And fourth, it put him close to New York, where, soon after the school year started, he talked to an editor named Mary Mahoney about publishing a journalistic account of the Cristianis on tour.

Mahoney worked for a small publishing company called Duell, Sloan & Pearce, which had published Ed Rice's second book two years before. The Pearce in the name was Cap Pearce, who had been the *New Yorker*'s poetry editor when Lax was there. Lax's idea was to try to publish his account in the *New Yorker* first, as a "Reporter at Large" piece, then bring it out as a book. Pearce and Mahoney were interested enough to advance him $500 for research.

So late that December, after grading final papers for his classes in composition, drama, and eighteenth-century literature, he traveled south, with Mack in tow, to visit the Cristianis at their winter headquarters in Sarasota, Florida.

Lax had stayed in touch with the Cristianis, seeing them from time to time, including when they came through Hollywood, but other than hanging out with them at their practice facility in Central Park, he'd never spent much time with them. Nor had he ever written a journalistic account of anything. He didn't know exactly what to take note of, so he took note of everything—from the snippets of conversation he overheard in a hotel bar to the menu for the family's Christmas dinner. His notes can be hard to decipher because he wrote them at various angles on odd pieces of paper while following the Cristianis around, but their clarity improves somewhat when he records the words of the book's proposed star, young Mogador:

> A bad performer wants people to say how good he is. Good performers want people to say how good people are.

> Things that are difficult to do on the ground we do on horseback.

> Other performers, what they can do by strength, they do, but they have no style or grace. Style is a way of making a hard thing look easy.

Where Lax struggled most was trying to describe the acrobats' intricate moves, his descriptions too confusing to create pictures in one's mind. It was only when he stepped back from the specific action and put it in poetry that the glory of the Cristianis—their talent, artistry, and grace—came through:

> Holding on the invisible wires
> On which the world is strung—
> Mogador brightly dressed
> And riding in the light
> While the music plays
> Is like the juggler at Our Lady's shrine
> Is like King David dancing before
> The Ark of the Covenant
> Is like the Athletes of God

Who sang their praises in the desert wind.

These early attempts to render the acrobats' art the way he saw it, according to his own perceptions rather than some supposedly objective journalistic approach, hint at the majesty and beauty in the *Circus* cycle to come.

———————

Lax returned to Connecticut College for the spring semester, but his mind was on his writing about the Cristianis. In a poem he sent to Van Doren that spring, he used the phrase *circus of the sun* for the first time. (The poem would appear in the *New Yorker* under the title "Circus" four years later—his eleventh poem in that magazine and the first of three about the circus to be published there.) Around this same time his friends and family began to notice a new calm in him. It's hard to say exactly why Lax felt so peaceful after so many unsettled years, but his increasing closeness to the Cristianis probably had something to do with it. Sometime that spring he arranged to travel with them through western Canada in June, and years later, when someone asked him when he'd been happiest, he singled out that month.

Before he could experience that happiness, however, he had to endure another sadness. On March 11, 1949, at the age of seventy-two, his father died. As with his mother's death, I've found no record of Lax's feelings about his father's passing, but I have to think that part of his great joy in traveling with the circus came from remembering his father introducing him to circus people when he was a child. He could show Siggie no greater honor than traveling with the kind of people he liked.

Another joyful event came between the end of the school year and the beginning of his travels with the Cristianis: on May 26, Ascension Day, he joined Rice, Freedgood, Robert Giroux, and James Laughlin at Gethsemani for Merton's ordination. Merton, Lax wrote to Van Doren, "is fuller of joy than any human being I've ever seen—very much himself—nothing removed but what blocked the light, or netted it in." Days later, when he joined the Cristianis, the same might have been said of Lax himself.

Despite a lifelong fear of flying, Lax took a plane to Saskatchewan, where Mogador picked him up to begin what would be a month-long trip from Humboldt to Indian Bend, Moosejaw to Medicine Hat. Both could be tongue-tied in social settings, but they talked at length throughout the month, mostly at night as they traveled in Mogador's old truck from performance to performance. With only sandwiches in a brown paper bag and a Thermos of coffee between them, they rode for miles in silence, their eyes on "the blond dirt road in the light of the headlamps," until Mogador spoke. Then Lax would ask him a question about the circus or some aspect of life and they'd begin to talk. As Lax would write in *Mogador's Book*, those long stretches of darkness Mogador was used to enduring alone were especially conducive to the kinds of thoughts that come "from the center of our being."

Although Lax was always the one asking questions, the one who wanted to learn from his younger companion, he saw these exchanges as beneficial to Mogador too:

It was, I think, a cooperation
with Mogador to coax truth from himself.
For the man one talks to
(when one talks to the inner self)
is not at all the man the world knows.
It can almost be said
he is not the man
the man himself knows.
He is part of him
(hidden in darkness)
very often the noblest part,
and very often
   very shy.

Lax might have been writing about the conversations he had with himself, and indeed talking to Mogador seemed akin at times to talking to his better self. But Mogador had a secret knowledge Lax desired as well: a *physical* understanding of a way of being in the world that Lax had already begun to think of as *pure act*. The manifestation of this understanding was his equestrian act:

We talked about the fact that
it wasn't the danger,

it wasn't the skill,
it wasn't the applause
that made the act what it was.
It was principally the grace;
the bringing into being,
for a moment,
the beautiful thing,
the somersault,
the leap,
the entrechat on horseback.

Although Lax was along just to observe, he ate and slept with the per-formers and, when the family would let him, performed as a clown called Chesko. Buried in his archives at Columbia are numerous photographs of the Cristianis and their children around the trailers they lived in on the road or performing, a couple of Lax in a tie, and two out-of-focus black-and-whites of him in clown costumes. In one he looks quite plain in a dark suit and normal shoes, the only clown effects the upturned brim of his hat and his painted face, but in the other he wears a wide-striped shirt, too-short pants, enormous shoes, and a cap turned sideways above what looks to be a bright red nose. The photos appear on a contact sheet next to two of Moga-dor. The contrast couldn't be more striking. Whereas Mogador looks proud and comfortable in his body, as you'd expect from someone who had been an acrobat all his life, Lax looks, well, humorous, his splayed-foot stance and long, limp arms reflecting lifelong awkwardness. It's easy to imagine him as a clown, especially with his good nature.

"You gotta like him," Mogador said about Lax's natural ability at clowning, "you don't teach anybody to have a funny walk and make good faces."

Lax described his clowning technique this way: "I walked around the ring. I hardly looked up at the crowd at all at first. Then I looked a little, scanning through the sea of faces for one familiar, for one that was watch-ing me. When I found a pair of eyes watching me, I watched them back, watched and waited, waited for anything. When they changed, I changed. If they smiled, I looked quizzical; if they looked angry, I looked shocked. If a child put both hands to his ears and waggled, I'd make a face at him and walk away." Sometimes he would lie in the dirt and gaze at a beautiful woman, "looking at her wistfully, thinking, and not thinking, of all the dreams of romance." Then, when she laughed, he would pick himself up, brush himself off, and walk away, looking back at her sadly.

One time he lay down in front of a family of farmers, propped his head on his hand, and stared at the family's two-year-old, who stared back at him "sober as a judge." The family leaned forward together to see if he could coax a smile out of the child, and when he did, they relaxed. He did as he did with the beautiful women—picked himself up, dusted himself off, and walked away—but this time when he looked back he saw the child following him.

Acting was one of the fields he'd considered going into when young, and he had appeared in a play or two in high school, so being in front of an audience again must have pleased him. At some point he learned to juggle, but it's doubtful he ever juggled for anyone but himself.

For that month he traveled with the Cristianis, all of the disparate strains in Lax's life came together for the first time. He was indulging his love of travel and taking notes for a piece of writing he felt truly mattered. He was spending his time with a large, talented Catholic family that was both dynamic and simple. And he was living day to day, moment by moment, with every activity new, every conversation a gift. Best of all, as he told Van Doren, the family, with their "unearthly sweetness and grace," had embraced him as a "poet and philosopher without portfolio."

Although the trip lasted only a month, it stayed with him the rest of his life. When someone asked in his later years how long he had traveled with the Cristianis, he answered, "Even till now."

———————

It might have been difficult to return to ordinary life in Olean or even New York after such an amazing adventure, but Lax never had to find out. Almost as soon as he arrived back in the States, he checked his fear of flying again and boarded a plane to the Virgin Islands. Three years before, Gibney and Flagg had gone to St. John on their honeymoon and, feeling it was a place Gibney might finally write the novel he'd long talked about, had rented a cabin by the beach without running water or electricity. Since then they'd spent a year as caretakers in a refurbished plantation house before moving into a storage shed on

Henley Cay, the slip of land just offshore where they were now. Needing a break, perhaps, from having only each other as company, they had invited Lax and Reinhardt, who'd just gone through a divorce, to come for the summer.

Gibney, who may have been the most broadly talented of Lax's Columbia friends, had yet to write his novel, but he hadn't been idle. In addition to working on the shed-cum-house, he'd made furniture, repaired engines and tools for the islanders, mastered the local dialect, and made friends with people across St. John. He'd also kept a journal, written frequent letters to friends, learned to fish with a spear gun, caught lobsters and turtles, and drunk heavily. By the time he stood waiting for Lax's plane to land at the small airport on nearby St. Thomas, he had probably argued with Reinhardt as well.

It's hard to know what Lax was expecting when he traveled to Henley Cay. He wasn't one to write about expectations. It may have been that he was just happy to have a place to stay for a while without having to pay for it, a place where he would be with good friends and wouldn't have to look for a job. Or he may have been hoping for a re-creation of the times with Merton and the others in the Olean cottage. If so, his hopes went unfulfilled. Spectacularly so.

Certainly these old friends shared many good moments—they swam and fished and visited local sights—but Lax's spare notes suggest a dispiriting number of alcohol-fueled arguments, especially between Gibney and Reinhardt. A sharp tongue had always been part of Gibney's quick wit, and the years at Henley Cay had sharpened it further. Despite the many things he was doing, he felt bad about not writing, and what was probably disappointment in himself came out as harshness toward others, especially when they talked politics. Reinhardt, who had become a communist, said less and less as time wore on.

While Reinhardt spent his days inside the house painting abstract watercolors that Gibney proclaimed a bastardization of his talents, Lax tried to read Aquinas and flesh out his account of traveling with the Cristianis. What he preferred to do, however, was climb up the hill to Gibney's workshop and sit alone writing poetry. From time to time he took the ferry to Charlotte Amalie on St. Thomas, once to be treated for an eye ailment the doctor said came from too much sun and once when a stomach problem landed him in the hospital. Whenever he could, he went to Mass at the Catholic church there, sometimes taking Reinhardt, the communist, along. After Mass one day the priest proclaimed that the following year, 1950, would be a Jubilee Year in Rome—a special year of blessing and celebration—and Lax heard a voice inside him say, "You'll be there."

In the evening martinis were the drink of choice and dinner was usually fish Gibney had caught, often by hand—mackerel, grouper, lobster. They usually spent the evening at home, but one night they crossed to St. John to visit a refurbished plantation house, perhaps the one the Gibneys had lived in. A "semi-drunk lady" drove them up to the house and showed them the ruined sugar mill, including the sugar vats slaves had carried up the hill years before. Lax's description of what came next captures the feeling of one of their calmer evenings together:

> Sat around living room watching cats & dogs. Husband poured martinis. All fearing hopeless conversation got crocked. Recited poetry. Listened to theory on how to sell stories. Got out old accordion & played old songs, some older, some either older than we remembered or too silly to have made an impression. Drank coffee. Ate dinner of cold ham & beans & melon. Sang. Laughed loudly. Danced drunk waltz with hostess. Spent interludes in bathroom putting drops in wind/sun irritated eyes. Eventually husband drove us home, wife sits in front with rum & water. Jokes all the way down hill. . . . Left them, took oar boat. Talked about how getting drunk was the only way out of that kind of evening.

That night he slept on the dock with Reinhardt and dreamed of owning a circus with Mogador. The contrast between his life on the road with the Cristianis and the drunken evening in an old plantation house couldn't have been starker. Still, he seems to have enjoyed much of his time in the Caribbean. He even suggested to Merton that St. John or perhaps Henley Cay would be a good place for a small monastery.

---

When Lax finally returned to the States for good, he didn't go to Connecticut or New York but to Olean, where he lived in his sister's house and worked on his book in a basement room at the St. Bonaventure library. Father Philotheus Boehner, who had helped Merton overcome his doubts about entering the monastery, had arranged the room for him and agreed to serve as his spiritual advisor. Lax was also attending Father Philotheus's class on Aquinas, perhaps hoping to continue the kind of close reading he'd done with Professor Kuhn at the University of North Carolina.

Over the next year Lax worked harder and more regularly on his writing than he ever had. "I've got quite a few words now on the acrobat book," he wrote to Merton early in 1950, "but still haven't tried to put sections or even paragraphs together." He stuck with it through the spring and summer and finally decided in early September that the book was done. It was still an uneven patchwork of prose and poetry with too much material left in, but he had done as much as he could. He was ready to show it to others.

Having stayed in one place, with one project, for longer than at any other time in his life, Lax was ready for a break. He decided to travel to Combermere, Ontario, where, after leaving Harlem, the Baroness de Hueck and her husband, Eddie Doherty, had established a lay apostolate and "community of love" called Madonna House. His intention was probably just to see the baroness again and spend time among loving people who shared her charitable approach to faith. What happened to him there, however, would send him on a journey like none he had ever imagined.

# Being a Presence in Postwar Marseilles

Lax believed deeply in the significance of dreams, likening their meaning for an individual to that of art for a community. To his mind, they communicated the soul's deeper thoughts and feelings in signs and symbols, bringing the resources of the subconscious into the waking world. One sizable box in his Columbia archives is filled with notebooks in which he recorded every dream for months, without explaining them. The important thing, he felt, was to observe closely, not interpret systematically.

Sometimes, though, a dream's meaning can seem clear. During one of our last times together, for example, he told me he'd dreamed I'd reassured him that "peace is a good thing to seek and love does conquer all"—a sign not of doubt, I think, but hope that I would carry the flag he and Merton had hoisted. And during his stay at Madonna House in the fall of 1950, the Baroness de Hueck had a dream about him that was not only clear but prescient, helping him make the kind of decision he had trouble making: about where and how to live.

———————

Madonna House was (and still is) governed by a credo called *The Little Mandate*, a distillation of the gospel the baroness said she received from Christ himself. Among its dictates are "Sell all you possess. Give [the proceeds] directly, personally to the poor. . . . Be simple, poor, and childlike. . . . Preach the gospel with your life—*without compromise!* . . . Love . . . love . . . love, never counting the cost." The baroness had lived the mandate herself by going to Harlem without knowing anyone there and renting a room in a tenement with no other purpose than to do what she could to help the people around her. She believed in what she called the *duty of the moment*: filling whatever need was right in front of you. That fall Lax's need was for a calling, a vocation, a way of living that would fit his inclinations and yet feel important, necessary. The answer to that need, as it turned out, was the baroness's dream.

As dreams go, it was quite simple, or at least Lax's understanding of it was. Since it was obvious he couldn't do anything else, the dream said, he should emulate St. Benedict Joseph Labre, the eighteenth-century Frenchman who, after trying unsuccessfully to enter several monasteries, felt called to live a solitary life of poverty dedicated to visiting the major Catholic shrines. Setting out with nothing but the clothes on his back, two rosaries, and various religious books, Labre visited all of Europe's famous shrines—Loreto, Assisi, Compostela—before restricting his peregrinations to those in Rome. When he tired, he slept on the ground. When he was hungry, if no one gave him food, he ate what he found in the garbage. He never begged, and even when somebody offered him something, he took only what he needed, giving the rest to others. When his manner of life had finally worn him out, he collapsed on the steps of Rome's Santa Maria dei Monti church and died in a nearby house. By then his extreme self-denial, humility, and devotion had convinced his skeptical neighbors of his sincerity and holiness.

I don't know how much Lax knew of Labre's life or how closely he thought the baroness was suggesting he follow it, but something about the dream and the manner of life it pointed to appealed to him. No doubt he remembered that voice inside him at the Mass on St. Thomas that said he would be in Rome for the Jubilee Year. The baroness advised him to ask his spiritual director for his permission and then leave for Europe on January 6, Epiphany, but the Jubilee Year would end before that and Lax wanted to depart immediately. So he hurried home to Olean to ask for Father Philotheus's consent.

Money might have been a concern, but coincidentally, or maybe providentially, a young woman Lax had taught at Connecticut College and talked to about Catholicism, an heir to the Colt family fortune named Teddy Flynn, had just married a Frenchman, Jean François Bergery, and wanted Lax to come to Paris to meet him. She offered to pay for his passage, his lodging, and whatever traveling he wanted to do, including a trip to Rome.

When Lax asked for his spiritual director's blessing, the answer was yes, he could go, but only if he promised to return to the States within the month. "Europe is an aging Roquefort cheese," Father Philotheus said. "Touch it quick and come back soon."

So began one of the stranger interludes in Lax's unusual life. I'm not sure how much he planned of what he would do when he left for France in late October, but his experiences on this trip would change his life significantly. His simple intention was to serve as godfather for his former student's son (and her too, it turned out), then go to Rome. But he had other desires as well, and after spending only a brief time in Paris, he headed for Lourdes. He might have been making a serious attempt to emulate Labre by visiting one of Europe's most famous shrines, or he might have wanted just to see it. In either case, he stopped at other towns along the way: Bordeaux, Pau, Carcassone, and Narbonne. He hadn't been to Europe in thirteen years and there was much to take in. Much to do.

Most of Lax's memories of that 1937 trip with Slate were hazy and pleasant, but one was still vivid and hard, and to truly live the new life he intended, the life the baroness had envisioned, he needed to move beyond it. It was a memory of fear—perhaps the most fear he'd ever felt—and he'd come to believe, or wanted to believe, that the words in 1 John 4:18 were true: *Perfect love drives out fear.* To rid himself of this particular fear and maybe fear in general, he had to return, with a heart full of love, to the place that had caused it: the dangerous, chaotic city of Marseilles.

As he remembered it, he and Slate had planned to spend the night there, but after several hours he had insisted they leave. He wasn't sure what exactly had frightened him, but he had felt it already leaving the train and it had grown stronger as they walked through town, reaching its zenith in a café near the port where the clientele and even the owner seemed sinister. Samaritaine, the café was called—named, ironically, for the man in Jesus's parable who helped a wounded stranger. In the Bible the parable follows Jesus's command to love our neighbors, and one of the lines in the baroness's *Little Mandate* was "Be a light to your neighbour's feet. Go without fear into the depths of men's heart. I shall be with you." Clutching that promise, determined to love instead of fear, Lax headed south to Marseilles.

It was the middle of the night when his train approached the city. The car he rode in was filled with Arabs, and a drunk or crazy Italian ran down the corridor talking angrily to himself. Lax must have wondered if he was being tested already, but he persevered, and just as the sun was coming up, the cafés opening, he stepped out onto the platform at the Gare St. Charles.

———————

To most people, postwar Marseilles, which had been heavily damaged in the war, was, as one paper put it, a world capital for "dope, whores, and street violence." It was the main French port on the Mediterranean, the center of the infamous Turkey-to-France-to-America heroin-smuggling operation called the French Connection, and the primary entry point for immigrants from North Africa. Yet, as M. F. K. Fisher points out in *Two Towns in Provence*, her book about life there in the 1950s, it was a city very much *alive*, with new building everywhere and a mingling of races, nationalities, classes, and characters unmatched in the world.

It was the first of these cities Lax expected and the second he found. Two days after his arrival, his fear clearly gone, he wrote:

> A lifetime has prepared me for what I have seen in the last two days—
> A lifetime of panting in America could not begin to tell me in the old terms what I have seen.
> By its minute to minute existence the city destroys philosophy and art—makes a mockery of sculpture & architecture. A religion of ritual—that moves in time & mysticism that leaps beyond it: gambling, bullfighting, fishing, sailing, buying and selling—stealing and apprehending—burying the dead with decorum and dispatch— dances, spectacles, the acrobatic art—card games—promenades & the ancient art of sitting & looking—all these have been developed to a high degree & hold an honorable place in Marseille. . . .
> The net maker next to me sings (romantic tango) & that is the song of the city. A song that rises naturally with the work—that is bound in with the net—it is not a prayer that rises above it—the city itself is a song & a prayer. . . .
>
> The great thing in Marseille is not the buildings it is the people. . . . All who live here walk the decks of their city with grace and equilibrium, the joy of acrobats and sailors.
>
> The city is full of Mogadors. . . .

Idiosyncratic punctuation aside, nothing Lax ever wrote expressed his true being quite as well as this. Not his old being—the privileged pre–*New Yorker*, prewar, pre-breakdown, pre-Harlem, and pre-Cristiani being that feared the city in 1937—but his new, simpler being, the one shaped and freed by all he'd gone through. He was thirty-five now, at the midpoint of life according to Dante and the Bible, and he was about to start living a life more expressive of his truer nature—a simpler existence focused primarily on love. What he saw from the train station steps at dawn and down in the streets of the war-damaged city was the longed-for, imagined city of God—the diversity, the beauty, the love. He had glimpsed parts of it before but never seen it all together.

So why was he able to see it now? To live differently now? What had changed? The key, I think, was his willingness to accept and even embrace poverty. Not the desperate poverty thrust upon people in the midst of scarcity and exploitation but the poverty that comes from simplifying one's desires and thereby reducing one's need to earn money. The poverty that trusts God and his people to provide. The poverty that empties oneself of prerogatives and privileges, establishing a quiet camaraderie with those with nothing. It is the kind of poverty Saul Bellow meant when he wrote, "If there were a beautiful poverty, a moral poverty in America, that would be subversive."

The reasons Lax chose this poverty were varied and complex. One was a natural lack of desire for things. Another was a strong dislike of work that didn't have clear meaning. A third was a firm belief that lessening one's needs makes it easier to hear and follow God. And a fourth was a long-nurtured love for those on society's fringes.

Since his days with Merton listening to jazz musicians jam, Lax had admired what he was now calling *pure act*, a natural living out of one's God-given abilities and potentials without the splitting-off of consciousness that might question or judge. His observations of the Cristianis had strengthened his belief that this was the ideal way to live, not only individually but also communally. Long before he reached Marseilles he had come to believe that all of life is connected and motivated by love, or at least potentially motivated by love. He believed that people sin and hurt each other not out of malice but out of ignorance of love. If all people could learn to see themselves as they are and act out of that awareness, they would live in harmony with themselves and others. Their thoughts and actions would flow together like the music of the jazz musicians and the movements of the acrobats. He was beginning to envision his own role, his own pure act, as something more than just writing, as a kind of coaching or counseling or even prophecy. He was not a musician or an acrobat, but he could write poetry and prose that spoke of the beauty of

God's world. God's people. And he could show those around him what harmony, grounded in love, looked like.

This way of looking at things didn't come together for him until he spent those first few days in Marseilles, a city that demanded he transcend fear and trust God. It was a city where sea met land, rich met poor, West met East, and past met future. A city that did what it did under the benevolent gaze of the Mother of God, as symbolized by the Notre Dame de la Garde on its highest hill. There in that city at that time not only all of his life but all of life in general converged.

Although the clarity of vision those few days in Marseilles gave him made Lax want to linger, he had to move on, at least for now. He had little money and he was due in Rome, where a Brother Octavius he'd met through Merton had offered free lodging at the Trappist General House. Wanting to show his love for humanity in some way before he left town, he started talking to men who looked down and out, hoping, but failing, to find some way to help them. When he told a friend later that these men liked him but he didn't seem to be doing anything for them, the friend replied that if they liked him, he was.

The day before he left Marseilles, he saw a young man—a boy, really—in an army jacket with his hands in his pocket, looking forlorn, and decided to approach him. The boy's hair was untrimmed, making him look wild and shaggy, but Lax didn't look much better: his own hair was hidden by a stocking cap, he hadn't shaved in three days, and the shoes below his black overcoat were broken down. To get a conversation going, he asked the boy where the waterfront was, and soon the boy, a Belgian named Marcel Lambert, was telling him how hard it was to find work, especially dressed the way he was. He was standing there in front of the post office, he said, because he'd arranged to sell a man his coat, but the buyer hadn't shown up. With nothing else to do, he told Lax he would walk him to the port. As they strolled along, Lax offered him a suit he owned. The boy must have been wary, but he followed Lax to his room anyway, and when they arrived, Lax gave him a shirt and socks as well. When the boy spied a duffel bag Mack had loaned Lax for his trip, he asked if he could have that too, but Lax said no. It bothered him to hold something back—how could he emulate Labre or trust God entirely if he did?—but he didn't feel the bag was his to give. Eventually he and the boy parted, but the guilt he felt at not relinquishing the bag stayed with him.

Lax spent only a week in Rome before heading back to the States. He didn't record what he did in the city, but it's a safe bet he visited its famous churches and took in Jubilee events. When he left, Brother Octavius invited him to come back for a longer stay, and by the time he boarded the *Vulcania* in Naples, he was already planning his return.

———————

With thoughts of a longer stay in Europe, Lax felt a more urgent need that Christmas to finish his circus book. He gave it to his cousin, Soni Holman, to read and she said there was too much "talk" in it. Next he showed it to his old *Time* magazine colleague, Alex Eliot, who suggested significant cuts. He was still hoping to send at least part of it to the *New Yorker*, but Eliot urged him to keep polishing it instead, making it something for the ages rather than a quickly forgotten publication. Unsure what to do with it, Lax took it with him on a bus trip to Washington, DC, to visit Mike Beam. There he contacted another North Carolina friend, Bob Butman, who had worked for the student literary magazine, and asked if he would come read it.

Butman found Lax staying with "a minor gangster" he'd met on the bus and some of his young friends in an apartment with only mattresses and folding chairs as furniture. Holding a bottle of twelve-year-old Scotch in one hand and an editing pencil in the other, Butman crossed out heavy blocks of prose and rearranged lines of poetry, knowing, as Eliot had known, that Lax's writing wasn't meant to appear as a "Reporter at Large" piece or a journalistic account of any kind but a poetic evocation of the wonder and magic of the circus and Creation. When he was done with his pencil and the Scotch, he handed Lax something close to what would be the final book.

*Now that that's done,* Lax thought, *I think I'd better go back to Marseilles.*

Returning to Europe so soon was no spur-of-the-moment decision. While wandering the ship's decks before his trip there two months earlier, Lax had run into his Hollywood friend Pat Laughlin, who was heading to Paris to study at the Sorbonne. They had promised to stay in touch, and now Laughlin had sent an urgent cable from Paris. He had contracted pneumonia, he wrote, and needed Lax's help getting on a homebound boat.

Eager as he was to return to Marseilles, Lax wouldn't have hesitated a moment except for two problems: he didn't have any money and his spiritual advisor had insisted he stay in Europe no more than a month. A conversation with Teddy Bergery took care of the money problem. She promised to pay his passage and give him funds to continue his travels when he reached Paris. Receiving permission from Father Philotheus proved more difficult. No matter how hard Lax tried, he couldn't reach him. (Unbeknownst to Lax, Father Philotheus had died.) Thinking time was of the essence, he talked to a local priest instead and, just to be sure, checked with a Franciscan. Both gave their okay, and on January 26, 1951, Lax boarded the *America* in Baltimore, headed for France again. Before he left, he called Mary Mahoney, the editor who had given him the advance for his book, to tell her it was almost finished. He must have told her it was going to be more poetic than he had originally proposed because she said, "Okay, but nothing fragmentary." He didn't let on that it was no longer the kind of book she was expecting at all—that it was, in essence, all poetry.

––––––––––

When Lax returned to Marseilles, he carried three things he hadn't had with him his first time there: $300 Teddy Bergery had given him in Paris, an alpenstock Laughlin had handed him before his departure for New York, and a determination to do something good no one had bequeathed him except perhaps the baroness or God. For Lax—and maybe Laughlin too—the alpenstock was like the ashplant Joyce's Stephen Dedalus used in *Ulysses*. As Lax tapped his way down the sidewalk toward the port, he imagined it a divining rod leading him to somewhere he could dig "a well for peace."

That somewhere turned out to be the Hotel de Calais, a flophouse a half-block off the Vieux Port that catered to drifters and sailors, immigrants looking for manual labor, and prostitutes working the narrow alleys behind the docks. The desk clerk when Lax arrived was the owner's husband, a black North African with graying hair and black eyes, "hangdog and belligerent."

"Are you an Alpinist?" he asked sarcastically.

"Yes," Lax said, "an Alpinist from Mars."

The man must have liked his moxie. He smiled and gave him room number five with a view of the harbor through the frame of the hotel's missing sign. The room had blue walls and red tiles, a solid bed, and a cold-water tap that shut itself off when you let go. An "ink-black water closet" was one step outside.

The window onto the harbor was the room's best feature. From it Lax could see the fishermen mending their nets along the port's broad apron, the fish market across the harbor, and the fortress-like church, Notre Dame de la Garde, perched majestically on the far hill.

"this is my home (and i have come a long way to find it)," Lax writes in an unpublished manuscript he would revise periodically over the next decade. Titled alternately "Acey-Ducey" or "Reflections of a Temple Dancer," the manuscript states that one of his reasons for returning to Marseilles was to write a book about his life there—a book that, in essence, would write itself. Referring to himself in the third person, he says, "So he's back to the place (the center of the world) with only one job (to write a book) and to find marcel lambert."

Why, you might ask, would his first thought be to find a boy he had barely met? First, he still felt guilty for not giving Lambert the duffel bag. During his brief stay in the States, he had mentioned the incident to Mack, who had said he should have offered it. Second, Lambert was the only person he had spoken to at length in Marseilles and he knew him to be in need. In other words, in the idealization of the poor that was part of Lax's vision in those days, Lambert was a prototype. Even while looking for a room he'd been thinking of him.

"lambert—young lion," he writes in his manuscript, "an angry young romantic—angry poet—hurt young lion—(he had hurt him more) not giving him the bag (he was bringing him) the bag—would find a room where he could live and write—where m lambert could come and go— room near the port—the sound of boats—horizontal windows—him writing—lambert either coming or going."

Lax's obsession with young Lambert is one of the odder aspects of his unusual stay in Marseilles. It's clear from several things he wrote that the chance to see Lambert again and give him the duffel bag fueled his desire to return to Marseilles. And it's tempting to view his obsession as evidence of latent homosexuality, his joy at living in Marseilles excitement at the prospect of doing whatever he wanted away from observing eyes. During this period of his life, after all, he tended to focus on specific young men, starting with Mogador. But there is nothing in Lax's journals to suggest that his interest in these men was sexual. What the journals do suggest is that he was becoming a kind of monk in the world, giving away what he had and living a chaste life.

The strangeness in this and other stories Lax set down comes from a hyperawareness in him that he was changing his life, moving from thinking about how he should live to living consciously according to his beliefs. He didn't go to the extremes Labre went to, but in its way his life was just as dedicated. The difference between them was that Lax believed in living joyfully among people, embodying his belief in a benevolent God. He had discovered that loving people was part of his true nature.

So Lax went out looking for Lambert, but before he did, he had one other need to take care of. Living where he was and the way he intended, he couldn't leave Teddy Bergery's money in his room, but he had no local bank and he knew no one in town. So he walked down to the Café de la Samaritaine—the place that had so frightened him—and asked the owner, an older man named Pierrot, to keep his money for him, doling out small amounts when he needed them. For whatever reason, Pierrot agreed and, according to Lax, kept perfect records. "Of course," Lax said to me, "we became great friends."

(Lax became friends with the man's son, Ernesto, too. When he passed through Marseilles again fifteen years later, wearing a beard this time, he sat down at one of the café's outside tables. Pierrot was dead by then, and the waiter who served him, someone he used to know, didn't recognize him. When Ernesto came out, though, he greeted Lax warmly, telling him how great it was to see him again. Lax felt happy and relieved until Ernesto said. "How's football?"

"Football?" Lax asked. "I'm sure it's fine but I don't know much about it."

"Come on," Ernesto replied. "A great Swedish football player like you?"

Lax fared better with a blind man he'd known who played an accordion on the Canebière, the famous boulevard running through the heart of Marseilles. When Lax saw the man still on the same corner, he said hello and the man stopped playing.

"Who's that?" he asked.

"An old friend," Lax said. "An American."

"C'est toi, Bob?" the blind man asked.)

With his money safe, Lax was free to dedicate himself to his search for Lambert. He found out that Lambert worked on a transport boat between Marseilles and Casablanca and started watching the buses that brought workers to the port. When he finally saw him, he told him he was living at the Hôtel de Calais and had brought him the canvas bag he'd wanted. One can only imagine what Lambert thought.

"I have to go now," Lambert said. "I'll see you soon."

"Wait a minute," Lax said. "Let me take your picture."

Lambert insisted he had to leave, but he stood long enough to "glower" into the camera.

Clearly this encounter was as awkward as Lax's first interaction with Lambert, but Lax was trying to do something new, something he hadn't been trained for and didn't do naturally. It's unclear whether he ever saw Lambert again, but in a photograph taken in Rome months later, Lax still has the duffel bag under his arm.

---

The four months Lax spent in Marseilles, from February through May, set the pattern for the next fifty years of his life: living simply among those at the bottom of society, watching and writing down his observations, offering peace and whatever else he could to those in spiritual or physical need. After years of wearing other people's outfits, he had found his own comfortable clothes. He'd given up worrying about making a living, believing that if he lived simply—simply lived—God would fulfill the promise of Jesus in the Sermon on the Mount: "Therefore I tell you, do not worry about your life, what you will eat or what you will drink, or about your body, what you will wear. . . . Look at the birds of the air; they neither sow nor reap nor gather into barns, and yet your heavenly Father feeds them."

The only physical element important to Lax was being where peace surrounded him or entered through him. Few would have called postwar Marseilles a peaceful place, but to Lax the violence, corruption, and sin were opportunities to extend peace more broadly. To bring harmony from disparate elements. Marseilles was like a dark downtown club and a bright circus tent. A celestial city and the ultimate lover.

In "Acey-Ducey" his poetic meditation on his time there, he writes:

(city, city,
i am in thy midst,

as a dream
in thy midst,

as a dream
in thy midst

and myself

in the midst

of my dream)

city, city
i ask thee
not to change

I ask thee
not to stay;
but only to be,

and to let me be
with thee

The entire meditation is both allusive and illusive. Instead of vignettes or clear pictures, Lax gives impressions and fleeting images, as if unable to decide whether or not he wants readers to understand what his time in Marseilles meant to him. He seems unsure whether something that matters to him matters only to him or might be important to others because he sets it down as important. He wants to remember it all, he tells himself, without losing a single fragment, yet he seems to sense that his experience can be important to another person only if it echoes something that person has experienced or might experience. What's important isn't the experience itself but the pursuit and finding of some kind of meaning in one's experiences. And for him, everything he did and saw and everyone he met in Marseilles radiated meaning.

What Lax remembered fondly through the years, I think, was how free he felt in Marseilles—from fear and expectations and responsibility. With Labre in mind and the alpenstock in hand, he walked the streets as a man of peace looking for other peaceful people. What he found was something else entirely: a group of immigrants and criminals who spent their days together in his tiny room—making it, he wrote to Merton, "like a Warner Brothers movie."

---

One of the first men he befriended was a Pole named Theo he would often drink with in a bar near his hotel, a waterfront place whose habitués included a leering Italian sailor, a man who always wore a Basque beret, and an accordion player from Paris on his way to entertain the diners in the restaurant upstairs. When he'd tired of the bar, Theo would take Lax to his shack on the other side of the city's Arab section, and, if they had money, they'd fill a bottle at the vintner's along the way, adding some meat or maybe *salade Russe* for dinner. In the light from a candle on a jar lid, Theo would talk about his days in Poland or read from an English grammar or sing songs from his days in the French Foreign Legion, yelling "Shit!" or "Phoque!" when he was feeling especially good. One night he announced in his terrible English that they were eating "duck."

"Duck?" Lax asked.

"Duck," Theo replied. "*Duck!* Bow-wow."

In another bar, the Tosca, Lax saw a big man with an angular Slavic face—the "type from a gangster movie: not really the brains, not really the lug, but a trustworthy type to strangle you from the back"—and asked the bar's owner if he was her husband. He wasn't, but the next day when Lax walked by, the man came out to greet him. His name was Georges, he said, and he was out of work. He wondered if could visit Lax in his hotel room later to tell him something on his mind.

"Can't you tell me here?" Lax asked.

"No," said Georges, looking skeptically around the port. They arranged to meet that evening, and when Georges showed up, he asked the question Lax may have feared and wanted: "Can I stay with you?"

———————

Georges was a Russian, as it turned out, but he'd grown up in Turkey and, like Theo, had joined the French Foreign Legion. Since then he'd done some smuggling but fallen on hard times. What he needed now was a little money to get started again. He had a lucrative plan, he said in Lax's room that first night, to smuggle clocks across the border from Belgium. If Lax would only help him a little, he'd set him up in a grand apartment with a view of the harbor.

As Lax watched and listened from the bed, Georges, who had been sitting backward on the room's only chair, took off his jacket, then his shirt, then his socks. "Do you mind if I wash my feet?" he said. Lax writes:

> the only water we had was cold but he was used to that. his feet were wide and square, his calves enormous. he washed and dried them with energy and attention (as though they were bergers he had been commissioned to strangle without a sound). In his old-fashioned European legionnaire's underwear he looked like a short Russian version of john l. sullivan or an acrobat in a taxidermist's window. His skin was a pale dead white but his flesh was firm; he was obviously as lithe as a cat and (in his musculature at least) as ferocious. His only signs of pathos were holes in his trousers (he showed them to me) and in his shoes and possibly in the white malnourishment of his skin.

When it was time for bed, Lax told Georges to sleep against the wall because he'd be getting up to go to Mass. Then he turned out the light and, lying in a bed beside this stranger who looked like someone who would "strangle you from the back," went to sleep.

I find Lax's actions and attitudes here more remarkable than almost any others in his remarkable life. Despite appearances, despite Georges's past, despite what was obviously an overbearing manner, Lax felt content to be with this man who had invited himself into his room. Why? He never really says, although these lines from his manuscript may contain a partial answer:

> georges was
> absolutely real
> absolutely self-contained
> absolutely unimaginative

"In the morning," Lax writes, "the sun came brightly into the room. Georges woke up first and looked toward me with a broad unaccustomed smile: 'hello, meester!' he said. 'hello, meester!' I said and got up to go to church."

That night Lax took Georges to a Russian restaurant he had found, and as they ate their borscht, Georges began to cozy up to a pretty Russian waitress. An accordionist began to play and then a singer began singing Russian songs. The night was just getting good when two "fox-faced cops" burst in and asked for everyone's papers. Georges had only an expired *carte de séjour*, so they took him away. When he didn't come back to the hotel that night, Lax felt bad because he'd picked the restaurant, but the next morning there Georges was, saying the arrest was nothing. The police, in fact, had extended his papers.

Georges suggested lunch at the same restaurant, and when they were through eating, a man and a boy came up to their table. When Georges greeted them like old friends, Lax realized the meeting wasn't accidental. They'd been in jail with Georges, it turned out, and they were worse off than he was. Whether Lax invited them or they invited themselves is unclear, but they spent that night in the quickly shrinking bed.

The woman who ran the hotel—*Madame Maman*, who came down in a flowered dress each night, her cheeks rouged, her hair in spit curls, her mouth sporting a broad gold-toothed smile—didn't care how many people shared a room as long as they all slept in the same bed, but four was clearly too many. So the two newcomers—a short Spaniard named Fernand with two fingers missing on one hand and a shy blond boy named Luigi who had tired of the poverty in his Italian hometown and wandered across the border—went to stay in a shelter. Each morning, however, they returned and the four of them spent the day together.

As time wore on, others came and went too. There was Kerkor the Pole who slept in the room next door, Ramon the Argentine who had worked on a cattle ranch, and Freddy the Greek who repaired all their clothes. Georges was the recognized chief of this unofficial crew—the maker of plans, the arbiter of squabbles, and the ensurer of equality at meals. He was the enforcer of cleanliness too—the difference, he said, between a useful crook and a "vrai clochard." He spent part of each day washing socks and shirts that Freddy would repair and fold and part of it explaining his schemes, to smuggle not only clocks from Belgium but also cigarettes from who knew where.

Most days they would meet for tea and bread at 6 a.m., then Georges would make the round of restaurants looking for work while the others went to the port for the same purpose. There was never any work to be had, so they would all return for lunch or sometime in the afternoon. Then Fernand and Luigi would sit at the open window looking into the room while Lax would stand beside them gazing at the harbor and they'd talk about their lives. Fernand, for example, said that he had tried to join a monastery once, had left Spain to get away from Franco, and had met Luigi while looking for a ship to work. When he wanted to think instead of talk, he'd take out a small mechanical frog and send it hopping across the window ledge.

When it came his time to speak, Kerkor told them of his dream of flying to America. He was only waiting for permission, he said, for his name to rise to the top of the list. He had a picture of the plane he imagined he would fly in and the address of the uncle and aunt he'd stay with in Ohio.

With Georges in control, the men were ritualistic about their meals. They'd start by sending young Luigi out with an old green wine bottle to pick up a liter of milk. When he returned (sometimes with a demi of white wine from the bar they would drink diluted with citronade), they'd pull the table out from the wall and Georges would sit down at it while the others sat on the bed or stood along the wall. On the table would be an opened tin of sardines and a long loaf of bread, surrounded by mismatched glasses. Georges would cut the sardines and deal them out on bread in a clockwise manner, each man waiting with a jackknife or kitchen knife in hand. When the can was empty, they'd drink whatever they had to drink that day and Georges would parcel out squares from a chocolate bar, if they had any chocolate.

Between meals they'd often dream together about sailing off somewhere. The sailing dreams came courtesy of another Russian who joined them from time to time, a man named Plekanoff, who lived with five thin kittens on a rotting boat he called the *Santa Margherita*. A Russian accordionist who stayed with him on the boat sometimes came along for meals. "This is the way to live," he'd say, "in poverty but joyous."

Clearly Lax was different from the men who gathered around him, but this seems to have been little more than a curiosity to them. They noticed, of course, that he had some secret source of money, but they seem to have accepted this as a matter of course. He was American, after all, and Americans were rich, weren't they? Crazy too. They may have wondered where he hid the money, but they never searched for it or tried to force him to tell them.

They were curious about the pictures he put on his wall—prints of a contemplative country scene and a head of Christ by Rouault, an El Greco Madonna, and a miniature by Jean Fouquet of St. John on Patmos writing the Apocalypse (which would inspire Lax to visit Patmos himself years later). When they asked about them, he said whatever came into his head and they seemed satisfied. Their curiosity was just that, without ulterior motive. They were simple men living entirely in the present, which was what Lax liked the most. Every day was the same, yet every day was different. An adventure.

When he wasn't with the men in his room, Lax was out walking the streets, where he met other characters and saw other sights. In his notebook he described the fights he saw, the café lights on cobblestone, and the scuttling of rats through gutters. He wrote of statues masked in lavender for lent, a shoemaker with an aluminum leg, and a monkey in an alley basket. He noted the sadness of the "lady wino," the cross-eyed whore who traveled with her mother, and the "hot white overshoes" of a little girl. "The omphalos of the world," he called this city he loved. "The convergence of nations."

Naïve as he could seem, Lax wasn't unaware that Madame Maman was a real madam or that the girls who gathered on the lowest hotel floor each night were there for a particular reason. He saw them, though, not as sexual objects or as fallen women but as people.

One person Lax felt particular sympathy for was a little girl with blond braids whose mother helped Madame Maman clean. Whenever the girl entered Lax's room, she smiled sweetly but her eyes were sad. The only thing that seemed to cheer her was Fernand's mechanical frog.

---

Perhaps no one intrigued—or frightened—Lax more than a homeless Yugoslav named Raymond. He was "a thing of terror," Lax writes, "a walking windmill" dressed in layers of coats who terrified the passersby he begged from. One misty day Raymond lurched toward Lax and his friends, and Lax, atypically, warned them to watch out for him. In his journal he calls him "a thing of menace, a figure evil, milton's own disconsolate satan." Yet he seems sorrowful when he writes of Italians and Arabs robbing Raymond of his coats while he slept in a doorway, and he notes with tenderness that although the other girls shunned Raymond, one, Yvonne, let him sleep in her bed.

There is one last figure who made a significant impression on Lax, a man he calls only Le Philosoph. Dressed in an army coat and tilted beret, Le Philosoph was northern-looking, with a ruddy face, a short white beard, and bright blue eyes. One day Lax came across him staring at the sea while wearing a work shoe on one foot and a bedroom slipper on the other. When Lax tried to take his picture, Le Philosoph scowled and breathed a low threat: "Police informers often end up in the bay." I've found nothing that says why Lax called this homeless man Le Philosoph, but he seems to have had great respect for him and his wisdom.

When Lax had been in Marseilles four months, he decided it was time to leave. Brother Octavius had offered him an indefinite stay at the Trappist General House in Rome and Merton had told him about a sanctuary in the French Alps called La Salette, where he could stop on the way to meditate. The one person outside his small group he told his plans was Le Philosoph. If he was hoping Le Philosoph would somehow confirm his decision, he was mistaken. "That's good" was all he said. "We all need meditation."

Georges, of course, had a different reaction. "You must not go," he said. But Lax insisted it was time. He was beginning to fall apart, he said—whether emotionally or spiritually or just financially, I don't know. "Okay," Georges said, "then tell me only in which direction you are going: north, south, east, west." When Lax said east, Georges told him, "I will find you."

---

By the time Lax actually left Marseilles, his friends were already gone. Luigi had begun to miss his home, and the men had pooled their money to pay for his passage. Once he'd departed, the others decided to head to Paris, where Georges claimed he had an apartment. From there, he said, they'd go to Belgium, where a friend of his was waiting with a fortune in clocks. Fernand and Ramon negotiated for several days with a driver who eventually agreed to take them for 1,500 francs. If we only had 3,000 francs, we could make it, Georges told Lax. By this point Lax was more than ready to see them go, especially Georges, who, he writes, "had become a frantic dictator in a realm as large as a life-raft." Before Lax could offer the money, however, the plan fell through. As always, Georges had another one: they would go to the train station and buy *billets de quai*, 20-franc tickets that would allow them onto the platform (though not the train). Then, when the train arrived, they'd sneak on and hide in the toilet.

They mulled this plan over for several days, and then one Sunday morning, taking nothing but what they wore or had stuffed in their pockets, they all left. Lax expected them back that evening, but they didn't return. Just before they walked out the door, Fernand reached in his pocket and took out his frog. "Give it to the little girl," he said.

About his time in Marseilles, Lax would write:

I have seen love
As a blinding flame
Whiter
Than sunlight on water.

## 12    Entering the Lion's Mouth

Of all the places Lax told me he had lived, the one I thought I'd never see was his destination when he left Marseilles: the Sanctuary of Notre Dame de la Salette. Early in my research, I found a postcard of it. Perched on a tongue of land high in the French Alps, it was surrounded by mountains and tall green hills with deep ravines between them. According to the map, it lay roughly between Grenoble and Briançon, secondary cities I had never even passed through. Getting there would be too difficult, I thought. Then one June my wife and I were visiting an old friend in northwestern Italy and I happened to mention it. Our friend had a car and wanted to see this place I said was so remote and peaceful. So we piled into her Renault and headed west from Piedmont, winding our way up and up to Corps d'Isère, the only nearby town. From there it was a twisting fourteen-kilometer drive to the glade at 5,900 feet where in 1846 two shepherd children saw a vision of the Virgin weeping. All around us, I knew, were stunning views, but the clouds were too low for us to see them.

Eventually we reached a parking lot and spied the pilgrims' dormitories and the towering basilica through the scrim of fog. Beyond a postage stamp of cleared land, the hillside fell away. I tried to picture Lax sitting in the sun beyond the church writing in his journal as I knew he'd done right there, but I couldn't, not entirely, until we took a picnic up a path beyond the statues of the children and the Virgin where the vision took place. The fields on either side of the ridge were dotted with wildflowers, and as we rose the clouds rose with us, revealing more and more of the panorama Lax enjoyed. We were there, I realized, in the same season he was, so what I saw was more or less what he saw: a fragile perch of spiritual peace surrounded by a patchwork of pleasing greens. Beyond the seemingly benevolent valleys that isolated the sanctuary's thrust of land lay a gray phalanx of white-topped mountains that kept the world out. If you wanted to shut yourself away, hold the world at bay, this was the place to do it.

For a while after leaving Marseilles, that's what Lax thought he wanted. He had tired not only of the men who gathered in his room but also of the city. He'd hoped to write a book while there, but he had written only poems. He'd gone to Mass each morning but lacked the fellowship a place like La Salette offered. The sojourn in Marseilles had been a pivotal period in his life—a time when he had pushed beyond his fears, decided for himself how he would live and, in his way, helped the needy—but he desired something more. What that something was, he couldn't say exactly. A greater focus on his writing perhaps. A more supportive spiritual community. Or maybe a publication of some kind where he could work with others. He must have suspected by then that however much he admired Labre's approach to life, it would never quite be his.

The idea of working on a publication had two sources. Near the end of his time in Marseilles, Teddy Bergery and her husband Jean François had come to visit and Jean François had asked Lax if he'd like to work for a literary magazine he was starting in Paris to be called *New-Story*. At the same time, Lax was thinking of putting out a small publication of his own, a broadsheet of poetry and art dedicated to peace he planned to call *Pax*.

Postwar Paris was filling up again with young American writers, drawn in part by stories of Hemingway and the others who gathered there in the 1920s and 1930s, in part by the eternal lure of Paris itself, and in part by how cheaply they could live there. Still fairly young himself, Lax too must have felt the pull—thinking perhaps, as others did, that Paris would offer the best of living in New York without the worst. Paris would be more expensive than Marseilles (or La Salette), but he would have a job.

Surrounded by other pilgrims, many of them simple people from the rural areas of France, Lax spent his time at La Salette in meditation and prayer, in gentle conversation over morning bowls of *café au lait* or frugal evening meals, and in writing—journal entries, poems, and postcards scribbled on that terrace by the church. He brooded about his future too, but sitting there surrounded by those hills and mountains, the world in which decisions were important must have seemed particularly remote. If he hadn't already made plans to stay at the Trappist General House in Rome, he might never have left La Salette.

But the time for Lax to settle down had not yet come. When May turned into June, he roused himself and set out on the road again, stopping in Turin, Milan, and Bergamo on his way to Rome. His time in Rome the year before had been too short to see much of the city and he planned to stay much longer this time. He didn't have much money, but the Trappists' invitation to stay as long as he wanted meant he didn't need much. Or so he must have thought.

The Trappists gave him a quiet room at the back of their large house on Via Santa Prisca and he settled in, writing on his little portable with the windows open to alleviate the heat. He loved everything about the house: the roses in the garden, the chanting in the chapel, and the roof with its view of the city. As the days wore on and the pages piled up, his circumstances seemed unusually ideal—he was living with monks without having to be one and he could pursue whatever he was interested in without having to worry about room and board. But one day, due to his own negligence, the idyll came to an abrupt end.

The problem began when the monks moved him to a room next door to the prior. Like most Italians, the prior was accustomed to taking a siesta in the afternoon, when Lax liked to write, the clatter from his typewriter drifting out into the hot June air. After enduring the clacking keys for several days, the prior asked Brother Octavius to speak to Lax, and then, when Lax continued to type, spoke to him himself, gently and modestly. For some reason Lax didn't heed either of these two warnings, and so a visiting Irishman told him bluntly it was time to leave.

---

So many events in Lax's life seem to have biblical parallels; this one, I suppose, would be titled *Expulsion from the Garden*. Never one to be angry, Lax felt only dismay. He was down to his last 2,000 lire—about $3. Teddy Bergery had told him if he ever needed money all he had to do was ask, so he walked to the Western Union office and spent a quarter of what he had left on a telegram that began with a single word: *Urgent*.

Then he waited. But no reply came.

Worried he might have to spend the night on the street, he took his camera and his only other significant possession, a black overcoat, to the Left Luggage Office at American Express while he tried to decide what to do. While he was there, a thin young man with a pimply face asked if he wanted to sell his camera. When Lax asked how much, the young man led him on a circuitous route to a bar where a fat man sat at a table in back. When Lax showed him the camera, a simple Brownie Reflector, the man turned it over and offered only a few hundred lire. Lax decided to keep the camera, but now he was back to where he had started.

He still had one hope, however. Before going to American Express, he'd arranged to meet a man he called Michael the Russian, an acquaintance perhaps of one of the men he'd known in Marseilles. The camera incident had made him late, and he reached their meeting point, the Bernini Fountain near the Spanish Steps, just as the Russian was leaving. Hoping perhaps for a handout or a loan, Lax asked if he could accompany Michael to his hotel on the fashionable Via Veneto, but the Russian said no. When Lax asked when they could meet again, the Russian said, "I'll see you when I see you," and Lax was alone once more.

Poor as he had been before, Lax had never been this low, this lacking in options. He sat down on the Spanish Steps and wrote a long meditation on *waiting*. Noontime came and went and he was hungry, so he wandered the side streets until he came upon a man selling tiny tomatoes from a wagon. On his way back to wash them in the fountain, he bought a bread roll with the last of his money. Then he sat down next to an American tourist in a Tyrolean hat and, without knowing what might come along, went back to waiting.

The shadows of late afternoon were crossing the square when he recognized a bearded man with a walking stick—a man he called "the knapsack prophet"—heading toward the fountain. He had talked to the man in St. Peter's Square the Sunday before but he wasn't sure the man would remember him. As soon as the prophet sat down, the American in the hat started quizzing him about his beard and his stick, but the prophet gave only enigmatic replies. "His eyes were a misty blue and looked far off," Lax wrote about him later, "yet when he had a point to make he would flash them at his opponent." When the prophet saw the name of Lax's camera, he asked if Lax knew what a *brownie* was. "A spirit," he said, "in the mystical language."

Lax doesn't record why he called the man a prophet or what caused him to follow him, but follow he did. Maybe he thought the man was truly mystical or maybe he looked like someone who knew how to survive on the streets. The man begged food from a convent, preached to children who gathered around him at a fountain, and stopped to pray in a church. When evening came, he took bread, milk, and cherries from his knapsack and shared them with Lax, crossing himself before every bite. After the meal he suggested they sleep on the long, broad steps of the Church of Santa Maria Maggiore. When Lax hesitated, the prophet said, "You should not be afraid of these hardships. Remember Dante and how he suffered for his vision. Remember the life of Benedict Joseph Labre, who is now a saint."

Lax doesn't record his thoughts at this moment other than his concern for his two possessions, the coat and the camera, but it must have been eerie to hear this man who seemed to be living so much like Labre mention the saint the baroness had told Lax to emulate. And Dante too, one of the writers Lax admired most. Did he know at this point that it was on the steps of a church in Rome Labre collapsed and died?

A crowd had gathered around the two of them while they ate, and when the philosopher paused to answer their questions, Lax slipped away. As he did, he saw what he thought was admonishment in the philosopher's eyes. Admonishment for what, he didn't know. For holding himself back? For not being willing to commit wholly to poverty? For not fully trusting that God would take care of him? He had moved to Marseilles as a way of conquering his fears and he thought he'd succeeded, but here he was clinging to something as small as a camera and the desire to sleep in a safe place. He wanted to believe that God's love was sufficient, as Labre had believed and Dante had written, but he was afraid and his fear made him feel ashamed.

As he walked, he chastised himself, and when he reached the Church of Santa Maria Sopra Minerva, he looked down at the narrow stone apron in front. I could sleep here, he thought, remembering the prophet's words: "You should not be afraid of these hardships." But he felt too distraught to lie down, so he kept walking. Eventually he came to another church where, on the cornerstone, he saw the words *Bocca di Leone*— Mouth of the Lion.

"I read it with fear," he wrote later, "and halted before it."

Signs were everywhere, it seemed. Biblical parallels. He thought of Daniel in the lions' den, how God had honored his faith by sending an angel to keep the lions' mouths closed. Standing there, he felt more afraid than ever before and he made a decision: he would enter the lion's mouth. He would trust that God would be with him.

———————

Although he records this decision, Lax doesn't say what it meant to him—whether it meant only letting go of fear or being willing to live with nothing. He walked away, praying, but he didn't go to sleep on church steps. Instead, when he saw a small hotel, he asked if he could have a room without paying. He would leave his passport and his camera there until he could find the money, he said, and the innkeeper took pity on him. The next morning, as he drank his coffee and ate a croissant, he felt ashamed again. His faith was not yet whole. Not yet pure.

After breakfast he headed back to the Church of Santa Maria Sopra Minerva to pray, and on the way saw two girls collecting contributions in cans. "Giornata di Dante," the cans said. It was June 13, the day in the *Commedia Divina* that Dante started his journey through Hell. Lax hurried on to the fountain to see if Michael the Russian might be there, but he saw the prophet instead, descending the Spanish Steps. He watched him glide across the square to the fountain and scoop water into his mouth, the morning sunlight glistening in his beard. When the prophet looked up, Lax greeted him, hopeful perhaps that they could reconnect, but the prophet turned without saying a word and started back up the steps.

———————

With his passport and camera held hostage and no money to redeem them or buy a meal, Lax went back to waiting, trying to trust God, and, as would happen many times in his life, the right person came along: a Columbia classmate. Although they hadn't known each other well, the man took pity on Lax, introducing him to an American named Peter who lived nearby. The Chilean artist Roberto Matta was using one of Peter's rooms as a studio, but Lax could sleep there at night, he said.

It turned out that Peter worked at Cinecitta, the Italian Hollywood, dubbing films into English, and harbored a secret desire to win the Prix de Cannes with a film of his own. One of his reasons for letting Lax stay in his house was to learn from someone who had worked in the real Hollywood. Lax didn't have much practical advice to offer, but he offered what he could: stories. One of his stories—about traveling with the Cristianis—came close to causing more trouble.

One day while they were driving in Peter's Jeep near the Forum, they saw a sign advertising a circus. "We can make a movie short of it," Peter said right away. "A day at the circus. A day in the life of a clown. How about that?" Few things excited Lax more than a circus, but he had no desire to get involved in the kind of thing Peter suggested. As he waited for the circus to arrive, his hopes that it might somehow save him were burdened by fears that Peter might ruin his interactions with the performers. As it turned out, he needn't have worried. Before the circus appeared, Peter had moved on to other things.

When the circus finally came, it came quietly, as a battered dump truck carrying a load of soil. None of the people in the truck looked to Lax like circus people, until a young blond man with a performer's muscles leaped from the back. From that day on, Lax went to the Circus Maximus every day for the month the Alfred Court Zoo Circus was in town. Run by a clown named Achille Zavatta, it was a French circus passing through Rome on its way to Pescara and other towns along the Adriatic Coast, and Lax began to hope that when it left he could go along. Although he still wanted to write about Marseilles, he hoped to start a new writing project: chronicling his travels with another circus.

In *Voyage to Pescara*, a combination of journalistic observations and poems that wasn't published until the year he died, Lax describes the acrobats arriving in an open convertible and, behind them, a long line of red trucks with gold lettering and roustabouts perched on tents on top. The trucks wound into the Circus Maximus, but the setup didn't begin until a blue-eyed worker with "sun-textured flesh" dropped his shirt on the field "like a blessing." As he had in his earlier cycle of poems, Lax sanctified the circus by connecting it with biblical imagery:

The circus is here
and this cloth shirt
is the first cloth to touch it;

the first
and smallest
curtain
of the
tabernacle.

"One of the central metaphors which *Voyage to Pescara* presents is that of the circus as the Tabernacle which Moses and the Jewish people traveled with in the desert," writes Paul J. Spaeth, curator of the Lax archives at St. Bonaventure University, in his introduction to the book in which the poem cycle appears. "The Tabernacle itself was a tent surrounded by an open court and was placed in the center of their enormous camp. Just as the priests ministered to the people out of the Tabernacle in the wilderness of Sinai, so the performers and workers of the circus are depicted as modern-day priests ministering to the needs of the people who come to watch."

Lax does indeed play with this idea, but unlike in *Circus of the Sun*, where the analogy between the circus and Creation becomes a controlling metaphor perpetuated throughout the cycle of poems, the Tabernacle theme appears only sparingly in *Pescara*. Perhaps because Lax spent much less time with the Alfred Court troupe than with the Cristianis and paid less attention over time to *Voyage to Pescara* than *Circus*, his chronicle is much less lyrical and evocative. Much of it reads like notes for a future work rather than a work itself. But it does tell us key things about his travels with this group of Frenchmen.

For one thing, he introduced himself as an American journalist, acquiring a cachet even his connections to other circus performers didn't offer. Whatever attraction being written about held for them, however, it's clear the circus people invited him along mostly because they liked him. During his travels with the Cristianis Lax had usually worked, but this time—traveling from Rome to Rieti, Aquila, Populi, and finally Pescara—he simply observed and took notes. With the Cristianis he'd always watched the shows, but this time he sat outside or went for a walk instead. He had grown too fond of the performers, he said, to watch their daring acts.

It wasn't the spectacle Lax liked anyway, so much as the circus atmosphere and people. One night when the evening's performance had ended, he reclined on his borrowed mattress and took it all in: "I lay still, watching the tent move in the slight breeze, shadows of the ropes in moonlight moving, as the canvas moved; looking, too, at the iron stake with hammered head. Lions, muffled in their cages, roared. The tent breathed heavily, creaking at the poles like a vessel at anchor."

Several small observations that didn't make it into the edited version of *Voyage* hint at the deep admiration and love Lax held for the circus people and the life they lived. In one place he writes that he spent the last of his lire on a pack of cigarettes for Harry, the worker responsible for slaughtering donkeys to feed the lions. A few pages later he set down the following observation without comment:

almost every night
william randal
a tall dancing
clown
in a pork-pie hat
and nono
a gentle dwarf
in a clown-suit
would walk together
to nono's wagon,
a little rounded
trailer
his father
had built for him
they walked
across the field
like friends from school
to the step
in front of
nono's door;
here, after
a last few
minutes of talk
william randal
by a push or a
nudge at the end of a joke
would lift him up
into his door

and say *bon soir*
*mon vieux*
while nono
blessed him
with his hand
and smile.

Much as Lax loved circus people and life on the road, however, there were times when his wandering and lack of a home made him feel unsettled. He'd been in Europe for most of a year by then, and one evening, while sitting outside alone during a sold-out show, he felt the divided nature of his current life acutely:

> I felt melancholy and yet untroubled; curiously estranged but at the same time at home. It was as though, sitting on this dark rock on a far-off hillside, I had been carried home for a few minutes to sit in the darkness of the hills I knew; hills I knew as well as my own blood, whose depths I had measured as well as my own heart's, but which in the end I knew no better than the hills around me now (no better and no less). For I was close to each, and far away. Almost weeping, yet with an endurable sorrow, I looked out over the valley, down into its darkness. Not far off down the road, in a rising mist, was the strand of lights which looped before the tent.

When the circus reached Pescara, where he saw the Adriatic Sea, he called Peter in Rome and learned that his nephew Dick Marcus and Bob Mack were on their way to Italy to see him. Much as he loved being with the circus, the pull of family was stronger. And so he said a sad goodbye to his new friends and, as Fritz and the others took down the tents, went to the beach for one last swim.

"As I crossed the road toward the ocean," he writes, "I saw the circus trucks rounding the corner and heading north toward me and San Juliana. Fritz was first, he honked and waved. Then the red truck of Robert the chauffeur; Nono the dwarf rode in it and leaned out of the window and waved. Then one, then another, until they had all passed. Then I walked toward the shore and looked out at the sea where the sun, slowly rising, laid down a white path of light."

Not far away, in the direction he gazed, lay the Greek islands where, a dozen years later, he would finally find the home he needed.

# 13    Paris, *Jubilee*, and Kerouac

Lax and I shared many loves, including a love of Paris. I spent so much time there during my travels, I knew it better than any city except my hometown of Seattle. One year George Whitman, who had resurrected Sylvia Beach's Shakespeare and Company Bookstore, invited me to stay in one of the rooms he reserved above his shop for young writers, but for some reason I didn't do it. Lax was much less hesitant to make a move like that, especially to a place where his hero James Joyce once lived.

By August 1951, when Lax left the circus in Pescara, Paris had revived its reputation as the number one destination for American tourists and English-language writers, including African American writers like Richard Wright and James Baldwin, who found it much more welcoming than Jim Crow America. Joyce was gone, of course, as were Hemingway and Fitzgerald, but the writers who called it home at some point during the 1950s included William Styron, Irwin Shaw, Terry Southern, Gay Talese, Allen Ginsberg, William Burroughs, and George Plimpton, whose *Paris Review* became the most famous—and enduring—of the literary magazines Americans were founding there.

Pleased as he was to be with family again, I suspect that Lax's departure from the circus was driven primarily by his belated decision to work on Jean François Bergery's new literary magazine, *New-Story*. Bergery had told him no doubt that the magazine's editor would be David Burnett, whose parents had founded *Story*, one of the most admired literary journals of all time. By the time Lax reached Paris in September, the magazine had already published works by writers like Baldwin and Ray Bradbury and even a piece of Lax's circus cycle titled "Circus of the Sun," the first time he'd used that name in print. He had every reason to believe the magazine would be successful. Beyond that, as usual, he needed money.

---

Mack and Marcus had purchased a cheap Renault in Paris and driven down the French Riviera before picking Lax up in Rome. They were on a lark and Lax was happy to travel with them and postpone taking another job for a while. He took them to Castel Gandolfo to see Pope Pius XII and rode with them as far as Milan before catching the train to Paris on his own while they went climbing in the Alps. A few days later they swooped through Paris to pick him up again and cross to London, where Lax's old friend Bob Butman had become an assistant to the playwright Christopher Fry. Fry's firm belief in God, pacifist leanings, love of theater, and strong connection to T. S. Eliot must have led to interesting conversations, but Lax left no record of them. Before long, while Marcus headed to Scotland, Lax and Mack were off to Dublin to take photographs for a pictorial companion to *Ulysses* Mack hoped to create. Then Mack went back to the States and Lax returned to Paris, planning to stay a while this time.

By the time Lax took up his editing duties, Burnett had left and a young Columbia graduate named Bob Burford had taken over. Among the writers Burford was planning to publish was a young man he'd met in his hometown of Denver, an unknown he thought showed uncommon promise named Jack Kerouac. Burford encouraged other editors to publish Kerouac's writings too, and when Lax came on board he pressed him to read them. Whenever letters from Kerouac arrived, he'd show them to Lax, who long remembered one in which Kerouac said he thought he'd call his generation the Beat Generation. Within a short time Lax himself was corresponding with Kerouac, beginning a friendship that would reach its apex five years later in New York. By then the deadly fame that followed *On the Road* was making Lax the kind of friend Kerouac needed.

----

Most of that first year in Paris Lax stayed with the Bergerys and then the Burfords. At one point he lived on a picturesque square called Place Dancourt. It was the perfect place for him—halfway between the artistic heights of Montmartre and the intriguing lower life of Pigalle, with a theater in its midst. His building was the former home of the Selmer brothers, famous for manufacturing clarinets, the instrument he played as a child. And the *New-Story* office was only a short distance away. He wasn't paid much for his work, but in those days you could live in Paris on as little as $80 a month, even without free housing.

Although he'd spent years writing for magazines of one kind or another, Lax hadn't worked as an editor since college or read submissions in the numbers he was reading them now. He'd never cared much for short stories, but he found he liked reading them in manuscript, even those by undeveloped writers. "You listen," he wrote to Van Doren, "as you would to a friend who stuttered." (In this same letter Lax mentioned Van Doren's son Charlie, who would become well known a few years later for his role in the quiz show scandals. Charlie had a fellowship that allowed him to live in Paris while writing a novel, and he and Lax met infrequently at a local café.)

During Lax's year and a half at the magazine, before it folded in February 1953, it became known as one of the best of the many English-language journals founded in the French capital in that decade. Three of its stories appeared in *Best American Short Stories of 1952* (edited, conveniently, by Burnett's mother, Martha Foley)—as many as the *New Yorker* and *Mademoiselle* and one more than *Atlantic Monthly*. (Only *Harper's*, with four, had more.)

But despite contributing to a successful enterprise, having an income, and being in a city he loved, Lax never felt entirely comfortable in Paris. It wasn't Paris itself but living in a city again, any city. So when the Bergerys introduced him to a young man named Jean Vanier who lived at a Catholic retreat center in the suburb of Soisy-sur-Seine, a half-hour train ride from Paris, Lax was quick to visit and, in short order, move there.

Vanier, who would go on to found L'Arche, a Christian organization that cares for mentally disabled children around the world, was at the time the twenty-three-year-old son of Georges Philias Vanier, a former governor-general of Canada who had become the Canadian ambassador to France. The center where he lived, L'Eau Vive, had been established as a place of contemplation and prayer by Père Thomas Philippe, one of Vanier's theology professors at Paris's Institut Catholique, with help from the Catholic philosopher Jacques Maritain. It was housed in what was left of a residence once owned by Louis XIV's lover Madame Pompadour. But while the buildings had once been grand, they were crumbling now and the living was simple. The only adornments were the plentiful wild-flowers brightening the unmown fields. In other words, it was the kind of place Lax had come to prefer. A photograph from that time shows him sitting cross-legged on the overgrown lawn in front a dilapidated stone building, the sleeves of his wrinkled work shirt rolled to the elbows, looking calm and content.

When Lax wasn't in Paris or at L'Eau Vive, he was often visiting his friends from the Alfred Court Circus, who wintered on a farm near Marseilles and performed in nearby towns. An unpublished manuscript in Lax's Columbia archives chronicles his interactions with his old friend Fritz and another circus worker, Harry, who worked for a while selling ads for *New-Story*. It reveals much about how Lax looked and felt at that time. "His face is thin," Harry says about him, probably during the time Lax was still living in the city. "His eyes are not the same. At Rome he was happy. He would come at 5 o'clock in the morning taking photos all day, talking to everyone, always happy."

"We were happy there," Lax says about their travels in Italy. "We are not happy here. We must find a place where the three of us can live peacefully."

During this period of his life, Lax was unusually sensitive about how he acted and spoke, feeling acutely any suggestion that he might have hurt someone. This sensitivity led to an almost painful analysis of his interactions with this group of circus workers. However complicated the relationships were, though, his affection for Fritz—like his affection for Mogador Cristiani—never wavered. "The Lord shines through him as through a window," he writes of Fritz. "The light must shine through a lot of hurly-burly, but it comes through clear and strong. I do not know whether Fritz is a saint, but I believe he is a man. His is a spirit living close to the earth, bound now to the earth, but capable of soaring above it. The earth, I feel, needs saints who are men."

The two men might have remained friends the rest of their lives had a falling-out with Harry not ended Lax's friendship with Fritz too.

––––––––––

Much as Lax liked living at L'Eau Vive, once *New-Story* folded he had no particular reason to stay around Paris, but he was unsure what to do next. "More and more I become a total clodhopper," he wrote to Merton, "saying yes when I mean no and driving along with no apparent fog-lights. Pray me out of weariness: I want to be agile for good."

The real problem was he didn't know what *doing good* meant at that moment. He dreamed of returning to La Salette, living and writing in a quiet room in a seminary in Corps, but he had hit a wall with his writing (or at least the publishing of his writing) and he wasn't sure devoting all of his time to it was the right choice. The publisher who'd given him the advance had rejected his circus manuscript, and when he sent it to Bob Giroux, the Columbia classmate who had published Merton's *Seven Storey Mountain*, Giroux said it "made him sad." "I wondered whether he sent it to you, " Lax wrote to Merton, "whether you had been saddened by it too, and whether that meant that after all, I was in an alley?"

But even as publishers were rejecting the book, the *New Yorker* was accepting parts of it. In addition to "Circus" that May, the magazine would publish "Sun Poem" in its August 15 issue and "Solomon's High Dive" on August 28, 1954. And Ed Rice was bending Lax's thoughts toward New York for another reason: that May he would launch a magazine there called *Jubilee* and he wanted Lax to help with it.

Since at least 1950 Rice had been talking to Lax about starting a lay magazine for Catholics patterned on *Look*, with three-quarters photographs and one-quarter text. This was the latest manifestation of a conversation that had been going on in one form or another since the two men and Merton and Reinhardt had had such a fine time working on *Jester*. As Rice certainly knew, Lax was a poor choice for a partner as far as practical matters went, but he was often brilliant in conceptual matters. Like Rice, he had experience in the commercial magazine world and he was deeply spiritual. Beyond that he had strong ties to many Catholic intellectuals and he was one of Rice's closest friends, someone Rice trusted entirely.

Rice laid out his approach to the magazine in a letter to Merton in June 1950. In essence he wanted to cover all of the wonderful subjects in Catholic and non-Catholic spiritual circles that the narrowly focused mainstream Catholic publications ignored—subjects like Friendship House, black Catholics, Russian Orthodox mystics, artists, visions, St. John of the Cross, and St. Benedict Joseph Labre—and he wanted to do it in a contemporary style, with large, quality photographs and illustrations.

Although he told Merton he wouldn't worry about his readers' intellectual level, the magazine he envisioned was clearly aimed at Catholics with intellectual and artistic interests—the kind of Catholics who had made Merton's autobiography a bestseller. The only problem was that the rich Catholics who might have backed his enterprise didn't think most Catholics were interested enough in intellectual matters for the magazine to succeed. Throughout 1951 and 1952, as Rice refined his plans, he worked tirelessly to find investors, but in the end he was forced to rely on the inventive but dubious approach spelled out on the first page of the magazine's inaugural issue in May 1953:

> In a plan inspired by the Social Encyclicals, the first 50,000 subscribers will receive one share of Class A stock with each one-year subscription, paying $5 for the package.
>
> As a charter subscriber, you will thus share in JUBILEE'S profits and its successes. Only 50,000 charter packages are being offered (many have already been bought), so reply immediately.

For those who weren't interested in having a stake in the magazine, a regular subscription cost $4 and the per-copy price was 35 cents.

The stock scheme helped launch the magazine, but it never brought in enough for Rice to pay adequate salaries or take one himself. Throughout *Jubilee*'s thirteen-year existence he was constantly hustling for funds, constantly fearing that each issue would be the last.

---

It's difficult to determine just how involved Lax was in *Jubilee*'s early days. For the first four and a half years of the magazine's existence (it lasted through September 1968, although neither Lax nor Rice was involved after 1967), he was listed as a "roving editor." Most of that time he lived in Europe, receiving $75 a month for sending in periodic articles and occasional photographs on subjects that interested him. His first piece for the magazine, a brief history of his favorite circus family called "The Incomparable Cristianis," appeared in the inaugural issue. Almost a year would pass before his second, a feature on a Little Brothers of Jesus congregation in the town of Berre-l'Étang near Marseilles. It featured photographs by a young man who had fled France with his Jewish mother during World War II, Jacques Lowe, who would go on to be President John F. Kennedy's favorite photographer. In an interview years later, Lowe gave an inkling of what it was like to work with Lax:

I told Lax which stories we were supposed to do: Catholic youth, Sisters of Mercy, a few others. He said, "Relax, relax, these are boring stories. We'll go see the gypsies, and the circus in the south of France."

"What do those stories have to do with *Jubilee*?" I asked.

"Everything has to do with *Jubilee*," he said. "Don't tell Rice, we'll just do the stories."

According to Lowe, the two hitchhiked to a gypsy encampment at Ste. Marie de la Mer and Lax went straight to the trailer of the King of the Gypsies. Using approaches he'd learned during his travels, he introduced himself as an American journalist and told the king that Lowe wanted to leave his camera with him while they looked around the camp. "I nearly pissed in my pants," Lowe said. "I had a single old Nikon with two lenses, the only camera I owned, but we left it with the King and, of course, it was safer there than it would have been in a bank vault. And we got a wonderful story."

Lax stayed in Europe as long as he could, but Rice kept asking him to return and he had no clear reason to be there, so in December 1953, he moved to New York for what would be a five-month stay. It was during this time, at a party hosted by Bob Burford's sister Beverly, that he and Kerouac finally met face-to-face.

Later in the 1950s, when Lax moved back to New York for a longer period, he and Kerouac would come to know each other quite well and talk about a wide range of subjects, but during their first encounters their conversations seem to have centered on Christianity and, more specifically, Catholicism. As he did for most of his adult life, Kerouac was living with his devoutly Catholic mother, and in those days before *On the Road* he was considering turning more fully toward Catholicism rather than away from it, as he did later. One of the things that initially attracted him to Lax was Lax's friendship with Merton, whose writings and monastic life Kerouac admired. As he and Lax spent more time together, he began to see Lax himself as a paragon of what a Catholic could be: a man devoted to both art and the search for truth who chose to live in poverty and simplicity. When Lax was about to return to Europe, he invited Kerouac to come live with him at L'Eau Vive (which Kerouac thought was some kind of monastery) and Kerouac considered it.

If Kerouac had had the money, he might have followed Lax to France that summer, but once Lax was gone, Catholicism lost its appeal. By the time he sent a long letter to Lax at Corps d'Isère on October 26, 1954, Buddhism had eclipsed Christianity in his affections, and the one thing that might have saved him from his sad end—a sober spiritual existence within a community of humble and simple believers—was lost.

"O no, Bob," he wrote, formally rejecting Lax's offer,

> I dont want to go to France too badly (Europe's precisely what I'm try-ing to get away from)—my interest is turning to the desert, next Spring I'll be there, in a hut, prove at last by example not only by words—Bless Jesus.
>
> . . . I'm no saint, I'm sensual, I cant resist wine, am liable to sneers & secret wraths & attachments to imaginary lures before my eyes—but I intend to ascend by stages & self-control to the Vow to help all sentient beings find enlightenment and holy escape from the sin and stain of life-body itself—I'm afraid of going to France—impatience is my chief weakness—but thank God I'm a lazy bum, because of that repose will come, in repose the secret, and in the secret: Ceaseless Ecstasy.

In a note following this letter in *Jack Kerouac: Selected Letters 1940–1956*, the editor Ann Charters quotes a 1954 entry from Kerouac's note-book in which he lays out a plan to reach Nirvana by the year 2000. It begins with giving up alcohol and "chasing after women" in 1954 and es-tablishing an "elementary diet" in 1955. I can't help seeing Lax's influence—and example—in these resolutions. He had seen how benefi-cial similar changes had been for Merton as well as himself.

In *The Long Slow Death of Jack Kerouac*, Jim Christy suggests intrigu-ingly that Kerouac's decision not to follow Lax and the more traditionally Catholic path Lax represented might have been the beginning of his de-mise as a writer. (Although they weren't published until years later, Ker-ouac had already written the books most critics consider his best.) "Kerouac had been corresponding with an editor named Robert Lax who was a convert to Catholicism," Christy writes. "When they finally met, the conversation was entirely on religious matters. When Kerouac ex-pressed his desire to go on retreat, Lax offered to get him into a monas-tery in France, but by the time it was arranged, Jack's head had been turned by Buddhism." Buddhism, Christy asserts, robbed Kerouac's writing of its magic, as terminology replaced "the Kerouac sound and distinct description—the thing described and the heart of the thing described."

In a long letter he sent to Kerouac around this time, Lax expressed a similar concern. The letter, written in the long sentences Kerouac favored, reveals so much about the relationship between these two men it's worth quoting at length. All of the idiosyncrasies in punctuation, capitalization, and grammar are Lax's:

> Dear Jack,
>
> thanks for letter, dont think from silences and taciturn answers that i don't appreciate or that they less than dwell with me, i walk around talking to you, most often just after noon, and it is too bad for us both you are not here, because at least it would be nice, anyway the cat and the diamond sound were wonderful, and most of what you said moved me, comme poetry; philosophy i don't know anything about, and anyway i think it is the heart not head that talks in your writing, and the heart is no dummy. (big mistake of wolfe and whole crack-up crowd was thinking they needed ideas, or at least that they needed to express or even masquerade them; homer didn't have any of that nonsense (as far as i know) and dante had the wisdom to take a cosmology he had been born into, understood and in his heart believed, more than adequately for him, and on the basis of that began to make music (with minor changes) as did bach; thinking now a good artist is (not impossibly) a conservative, not in the final impact of what he has to say (which is said in talking about roses) but in bringing from his store old thing and new; the whole vocabulary of your heart is christian and Catholic; it would surprise me if you (or anyone we know) could ever become more than a pocket-book buddhist; anyway i don't for the moment think it's new ideas we need but a neat neat clarification of our own old ones.

It is easy to see the influence here of Brahmachari, the Hindu monk Lax and Merton knew back in college—his advice to study one's own tradition first.

Kerouac must have told Allen Ginsberg about his plans to join Lax in France because one night that summer Ginsberg had a dream in which he visited Lax "in a large secular monastery near Paris." In the dream Lax had given up writing poetry to run the place. "He is empty so he has taken on this discipline," Ginsberg thinks in the dream. "I am his prob-lem—I realize we all are."

---

However much he enjoyed talking to Kerouac and being with old friends like Rice, Lax wasn't comfortable living in New York again, and the only work he really wanted to do was write, so on May 14, 1954, he returned to Europe, where his heart had been all along. For once he knew exactly where he want-ed to be: in a little room off the hallway in the seminary in Corps, just down the hill from the Sanctuary of La Salette. Solitude was calling.

Lax spent the next year and a half hidden away in an area he called the most peaceful place in the world. It was there, on October 13, 1955, that Mark and Dorothy Van Doren found him living, as Van Doren reported to Merton the next day, like a man in paradise:

> I called from a neighboring town to make sure he was there. He was, and the next morning we arrived by car to spend two very happy hours with him, mostly in a little visitors' room where we had coffee in bowls about the size of your head, but also, just before we left, in the garden where Bob knew the names of all the vegetables and flowers. He named them like Adam, then photographed us standing among them.
>
> He is in a fine state, I think, but fears he will have to go back home before too long. Apparently he could stay there forever, looking at the mountains and the trees.

While Lax lived in Corps, his "roving" work for *Jubilee* provided an income well above his modest cost for room and board, so he could have stayed there indefinitely. But much as he loved his quiet life among the seminarians, he was still restless. Still unsure where he should be. The Little Brothers of Jesus had offered him a kind of hermitage not far from Marseilles, where he'd be near his circus friends' farm. Someone else with land in Normandy had invited him to stay there. Then there was Paris, especially L'Eau Vive, where he went whenever he could. And of course Rice was always calling him back to New York.

In those days there was a Carmelite in Paris named Père François de Sainte-Marie, who offered spiritual guidance two afternoons a week at Saint-Joseph-des-Carmes Church. Lax knew the father to be a wise man, so he went to him with the question of what to do. Père François listened calmly, then drew a circle, dividing it into several segments and writing the name of one of Lax's choices in each. For this many months of the year you go here, he said, then for this many months you go there. The plan seemed feasible to Lax, but before he could put it into practice, he received an urgent telegram from Rice. *Jubilee* was growing rapidly and he needed Lax's help.

"I went right back," Lax told me. "There was no question about it, just as there hadn't been when he wired for me to be baptized. I'd learned long before that if Rice said something it was probably a good idea."

———————

Not long before Lax left Corps for good, one of the most significant of the many fortuitous and usually serendipitous meetings that happened throughout his life took place. A young Swiss photographer named Bernhard Moosbrugger and the young writer he often worked with, Gladys Weigner, were in Paris visiting Gladys's husband Fritz, who had gone there to paint, when they met Teddy Bergery. At the time, 1955, they were hoping to start a newspaper focused on peace. They thought of it not as an international newspaper but what they called a "supra-national" newspaper, seeking greater world understanding by making links between continents. When she heard their plans, Bergery told them they had to talk to her old professor, Robert Lax. She showed them a yellowing photograph of Lax, and when Fritz said he had a good face, Moosbrugger and Weigner set off in search of him.

They found him at La Salette, in the garden Van Doren had written about, sitting next to an old lion tamer. When they told him why they were there, Lax suggested he go with them to their hometown of Zurich to talk about their plans. Moments later they were off, not knowing they were starting a friendship—and eventually a publishing partnership—that would last the rest of their lives.

Lax spent almost two weeks in Zurich talking to his new friends about their project, going to a circus that came through town, and teaching Moosbrugger to juggle. Although he shared their excitement, he had watched Rice struggle to launch *Jubilee* and knew that starting a publication wasn't easy. When they told him they had no money, he suggested they find their way to the States, where he would introduce them to Rice.

So that's what they did. An American presidential election was coming up and they found a magazine willing to send them over to cover it. Rice did what he could to help them, improving the English translations in their prospectus and giving them funding tips, but despite some interest from the Ford Foundation, the money never came through. When they returned to Europe, they took with them only a name an African priest had suggested for the paper, *pendo*, which, in Swahili, means *love*. They would never publish the paper, but years later they would start a publishing house, in part to print Lax's work, and they would call it *Pendo*.

---

Lax arrived back in New York on December 20, one day later than his return two years before, but he didn't start working regularly at *Jubilee* until he had visited Olean. *Regularly*, of course, is a relative term when talking about Lax. His *Jubilee* colleagues saw him as a kind of rarefied spirit, appearing for a while and then vanishing, either into his office or into the city. His approach to work frustrated Rice, but the *Jubilee* staff found him to be a comforting, even sanctifying presence.

"He was tall and thin, with large teeth and a long, bony horseface that had its own rough beauty," Richard Gilman wrote, "and he walked in a loose-jointed, hurrying manner, perpetually leaning over as though in search of something valuable that might be on the ground. Though he could be dour at times, he could also be extraordinarily funny, with a Jewish, almost Talmudic, flavor to his wit, heavily involved as it was with self-mockery and verbal capers. (I remember a postcard he once sent me that bore only these words in elegant script: 'Where There's an Oy, There's a Vey.')"

The most striking thing about Lax in photographs taken in those days is how thin he is, especially his face, with its long prominent nose, cratered cheeks, and deep-set oval, almost Asian eyes. His hair is still dark but has receded to the middle of his head, the smooth roundness of his forehead giving his face the shape of an inverted pear. There is something otherworldly about his looks at this moment in his life, as if he were only visiting this human community going about its human activities. They are not the looks of an angel, as some would have you think, but of an alien, a being whose natural environment is elsewhere.

When Lax did work, the work he did was sharp, particularly his editing, a skill he'd honed while whittling down his own work. "Lax's idea of a perfect editing job was to slash through the whole piece with a red pencil, until only one key word or, at most, sentence was left," Wilfrid Sheed wrote. "He was generally right in his choices but we couldn't afford the blank space."

"If you worked with Lax you didn't need Strunk and White," the photographer Charles Harbutt said. "My eight pages of pictures and his forty words caught the whole story." Oona Sullivan, a *Jubilee* secretary and later editor, told me that Lax once reduced the history of the Catholic Church to one page. Later he edited the Bible to a single sentence: "God is love."

During the six years Lax worked for *Jubilee*, it was an important voice in American Catholicism, giving lay Catholics a perspective on living as a person of faith in the modern world refreshingly free from Church sanction. Beyond that it looked much better than other Catholic publications, with pleasing layouts and an abundance of quality photographs. Rice couldn't afford to pay much, but he had a keen eye for talent and was adept at persuading some of the best young writers and photographers in New York to work for him. He took risks too. With its unsanctioned and often controversial approaches to hot-button Catholic issues, including birth control and the atomic bomb, *Jubilee* was like an unruly child raising a ruckus in the rumpus room.

That chaotic, creative mix wasn't just on its pages. Inside the magazine's main office, where the air often smelled of sauces being made in the Chinese restaurant downstairs, impromptu parties were always erupting. "Our artists and writers were a bit crazy," Rice told one interviewer. "They could not have worked on a staid magazine. Actually *Jubilee* was a kind of extension of *Jester*—an unstructured creation."

Sheed paints an even more colorful picture: "At *Jubilee*, we strove to outslob each other in dress—if neckties were worn, it was around the waist—and my own particular makeshift office consisted of a drawing board in the middle of a clearing, from which I could hear every conversation in the joint. Rice had practically a real office, in which we tended to eat sandwiches, and Robert Lax had another next to the fire escape, so that he could duck onto it and crouch when he didn't feel like visitors."

Of all the young talent at *Jubilee*, the person Lax became closest to was an illustrator and designer named Emil Antonucci, who would end up being more important than any other single figure in the development of his career. A descendant of Sicilian immigrants with a gentle personality and a fine arts degree from Cooper Union, Antonucci was looking for work in the early days of the Korean War but hesitant to take a full-time job because, although he had filed to be a conscientious objector, his draft status was uncertain. He tried to survive as a freelance designer of book covers but work was hard to come by. So he put together a portfolio of what he'd been able to do and, since he was a Catholic, took it to the Catholic publishing house Sheed & Ward. They didn't have anything for him, but they'd heard that Rice was starting a Catholic magazine, so they sent him to *Jubilee*, where, in the early months of 1954, he met Lax.

Given how gentle both men were, they must have taken to each other right away. At some point, Lax—"with his usual grave modesty," Antonucci said—showed his new colleague some of his poetry, maybe even the circus cycle, which he was circulating to friends and anyone else who would read it, still looking for a publisher. Reading Lax's work, Antonucci told me fifty years later, was a turning point in his life. He knew right away that he had to get it into print.

Shortly after their first meeting, Antonucci was walking down Beekman Street when he saw a hand press in a printing equipment company's window display and fell in love. The company was willing to sell it and he had a place to put it—the basement of his family's house—so he bought it with his last few dollars. The machine was an old Washington model used as a proofing press in the 1880s, virtually the same kind Benjamin Franklin used. What Antonucci liked most about it was its simplicity and the sense that he was making something by hand, adding creative value to whatever he might publish. He had to print each sheet manually, and each impression took a full minute, so he couldn't print anything long or elaborate. He knew right away that Lax's poetry, with its spare beauty, was just right for it.

When Antonucci told Lax about the press and suggested they publish a book together, Lax of course said yes. This was in the spring of 1954, however. Before anything could happen, Lax was on his way to Corps.

Their plans and even their association might have ended there if Antonucci hadn't gone to the New York Public Library one day and happened upon something called the Spencer Collection. Many of the best painters in France at the time were doing illustrations for finely crafted, limited-edition books intended to show off their art. Several of these were in the Spencer Collection and when Antonucci saw them, his life changed. "I realized there was a relationship between the fine arts and books," he said. "It was a dream."

To find his way into that dream, he applied for a Fulbright grant to live in Paris and study deluxe editions of these kinds of illustrated books. Then he took a handful of poems about trees Lax had sent him, added his own woodcut illustration, and printed them on paper made from Japanese magnolia trees. When the Fulbright came through, he tucked a few of these tall, skinny chapbooks into his bag and took them to Paris. It was there, in the City of Light, on his way back to *Jubilee*, that Lax saw his work in a stand-alone form for the first time.

Lax's mother's family, the Hotchners, in 1901. *Back row*: Henry, Rebecca (Betty), Maurice, Celia; *front row*: Sol, Rosamund (Roz), Hedwig. Courtesy of Soni Holman Fink

Lax's family at the time of his birth. *Back row*: Gladys (Gladio), Sally (Sal), Sigmund (Siggie); *front row*: Robert (Bob) in his mother Betty's arms. Courtesy of Connie Brothers

Lax with his mother, Betty (*center*), and sister Gladio on a boardwalk somewhere after the Lax family's move to New York City in 1928. Courtesy of Connie Brothers

Lax with his spiritual advisor, Father Irenaeus Herscher, outside the Friedsam Memorial Library at St. Bonaventure College (now University), where Lax worked on his first book, *The Circus of the Sun*, in a basement room in 1949–50. Courtesy of St. Bonaventure University

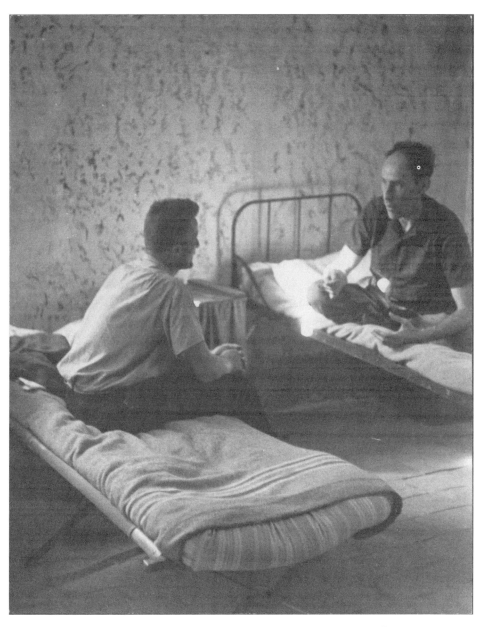

Lax (*right*) with an unknown acquaintance during his three-month sojourn in Marseilles in 1951. Courtesy of the Robert Lax Literary Trust, from the Robert Lax Collection at Columbia University

Bob Mack (*left*) and Lax in Rome in August of 1951. Note the duffel bag under Lax's arm.  Photo by Dick Marcus

Lax on the overgrown grounds of L'Eau Vive, near Paris, where he lived in the 1950s. Courtesy of the Robert Lax Literary Trust, from the Robert Lax Collection at Columbia University

*Left to right*: Ad Reinhardt, Thomas Merton, and Lax at the Trappist Abbey of Gethsemani in 1959. Courtesy of The Merton Legacy Trust and the Robert Lax Literary Trust

Emil Antonucci (*right*), who published Lax's early books and chapbooks, bidding him goodbye as he departs for Europe in the 1960s. Photo by Stephanie Rancou

Limnina the "rug girl," one of Lax's first friends on Kalymnos, with a young helper outside her house, in the mid-1960s. Photo by Robert Lax, from the Robert Lax Collection at Columbia University

Lax in one of his many Kalymnos rooms, with one of his many cats, in October of 1972. The rug is probably the one Limnina wove for him. Photo by Jim Sugar

Lax with the author and an unidentified cat outside his house on Patmos in 1992. Photo by Sylvia McGregor

Lax going shopping on Patmos in 1996. Photo by Nancy Goldring

Lax writing on his bed on Patmos in 1997, three years before he died. Photo by Judith Emery

# 14   Inspiration in a Greek Diner

One day in the spring of 2013 a stiff brown envelope with a large red label saying *DO NOT BEND* arrived at my door. Inside, sandwiched between thick pieces of cardboard and wrapped in a covering of cellophane, lay a twice-folded piece of fifty-five-year-old newsprint 46.5 centimeters high and 30.5 wide. Its mere existence seemed phenomenal to me; that Lax and Antonucci had conceived and created it, a miracle.

One of the craziest things I discovered in my research into Lax's life was the collectibles market for his poetry. I always assumed that literary collectors were interested only in that signed first edition of Joyce's *Ulysses* or one of those J. D. Salinger letters. What I learned is that fame is only part of the equation; scarcity is important too. If the scarce item is also fragile, so much the better. Since all of Lax's early publications were small-run labors of love assembled and printed by Antonucci, the current prices are often astounding. The single broadsheet I bought—issue #3 of a publication called *Pax*, with poems by Mark Van Doren and Peter Lewis (a nom de plume Lax sometimes used) down one side and an Antonucci illustration of twenty-one orange balls down the other—was a bargain at $50. Other issues of the same publication, which originally sold for 20 cents, were being offered at $200 or $300 if the writing in them was original work by Merton, Maxwell or e. e. cummings, $1,000 if it was by Kerouac. I don't know if knowing this would have made Lax laugh or despair.

---

Lax started thinking about creating *Pax* when he was still living in Marseilles. His idea was to promote peace by publishing the works of poets and artists he admired. The poems and art didn't have to be about peace, he felt, because poetry writing and art making were already peaceful—and therefore peace-promoting—activities. By the time he moved to Paris in 1951, he already had poems for the first issue from Merton and Van Doren. For his own contribution he was trying to choose among three poems, including what would have been the first excerpt from his *Circus* manuscript to be published. In the end he did choose that one, but by the time that first issue of *Pax* came out—five years later—the poem had already appeared in the *New Yorker* and other *Circus* poems had been published too.

While working at *New-Story*, Lax shared his ideas for *Pax* with Burford, who helped him plan it. Thanks to Burford, who had no qualms about approaching anyone, by the time Lax sent a dummy copy to Van Doren in early 1953 he had verbal commitments from Matisse, Chagall, Léger, and Breton to contribute art. A year's subscription would cost $1, a single issue 10 cents.

Lax envisioned a monthly three-page magazine on light paper with a first run of fifty thousand. Unfortunately he was a better dreamer than marketer. Although he was able to sell a few subscriptions to friends, what came in wouldn't have financed fifty copies, let alone fifty thousand. He had to wait until he was back in New York, where he could use leftover paper from *Jubilee* and had Antonucci to help him.

When the first issue finally appeared, in late 1956, it bore the three original poems but had been scaled back to a one-page broadsheet mailed to a few supportive friends. Other issues followed—eighteen in all between 1956 and 1962 and three more in the 1980s—but instead of monthly they came out infrequently, whenever Lax and Antonucci could get one together, and the price was slightly higher: five for a dollar.

*Pax* didn't send shockwaves through the literary community or convince nations to lay down their arms, but each issue was greeted with delight by those who received it. The writing Lax coaxed out of friends such as Merton, Kerouac, Maxwell, and cummings was worthy of publication in the finest magazines, and Antonucci's imaginative designs added significant value, giving each issue a distinct look.

———————

The years Lax spent in New York between 1956 and 1962 would seem on the surface to have been settled and gratifying years of work for *Jubilee*, but they were some of the hardest years of his life. He was entering middle age now and he still wasn't sure what he should be doing. For the most part he hated living in New York, hated all the city stood for as well as the need to work at something other than his poetry each day. Eventually he stopped writing poetry altogether and gave up on finding a publisher for his *Circus* manuscript. After a trip to Kentucky to see Merton in May 1956—the first time they'd seen each other in seven years—he stayed in a third-floor walkup on the Lower East Side and seemed to endure his life rather than really living it.

The apartment was one of two *Jubilee* kept as "hospitality suites" for writers or guests coming through town. According to Tom Cornell, a Fairfield College student who spent a night there that spring and eventually moved in, the lightbulbs were all burned out and Lax found him a bed by putting his hand on several to see if anyone was sleeping there. The building had been condemned after World War I but reopened during the housing crunch after World War II.

"There was only one w.c. for the four apartments on our landing," Cornell remembered. "There was a bathtub in each kitchen, with a lid that served for food prep. There was no heat or hot water. The rent was $20.68 a month. The people in the other *Jubilee* apartment [Bernhard Moosbrugger and Gladys Weigner] were given a key to ours so they could use our stove and refrigerator. Very chummy, but, oh, so cold!"

Both Cornell and another roommate, Joe Rush, worked with Dorothy Day's *Catholic Worker*, and during this time Lax himself came to know Day. His archives include photographs he took of her being arrested. But he was never more than a fellow traveler, one of many Catholics who hung around the *Catholic Worker* headquarters because, as Oona Sullivan—who worked at different times at *Jubilee*, the *Catholic Worker*, and Friendship House—told me, those were "the only places for liberal Catholics to go in those days."

Although Lax was mostly silent when he was at home, he was "a presence," Cornell writes, teaching this younger man by the gentleness of his movements how important a simple presence can be. "That glum, bitter cold winter of '56–'57 subdued us all. There was not much of Lax's playful nature on show. I huddled in the only stuffed chair we had, with my overcoat on, reading Herodotus in Greek, while Lax stalked. He needed space to walk back and forth to compose his lines. Finally he and Joe [Rush] found a heated apartment on Ludlow Street that had a corridor he could walk. But by then the cold had seeped into Lax's bones, always to burden his health."

The new apartment was actually a couple blocks west on Norfolk Street, near the Williamsburg Bridge and maybe two miles from where Lax's cousin Soni was living. The difficulty Lax had making decisions during this time is illustrated by a story she tells of inviting him to her place for dinner. They went out together to buy lamb chops from a butcher near her apartment and ate a meal she remembers as ordinary. Normally Lax didn't visit that area except to see her, but a couple months later she ran into him on the street. When she asked where he was going, he said, "I wanted lamb chops." For two months, whenever he felt like lamb chops, he had walked to her apartment and followed the route they'd taken to her butcher.

Antonucci tells a similar story. Whenever Lax went to lunch with his *Jubilee* colleagues, he waited for someone else to order and then ordered the same thing. When they realized what he was doing, they'd sometimes wait until he had ordered his copycat dish, then change their original order to fluster him. According to Rice, Lax wasn't indecisive so much as eager to please, his order a show of support for someone else's decision. Sometimes he'd accept three or four invitations to dinner on the same night, just because he didn't want to turn anyone down, and when the evening came, he would either send a written excuse to all but one or not go out at all.

———————

Lax stayed with Rush through August 1957, when he came down with rheumatoid arthritis so bad he couldn't work anymore. Wanting to spend less time thinking about what he was eating so he could focus on what he should do, he had started to consume only dairy products. His extreme diet sent him to a hospital in Buffalo and then to Olean to recover. To lower his sedimentation rates, his Buffalo doctor put him on Butazolidin, a powerful analgesic and anti-inflammatory that was relatively new at the time (and, because of its dangerous side effects, is used now primarily to treat horses). After taking it for a while, he was able to manage his condition by taking aspirin and vitamin C—and, of course, changing his diet.

Lax suffered from several physical ailments during his years in New York. They may have been the cause of the glum silence Cornell noted, but a more likely cause was the feeling he had of being trapped in New York. He needed money and he wanted to help Rice, but his real desire was to be on his own somewhere else and just write.

"So many haven't found themselves—the eternal struggle," his uncle Henry Hotchener wrote in an encouraging letter. "You're not one of them, for you understand the innerness of all life. And are more and more beautifully expressing it through every line you write. Do keep on, despite the obstacles that confront you, as every other genius." Encouragement came from others too, but Lax's battle was as much with himself—his desires, his habits, his lack of a clear vocation—as with his circumstances.

While he recuperated in Olean, Lax tried to write about Marseilles but couldn't find the right approach, and he couldn't focus on anything else for very long. He enjoyed working on *Pax*—sending copy to the *Jubilee* secretaries, who maintained his subscriber list and put out new issues according to his instructions—but the lack of publisher interest in the *Circus* manuscript continued to sadden him. His despondency deepened in late February 1958, when Bob Mack, who was the most physically vibrant man he knew, died at forty-five.

The only thing that brought Lax real pleasure during this time was journaling. So he journaled, sometimes twenty or thirty pages a day. When he told Merton it seemed the calmest and "most legitimate" thing he could be doing, Merton encouraged him to journal even more, telling him it was his way of fulfilling David's call to sing a new song to the Lord.

What Lax didn't realize yet was that a truly new song was on its way. The people he knew in New York, the experimental atmosphere there, and even his bout with arthritis were helping to bring it forth. The arthritis (caused by insight, Rice joked) seemed nothing more than an awful affliction, but it freed him from the daily work at *Jubilee* to spend idle days in Olean. Those idle days allowed him, however haltingly, to give concentrated thought to his poetry again. And it was that concentrated thought, coming so soon after the stimulation of New York, that nudged him toward the kind of experimental writing he would do the rest of his life.

The poems Lax wrote in Olean during the fall and winter of 1957–58 weren't his best—most of them fell somewhere between his naturally spare style and some idea of how poetry should sound borrowed from someone else—but in time they became sharper and more concrete. What was most important wasn't the work itself but the thinking he was doing about it, most of it during those long journaling sessions. Despite taking over as executive editor of *Jubilee* when he returned to New York in the spring of 1958, he found himself feeling freer and more directed as a poet. It helped, of course, that Antonucci had good news for him: he had received a Guggenheim grant he would use to publish "the long abandoned circus book."

---

From the time Antonucci first read Lax's poetry, he was determined to see as much as possible put into print. His efforts in this regard started with the hand-press publication of "Tree," copies of which he delivered to Lax in France. When his own time in France ended, he returned to New York, arriving a few months after Lax. There, while earning his living doing illustrations and graphic design for *Jubilee* and other publications, he picked up where he'd left off, printing hand-press versions of three other Lax poems—"Juggler" (four pages, 1957), "Question" (four pages, 1958), and "Oedipus" (twenty-eight pages, 1958)—each with his own woodcut illustrations.

With the hand press he could publish only short pieces with small print runs, but he knew Lax was having difficulty finding a publisher for his longer circus work, so he applied for a Guggenheim to print experimental books and, when it came through, put the whole $4,500 into publishing a hardcover version of what would be called *The Circus of the Sun*. He found a quality printer willing to do small runs, Joe Blumenthal at the Spiral Press, and laid out the pages himself, alternating poems in straight type with others in italics. He added his own simple line illustrations at the beginning of each section and put starkly dramatic black-and-whites by the *Jubilee* photographer Charles Harbutt on the covers: an elephant silhouette beneath a dark circus tent and a full moon on the front, a high-wire acrobat in front of bright tent lights on the back. Just when Antonucci thought everything was done, the printer called to say they didn't have a publisher's name on the title page. Antonucci knew that printers started out as apprentices and became journeymen next. He figured he'd graduated to this second level, so he called it Journeyman Press.

The galleys arrived in August 1959. ("Most beautiful," Lax wrote in his journal.) The book was just sixty-four pages long but it would sell for only five dollars. The print run too was modest, just five hundred copies, each one signed by author and artist. When Lax and Antonucci picked them up, Blumenthal hefted one in his hand. "I'd say you'll sell a hundred copies," he said.

I haven't found a journal entry recording Lax's feelings the first time he held a copy of *Circus of the Sun*, but it must have been unusually satisfying. Seeing one's first book is a thrill for any writer, of course, but *Circus* was more than just a book. It was a burden relieved, a past life finished. He was forty-three years old, and now, thanks to Antonucci, he had tangible evidence of his art and talent. Evidence too of his faith, expressed in poetry Denise Levertov called "dreamlike and vivid."

"The effect of 'Circus of the Sun' is the same as the effect of the first chapter of Genesis," wrote William Packard, the future *New York Quarterly* editor. "There is movement and truth because there is order and purpose."

Mark Van Doren thought the book filled with grace, and William Claire, who reviewed it for *Stars and Stripes* (and would later dedicate an entire issue of his literary journal, *Voyages*, to Lax's writing), praised it for "evoking the wonder and the beauty of motion and people and ideas and faith as they come to expression in the lives of the people who work under the big top."

e. e. cummings, who chatted with Lax when their paths crossed in Washington Square Park, liked the book so much he invited Lax to tea to talk about it and circuses, which cummings had written about too.

Unsurprisingly Merton was the book's biggest fan. "It is one very fine book, all the way through completely fine," he wrote to his friend, "and it says real good all that you have been wanting to say, and that is a lot, because you have been wanting to say more than most people who are content with selling somebody something for some money."

Merton made a habit of recommending the book to anyone he thought could appreciate it or make it more widely known, including

James Laughlin and Boris Pasternak. Even so, it sold poorly, as the printer had predicted, despite reviews in *America* and *Commonweal* and a prize for its design.

---

Before Antonucci received his Guggenheim, setting in motion all that led to the publication of *Circus*, Lax had dithered over the manuscript for years. The need to come up with a final version must have caused him panic but it also seems to have quickened his blood and given him confidence. Over the winter of 1958–59, as he worked more regularly at *Jubilee* and made final *Circus* decisions, he continued the writing he had been doing in Olean, turning his journal into a laboratory as he worked toward a new poetics he could truly call his own.

"Most people think of writing as a message to people to get them to think or respond in a certain way," Antonucci said about his friend's poetics shortly after he died, "but Lax's intention was to explore his own mind—to examine how his thoughts worked, how he perceived the world. Whether a reader understood that or was changed by it wasn't really important to him. He wanted an audience, of course, but on his own terms. He wasn't trying to persuade anybody about anything."

In the late 1950s and early 1960s, when he was working most closely with Antonucci, Lax was coming to a similar conclusion. After his months in Olean he focused more intently than ever on what for him were twin ideas: the need to seek God constantly and the need to state his true thoughts in words that were all his own. Seeking God and seeking his true self were essentially the same pursuit, he thought, since the purpose of life is communion with God. To say what he really thought—to *know* what he really thought—he needed to spend more time in prayer and contemplation.

This may sound like a simple idea, but it wasn't to Lax, who believed himself to be connected to and yet distinct from God. His desire in watching the world and watching himself was to see the manifestations of God in the common life outside and inside himself. What bothered him most about living in New York were the ceaseless distractions, empty philosophies, and false desires that made it hard to see clearly and listen well.

The greed and possessiveness around him bothered him too, less because of what they caused people to do to others than what they caused people to do to themselves. In that long meditation on poverty I quoted several chapters ago, he writes:

> Deprived of *being* we have recourse to *having*, which is indispensable for us, and good, as long as we know how to use it largely and simply for our real needs. But there is a danger: *having*, in giving us many things (burdening us) weighing us down, gives us the disastrous illusion of making up for our deficiency of being, and we are always tempted to look for a (consistency) in it, to attach ourselves to it as to a security, and to accumulate more and more . . . instead of turning ourselves, as empty as possible, toward the Source of being who alone is capable of satisfying our thirst and giving us happiness joy blessedness.

What Lax truly wanted to do was return to somewhere like Corps where he could live simply and cheaply—being without having—receiving whatever graces came. But he had made a commitment to Rice and he hadn't figured out yet how to live without income, so he did what he thought was the next best thing: moved from the city with its many distractions out to Jackson Heights in Queens. There, with a group of religiously minded Catholics, he lived just a mile from the Elmhurst neighborhood he'd lived in as a child.

The new apartment was one of two lower units in a four-unit complex on a street of identical buildings. Each unit had three bedrooms: two in front and a quieter one in back. Lax had the back one all to himself, but it was no paradise. The walls were covered with overly delicate roses and the floor was a depressingly green linoleum. What few furnishings he had were gifts from friends: a chest of drawers, some bookshelves, a record player. Everything else was easily movable—boxes of journals and poetry, a portable typewriter—as if he intended to flee at any moment. Maybe he did. It's hard to imagine a blander environment or a life less suited to his propensities. To make matters worse, by the spring of 1959 his roommates were getting on his nerves and he could feel his arthritis flaring again. Tired of taking the subway each day, he thought about moving back to Manhattan. But he stayed where he was, giving himself the following instructions:

set yrself a time of day to read torah/
study/
and use carbon paper/
and take walks/
and speak little/
and work well/
breathe deep/
bear fruit well/
eat/
not much but
often/

During this time he began to read a new translation of *The Midrash on Psalms*. The Psalms had long been a model for his own poetry, and he felt comforted by the midrash idea that all of literature—in fact all of life— should be a commentary on the Bible. His comparison of the Old Testament with the New had convinced him that progress toward God was an upward movement through the stages of Power and Wisdom to Love, and he tried to find signs of that movement in what he called the "carbuncles" around him.

At the end of June 1959, shortly after visiting Merton with Reinhardt, he moved with a single housemate into a quieter apartment next door, but he still felt at odds with his environment. While Antonucci imagined the bland, identical houses in Jackson Heights to be "filled with probably smouldering and wildly various lives," Lax saw only dullness and busybodies who spent their time being suspicious of others. Welcome as the greater solitude in his new residence might have been, it made the split in his world more severe. Weekdays he rode the hated subway into the city and did his best to help Rice run *Jubilee*. Nights and weekends he stayed alone in his room or went for solitary walks around the neighborhood. Sometimes he just listened to Indian music or, more often, Bach. He liked Indian music because it seemed both "primitive" and highly civilized, but it was Bach he truly loved, Bach who inspired him as an artist because he saw and expressed the whole of creation.

When he wrote for himself in those days, he wrote about his life, trying to figure out who and where he was. Writing about himself, he thought, helped him see where he was running in circles and where he was moving upward. His fear of running in circles was especially strong because he was

living so close to where he had lived as a child, but he was aware that re-
turning to a familiar place might help him see how he had changed too:

> you never
> step into
> the same stream
> twice
>
> nor even
> into
> elm-
> hurst

Agonizing as it was for him to spend half of his time immersed in the
overstimulating social world of Manhattan and the other half in relative
seclusion in a cookie-cutter house on an unimaginative street in Jackson
Heights, this clear-cut division was exactly what he needed to see himself
clearly and, ultimately, act decisively. It was the difficulty of the division,
in fact—the anxiety it produced—that forced him to act to resolve it.

By the end of 1959, whatever interest Lax had once had in running a
magazine, attending parties in Greenwich Village, or pursuing "success" as
America defined it—even as a writer—was gone. Over the past three years
he'd seen Bob and Nancy Gibney's marriage end in divorce as Gibney sank
deeper into paranoid self-loathing fueled by alcohol; watched Kerouac re-
act to his own success by sinking into an embarrassing despond of drunk-
enness and dissipation; witnessed the awful effects on Rice of money
worries and criticism from conservative Catholics; and, in recent weeks,
followed the unfolding quiz show scandal engulfing his young friend Char-
lie Van Doren. He was sick of what he had to do to make a living, sick of the
world he felt forced to live in, sick of America—not of the people he knew
or Americans in general but of what America's culture, especially its busi-
ness culture, did to sensitive people with talent. This sickness went hand-
in-hand with fear: for his own talent, his pursuit of God, his life.

---

Like everyone connected to the Van Dorens, Lax was extremely proud of
Charlie's success on the quiz show *Twenty-One* in 1957. His pride turned
to elation in early 1959 when Charlie read from *The Circus of the Sun* while

featuring the Cristianis on a culture segment he'd been asked to host for NBC's *Today* show. Then came the news that Charlie had been fed the quiz show questions in advance. When Lax found out, he didn't know what he could do, but he knew who—or rather *what*—was to blame. "As soon as I heard about it I went over to the church and prayed," he wrote to Mark Van Doren in October 1959, "and that's what I've continued to do. I won't bother you with any of my ferocious sentiments nor yet too much of my arcane gnosis that these things are all arranged so Babylon can fall again: Babylon, Arkansas & N.B.C."

A couple days later he sent Van Doren another note: "[Charlie's] just like Gulliver in a crowd of Lilliputians: he'll show them what they are and who he is."

Then, on November 2, after Charlie had finally admitted his part in the scandal, Lax sent him these words:

> If by some crazy miracle you had been "totally innocent"—I wouldn't have known how you felt—but now I do.
>
> Have always (as you certainly know) admired you—but now much more.

When I interviewed Charlie forty-four years later, he still remembered—and cherished—that note.

Rice and the others at *Jubilee* continued to admire Lax for his intelligence and spirituality, but the more dissatisfied he became with his work, the more frustrated they became with his laissez-faire approach. He came and went when he wanted to, edited idiosyncratically, and often pursued his own interests instead of magazine business while at the office. One of those interests was *Pax*. Another was his publishing with Antonucci.

It's impossible to overstate Antonucci's importance to Lax during the last two years he lived in New York and, in a slightly different capacity, the years after that. In addition to publishing Lax himself, he promoted him to editors and bookstores, negotiated publication arrangements, and, most important, lavished him with praise. For Antonucci, who was young and believed wholeheartedly in the value of art, Lax was a pure artist unencumbered by commercial concerns. He honored everything Lax did and considered it a privilege to work with him, even if that meant paying for things himself. While trying to build his own career as a designer and illustrator, he promoted Lax tirelessly without being paid a penny.

But even Antonucci's partnership and promotion couldn't make Lax want to linger in New York, where he felt mired in a workaday world awash in materialism. In fact Antonucci's enthusiasm for his poetry strengthened his desire to escape. The stronger that desire grew, the uglier the world he lived in looked and the more despondent he became. Some nights he'd stay in one of *Jubilee*'s Manhattan apartments and go on nighttime walks that left him standing in front of luggage stores or brooding over coffee in Greek diners. One cold night an old Greek waiter offered him a cigar. Lax tried to refuse it but the man insisted, so he took it, and soon the waiter was talking about his homeland. It was beautiful and warm, he said. It never snowed. He went on to describe the landscape and the people, then said, "You ought to go there. You ought to go to Greece."

Lax doesn't record what he replied but months earlier, when his *Time* colleague Alex Eliot had been brooding over what to do with his own life, Lax had encouraged him to go somewhere where he could write freely and Eliot had chosen Greece, in part because it was cheap.

Beautiful, warm, and cheap—what better place could there be?

# 15    A New Poetics

On a late June day in 2003 I ignored the lifeless papers waiting for me in Lax's Columbia archives and caught the subway to 14th Street to meet the most important living connection to his days in New York, Emil Antonucci. The temperature hit 90 that day and I was sweating more than was comfortable as I approached Charlie Mom, the West Village Chinese restaurant he had suggested. We had spoken by phone, and of course he'd agreed to meet me but I didn't know what to expect. He had declined other interviews, I'd been told, because his decades of work on Lax's behalf had gone unacknowledged in a prominent collection of Lax's poetry. He was still angry. Still hurt. Would he be guarded or evasive, I wondered, or would he trust me?

As I approached the restaurant, I saw him from down the block. I knew it was him because I'd seen a picture somewhere—the black hair, the round face, the dark skin. I was still several steps away when he glanced in my direction and, without a moment's hesitation, smiled. I knew then that we'd get along fine.

Charlie Mom's was mostly a takeout joint with a compact seating area. We sat at a small table next to a brick wall, our voices soft at first, then rising above the increasing din. Some people thought he was Chinese, he said, making conversation, and I could see it. His eyes were more horizontal than most Caucasian eyes, his nose was broad, and his skin had that reddish-yellow tone that could be Native American too. His face, in fact, could have put him in any number of races or cultures, but he was Sicilian, he told me, through and through. That was the reason, he joked, he was still angry three years after Lax had died.

He said he was angry, anyway, but once we got talking, all I saw was affection for Lax and a kindness that ran so deep I knew exactly why he and Lax had been good friends. We wound up talking for almost three hours, and he would have gone on longer if I had wanted to, just to help me. Before he had come to meet me, he said toward the end, he told a

good friend of his, "The first thing will be to decide if I can trust him."
Obviously he did.

A few weeks later two large packages came in the mail. One held an
assortment of old Lax books Antonucci had designed and published, in-
cluding one of the original five hundred copies of *The Circus of the Sun*,
signed "For Michael, Emil." The other held audiotapes of Lax reading his
poetry—readings no one had ever heard. Along with them came a note
saying he would look for other materials. Before he could find any,
though, he died.

----

Even in his seventies Antonucci radiated the kind of creative energy that
characterized New York City during the years he and Lax collaborated
there. New York was not only the U.S. center for commercial art and
publishing in those days but home to a growing number of small presses
and experimental artists. Eager as he was to leave New York, Lax would
say later that he could not have written the breakthrough poems that
appeared in his second full book anywhere but there. And it's doubtful
Antonucci would have felt inspired to do what he did with Lax's work in
many other places.

The change in Lax's poetry over those years was so severe, Denise
Levertov, who had praised his *Circus* cycle, said it saddened her. Others
just shook their heads at it. Lax didn't care. He had been looking for a
style, an approach, that reflected more accurately who he was—how he
saw the world—and the stripped-down, vertical style that came out of
this period fit his perspective perfectly. An added benefit was that he'd
never have to consider commercial concerns again. His new poems
were so different, so seemingly simple and yet unique, only other avant-
garde artists could appreciate them. And at first only Antonucci would
publish them.

----

Many artists Lax knew during these years influenced his development,
but the two who made the most impact were Kerouac and Reinhardt.
Kerouac helped him think differently about how he wrote, and Reinhardt
helped him find his way beyond artistic conventions.

It was after Lax's return from L'Eau Vive in 1956 that he and Kerouac became good friends. In his forties already and a committed Catholic, Lax attended few of the parties at the center of the Village scene except when Kerouac came to town and coaxed him out. "I'd usually find him at the apartment of a friend, downtown," Lax said, "in one of the 'villages' during a moment's lull in a party that had been going for a day or so, and might go on for several more; I'd stay around for a couple of hours of wine, song, and high-flying conversation, then get back home." They often talked by telephone too. During one of their conversations Kerouac handed the phone to Ginsberg. "Lax," Ginsberg said without introduction, "do you believe in God?"

While convalescing in Olean a short time later, Lax wrote the following and sent it to his new friends:

POEM
(for Jack Kerouac and Allen Ginsberg)

The monks and cokies sought him
        in their ways
(The ways were rough; the ways
        were never plain;)

They sat up all night begging
        him to be:
To show himself, that is, to
        come in fire;

At last he did come caroling
        down the skies,
And sent them screaming

For yosemite.

The poem was typed, but Lax added the following in a handwritten circle: "In love and games of the imagination. What we are doing doesn't matter so much as what we're pretending to do."

———————

Lax's main attraction for Kerouac seems to have been the purity and simplicity of his spiritual pursuit. When Lax asked him to write a jacket blurb for *The Circus of the Sun*, Kerouac wrote, "Robert Lax, simply a Pilgrim in search of beautiful Innocence, writing lovingly, finding it, simply, in his own way." Almost equally attractive were Lax's friendship with Merton—the two of them talked about going to visit him together—and his devotion to Catholicism. It was the last of these, no doubt, that caused Kerouac to invite Lax to spend the Christmas of 1958 at the Northport, Long Island, house he shared with his mother.

As Lax told the story, he arrived in Northport by train on Christmas Eve and Kerouac picked him up. They entered the house by the back door, and there was the formidable woman everyone called *mamere*, looking "just like him." She had an obvious love for her son, Lax thought, a love that had made her skeptical of her son's claims about his friends. "This is Bob Lax," Kerouac said as the two shook hands, "he's a saint." His mother fixed Lax with a weary smile. "Everyone he brings out here," she said, "is either a genius or a saint."

Despite her skepticism, Lax found much to like in her. She was as talkative in person as her son was on the page, and, like him, she could tell a good story. In the one Lax remembered, she asked a clerk at the supermarket one day if she knew where to find a kitten to adopt. "Right here," the young woman said, leading her down into the basement of the store where the family cat had just given birth. Of the four or five kittens there, mamere felt drawn to one that was tiny and feeble.

"You don't want that one," the clerk said. "He'll only live for a day."

"Well, he's going to have one very nice day," mamere replied.

The cat had grown big and fine by the time Lax visited.

Lax and Kerouac stayed up until five in the morning in Kerouac's attic room talking happily "about everything." They read passages they liked from *Finnegans Wake* and Kerouac read some of his unpublished poems, including a long poem he'd written on a beach in California that reproduced the sounds of the sea (something Lax would do himself in more than one poem years later). Sometime after midnight several teenagers Kerouac had befriended in the neighborhood stopped by, and they all ate cake and drank wine together. Lax hung around a while the next day before returning to his Jackson Heights home, thankful no doubt to have spent such an intimate time with a writer he admired.

Kerouac never addressed Lax's writing in print, but as early as February 1958 he was aware of Lax's distinctive emerging style. In a letter to Don Allen at Grove Press about putting together a "big hep review" of Beat works, he suggested specific works from Ginsberg, Gary Snyder, John Clellon Holmes, William Burroughs, and many others, ending with:

A
lil
beato
pome
by
Bob
Lax
mebbe
too

Lax never published anything on Kerouac's writing either, but in several journal entries and in conversations years later he expressed admiration for Kerouac's approach. In a September 2, 1973, journal entry he summarized Kerouac's method and its effect:

the big thing, says j ker, is to have a scene in your mind, some whole scene in your mind, a whole epiphany, & write from that, not hurrying to reveal where & what it is. Keep it there as a source of strength, a shaping force for the way things go, for the direction eventually all things take. you're writing about something because you are writing about something, but you're in no hurry to reveal what that thing is; not yet, not till it's ready. (until i've circled around a subject a hundred times or so, you'd hardly know what it was until i landed.) but all the circling helps: helps you know what it is when we land there, & helps me land just right.

Just over a month later, in an entry about different kinds of writing he liked, Lax wrote:

the reckless writers (reckless riders) may be exemplified by henry miller and kerouac: both really reckless and really great. They're like the wild horn players in jam session jazz: the "knockout-guys" of the thirties: jimmie mcpartland and others: given to blowing hard fast hot wild extempore, and always seeming to drive toward a kind of epiphany at the end. Jackson Pollock was that kind of painter: in spite of great knowledge of technique, he painted as he drove, like a wild man (or so we are told). Louie Armstrong drove hard too, but with more control, and probably in the end better further deeper than knockout wildmen. I wouldn't compare him to henry miller. I'd rather compare him to rabelais in all this. spontaneity, humor, good humor, and drive, but at no point a real loss or willful slackening of control.

Refining his view of spontaneity versus control a little further, he wrote:

I think when perfection has gone too far, the spontaneous writers have to come in, like barbarians, & break it all up again. That's their function, and some are born, and given all grace to perform it. but imperfection can never be an end in itself: perfection can, or within its own self-imposed limitations it can. And so, imperfect writing will always at a certain point begin to lick itself, and work, at a pace of its own, toward perfection. Artless writing will work toward art: there can be no lasting art of "artless writing." And since there cannot be, why not start at the beginning with canons of perfection? Why not? because without the volcano's flow as a base our ideas of perfection will be too limited to be of much worth: we will go out with butterfly net to catch a whale. The whale, beloved, is the human spirit, and it will not willingly enter its own small traps.

Consciously or not, Lax was looking for a way past the hesitation and second-guessing he felt characterized his writing, and Kerouac's approach, with its bypassing of the mind's editor, looked promising. But Kerouac's writing was garrulous and choked with words, while Lax's instinctive style was lean and elegant. How could he let himself go and yet preserve the essentials of his own style? This was the question he needed to answer to free himself as a writer.

Lax and Kerouac seem to have been closest during the two years after *On the Road* came out. (Lax was in Olean when it appeared; he returned to New York to find that Kerouac had become famous overnight.) A few months later, in May 1958, Lax wrote poetically and somewhat sadly about his friend being beat up in "another village brawl." Kerouac was extremely sensitive, Lax wrote, but good, and then he described him as he saw him:

has big blue calm
and questioning eyes

calm closed mouth
relaxed and set
sometimes a small
quaint smile

his nose though maybe
broke is straight and snub
an irish more than french
canadian nose

eyes are special
writer's (contemplative)
eyes, and chin
(determination)
strong

wonderfully fused
of gentle
and aggressive

The next year, 1959, at the height of his popularity, Kerouac contributed a short piece about his older brother, "Gerard," to *Jubilee* and a poem called "Hymn" to *Pax*. Above the poem (the only writing in that issue of *Pax*) Lax ran an illustration by the abstract artist Dave Budd, one of the key artists and writers—including J. D. Salinger and Samuel Beckett—influencing his thinking about art and writing at the time. Budd was never as well known as Reinhardt or other abstract painters, but his work is in major museums around the world. As Roberta Smith wrote in his obituary for the *New York Times*, he "was best known for enormous horizontal canvases covered with thousands of small, thick strokes of paint. Usually monochromatic, with black or dark blue being favorite shades, these strongly tactile surfaces combined aspects of Abstract Expressionism and Minimalism while also being indirectly naturalistic. Their shifting rhythms and often mesmerizing textures could evoke gently swelling waves, dunes or hills." This description is eerily similar to later descriptions of Lax's poetry.

Budd and his wife, Corky (one of the Cristiani family acrobats), had moved to New York from Sarasota, Florida, in 1952 to further the painting career he began after watching a video of Jackson Pollock. Until they moved to Paris in 1960, Lax was a frequent visitor at their apartment and in Budd's studio, where he met many artists active in abstract and minimalist circles. Willem de Kooning and Robert Motherwell, among others, became friends and influences, but it was the artist Lax had known since high school who made the greatest impact on his life and work.

———————

When Ad Reinhardt is remembered at all in art discussions these days, it is for his last paintings, an extended series of apparently identical black-on-black squares that seemed to reveal the limits of abstract art. These came after he had painted red-on-red and blue-on-blue paintings in a similar way. Although his paintings still hang in many of the world's major modern art galleries, he and the enigma of his work are considered by most art critics to be emblematic of a bygone era. Yet Reinhardt, who had an extraordinary knowledge of past and present art, had an influence on art making and art history through his writings, teaching, and practice that went far beyond the reputation he's been assigned.

"If Reinhardt repeated himself, becoming increasingly insistent," writes Barbara Rose in an introduction to his collected writings on art, "it was because he saw, more clearly than anyone else, that the values of aesthetic detachment and moral integrity, of rationality and civilized awareness to which his own life was dedicated, were besieged on all sides by the rising pressures of commercialism and media culture."

Reinhardt championed an idea of art as individual and self-referential. His movement toward extreme abstraction was an attempt to rid his painting of secondary considerations and representations, anything that couldn't be found in the art itself. As a result you can't glance at his work and move on; you must linger and look and find a wordless relationship to it in yourself.

Lax had always considered Reinhardt the consummate artist—the one artist to emulate if you were going to be an artist yourself—because of his absolute devotion to his art. They had become good friends over the years, and now that Lax was living in New York again, he spent as much time with Reinhardt as he could. His letters to Merton are filled with references to him.

It was during this period that Reinhardt was simplifying his painting more and more, moving inexorably toward the mostly black canvases that would make him famous. He was also putting together the "manifestos" on art that contributed to that fame. It's clear from things Lax said at the time and in later years that Reinhardt's painting and his ideas influenced him greatly. But Reinhardt's greatest influence had nothing to do with his actual art or any ideas he expressed about it. What impressed Lax most from the time he first learned of Reinhardt was how completely dedicated his future friend was to art. Reinhardt's example convinced Lax of two things: being an artist was a viable way to live and being a true artist meant giving everything to your art.

"He was a serious artist," Lax told an interviewer years after Reinhardt's death. "He worked hard and well at what he was doing. . . . He had never been any place where he hadn't been the best student but that didn't keep him from constantly developing and being very interested in his own work and in all the work around him." In the same interview Lax talked about watching Reinhardt at work: "He was so concentrated in his work it sort of created an atmosphere around him. . . . You wouldn't think of talking or of doing anything but breathing easily while he was painting."

During his years at *Jubilee*, Lax would often escape the noise in the magazine office by walking over to Reinhardt's studio at 732 Broadway, with its high ceilings, huge windows, and Imax-like view of Waverly Place. There they'd each do their own work, talking occasionally, until late afternoon, when Reinhardt saw that the light was just right for painting. He'd paint for a couple of hours then, with Lax staying to watch or drifting home. "I think he really liked looking at the paintings some time after the sun had gone down," Lax said, "in the softest possible light. That's when he really liked them."

By this time Reinhardt, who had passed through several phases in his career as a painter and several more in his progression from avowed communist during the 1930s to dedicated champion of artistic freedom against the capitalistic commodification of art, had turned from the collage work he was doing in the late 1940s to the geometric and monochromatic works that culminated in his late-life black paintings. While the black paintings puzzled others, Lax both understood and appreciated them, in part because he had followed Reinhardt's development throughout his career.

At Columbia, Lax had attended Meyer Shapiro's lectures on art history and an Irwin Edman course on aesthetics with Reinhardt, and they'd gone together to talks by Gertrude Stein and André Malraux. During Lax's later years in New York, he accompanied Reinhardt to dozens of gallery openings, meetings at the Artists Club, and the Chinese operas Reinhardt liked. Reinhardt wasn't one to keep his opinions to himself, so Lax must have had a thorough grounding not only in all his friend did but also his reasons for doing it. During those long afternoons in the Broadway studio, Reinhardt would sometimes read his latest manifesto to Lax, not for commentary but for the sense of an audience, to hear how it sounded. Afterward he would critique it out loud himself before setting to work on it again.

It's impossible to say which of Reinhardt's ideas affected Lax most, but a look at how his own art changed and remarks he made later in life suggest that the ideas contained in what may be Reinhardt's most famous statement, "Art-as-Art," were among the most influential. The statement was published in the December 1962 issue of *Art International*, but Reinhardt had been working on it for a long time and it's highly probable that Lax heard at least parts of it prior to December 1960, when he experienced what he recognized immediately as a breakthrough in his own work—a breakthrough with unmistakable connections to the abstract and minimalist work Reinhardt was doing at the time. In later years Lax accepted his adoption by the so-called concrete poets as a kind of elder brother, but he always insisted that *abstract* was a more accurate description of his mature poetry than *concrete*—*abstract* as Reinhardt used the term.

Reinhardt begins "Art-as-Art" with these lines:

> The one thing to say about art is that it is one thing. Art is art-as-art and everything else is everything else. Art-as-art is nothing but art. Art is not what is not art.
>
> The one object of fifty years of abstract art is to present art-as-art and as nothing else, to make it into the one thing it is only, separating and defining it more and more, making it purer and emptier, more

absolute and more exclusive—non-objective, non-representational, non-figurative, non-imagist, non-expressionist, non-subjective. The only and one way to say what abstract art or art-as-art is, is to say what it is not.

The one subject of a hundred years of modern art is that awareness of art of itself, of art preoccupied with its own process and means, with its own identity and distinction, art concerned with its own unique statement, art conscious of its own evolution and history and destiny, toward its own freedom, its own dignity, its own essence, its own reason, its own morality and its own conscience. Art needs no justification with "realism" or "naturalism," "regionalism" or "nationalism," "individualism" or "socialism" or "mysticism." or with any other ideas.

A few paragraphs later he writes:

The one thing to say about art and life is that art is art and life is life, that art is not life and life is not art. A "slice-of-life" art is no better or worse than a "slice-of-art" life. Fine art is not a "means of making a living" or a "way of living a life," and an artist who dedicates his life to his art or his art to his life burdens his art with his life and his life with his art. Art that is a matter of life and death is neither fine nor free.

And he ends the piece with this:

The one standard in art is oneness and fineness, rightness and purity, abstractness and evanescence. The one thing to say about art is its breathlessness, lifelessness, deathlessness, contentlessness, formlessness, spacelessness, and timelessness. This is always the end of art.

Although he would modify it later for his own use, this approach to art—the third excerpt in particular—seems to have spoken to the deepest part of Lax's soul, freeing him not only to write as he wanted to write but also to live as he wanted to live. In a journal passage a decade later he wrote that during his last years in New York he all but worshiped the idea of art having no connection to life. As we will see, many other Reinhardt ideas resonated deeply inside him too.

---

While Lax was absorbing and admiring Reinhardt's highly controlled, abstract approach to art—an approach that would nudge him in a mini-

malist direction—he was also feeling attracted to what seems the oppo-
site extreme: Kerouac's freewheeling prose, with its long sentences and
spontaneous celebration of the experience of life. Throughout the pivotal
years of 1958 through 1960 he thought deeply about both, his thinking
modified and expanded by admiration for Salinger and Beckett as well.

Although his subsequent work has more in common with the mini-
malist approaches of Reinhardt and Beckett, Lax would never have felt
free to write the way he did later if he hadn't been exposed to Kerouac's
belief in writing fast—that the first thought is always the best thought—
and Salinger's example of writing in a natural language and style. Ker-
ouac's approach released him from the overthinking and hesitation he
felt robbed his writing of a natural flow, and Salinger's, as he wrote in his
journal, freed him from his "laconic"—and "dogmatic"—"slumber."

———————

One of the first clear signals that Lax's thinking about writing was flowing
in new directions came near the end of his long convalescence in Olean
in late 1957 to early 1958. On Sunday, March 22, 1958, he set down the
following journal entry/poem, titling it "CHERUBIM & PALM-TREES"
and later adding a handwritten note—"for Jean-Louis Kerouac":

what i want to say
to (jean-louis) is:
if yr really
a jazz writer,
then stop
thinking about
literature
and think
about music.

music can speak,
and words played
like music can speak;
but words played like
music are not the same
as words just played
like words.

words played
like music
have meaning
as words,
like words
and music,
but not the same
meaning
and not
the same value
as words
just used
like words.

words played like
music
are poetic words;
words played like
music
are themselves
a kind of
music.

they are fetched
words,
fetched from deep
like rocks
and fish,
not hunted down
like quarry.

they are words
to cry,
are lyric words,
words which
hold a feeling.

any word
any word at all
can sing,

but some are strange,
as dinosaurs
are funny
when they
fly.

what we are talking
about is the kingdom
of heaven:
a jam-session
civilization,
a civilization
of jazz.

a culture
of new
and spontaneous
music;
spontaneous
order of
play.

a civilization
in which each man's
songs
and each man's
dances
are new
spontaneous
his own
individual
(not to be
copied)
yet filled
with grace
and decorum.

a jam-session
of the
just

where each
is filled
with wonder
for the
other

where all
delight
in the all
and the
Maker
of all.

how will this begin,
it will begin
by prayerfully
beginning;
and by a prayerful
beginning,
it is even now
begun.

the instruments
are tuned,
the first notes
sounded,
even now
the music
has begun.

how many players
does it take for a session?
one, two or ten
as many as can play;
one, two or ten
and all will have
their licks.

the tune,
the tune
is always

the same;
the music
is always
different
and new.


jazz
doesn't do
any work
at all,
no work
at all,
just sing.

jazz
doesn't hoe
any fields
or plant
any crop.

jazz lies back
to sing its song;
jazz leans forward
to hear the tune;
jazz doesn't walk
it dances.

jazz is made
of sound and
flame;
jazz is made
of vision
and song.

jazz rejoices
in the judgments
of the Lord
and waits for His
epiphanies

jazz is for
the outer temple,
for the courts
of the house
of God.

While this poem is not significantly different from poems Lax had written
before, it contains hints of what he was learning from Reinhardt about repe-
tition and limiting the elements of one's art, especially in the verse: "the tune,
/ the tune / is always / the same; / the music / is always / different / and new."
Its content, especially near the beginning, shows both the influence of Ker-
ouac and Lax's emerging ideas about his own different approach.

When he tells Kerouac to "stop thinking about literature and think
about music," he is talking to himself too. There is a hint of Gertrude
Stein in his statements that "music can speak, / and words played / like
music can speak; / but words played like / music are not the same / as
words just played / like words.—words played / like music / have mean-
ing / as words, / like words / and music, / but not the same / meaning /
and not / the same value / as words / just used / like words.—words
played like / music / are poetic words; / words played like / music / are
themselves / a kind of / music." He is working to free words from their
conventional place as words, as we think of words, and letting them
come out as music comes out in a jazz jam, flowing, being, not symbol-
izing but having meaning in themselves, a poetic-lyrical-musical mean-
ing inherent in them because they are "fetched from deep" rather than
"hunted down like quarry." They rise naturally rather than being con-
sciously chosen and so they "hold" a feeling rather than express one.

What I see Lax working with here is that old idea of *pure act* but ap-
proached in a new way that is at once more conscious and less conscious.
He is reaching one hand toward Reinhardt's meaningful simplicity and
the other toward Kerouac's unmediated spontaneity. If he can bring his
hands together, he believes, he will hold the horn that announces the
kingdom of God—the horn Louis Armstrong blows, as Lax expressed it
in the following entry, from December 6, 1958:

why did they
all shout:
louis

is de
lawd?

because
there was something
prophetic
about his trumpeting:

to be that right
is to be at one
with the source
of all good
things

hit it!
higher
and higher
and higher:

to be that high
is to be at one
with the source
of all true
blessings

that is why they shouted
when louis hit the
high notes:
they thought
the roof
would open
and the angels
would burst in

Lax had been waiting all of his life for the roof to open and the angels
to burst in—for a clear revelation about his own life—but it hadn't come.
What came instead was an ability to watch patiently, to consider and
wait. He was learning to be content with that. "I prefer the long specula-
tion," he wrote that December, "to any kind of answer not accompanied
by thunder and lightning."

In the spring of 1959, in an attempt to write about his journey from Mar-
seilles to Rome in 1951, Lax abandoned the vertical style he used in so much
of his poetry and wrote lines across the page. Using hash marks to break
the lines into several-word segments—approximations, perhaps, of poetic
lines—he continued to write in this fashion through May. In his March 22
entry he explained his intention: "No more inching along down the page /
not for today anyway / maybe pretty soon not even no hashmarks / all those
things are signs of hesitation / hesitation for thought / thought is a great
thing but a rush of words is sometimes even better especially if it is without
any words like sometimes / awfully hard to read later but what emerges and
habit one gets in from writing right straight ahead may be worth all that."
Later in this same entry he gets to the heart of what this approach means
for him and how he envisions his own writing—his own project, if you will:

> not by deep breathing and lots of brandishing the pen will the page be
> beautiful and weighty but through clarification of the soul /// the need
> to speak and its expression in true speech / the words will look good
> on the page when they express the true meaning of the writer speak-
> ing in a serious vein. the words will look right on the page when the
> whole being the whole mind of the writer goes into his work word by
> word and minute by minute / when his whole weight comes down on
> the key with the care of a chinese writer painter making a character
>
> and he will speak as he thinks at that time and the speech will have
> balance even as the thought does and the writing will have maturity
> even as the writer
>
> and the writing will have a pace of its own not ahead of the think-
> ing and not too much behind
>
> and the question of space will take care of itself for the writer will
> be himself and his space will be his own
>
> no it is not a race against time or even a race against kerouac it is a
> race to get something said it is like a beginning of breathing / it is the
> beginning of the one continuous conscious activity for which we feel
> this enthusiasm and to which we can give this devotion

Near the entry's end, after considering the pros and cons of speaking
or writing without hesitation, he seems to come out on the side of weigh-
ing one's words, before setting down one more lesson from his attempt at

spontaneous writing: "it is good nonetheless to see how many words go into a sentence before the rhythm drops." This idea of natural rhythm in a string of words will be central to his work in the years ahead.

"i feel like demosthenes," he writes in the entry's last line, "practicing speaking on the seashore and him with a mouthful of pebbles."

------

Over the next year and a half Lax would add the approaches of Beckett and Salinger to his pile of thoughts about writing, the last of the necessary fuel for the bonfire to come. Beckett, of course, had once been an amanuensis for Lax's hero, James Joyce. The first time Lax mentions him in his journal, on May 19, 1959, he praises not his style but his point of view and what he does with it: "What I like about Beckett is his dim view of everything. From which he creates, from many dim views, a brilliance." Lax's own infrequent battles with illness and depression seem to have given him an understanding of how Beckett saw the world and why, as well as an appreciation for Beckett's ability to express his view directly and satirically at the same time, seriously and yet with humor. In a later entry he compares what he calls Beckett's greatest novel, *The Unnamable*, favorably to both *Gulliver's Travels* and the Book of Job.

In Salinger Lax saw and appreciated what so many New York writers and readers saw and appreciated in those days: that he seemed to write in what Lax called "my language, our language." On June 6, 1959, after reading a Salinger story in that week's *New Yorker*, Lax explained that Salinger's Seymour Glass "had a good knowledge of the new york idiom, and that is largely it; he doesn't talk like someone who is writing in a bad translation from german or japanese; he doesn't talk like an idiot boy stammering out a dream, or like ralph waldo emerson setting down some immortal words for an essay." Lax contrasts Salinger's readable style to his own, often intentionally cryptic approach, noting that Salinger reminds himself that what he writes is meant to be read. Lax's takeaway from this seems to be: Write simply and naturally, not trying to sound like anyone but yourself.

------

"i am hard at work, i say on this project," Lax wrote to Merton on Valentine's Day 1960, "hammer and tongs hippity hop all night and all day slugging like old ben in the last twelve rounds. no sooner do i hop off

the subway and slide down the street than i am home back at the type-
writer again hitting away as fast as i can, all my impressions, every last
fugitive encounter with those far-off places, those half-imagined scenes.
i am getting i feel to the root of the matter, the heart of the business; as
shucking off shells and getting to the real nub."

The "project" was another attempt to write about his days in and
around Marseilles, this time without fussing over every word. As this
excerpt, set down in March 1960, shows, he was moving closer to the
extremely vertical, repetitive-word style that would later define him,
yet he hadn't quite worked it out:

> an ancient look
> a foreign look
>
> ancient foreign familiar
> all at once
>
> what is it that
> I recognize
> in the
> city
> ?
>
> the face
> of this
> city
> is
> familiar
> to me
>
> fear
> and fascination
> love
> (and
> enchantment)

As he continued to write, often in fits and starts, over the next sev-
eral months, he kept thinking about the writers discussed above. His
thoughts culminated in a long entry on November 15, 1960, that in-
cluded the following:

kerouac, salinger, beckett

one thing they all seem to have in common is the idea of starting in and plunging right ahead as fast as possible each in his chosen direction; kerouac helter skelter with plenty of slang, french canadian insights and great uncooked gobbets of experience (everyone is thanking robert lowell for that one); salinger goes right ahead sounding as much like new york (and the newyorker) and himself as possible, inventing as he goes along and probably biting his fingernails a good deal between paragraphs; beckett proceeds from sentence, story to story, dream to dream with a mad methodology, always explaining his transitions (his work is a series of transitions) always adjusting and readjusting his sentences in full view of the reader, his style is his own, but an eighteenth century style, as clear, as nearly transparent as swifts. his only near competitor, and he has chosen not to be too near, is s j perelman, who also writes in the style of dick whittington's cat, but his pieces are short and his material (unfortunately) trivial. of the three writers the most stylized, and perhaps the most successful in saying what he means, is beckett. as a result he also seems to be the one who has the most to say.

A little farther on, after adding J. C. Powys to his list, he gets to the heart of what he has come to see as the source of his own hesitancy and hiding in writing: "all of these writers talk of themselves but all in a way that dispenses right at the beginning with every symptom of self-consciousness."

The entry ends with a series of paragraphs and a short imaginary dialogue that are as self-revelatory as anything Lax ever wrote, expressing as they do his insecurity about his background—the fears of a middle-class scholarship boy lacking the confidence of the born-to-lead upper class and the perceived authenticity of those at the bottom of the social scale. He broaches the idea of embarrassment, reflective of a fear of what others think, by stating that "the decision never to use an embarrassing word can result only in sputtering and silence." The statement that follows this, with its focus on some unstated perception of "poise" and "style," deepens the feeling of worry about someone judging him: "the way to poise and style in writing is by frequent and easy practice of it." Notice the distancing use of "one" rather than "I" in the next sentence: "one thought to avoid the embarrassments of prose by the composition of verse, but this evasion is also a delusion." Then comes the short dialogue with himself, a form he had used before and would use much more often in later years:

> my real trouble then is an inability to write, an unwillingness to talk; an unwillingness to talk like a plebian, or worse, a middle-classer, and an inability to talk in any other way.
>     why? aren't you proud of being a middle-classer?
>     no, why should i be proud?
>     are you ashamed?
>     (i have been made to feel ashamed)
>     by whom?
>     by schnobs.

The perceptive grammarian will notice several signs of hesitation and, okay, shame here: the extra-long pause caused by the semicolon in the first paragraph, just before the admission of class consciousness and its consequent fear of inferiority; the encasing of the admission of shame in parentheses; the resorting to humor to pretend a lack of seriousness in that last word, "schnobs," and even the use of the dialogue itself rather than a straightforward addressing of what he sees as his problem.

Was it the admission of this fear, however couched and qualified, that freed him? Or was it simply a desperate need to do something that pleased him? Whatever it was, a few days later the angels Lax had been waiting for began to sing—not from the roof but from his soul. While walking down the street one day he picked up a rock. "One stone," he thought, realizing right away that this thought and the words that expressed it were a thought and words he felt sure about. The thought was definitely his. The words too. There was nothing ambiguous or pretentious or the least bit shameful about them. "One stone," his mind said again, and the words seemed as true and simple as the truest and simplest parts of his soul. Ineffable. Pleasing. Concrete and abstract at the same time. High and low. "One stone"—the words came again, and then:

> i lift
> one stone

one stone

i lift
one stone
and i am
thinking

i am
thinking
as i lift
one stone

one stone
one stone
one stone

Obvious and even facile as what he was thinking seemed, Lax recognized that it had a rhythm, that it was in fact a kind of poem, a new kind of poem, a new beginning—at least for him—and he hurried home, as hurried as Lax ever went, to set down his thoughts. To set down this poem.

The final poem had nineteen stanzas of two to four lines each, all fashioned from the eight words above. The last five stanzas were these:

one stone
one stone
one stone

one stone
one stone
one stone

one stone
one stone

one stone
one stone

one stone
one stone
one stone

It wasn't going to set the world on fire, he knew that, but it was a fire of sorts to him, the kind that appeared on the apostles' heads at the first Pentecost. Did he know in that moment that his life had changed? The question is hard to answer, but over the next three months, as he wrote poem after poem in the same simple style, his confidence grew, as did his determination to leave New York—to go where he wanted to be: Europe.

# 16 "Original Child Bomb" and an Island Home

Among the places I considered staying to write my novel on that 1985 trip to Europe were Berchtesgaden in southern Germany, Salema in southern Portugal, Lecco in northern Italy, and Paris. I'd been to Berchtesgaden in winter and liked it; Salema was warm and easy; I had friends in Lecco; and Paris was Paris. In the end I chose to stay in Greece because I'd wanted to live there since high school, when I saw a movie set there; I'd long been interested in Greek mythology and history; I thought it would be warm; and it was *cheap*.

Lax's reasons for going to Greece and eventually staying there were similar, I think. I don't know that he'd seen any movies set there, but he'd received a classical education, he knew it would be warmer than New York, and he'd learned from Eliot's letters that it was cheap. There may have been another draw too: when he had made up his mind to go and found the courage to tell Rice, he proposed writing an article for *Jubilee* on the monasteries of Mt. Athos. Some of his friends thought he might enter one after writing about them, but I think he was simply curious because Merton had mentioned them and because he was hoping to live a more solitary life.

Although Lax has often been called a hermit, a *solitary* might be a more accurate term. Even in groups there was always something remote about him, a reserve that made him seem, as he described himself, *unisingular*. If moving to Greece was an attempt to radically alter his life, as I think it was, one of the main things he was searching for was a simple place where he could be both solitary and in touch with people.

Lax never articulated a philosophy of solitude, but as was often true in his life, he found his articulation in something Merton wrote. A few months before his departure for Greece in 1961, a small, privately published book called *The Solitary Life* arrived. In it Merton makes a persuasive case for the hermit-like existence he himself would eventually pursue:

The miracle of the desert fathers was precisely that a man could live entirely separate from the visible Christian community with its normal liturgical functions and still be full of the charity of Christ. He was able to be so only because he was completely empty of himself. The vocation to solitude is therefore at the same time a vocation to silence, poverty and emptiness. But the emptiness is for the sake of fullness: the purpose of the solitary life is, if you like, contemplation. But not contemplation in the pagan sense of an intellectual, esoteric enlightenment, achieved by ascetic technique. The contemplation of the Christian solitary is the awareness of the divine mercy transforming and elevating his own emptiness and turning it into the presence of perfect love, perfect fullness.

Hence a Christian can turn his back on society—even on the society of his fellow Christians—without necessarily hating society. It can be, in him, a sign of love for his fellow man to leave the company of others and live alone. This withdrawal should not be a rejection of other men: but it may well be a quiet and perhaps almost despairing refusal to accept the myths and fictions with which social life is always full—and never more than today.

The book lifted Lax from his malaise, if only temporarily. "It fits my present needs," he wrote to Merton, "as if designed for them. the solitary life is the life, all right; it's the only life for me." He was already spending much of his time alone, but his aloneness had a sadness to it; Merton was describing a solitary existence filled with peace and joy. To make that kind of existence possible, Lax felt more than ever that he had to leave New York.

———————

Around this time one of Lax's artist friends, Harry Jackson, asked him to pose for a life-size painting Jackson called *Portrait of the Poet Robert Lax*. In the portrait—a full-length, realistic portrayal that appeared in the exhibition The Continuing Tradition of Realism in American Art—Lax is dressed in a dark suit with a thin tie, his arms crossed over his chest. His pose is stiff and his gaze dubious, as if to show his dislike of his business attire and what it signifies. He appears much as he did when younger, except his black hair has receded so far from his forehead it looks like a yarmulke, and the beard below his chin bears two white streaks. The beard itself seems a sign he's ready to move beyond

the conventional life he's been living. Years later a Carmelite priest re-
membered Lax in the months before he left for Greece as a "bearded
man in a long overcoat" who came to early morning Mass. "I felt sorry
for him," the priest wrote, "because he seemed so cold in the New York
winter."

As he shivered through that winter, Lax began to feel sorry for him-
self. "Say prayers plenty poor old Laxos," he wrote to Merton in February.
"Strange dark fellow all time lighting coattails." The one thing that
cheered him was the thought of going to Europe. When he finally shipped
out in April 1961, having decided to make an exploratory trip instead of a
permanent move, he felt lighter and more hopeful even before the ship
left port.

*1961*

---

Although he intended to describe his travels to his friends along the way,
Lax wrote few letters or even journal entries during his weeks in Europe.
The journal entries he did write were fragmentary, giving little evidence
of what he did or thought, even when he crossed to Greece at last. One
reason he wrote so little about Greece itself was that Greece—or, more
accurately, Greeks—disappointed him. After three weeks with the Eliots
in Ekali, a suburb of Athens, he returned home in mid-June unsure about
this country he'd been dreaming of.

From Ekali he made excursions into Athens and the surrounding ar-
eas, sending Van Doren a postcard from "owl-haunted Delphi." Here
were the classical sites Van Doren had helped him discover. Here was the
mythical land. But oh, those touchy Greeks!

Back in the States, Lax felt less sure about what he should do than be-
fore he'd left. All he knew was that he didn't want to live another year in
New York and he couldn't stand to look at any more *Jubilee* copy. He did
the work he had to do, however, putting away his earnings until he heard
the siren call of Greece again.

---

While he contemplated making a more permanent move, Lax spent as
much time as he could writing poetry and working on *Pax*. Before his
spring trip he had exchanged several messages with Merton about pub-

lishing a poem that would become one of Merton's most significant and best-loved pieces of writing. The discussion began on January 14, 1961, when Merton typed the following line into a letter to Lax: "In a minute I write a solemn awful ballad about bomb, to be recited in a cavern."

Although Merton didn't elaborate, Lax knew the bomb he was talking about was the atomic bomb. In a letter sent the previous October, Merton had praised a writer named Gordon Zahn for writing "coherently" about modern approaches to war, Lax's first indication that his friend was thinking about these matters. "It comes to mind that at least one issue of Pax these days ought to be about this subject," Merton wrote. "A broadside of about twenty statements about something. These I think I will sit down and make under one of the trees when I get a lucid interval."

By the end of January Merton had found enough lucid intervals to set down not just twenty but forty-one statements about the bombs dropped on Hiroshima and Nagasaki, forming them into an experimental prose poem unlike all but one of the mostly lyrical poems he had written before. In a measured yet bitingly sardonic tone, the poem, "Original Child Bomb: Points for Meditation to Be Scratched on the Walls of a Cave," criticizes the development of the bomb and the decision to drop it by calling attention to the words and actions of those responsible.

Lax saw the text of "Original Child Bomb" for the first time in February, when Ed Rice brought it back from a visit with Merton at Gethsemani. "Original child is come down from 96th st [where Rice was living] explode all over Pax office," Lax wrote to Merton. Excited as he was about publishing it, however, he didn't do so right away. The reason isn't clear. Lax was slow to get things done at the best of times and he was busy making plans to leave New York, but there are hints in their letters that Merton continued to revise the poem too. Whatever happened, the poem was still unpublished when Lax left for Europe in April. In a shipboard letter he promised Merton to print it "the minute I get back."

Given that they communicated mostly through infrequent letters written in a whimsical and sometimes cryptic style, it's doubtful that Lax fully understood Merton's concerns about this particular poem. Although Merton had decided that it was time for him to address contemporary issues, he wasn't free to address a particular issue just because he wanted to. He had taken a vow of obedience. Anything he sought to publish had to be approved by his order's censors, and he had come close to running afoul of them already.

A few weeks before writing "Original Child Bomb," he had set down another poem in a similar style, his first attempt at finding what he called a "cryptic and poetic" way to express his concerns about world affairs. Written from the perspective of the camp commander at Auschwitz, "Chant to Be Used in Processions around a Site with Furnaces" uses the same nonlyrical, matter-of-fact voice and ironic approach, and the effect is equally chilling. Although the censors hadn't passed it and Merton didn't intend for it to be published, he sent it to Dorothy Day, and somehow it made its way into the *Catholic Worker* newspaper.

Unsure how the censors would react to his newfound interest in social concerns, Merton was mortified by the publication. Determined to be more careful the next time, he chose *Pax* for "Original Child Bomb" because of its relative obscurity.

It is unclear when the censors approved "Original Child Bomb" for publication, but on June 17, 1961, about the time Lax returned from Europe, Merton wrote, "That Atom Bomb I sent, it is timed. It was forbid and then it was release. It was in and out of the dogshed, where pipes are lit and extinct. It is now released." A gentle but less than subtle nudge to Lax to get moving.

Lax arranged for Antonucci to illustrate the poem and design the *Pax* issue it would appear in. Meanwhile Merton was talking to James Laughlin at New Directions about publishing a paperback version using the same illustrations. Then Lax received a letter from Lawrence Ferlinghetti saying that Merton had approved publication of the same poem in his *Journal for the Protection of All Beings* if it didn't conflict with *Pax*. It turned out that Laughlin had mentioned the poem to Ferlinghetti on a visit to San Francisco. Although saddened by this turn of events, Lax was ready to give the poem up until, on June 30, Merton wrote, "[Laughlin] say Ferlinghetti wants to do in magazine, but I say no. This no fooling, first was promise to Pax, second censors walk on eggs all over the lot refusals in thousands before final consent I get in jail quick. They allow printing but discrete."

Finally, on July 7, Merton sent Lax "the final revised adapted cutrate paperback fusion fission" (i.e., version) of the poem. "It is longer," he wrote, "it sways more, it leaves out a sentence and adds a score, it has more swing to it, it lilts. It is my lyric to the new age."

Lax's response was characteristically simple: "this latest version of the bomb is by far the most magnificent. i am ravished anew." A little over a month later he announced to Merton that the poem was at the printer.

In a letter to the *Catholic Worker's* Jim Forest sent about this time, Merton elaborated on what he called "a loophole in the censorship statue": "When a publication is very small and of very limited influence (and this is not defined), articles for it do not need to be censored." Whatever the definition, *Pax* would qualify.

"New censor regulation say can publish in small magazine without having to go through censor," Merton wrote to Lax. "You willing to print my collected poems from now on?"

It's interesting to speculate what might have happened if *Pax* had indeed become the outlet for Merton's "collected poems" and controversial writings, but it was not to be. Lax informed him in a spring letter that he would return to Europe in September, making further publication of *Pax* impossible, and on June 4 Merton wrote in return that he had been forbidden to publish anything more about war.

Merton's silencing and Lax's departure closed a chapter in their friendship as well as their individual lives. They would continue to write to each other and even see each other two more times, but from then on they would live on different continents, their deepest concerns the same but their thoughts on different matters.

---

While he waited for his September departure, Lax visited friends and places he would miss. One was the *Catholic Worker* headquarters near his old East Village apartment, where he listened to readings by Ginsberg and Brother Antoninus and gave one himself. He read on an ABC Sunday show devoted to five Catholic poets, and did other readings at the Paraclete Book Center and in Greenwich Village cafés. Among the poets he mingled with at these venues was a young admirer named William

Packard, who would champion Lax's work when he founded the *New York Quarterly* a few years later.

---

One of the last things Lax did in New York was work with Antonucci to publish another book of his poetry, this one containing only recent poems in his new, more experimental style. He chose to call it *New Poems* not just because the poems in it were recently written but also because they were a new kind of poem, precursors of what many who called themselves "concrete poets" would write later. As usual Lax didn't trust his own sense of which poems might speak to a wider audience, so he asked Antonucci and Maxwell to help him choose. Among those that made the cut, one was just the word *is* printed vertically, in clusters of seven or three, twenty-seven times. Another was twelve repetitions of *river* flowing down the page. Others were gnomic statements ("The Maximum Capacity / of this room / is 262 people // 262 people // The Maximum Capacity / of this room / is 262 people") or humorous vignettes:

"are you a visitor?" asked
the dog.

"yes," i answered.

"only a visitor?" asked
the dog.

"yes," i answered.

"take me with you," said
the dog.

By the time the book appeared (to no fanfare at all) in the late spring or early summer of 1962, little of Lax remained in the States except his body. His formal goodbye, you might say, to the life he'd been living and the lyrical way he'd been writing was a gently satirical poem called "Ah! The Nature Poets," published in the journal *Approaches*. Nature would be central to many of his future poems, but it would be the simple nature of the Greek Islands rendered in even simpler verse.

When, on September 7, 1962, Lax finally boarded the passenger ship
*United States*, having paid $207 for a third-class ticket, he was bound for
Greece. Friends from his Paris days had invited him to travel with them
in Spain, but he figured he had enough money to live for three months
if he went straight to the islands, so that's what he did. It's hard to say
whether he knew he might never go back home, but it's worth pausing
here to consider the import of what he was doing at the relatively late age

of forty-six. With little money in his pocket and none in reserve, with lit-
tle knowledge of the country he was going to and few friends there, with
no job awaiting him and none to return to, he was setting out to do noth-
ing but write poetry and live as simply and purely as he could. At some
point—either then or in subsequent years—he made a conscious decision
to live a financially insecure life outside the United States for the rest of
his days. Part of the reason lies in all he experienced before 1962, the rest
in all that came later.

Despite its significance, Lax's voyage to Europe didn't begin well. Before
the *United States* had docked in Le Havre, he was seriously ill from food
poisoning. He wound up in a hospital in Rouen "feeling," he wrote later,
"as near death as ever in my life." Awful as the illness was, it had one
positive effect: his recovery left him with an almost religious feeling of
renewal, as if the poison left from his old life had been purged from his
system.

Brief stops in Paris and Zurich were all that slowed him in his return
to Ekali, where he stayed with the Eliots until almost Christmas. Once
he was back in Greece it didn't take long for him to decide he wanted to
stay as long as he could. The problem was how to afford it. Greece was
incredibly cheap in those days but it wasn't free, and he couldn't stay with
the Eliots forever. He wrote a couple of articles on Greek priests for *Jubi-
lee*, but *Jubilee* work didn't pay enough to support him and he had left
New York so he wouldn't have to write what he didn't want to write. The
only solution, he decided, was to do something Antonucci had encour-
aged him to do: apply for a Guggenheim.

His proposed project, he told Van Doren, would be a book of poems written during his travels that he might call *The Night Sea Journey*. "they've been rolling out of me ever since I got to the mainland," he wrote—narrowly vertical, sometimes cryptic poems that read like aphorisms or mini-travelogues. One was "what he / was really / doing // was kind / of an edi- / torial job // on the / (world)." Another was "white / birds // across / the / water // veered // & // dis- / appear- / 'd."

In a letter to Merton asking him to join Antonucci and Van Doren in writing letters of support for his application, Lax gives the first hint that his feelings toward Greeks have changed and, although he has no money, his stay in Greece might be a long one. "Here is absolutely capital," he writes. "The breezes, the landscapes & above all the people themselves, though Greek. From here, toward spring, I think to Mt. Arthur [Athos]—before that perhaps to Patras & meme Mytilene. I am writing every minute of time—new poems, more poems. Of money, as they say here, tipota [nothing]. (One eats like the birds. One eats, in fact, birds.) One sings. One is contented."

The idea of traveling to Mytilene—Mytilene is actually the main town on the island of Lesbos, but Greeks often use it to refer to the island itself—came from the activity Lax enjoyed most when he wasn't writing poetry or journaling: visiting tavernas and meeting Greeks. These excursions to local places produced his first independent conversations with the people he would live among for the rest of his life and, as was usual with him, led to gifts and invitations. One time a group of men sent herbs to his table because they thought he was an Orthodox priest and, when they found out he wasn't, invited him to get drunk with them. Another time a few words in Italian to a man who reminded him of his old circus friend Fritz led to a conversation with a table of laborers. They had all come to Athens from elsewhere to work, they told him. When he asked the Italian speaker, who was now his interpreter, where they were from, the man said, "*I am from Mytilene. Would you like to come there for Christmas?*" Not yet used to Greek islanders, who are prone to spontaneous gestures, Lax was taken aback, but he didn't want to disappoint the man so he said yes. By this time the Eliots' Greek nanny had taken it upon herself to educate him in Greek ways. When she heard he was going to someone's house for

Christmas, she told him to take some cloth for the man's wife. "Take red," she said. "Island people like bright colors."

---

Lesbos/Mytilene is a mountainous island in the northern Aegean a few miles off the Turkish Coast. Known for its olive trees and ouzo, it was once home to the classical poet Sappho and a stop on St. Paul's third missionary journey. For Lax it was the portal to the Greek islands. He knew that once he was there he'd be tempted to keep going, visiting other islands he'd heard or read about, but he didn't want to float from place to place. He wanted to get to know one place well. So he told himself that if he went to Mytilene for Christmas, he'd stay at least through Easter.

Red cloth in hand, he boarded the local ferry for the twelve-hour ride, but when he got to the other end no one was there to meet him. Either he had neglected to tell the man (who isn't named in the journals) he was coming or the man had simply forgotten. Nonetheless, when he found the man's house, the man's wife plopped a big bowl of soup and two spoons on a table and, while Lax and her husband were eating, evicted her four daughters from their bedroom. The next day the man took Lax into town and found him an upstairs room in a house where a fisherman lived with his wife and their small daughter.

Soon Lax had settled into the life he'd dreamed about, writing and going for long walks on which he talked to anyone who would talk to him. Over time he became good friends with a policeman from Crete named Carlos Petrakis, who began to teach him Greek. In the spring, when the winds and rain that batter the islands in winter had given way to sun and gentle breezes, he started spending long stretches of time outside—more, in fact, than ever in his life. Some days he hiked the hills for ten or more miles, scrambling from rock to rock. The freedom to write whatever he wanted, the stimulation of a new yet ancient environment, the simple food and the time outdoors combined to make him happier than he had been in a long time. Maybe ever.

When Petrakis returned to Crete for a visit that June, he invited Lax along, and for the first time Lax had a chance to compare islands. Before they left Mytilene, someone gave them an octopus they hung over the side of the ferry and convinced the captain to roast for them. On deck and again on Crete they slept in the open, and people squatted to talk to them or give them things: an apronful of ripe almonds, loaves of fresh bread, water from a local well. One time on Crete a man stepped down from his donkey and insisted that Lax ride it to the beach they swam at every day. Every swim, every gift, every sweet encounter increased his desire to stay in Greece as long as he could.

The ferry back to Mytilene stopped at Patmos, and Lax, who had a picture of St. John on Patmos pinned to his wall in Marseilles, got off to spend a few days there. He had certainly heard the old saw "Beware of Greeks bearing gifts," but on Patmos the gifts kept coming—an old woman's bouquet of flowers, a boy's aromatic plant, a farmer's wife's cluster of grapes—and he was thankful for each one. Even the religious people bestowed their goodness on him. His visit corresponded with that of the Orthodox Greek Church's ecumenical patriarch, Athenagoras I, and when Lax followed the crowd to a banquet in his honor, Athenagoras invited him to eat with him.

Another two decades would pass before Lax settled permanently on Patmos, but in the coming years he'd visit the island frequently, staying for days or weeks at a time. Although Mytilene and then Kalymnos were more appealing at first, Patmos always called to him—in part, no doubt, because of its association with St. John, whose deep commitment to God and solitary revelation of great truths reflected Lax's desires.

Unpretentious people, spontaneous gifts, a simple yet majestic landscape—nowhere in the world had pleased Lax as much as these islands. When he settled back into Mytilene, he hoped to stay there indefinitely.

---

Late in the year, however, Gladio asked him to accompany her daughter Connie, who was spending her junior college year in Florence, on a two-month trip through mainland Europe. Lax took her to his old home, Marseilles, hoping it would be warm, but it was cold, so they searched for warmth throughout the south: Barcelona, Granada, Algeciras, and Gibraltar. After spending a night in a frigid fourth-floor walkup with only a bare bulb for light, they started sleeping on the train, where Connie asked her physically awkward but entertaining and perspicacious uncle questions about life.

One stop on their travels was Paris, where they visited Dave and Corky Budd. Budd was working on a project with the Beat writer William Burroughs and wanted Lax to meet him, so they had dinner together. Unfortunately Burroughs brought along his writer and painter friend Brion Gysin, and the two of them were dismissive of Connie, ruining the evening.

After Lax returned Connie safely to Florence, he learned that for just a dollar more he could take the boat he planned to take to Athens on to the island of Kos. Kos was much closer to Mytilene, so he paid. That may have been the most significant dollar he ever spent. Although he would visit Mytilene many times in the years ahead, he would never live there again. It wasn't Kos that stole his heart but the nearby island of Kalymnos, where, the moment he touched sole to soil, he felt at home.

---

By this time Lax had lived in Europe well beyond the three months he'd hoped for. The natural question is: If he had so little money, how did he do it? The simple answer: On the islands, at least, things cost less than he expected. The rent on his house in Mytilene was only $3 a month and food was just as cheap. Beyond that he spent almost nothing on anything that wasn't essential, even clothes. He didn't receive the Guggenheim he'd applied for, but a little money trickled in. He inherited a meager amount, and several relatives sent gifts, viewing their giving not as charity but support, a sign that they believed in him and what he was doing.

Influenced perhaps by Kerouac, whose works of fiction were a thinly veiled mythologizing of his own life, Lax had begun to think of his prose writing as a series of "novels." But whereas Kerouac heightened the action and exaggerated the characters to make his works more dynamic, Lax merely set down what actually happened. As a result his accounts of his brief time on Kos in March 1964 and his move to Kalymnos later that month lack suspense and a noticeable arc. They give a good sense, however, of his observations and thinking as he entered what may have been the happiest period of his life.

He arrived on Kos at 6 a.m. on February 26, 1964, taking a tender in from the ferry and immediately meeting a man who offered him a hotel room for 25 drachmas instead of the usual 32 (80 cents instead of $1).

The man left Lax alone in a café for a moment and when he came back asked where his luggage was. Lax had left it on the dock, assuming someone would bring it to the café for him. "He seemed momentarily alarmed," Lax wrote, "that I should have left it unattended."

The incident is trivial, perhaps—the luggage was still where he left it—but his recordings of it and other equally mundane episodes chronicle his education in the ways of Greeks, and Greek islanders in particular. Here, for example, he learned four provisional and contradictory lessons: (1) You can't assume anyone will take care of you; (2) people will take care of you; (3) items left unattended are not safe; (4) items left unattended are safe. At the core of most of these lessons lies the question Who can you trust and how much? When I met Lax twenty years later he had learned most of the lessons well enough to teach me, but that central question had never been entirely answered. In his dealings with Greeks, he followed Jesus's instructions to his disciples: Be wise as serpents and gentle as doves.

The room the man led him to was clean and had a good bed, so Lax took it and went out to explore like any tourist. When he came to a park, he entered it and was struck immediately by the beauty and power of the world around him. "The walk through the park was overhung with trees, not blossoming, but with aromatic buds, extremely fragrant in the early morning," he wrote. "It felt like spring. There was dew on the grass as I walked toward the ruins of the temple, and complete silence in the town. In the center of the field I sat down on a huge ancient stone and looked about me: trees, the sound of the sea, columns, truncated and fallen, domes in ruins, an arch that led to the market square; above the trees a minaret, reminder of the turkish occupation. In the silence and dim light the place seemed charged with life. What would it be like when the inhabitants of the town awoke?"

I copy down this rather simple description of an idle moment in order to pause with Lax and consider the scene. He is alone with the dew and the stones and the sounds of the sea on a fragrant morning. In the silence and early light the world seems charged with life, even before the local people awake. He has been living in Greece for over a year, but he feels something different about this place. About these islands called the Dodecanese. A few days from now, when he crosses the narrow strait separating Kos from Kalymnos, the quiet pleasure he feels will deepen into something it would not be preposterous to call love.

---

Lax spent most of February on Kos, walking and talking to people in "pidgin Greek"—the soldiers patrolling the waterfront and the men in cafés where he wrote and worried about finding a cheaper place to stay. Occasionally he rented a bike for 7 cents an hour and rode to the island's main sight, the Temple of Aesclepius. To get there he had to pass through a Turkish village, and on his third time through he stopped for coffee.

This may be a good place to note that Kos, like all of the Dodecanese, lies just a few miles from Turkey; that even today the Greeks, especially the Greek islanders, retain a fierce ethnic memory of the hardships inflicted on them during four hundred years of Ottoman domination; and that tensions between the Greek and Turkish governments were high in those early days of 1964. In late December 1963 fighting had broken out between the ethnic Greeks and ethnic Turks on Cyprus, prompting a threat of Turkish invasion. The U.S. government had intervened and Great Britain had agreed to stand between the hostile parties until a UN peacekeeping force could be dispatched in March 1964. Because the Greek government, backed by the majority of the Greek people, claimed Cyprus to be a part of greater Greece, trouble between Greeks and Turks on Cyprus meant trouble between the countries of Greece and Turkey. In the coming years the "Cyprus problem," as it was called, would plunge Greece into the darkness of a military dictatorship and cause Lax a host of unforeseen difficulties.

Lax's narrative of his days on Kos makes no mention of military jets, but with Turkey a mere five miles away he must have heard and seen planes from both countries. Unlike the ethnic communities themselves, he didn't distinguish between Greeks and Turks other than to feel an affinity for the latter based on their relative poverty and outsider status.

Lax doesn't record whether he spoke to anyone that first time he visited the Turkish village or during a subsequent stop at a "milk place" there for yogurt, but his attraction to the Turkish residents is obvious. About the yogurt shop, he writes, "There are fancier places in town for yoghourt [sic], but this one feels to me the most authentic." What he means by "authentic" is left to the imagination, but he seems to be looking for that organic connection to life he saw most clearly in the Cristianis and found most often among the poor and less educated. Finding what was most authentic in life, he thought, would help him find what was most authentic in himself—in his soul, his mind, his spirit. When he found that, he would be in touch with his truest self, the self in touch with God.

One day after his first visit to the Turkish yogurt shop, he returned to the Turkish village on foot and this time engaged a café owner in conversation. It was the day after a strong speech on Cyprus by the Greek prime minister, George Papandreou. No one mentioned the speech, but Lax could feel the bitterness and wariness in the Turkish patrons. Sitting by a whitewashed wall in the shade of a tree, the café owner talked primarily about the hardships of island life. Even Greeks were abandoning Kos, he said, because there were no jobs and prices were high. For Turks it was even worse. Although there was electricity in the Greek town, there was none in their village.

The other Turks listened silently until the owner mentioned the Italians, who occupied the Dodecanese from 1912 to 1943 (the reason many islanders spoke Italian). "Things were better then," he said. "The Italians made no distinction between Greek and Turk." At this point a young man spoke up. "You'd better be careful," he said, "or you'll go to jail for that kind of talk." But the owner talked on, and when he had to go back inside for something, the young man and his friends stared at Lax. Prudence being the better part of valor, Lax bid them goodbye.

---

Throughout his time in Greece, until he had a house of his own in his later years, housing was a constant concern for Lax. He moved frequently for a variety of reasons, but the main reason was usually cost. He was able to live without new clothes and he ate simply and therefore cheaply, but housing was a fixed and at times expensive necessity. With no firm prices on anything, even hotel rooms, the cost usually depended on bargaining based on a mutual sizing-up. Unfortunately Lax wasn't much of a bargainer, and his desire to please often made him an easy mark. It could lead to humorous situations too, such as he faced on Kos.

Wanting to move out of what he thought was a relatively costly hotel room, Lax asked a man in a pastry shop if he knew of an inexpensive room. Thus began a quest that was part *Alice in Wonderland* and part fairy tale. The man took him to a neighbor who offered him two rooms, but the mattress in one sagged under a pile of metal and the man's son was already living in the other one. Plus they were too expensive. The man found him a third room, but this one was too noisy. Still wanting to help, the man took him to a waterfront hotel that was cheaper than the one he was staying in, and the hotel owner showed him three other rooms, one of which had six beds in it. When Lax said that they were too expensive, the owner offered to give him any bed in any room for 10 drachmas, with the caveat that he might have to share his room at times. A decision like this was designed to bring out the indecision and worry in Lax. The hotel was old and made entirely of wood, he thought. It might burn. And what about his possessions—his typewriter and camera? He wouldn't mind staying in a room with five Greeks if they were stationary because Greeks were respectful of other people's property, but a transient population might be different.

Dissatisfied with his choices, Lax asked a yogurt seller if he knew of a good cheap room. Before the yogurt man could come up with anything, Lax decided to stay where he was, making a deal with his original hotel owner to pay 20 drachmas a day. This might have been the end of things anywhere but on a Greek island, where word of mouth travels fast. A day or two later a dockworker asked if he was still looking for a room. When Lax gave an ambiguous reply, the man introduced him to a colleague who offered a room in a new house with a large new bed, a kitchen, and a courtyard. The colleague asked how much Lax wanted to spend and immediately accepted the 500 drachmas a month Lax proposed, which of course made Lax worry he'd overpaid. Nevertheless he gave the man a 100-drachma deposit.

When Lax found the courage to tell his hotel owner what he'd done, the man said he could have his current room for the same price. Now he was really perplexed, but he thought a less transient environment would be better, so he moved his things to his new house one by one—his typewriter first, then a piece of luggage—hoping no one would notice. The owner of the new house had told him he'd have it all to himself, but when he had finally settled in, he found a family living across the hall. He stayed just a week before moving to the six-bed room in the flammable hotel. The house was too clean and orderly, he told himself, and besides the owner of the flammable hotel was a Turk. "A sad Turk, as it turned out," he wrote in his journal, "because I had gone off without a word and left him holding a room for me."

In the end he pleased one Turk and made a half-dozen Greeks suspicious, mostly through indecision.

Settled at last in a big room with a large window overlooking a market and the harbor, Lax turned his attention to observing local life, including his own, and writing about it in his journal. He noted one day, based on sounds from the barbershop below his room, that barbershop life in Greece had less to do with cutting hair or shaving chins than sitting around in commodious chairs talking. He made similar observations that day about the sellers in the market, the fishermen in the harbor, and the soldiers he walked among along the waterfront. Then, addressing his anonymous reader, he set down four lines that reveal what moving to Greece meant to him: "This doesn't sound like me at all, you say? Good. It's cost me a terrible effort all these years to sound like me, and I've only now decided to give it up. That goes for looking like me, dressing like me, and preferring the kind of thing I prefer." He wasn't giving up on being himself, only on the mistaken belief that there was some single way of being himself he had to pin down.

From his room and during his walks, he began to pay increasing attention to a particular fishing boat and its crew, who seemed the liveliest and most interesting people in town. This was the beginning of an admiration for Greek fishermen that would last the rest of his life. In time he would come to see them—and the sponge divers he met on Kalymnos—as the closest thing in Greece to the Cristiani acrobats. "Lively they seemed, and friendly among themselves," he wrote in his journal, "but not communicative, as many Greeks are, outside their particular circle; they seemed to be in a world apart, like a crowd of flying Dutchmen." Except for the reference to Greeks, he might have been writing about Mogador and his family. It was inevitable that he would try to get closer to them.

The fishermen seemed more approachable in the morning, when they mended their nets, so one day he went up to them and asked where they went at night. A young man who spoke Italian answered him but offered nothing more, and Lax walked away disappointed. A short time later, though, he was telling a dockworker friend about the boat and his desire to go out on it. The dockworker called to a group of men sitting in the same café. One of them, a thin, friendly man, was a crewmember. "Could this American go out with you sometime?" the dockworker asked, and the man said, "No problem." The next day Lax saw the thin man standing with "a fat man with a big moustache and a hundred sweaters" and asked if he could take their picture. It was the first of many portraits he would take of Greek fishermen and their families in the coming years.

Lax doesn't record whether he ever went out on the fishing boat, but the fat man in the sweaters became his friend, the first of many fishermen and sponge divers who would school him in island ways. As he came to know and be known by more of the townspeople, he began to relax. The men in the Turkish village, which he continued to visit, grew less suspicious of him, and the town in general, he wrote, seemed "reconciled to my presence." The only difficult relationship was with the owner of the house he had fled, who couldn't understand how he could move from "a house as (splendidly made) as his." The owner of the hotel he had left surreptitiously seemed less civil too. These were the first of many islanders who, in the years ahead, would find Lax's actions suspect.

Although his time there was brief, in the month Lax spent on Kos he established the patterns he would follow while living on other islands in subsequent years: walks along the waterfront and into the countryside, a preference for fishermen and others at the bottom of the social scale, movement from room to room in search of the best environment for sleeping and writing, examination of his writing approach and his inner life, and journal descriptions of the life around him.

Discovering and embracing his inner life while doing the same with the life outside him, reconciling one to the other, was one of his chief goals. What he sought was a harmony that had always eluded him. "having all the words in your vocabulary come together and having all the parts of your being come together, seems to me the main point of writing, and in fact of being alive," he wrote. "trying to bring all these divergent things into harmony, like trying to make peace in the world, is the constant (if even unconscious) endeavor of every being in it."

This endeavor became more tangible to him late in March, when the rain turned to sunshine and he made the crossing to Kalymnos at last. There, in the days ahead, he would find the harmony—the reconciliation of inner and outer life—he had long sought. He would swim in it, dance in it, and sing its praises for the next ten years—until the hammer of circumstance fell unexpectedly upon it, smashing his crystal cathedral.

# 17    The Sorrow of the Sponge Diver

During the many years I knew him, Lax suggested several times that I go to Kalymnos, but I never did. I guess I always figured time on Kalymnos would be time away from Patmos, and I loved being on Patmos. It wasn't until I returned to Greece six years after his death that I finally made the crossing that had been so important to him. So many years had passed since he'd lived on the island, I didn't expect to find anyone who remembered him, nor did I expect the island to impress me. I was wrong on both counts.

Although climbers have discovered the towering crags that dominate much of the island and the main town of Pothia has become a fairly large place, Kalymnos still isn't on the main tourist route. It has no classical sites or chic resorts, and until a few years ago it lacked an airport. The ferry ride from Athens takes twelve hours, and when you arrive all you see is a U-shaped harbor and a sprawling main town backed by endless empty hills, several high enough to call mountains. Lying closer to Turkey than to anywhere important in Greece, the island has an almost forgotten feeling. How much more remote and forbidding it must have seemed when Lax stepped ashore in 1964.

He made the four-hour crossing from Kos with a roly-poly young Turk he'd met at his hotel named Stellio, who had friends on both islands and smoothed the transition for him. When Lax had trouble with the language, Stellio translated for him, and when Lax had questions about the island's main industry, sponge diving, it was Stellio he turned to for answers. In fact the most important attribute Stellio offered wasn't his friendliness or his knowledge but the fact that he was a sponge diver on an island where sponge divers were revered.

Lax found many things about Kalymnos attractive, including its remoteness from the American-driven world of commercialism and advertising and its robust people, but the thing that attracted him most was the island's culture, based as it was on occupations linked to earlier times and the sea. He sensed right away that the island's long-standing position at the center of the sponge-diving industry had given it a unique sense of pride and cohesion. The self-doubt and yearning for change he found elsewhere in Greece were absent here. Kalymnians lived happily as they'd always lived: by ritual and routine, tradition and training. With deep-seated values and expectations to guide them, they were free to live spontaneously, in the moment.

Of course Lax arrived on Kalymnos during its most dynamic days: a few weeks before the sponge-diving fleet left on its annual voyage. In 1964, after decades of increasingly aggressive harvesting, the boats had to travel to the waters off Libya to find the quantities they needed, and they usually set sail on their seven-month voyage just after Easter. That year, though, Easter came late and they would be leaving earlier. Divers and captains were already gathering from all directions, some from home islands where sponge diving had died out years before and some from Athens or elsewhere where they had family. The influx of young, able men gave the island an added energy, as did the final preparations for departure. Boats were being overhauled and outfitted. Divers were drinking and dancing away their pay. And captains were strutting importantly along the waterfront.

As he watched them and got to know them, Lax came to see the divers as more like his circus friends than even the fishermen were. Like acrobats, they practiced a specialized and dangerous art, the ins and outs of which were known only to those who performed it. Stellio, whose brother had died diving for sponges, said he once wrote a book about diving, but his captain paid him 5,000 drachmas to tear it up. It exposed too many secrets, he said, especially the awful conditions the sponge divers worked in.

The dangers of diving were on display on the streets Lax walked with Stellio: men using canes or crutches, others in wheelchairs, paralyzed from the waist down. This daily reminder of what might happen added to the pre-sailing frenzy. "stellio's attitude is fatalistic," Lax wrote, "you're only here for a day."

For Stellio, living for the day meant being generous. He gave children money, bought men drinks, and added sizable tips to café bills. The divers received their pay in advance—upward of $2,000 for seven months' work—and most of them spent it as soon as they got it. Carrying wads of cash around town, they bought their wives jewelry or furs and spent their evenings betting on cards.

Lax did his best to take it all in. He rented a room in a house he shared with a high school teacher and a bank clerk. When they went to their work in the morning, he set about his: walking, observing, asking questions, and writing everything down. He understood that what he was witnessing was unique, so instead of working on poems, he recorded and photographed a way of life that has now vanished.

Everywhere Lax had gone in Greece people had greeted him, but he had never received the kind of welcome he did on Kalymnos, where strangers were rare. People of all ages approached him to ask him questions: Where was he from? Did he know Greek? Why was he there? His nationality and interest in Greeks gave him a special status. People wanted to be seen with him and call him their friend—not only those at the bottom but those at the top too, including the sponge-diving captains. Their intrusive interest in him didn't bother him—everyone on the island knew everything about everyone else, he reasoned, and this was their way of coming to know him too—but one question should have given him pause: Were he and Stellio friends because he was American and Stellio Turkish? In another time and place the question might have been harmless, but this was an insular island near the Turkish coast when relations between Greece and Turkey were tense. Suspicion, born of fear, was rife, especially of outsiders, and it was widely believed that the U.S. government favored its nearer-to-Moscow ally.

There are hints in Lax's writing that he was aware of the xenophobia around him. It was important, he knew, to be seen as part of the island community, inside rather than outside the normal rhythms of life. Once he'd decided to stay on Kalymnos, he did what he could to make the people comfortable with him. That he never entirely succeeded had less to do with who he was than with history, prejudice, and the tendency of human beings to act out of fear when times turn dark.

———————

One of the first people Lax came to know on Kalymnos was a teenage girl named Limnina who worked all day making rugs. Her loom was in a small house at the far end of the harbor where the fishermen lived. This was the town's poorest area and so it was the one Lax preferred. I'm not sure how he and Limnina met, perhaps by exchanging smiles as he walked by, but once they'd had their first conversation, he stopped to chat with her often. "she sat at the loom and pushed the shuttle and worked the treadles with her stockinged feet," he wrote about one of their early encounters, "(the stockings were worn, the dress much mended, but she was looking beautiful)."

He was always walking, she said to him that day, the two of them speaking in Italian. "Walk, walk, all day, and I, all day, just work."

"I've been working," he said, "and now I'm walking."

"You work and take walks," she said. "I only work."

The girl was only seventeen, he wrote in his journal, but she looked older. He took pictures of her, and they talked until they ran out of things to say. "Come back tomorrow," she said when he left, and so he did.

Lax never recorded what exactly he liked about Limnina, but it's clear from his writings that she was one of his favorite people on the island. Maybe it was her truthfulness or her teasing. Maybe it was her vigor or lack of guile. Maybe it was just that she seemed to like him too, unconditionally. Whatever it was, she was one of only a handful of people he wrote about to Van Doren. In their correspondence they called her simply "the rug girl," and Van Doren, sensing Lax's attraction, joked that he was in love with her. The question of when he would kiss her became a running joke. But while there was nothing romantic about it, Lax's friendship with Limnina went deeper than this type of banter suggests. Early on she told him she'd make a rug for him and did so right away. Other than his clothes and his typewriter, it was the only item in his room he owned. Whenever he left the island, he wrote to her. And ten years later, when some of the islanders threatened him while he was away, it was a letter from her that warned him not to return.

Another of Lax's early friends was a former diver named Paul (Paulos) who gave him two sponges for coaxing an American tourist into his sponge shop. Lax would run into Paul often on his walks along the waterfront, and the two would retire to a café to talk in a mixture of Greek and Italian. Paul was in his midfifties and served as a kind of unofficial town leader, so he was a good man to know. He was a musician too, a "fiddler" who played at celebrations such as the party the town would host the night before the divers departed.

Among the divers Lax came to know before the fleet sailed, one of his favorites was a Turk named Mehmedi who lived in the Turkish village on Kos and remembered seeing him there. A red-faced man with fat cheeks and black eyes, Mehmedi liked to wear floppy hats and dark glasses even in a café. When Lax took pictures of him, he stared into the camera "as though he wanted to be a movie heavy," but when he talked, his talk was as simple as that of a farmer or fisherman. It was this simplicity, which he found in so many of the divers, that attracted Lax most.

Much as he appreciated the divers' and fishermen's simplicity and innocence, however, Lax also enjoyed the livelier and often grittier preparations, maneuverings, and celebrations taking place in the run-up to the divers' departure. The weeks before the divers left were the busiest of the year, both in the main town of Pothia and in the town up the hill where most of the divers lived, Chora.

The first time Lax visited Chora, he went with a sponge clipper—a specialist at snipping the roughness from raw sponges to make them attractive for sale—who called himself Charles. The town was blessedly free of visitors that day, a sleepy place where farmers relaxed on café terraces, and Lax thought he might move there. But when he returned at night a week or so later, the atmosphere was completely different. This time he went with a local named Yorgos who told him that nothing would happen until later in the evening. Sure enough, around 10 p.m., the lights in the café they were drinking in went down and colored spotlights shone on a couple dancing. It was the first time Lax had seen a man and a woman dance together in Greece, a sign that the usual strictures of Greek life didn't apply in this divers' and captains' lair in the days before they set sail.

Not long after the dancing began, the captains arrived in their proud fashion, spreading out and commanding the room. When Lax asked one of them if he had ever been a diver, the man replied that he had always been a captain, just as his father had. "A captain is a captain," he said. "A diver is a diver."

---

Before long Lax had learned that the various preparations and impromptu parties taking place around the island would culminate in two major festivals: a smaller feast on May 3 to commemorate Easter, the most important religious holiday in Greece, and a grand celebration two weeks earlier to mark the departure of the sponge-diving fleet. The fleet celebration would include visitors from the national government, including the son of the current prime minister, as well as free food and music. When the fleet was ready to depart, priests would bless the boats and families would line the docks, the women in black and crying as if in mourning. "It's like going off to war," a man told him.

While he waited for the grand event, Lax spent his time taking pictures and learning all he could about sponge diving. His main informants were Charles, Paul, Mehmedi, and a captain named Nicos who spoke Italian well. Some of what they told him was contradictory or vague, but he recorded everything he heard, hoping it would cohere. As he wandered through the maze of busyness around him, he began to think of it all as a movie being made, with the captains as directors, the divers actors, and the boatyard a giant back lot.

The men painting the hulls, fixing the engines, and maneuvering the boats into the sea received nothing for this work, he learned. They were paid only for their time on the boat and then less than half what the divers were paid. Boat trips could vary but usually lasted seven months, during which the crew went to shore just twice for supplies. The rest of the time they drank water from huge barrels filled and secured on board before departure, drinking—and eating—only at night. Their meals usually consisted of little more than beans, beef jerky, and a kind of hardtack baked into loaves. Although alcohol was forbidden, fights would break out, often after discussions of who was paid what. Seven months was a long time for young men to be alone together in a small, waterborne space.

Once they reached the sponge beds off the Libyan coast, the divers took turns diving, usually making three dives a day. Most wore suits made of cast iron and a rubberized material with helmets and an air house connected to a pump on the boat. Iron shoes allowed them to sink to the bottom and a rope around their waist gave them rudimentary communication with the crew on board; they'd tug it a specific number of times to indicate one desire or another. Some wore a different, porous suit, but it couldn't be used for long and not for the deepest dives.

These diving suits had been developed within the past fifty years. Before that divers wore only bathing suits, lowering themselves by clutching large rocks or having the rocks tied to their back. The suits were necessary now to reach the deeper beds where there were still sponges, but they were more hazardous to the divers. The deeper they went, the stronger the water pressure on their body and the more susceptible they were to the bends if they came up too fast. The crudeness of the aeration system kept the carbon dioxide the divers exhaled from clearing the hoses, meaning they breathed much of it back in. They wouldn't feel anything in the water, but once they'd been back on deck a few minutes, blue and black marks would appear on their skin. Starting around the hips or the ribs, these were the first indications they might be facing paralysis or even death.

The divers and captains had learned to look for these marks right away, of course. The divers avoided getting tanned or sunburned so the marks would show clearly. Sometimes they'd smoke right away because nicotine brought the colors out quicker. If the marks appeared, the crew pumped fresh air into the diver's lungs, hoping to forestall the more serious effects. Some divers who had been close to losing their livelihood and even their lives went back to work the next day. Others lay in a hospital for months but eventually recovered.

"It's a difficult business," Mehmedi said one day. "A dangerous, difficult occupation."

"Is it difficult to learn?" Lax asked.

"You can learn it in ten minutes."

The alarmingly high incidence of paralysis and death among divers, especially in the early days of the diving suits, when the deadly effects they produced and the ways to prevent them weren't understood, had produced a stoical acceptance of suffering in the divers and Kalymnians in general. Every October families waited in dread for the fleet's return, hoping and praying this wouldn't be the year their loved ones wouldn't come back. Widows wearing black were as common on the streets as men on crutches. Some women took to wearing black even before their men died, anticipating the inevitable. This resignation had a different look in Chora, where the motto was Live for today, for tomorrow we die. "an ancient attitude half-believed and kept alive," Lax wrote, "by all who can profit from it."

When Lax asked why some divers got the bends and not others, he was told the problem came from staying down too long at too great a depth. "I don't know if it's the competitive spirit that makes them stay down longer," he wrote, "or whether it's anything as simple and poetic as fascination with what they see." The greatest danger, a tightrope walker had once told him, was "to get happy up there."

---

Enthralled by all that was going on in town, Lax moved to a new hotel closer to the center where his room had a much better view. Unlike on Kos, the owner of his first hotel shrugged off his leaving. "If it's better for your work then you've got to move," she said.

One night, after listening to a visiting Frenchman complain about American kids in those mid-1960s years running around the world "barefooted, straggly-bearded, wearing blue jeans and ripped shirts," Lax walked out into the dark Greek night, thinking perhaps that those wandering kids were doing exactly what he was: looking for something more real than the lives they saw people living back home. The sea was gentle and the stars were out and it came to him suddenly that Greece was a place that hit you "right in the roots." Everything there was real.

The Frenchman had little good to say about Greeks either. They had no culture of their own, he said. All of their food and music and even their coffee came from the Turks during centuries of Ottoman domination. "They only have the very ancient times to hold onto as their own," he said, "and that is why they hold on to them so strongly." His comments bothered Lax, in part because so much of what the man said seemed to confirm his own view. But Lax saw defiance in the Greeks too, a pulling away from Oriental ways, not to become European or American but out of pride in being Greek. After watching a Greek potter make beautiful things from a pile of poor clay and a broken-down wheel, he set down a long contemplation on the relationship between art and life, deviating for the first time from his old friend Reinhardt. Reinhardt believed that life and art had little to do with each other, but Lax had acquired a different view.

"there is no such thing as an artless life," he wrote, "nor can art, as the product of man, be utterly divorced from life. . . . both life and art are a voyage of discovery, and wherever the land may be of our ultimate arrival, it is hardly likely to be (or seem) those indies for which we set sail."

Much of his meditation is abstract, but it reflects the concrete decisions he faces: Should he simply record the life around him as it happens or make stories and poems from it? Should he create his own life through conscious choices about where and how to live or let it flow like a falling river, watching and plucking the art from it?

Lax had been on Kalymnos for over two weeks by this time, but he was still trying to figure it out. What intrigued him most was the social scale. The captains and businessmen seemed to be at the top, with the fishermen below them and, at the bottom, without skills beyond their physical strength and their courage, the sponge divers. "they are at the bottom rung of the social ladder (as close to the floor of the sea as the sponge they dive for)," he wrote, "but they are also (in some sense) the heroes of the town. . . . they are, after all, what gives it its existence: no sponge, no captain, no sponge, no clipper, no sponge, no seller, and so, no town."

Every activity in town now seemed oriented toward the fleet's departure and the upcoming festivals. Workers rolled barrels for water or kerosene down the street at all hours. Men in white helmets climbed onto balustrades to string up white lights. And sheep appeared on the road with bright red daubs on their heads, a sign that they'd be slaughtered. The bars and cafés were filled with captains having a few last drinks with each other. The captains were "the real aristocracy in town," Lax thought, most of them "gentle, smart and well-organized." When he expressed this opinion to Paul, however, Paul disagreed. "I've been watching captains for forty years now," he said, "and most of them are shits."

There was a kind of courage and sureness in everyone and everything, Lax thought, even the cats. He watched one take its time deciding whether to leap onto a boat and then leap with sure-footed agility. The people were the same, no matter their age. When he tried to help an old man off a boat, the man waved him gently away. "We know how to do it," he said.

By the middle of April signs of the coming festival were everywhere. The curb along the waterfront and the town's main pier had been painted white, blue-and-white banners hung between the telephone poles, and a brass band was practicing its welcoming anthems nonstop. Sponge-diving boats were venturing out to retrieve *fusces*, a rubbery kind of seafood brought up from the bottom of the sea, to be used as hors d'oeuvres, and the hotels were filled with visitors. As he passed below Lax's window on the 17th, the town crier announced that the festival would begin at 5 p.m. the next day.

When Lax went outside that next morning, the town was full of people strolling, many of them dressed up. Radio stations in Athens had announced the festival, and the ferry that day was full of people, including a film crew. An English-speaking boy painting a welcome sign by the harbor told Lax he could go out on one of the boats to greet the visiting government ministers if he was down at the dock at 4 p.m., but Lax had learned that nothing on Kalymnos began at a specified time, so he kept his eye on the waterfront and when he saw the activity on the pier increase, he hurried down. The boats were about to take off and he was just able to squeeze himself onto a small one.

The boat he was on was full of boys, all of them able-looking except the last one aboard, a handsome boy who limped so badly he could hardly walk. Despite his affliction, he had a hardiness and joyous spirit that put everyone in a good mood. "he came to sit in the front of the boat," Lax wrote later, "and his feeling of glowing anticipation seemed to be what finally got us into motion." Like many in town, the boy had been paralyzed, not from diving this time but polio. His name, Lax found out, was Lefteri (*freedom*) and his father, Pandelis Ghenis, was captain of the entire fleet.

Although the government officials weren't scheduled to arrive until 5, the boats set out at 3:30 and passed the time racing each other until 3:30 became 4:30, 5:30, and then 6. By then the light was fading from the sky and the evening was growing cold. The officials were supposed to have flown to Kos and taken a boat from there. Maybe their plane never arrived, some speculated, but no, a report had come in that they'd made it safely that far. Maybe they attended a festival on Kos, others said, but again the rumor was quashed; the only festival on their schedule was the one on Kalymnos. When the horizon remained empty, boats started heading in. Before they had reached the dock, however, a new rumor spread: the officials' boat had been sighted! Mast lights went on and everyone looked toward Kos, peering through what was now black night. Which light was it? they wondered. The green one in the distance? Lax's boat flashed its light, and a white light above the green one flashed back. Then, like a shot, the officials' cruiser passed by, so close they could reach out and touch it. The officials waved from the deck as the divers and captains chanted the prime minister's name: "Papandreou! Papandreou!" The dynamite blasts the island was known for at Easter boomed from the hills, filling the air with the smell of cordite as church bells rang counterpoint and newly strung lights flashed in contrasting rhythm. Fires flared and bigger booms sounded from other hills, while down by the water a growing crowd shouted.

Once the government cruiser had landed, everyone moved down an alley to the open square in front of the cinema, where the officials appeared on a balcony. "This is an honor unique in the history of the islands," a local man announced. "It promises good things for us." Among them, he said, were better roads and a first-class hotel. The crowd cheered. Then came the introductions of the "great men," one of whom was from Kalymnos, followed by a speech by the prime minister's son, Andreas Papandreou (who would lead the government himself in the 1980s, when I first visited the country).

When the public introductions were over, the officials ducked back inside and those who had been invited, as well as those who hadn't, tried to squeeze through one of two doors to a garden where a reception would be held, including the singing of sponge diver songs. Lax hadn't been invited but a policeman at one of the doors let him in, and when a captain friend saw him holding a camera, he motioned him toward the front. Someone there asked if he was a correspondent, and when he said yes, he was directed to the area reserved for the press, taking his place between a folklore professor and the editor of an Athenian magazine called the *Fishermen's Gazette*.

After a roast chicken dinner, speeches, and dances by girls in native costume, Paul and a zither player made their way to the front. Joining them was the fleet captain, Pandelis, Lefteri's father, who, it was announced, would sing the songs the early sponge divers sang as they rowed out to sea.

"the captain threw back his head, but lightly," Lax wrote about what came next, "and sang a song whose major refrain was da-da-diddi-la-ta-ta. a cucumber-shaped man of medium size, and a pleasant, porpoise-like face, he sang without effort . . . da-da-diddi-la-ta-ta, da-da-diddi-la-ta-ta, a comic song with a persistent, agreeable refrain. the crowd recognized it as their song, their nearly most inner, most sacred series of jokes (rough jokes but living in their hearts with the sanctions of time); they recognized pandelis as a hero among them."

When he had finished the first song, Pandelis sang a second, with the crowd clapping and joining in. The program ended a short time later, but Lax wasn't ready for such a marvelous night to be over. He wandered the waterfront for a while, exchanging greetings with others who seemed reluctant to let go, and heard one of them say, "A beautiful evening, but tomorrow will be even better."

The next day, a Sunday, was gray and cold, and after the government officials left in their cruiser, nothing at all seemed to be going on. But as Lax lay in his room, he felt something stirring. When he went back outside, some of the dancers from the night before were dancing again. He saw Paul watching them, and when Paul saw Lax he whispered, "In a little while, go up to Chora, to a cafe called Eleni." Lax headed back to his room to get film for whatever might happen and thought about resting for a while, but something told him to head back outside. When he did, he saw two taxis about to depart. The first was full, but he managed to squeeze himself into the second just before it took off. A moment later he felt a tug on his sleeve. It was Paul. The taxi was full of sea captains.

————————

Café Eleni was on a side street Lax wouldn't have found on his own. As soon as they entered, Paul and his zither-playing friend walked straight to a table set up for them. Nicos, the younger captain Lax had come to know well, called to him from a corner and started to tell him what kind of party it was. "Almost everyone here is a captain," he said. "We get together like this for just one evening before we sail, and sing." He poured Lax a beer and they clinked glasses, sitting back to watch the show: Paul with his violin, the zither player, and Pandelis at its center.

"now the captain started to sing," Lax wrote in his journal, "a different sort of song from those he had sung at the party: the rhythm was as strong, the repetition as frequent, but the mood was melancholy: ah-khee, ah-khee: alas, alas. there were no jokes in this one, in fact there were very few words in the long lament. nicos joined, they all joined in the sad, yet not too sad, refrain: one could easily picture the long nights at sea, the troubles of a thousand years but there was the strength of the sea in it too: long waves, long nights, on the bosom of the sea."

While this was going on, a sheep wandered into the café with a small girl behind it. A few minutes later the girl reappeared with a freshly flayed sheepskin in her hands. "There'll be roast lamb tonight," Nicos said. Before the lamb appeared, however, a film crew arrived: a young director, his camera and lighting assistants, and a "theatrical-looking" woman in a black gown. Along with them came the folklore professor from the night before and two young assistants carrying recording equipment. When the filming began, it was interrupted a number of times, first because Pandelis stumbled over his introduction of the musicians and the songs, then because Paul wanted to make sure the professor wasn't planning to sell the recordings for a profit. The professor assured him they would go to the library of an academy in Athens, where they would be accessed only by students and researchers.

Before the professor had finished speaking, men carried a flaming brazier into the room and two boys brought in the freshly slaughtered lamb. An old seaman carrying a lobster followed. By this time the taping had begun again, and when the old man handed the lobster to the chef with a shout, the captains around him hissed.

"What's the matter?" he asked.

"The tape," someone explained.

"The hell with the tape," he said.

An argument ensued, and when the seaman had been shouted down, he continued to complain, making it impossible for the recording to continue. Finally the theatrical woman in the black gown sat down beside him. "Sponge-divers are now, and have always been, known throughout the world as gentlemen," she cooed. Moments later the seaman was being recorded himself, singing a sponge diver's song.

When the recording of the songs ended, the movie crew took over, filming not only Pandelis and the musicians but also the crowd, and then the evening started again, the singing uninterrupted and unmediated now. By this time, though, Lax was tired. Taxis were waiting outside, but none of the drivers wanted to leave with just one passenger, so he wandered the darkened streets, where he saw a tailor sewing and listening contentedly to the music filling the night. It was coming from all parts of Chora now—from the young divers' nightclub, the old divers' nightclub, and the captains' taverna. The old divers danced old dances to the sounds of drums and tambourine while the young divers danced to bouzouki, and from a side street the captains sang their sea songs "solemn and merry, solemn and slow." The captains' song rose from beneath the others, Lax wrote, lifting them and dropping them "new-born on the hills of chora . . . cleansing the night."

When his steps brought him back to the captains' café, he stopped outside to listen. There, behind and beneath it all, he heard the roar of the sea.

---

The folklorist left the next day, but the film crew stuck around for a while and Lax was able to watch them film divers entering and leaving the sea. One of the divers told him the rules: Each diver had his own limits of depth and time, but usually they made three dives a day, lasting fifteen, eleven, and then eight minutes. The diver told the boy who held the rope how long he planned to stay down, and when the time ended, the boy started pulling. Sometimes, though, the diver saw a sponge he wanted on his way back up and signaled that he wanted to stay longer.

"Wouldn't it be better to come back up and go back for it later?" Lax asked.

"It *would* be better to come back up and go down for it later," the man said.

"Then why would he stop?"

"It's hard to explain," the man answered. "It's like a girl. A magnet."

When Lax asked Paul the same question, Paul held his hand up and stared at his wiggling fingers. "Some people like girls and some like wine," he said. "This crowd, they like sponges."

"When you've been down too long or too deep," the diver who told him the rules said, "you don't die down there. You don't die while they're pulling you up. You die when you're up—when they unscrew the helmet and the air rushes in."

The first boats left on April 26, one week after the festival. All that week Lax watched the captains checking machinery, signing papers, and giving orders. Divers who had disappeared kept reappearing, "as clowns do, out of a tiny car." They huddled with their wives, giving last-minute instructions. Then the day came. Crowds gathered at the port, mostly families and captains and divers who would depart later. Before the boats left, they circled several times, everyone on sea or land waving. One woman cried, but mostly the people being left behind watched with composure.

"It's a sad thing to see," Paul said, "all of them going away for seven months and only God knowing which come back."

The boats did not go off in the form of the cross, as someone had told Lax they would. "it was more as though they had evaporated," he wrote, "and the crowd, as quietly, went home." When he walked through town later that day, the cafés looked abandoned. "only a part of the crowd had gone," he mused, "but it was the livelier part."

It was Palm Sunday and, out of deference to Holy Week, the cafés kept their music off. Feeling forlorn, Lax walked out to Agios Stefanos, where the fishermen lived. When he passed the small house where the rug girl worked, he saw the door open. A kerosene lamp lit the interior where the girl, her mother, and her brother were "squatting around a low chest or table, eating from a single white casserole, a loaf of bread at their side."

Lax had already eaten, but when they invited him to dine with them he sat down anyway. Mikali, the brother, wore a brown work shirt, the girl a white flannel nightgown, and their mother her usual black dress. "the light was beautiful," he wrote later, "and again they looked as though they had been, and would be, forever."

They told him he should go to the fishermen's church on the nearby hill and so he did, climbing the steps to the overfilled chapel. There he sat on a stone bench with two fishermen, listening to the chanting inside and gazing out at the sea.

————————

That Thursday, Holy Thursday, a captain named Theophilous invited Lax to come with him to an island Lax had hoped to see, Pserimos, where the boats that had left Kalymnos were biding their time before the long trip to Africa. All of the divers were on one large boat, and when a friend of Mehmedi saw Lax coming, he went down into the hold to fetch him. They spent what time they could together, with Lax taking pictures and Mehmedi showing him the tiny room the fleet's captain slept in. "it looked like a trappist or carthusian cell," Lax wrote, "like a bed in the earliest trailers or a gypsy caravan. . . . i didn't see where mehmedi and the others slept but can pretty well imagine."

Lax saw Mehmedi and the other divers once more, the next day, when they made a last pass by their homeland, circling the harbor and shouting goodbye. The departure took place on Good Friday, the day Christ died.

# 18    A Saint of the Avant-Garde

On the second floor of a stone building near the Kalymnos harbor lies a small museum dedicated to the island's sponge-diving days. According to the museum's founder and curator, Harilaos Billiris, those days ended in 1972. Until then, he told me, things were good. Money flowed in not only from sponges and fishing but also from "elephants"—islanders who had spent their working lives elsewhere and returned to die, bringing their savings with them. Back then, he said, "no one thought at all about tourism."

When I met him in 2006, Billiris was only sixty-five, but as soon as I said I was working on a book about an American who had lived there in the 1960s and 1970s, he remembered Lax. Billiris was a young man then, of course, and didn't know Lax well, but he recalled a tall man with prominent teeth who wore loose pants and wide-brimmed hats. "He was a simple man," he told me, "who never gave offense to anyone. He could get people talking about themselves or the island without pushing them. With just a smile. I didn't know much about him. I don't think anyone did. He was with you for a short time and then he was off. He liked to be alone." Billiris thought a while and then added, "He was intelligent, I remember. He liked to talk a little philosophy. And he wrote poems."

---

After the fishing fleet left that first spring, Lax flitted from island to island for a while before settling permanently on Kalymnos in July 1964. Having rented the upper floor of a house in the hills, he usually spent his mornings writing poems and his middays napping before taking a 10-cent taxi ride into town. There he would swim and talk to people in cafés, many of whom assumed he was a local who had emigrated and was back home visiting his family. He enjoyed being treated like an insider but he liked being an outsider too, free to come and go at will. He wouldn't commit himself to staying on Kalymnos, yet stay he did—for most of the next ten years.

His most faithful correspondent during this period was his old professor, Mark Van Doren, whose admiration for him had grown exponentially over the years. They had always stayed in touch through letters and occasional visits, and Van Doren had always encouraged him by praising his writing—even dedicating a book to him—but now their relationship deepened. It was Van Doren to whom Lax sent his poems and journals first. While Van Doren appreciated what he called the "power" of the poems, he felt their limited vocabulary kept them from expressing as much as they might—until, that is, Lax sent a copy of a long, spare poem called "Sea & Sky." Written in Mytilene in 1963, it wasn't published until 1965, when Lax's Columbia classmate James Fitzsimmons devoted 117 pages of his literary journal, the *Lugano Review*, to it. "A grand poem," Van Doren wrote back. "Homer would have liked it."

Slow as this lover of traditional poetry was to appreciate Lax's poetic innovations, he saw the value of Lax living in and writing about Greece right away. "Your summer chronicle was very sweet to have," he wrote the first year Lax lived in the islands, "and I agree with Tom [Merton] that you should stay there as long as they let you. . . . We want you to be happy, and that is maybe the best place." A year later, after saying that he would never nag him about coming home because he was so obviously in a place he loved, Van Doren signed his letter for the first time "Love, Mark."

"About coming home," Lax wrote in his first letter describing Kalymnos, "it feels like I'm there." He credited Van Doren with inspiring his love of Greece, perhaps because Van Doren had gone there first or because his teaching had ignited a love for classical things. "i feel (sometimes) like your delegate here," Lax said, "(as long, at least, as i'm not just being my own damn fool). the glasses of water continue to pile up beside the coffee cups; the courtesies continue to be overwhelming, and i'm recording them, every one, for you."

Later in his life Lax told young writers not to write for publication or some general crowd but for one ideal reader. His was Mark Van Doren.

---

Lax's only extended time away from Kalymnos the next few years came in April 1965, when he spent a month and a half in Pietrasanta near the Tuscan town of Lucca. The invitation came from a friend of Alex Eliot, a priest turned sculptor named Père McGlynn who provided Lax with an Alfa Romeo and a housekeeper. One of the other guests was Harry Jackson, the artist who had done the life-size painting of Lax in New York. Jackson, who would soon reinvent himself as a sculptor of the American West, was there to learn the lost-wax sculpting method Pietrasanta was known for. Between writing sessions and conversations about art, Lax took advantage of his proximity to Puglia to visit Padre Pio, the elderly Catholic holy man who had long inspired him.

It was during or just after Lax's time in Pietrasanta that James Fitzsimmons published Lax's long "Sea & Sky." Each 8-by-10-inch page had a dribble of words and syllables down the left side; the rest was white space.

One typical page had only this:

all
dreams

one
dream

all
dreams

one
dream

the
sea-
sons

the
sea-
sons

the
sea

In a letter to Father Irenaeus, who had read the poem but didn't understand it, Lax wrote, "I'm not sure I understood it either (in a literal sense) or that anyone could be expected to. I agree, though, with your friends who compared it in some way to music (whether good or bad music): it may not 'say' a particular thing; but if listened to again & again (even without great attention), it begins to wake things up in the listener (and to put others to sleep that have been awake long past bedtime)." What's most significant here, I think, is that he says "listened to" rather than "read." His spare poems become much more powerful when read aloud. One friend compared "Sea & Sky" to a Brancusi bird in flight.

Fitzsimmons would publish another significant Lax poem, "Black & White," the following year but balk after that. It wasn't that he no longer admired what Lax was doing, simply that he couldn't justify publishing Lax's hyperspare work without running more columns on each page, thereby lessening the poetry's power. He did, however, pass his friend's poetry on to people he thought might publish it, including the English poet and editor Ian Hamilton Finlay, who included several Lax poems in his small but influential new journal *Poor. Old. Tired. Horse.*

By this time John Ashbery had already published four Lax poems in *Locus Solus*, and other poems were appearing in journals edited by Aram Saroyan and Stephen Bann, among others. Finlay, Saroyan, and Bann were all part of a group of poets who came to be called "concrete poets." Recognizing a fellow traveler, they adopted Lax into their group as a sort of elder statesman or, as Nicholas Zurbrugg, founder and editor of *Stereo Headphones*, dubbed him, one of "the new 'saints' of the contemporary avant-garde."

Lax never felt comfortable with the label *concrete*—he saw his work as abstract rather than concrete and preferred the term *minimalist*—but he could see the advantages of being attached to this avant-garde group and didn't fight it. His connection to the group was cemented, so to speak, in 1967, when Bann included him in a London publication called *Concrete Poetry: An International Anthology*. The following year Mary Ellen Solt became the first person to write critically about his work, including it in a discussion of poets such as Emmett Williams and Aram Saroyan in *Concrete Poetry: A World View: United States*.

In a letter to Solt, Lax traced his movement toward the spare, vertical approach he was becoming known for through several publishing milestones: his *New Yorker* poem "Solomon's High Dive," in which one word (the longest word in Italian, according to his circus friends), *precipite-volissimevolmente*, drops down the page letter by letter; his 1962 book, *New Poems*; his poems in *Locus Solus* and the *Lugano Review*; *Sea Poem*, a chapbook issued by Finlay's Wild Hawthorn Press in 1966; and two chapbooks published by Antonucci's Journeyman Press, *Thought* (1964) and *3 or 4 Poems about the Sea* (1966).

The letter references other signs of growing interest in his work too:

> A recording of him reading and commenting on his poetry made for the Library of Congress at a studio in Athens on November 18, 1965 (four reels totaling almost two hours). The commentary here was his first public attempt to talk about his aesthetic.
>
> A recording of him reading excerpts from "The Circus of the Sun," "Black & White," "Sea & Sky," and other poems for Harvard University's Lamont Library made early in 1966 (three reels totaling close to an hour and a half).
>
> A production of *Drama: An Abstract Verse Play*, an unpublished radio play broadcast on the BBC's *Poetry Now* program in January 1966.

In the midst of all this activity, on November 30, 1965, Lax turned fifty, as Merton had earlier in the year. But whereas Merton was in and out of the hospital that year and feeling the restless pull of physical love (this was the year of his affair with a nurse), Lax was entering one of the calmest periods of his life. Yes, his restlessness still took him from island to island and even country to country, but he had finally found somewhere that felt like home and he was finally writing just what he wanted to write. Writers and editors were encouraging his experimental approach, and he was feeling better physically than he had in a long time. The arthritis that had dogged him back in the States was better (although it would recur late in 1966, causing such pain in his ankle and instep that an Athenian doctor put them in a cast), he was swimming and walking regularly, and the ghostly paleness that had always been one of his distinguishing characteristics had darkened into a radiant tan.

As he grew more comfortable with Greek island life, Lax found it easier to settle into his writing—not just the descriptions of local activities and beliefs he had concentrated on at first but also the questions and explorations that took him deeper into his own being. In an undated letter to a friend sent around this time, he wrote, "solitude and writing: it took me three years to find (creep up on) any solitude or get any quiet writing done. before that i was standing on my head, writing into little notebks as we careened through mountain passes; wearing earplugs, sleeping with blinders, trying to make noises of my own to drown out neighbors. you do get some quiet in winter if you've found the right place; but a lot of your time is spent in the arts of survival. (this is not a complaint.)"

His search for "the right place" must have been a source of some amusement to the Kalymnians. His letters to friends are filled with announcements of new houses: in the hills, by the waterfront, in the middle of town, away from town. Sometimes he kept two at the same time—one for sleeping and one for writing—and once he had three. One of his favorites seems to have been the one by the harbor he moved into in February 1966. From it he could see workmen walking to the shipyard, women heading to the grocery store, and the "square cement hut" where Limnina wove her rugs. Across from him was a large area where sponge processors dried their sponges, children played, and, in the late afternoon, fishermen prepared their lines for the next day's catch. While he watched these others at work or play, he could hear the clanging of the blacksmiths in their "little smoke-blackened shed" and the hammers and clippers at work in the sponge warehouse downstairs. It seems clear from his cheerful descriptions of the sounds and activities around him that Lax enjoyed the noise and bustle, even if it kept him from getting work done

Throughout 1965, 1966, and 1967 Lax's journal entries veered between descriptions of the Greek island life around him and explorations of his own thoughts on how to live. Many times the external and the internal came together as he learned from watching the acting-out of rituals and variations in this old traditional culture. In the summer of 1965 he wrote:

the (town)
is the
sum
of all
the
things

that all
the in-

habitants

in all
(these
years)

have
learn
'd

This view of Kalymnos as a manifestation of his belief that humanity was in the process of perfecting itself—a belief reinforced by his reading of Pierre Teilhard de Chardin at the time—reappears many times in his journals during these years. The Cristianis had been an extended family living out his *pure act* beliefs; here was an entire community doing so. He wasn't blind to the misdeeds he witnessed, but he was so convinced of the islanders' basic goodness, so impressed by the confident, robust way they went about their lives, he felt sure they would work out the imperfections in time. He idolized them and idealized them, viewing them through a pleasingly hopeful naïveté that would have dire consequences.

As the following passage, written on July 23, 1965, shows, he wasn't unaware that his glasses were tinted rose, but he wanted so much to believe in the simple truths he was seeing—truths he'd first felt were a possibility as far back as his days in Marseilles or even New York after college—that he tried not to notice the lenses:

> though it's obviously a dream-world, and all my own,
> the best i can do is describe it. the attempt may be
>
> to touch my foot to the ground: it may be something else,
> to give to airy nothings etc a local habitation.
>
> the place supports the dream, the dream, the place.
>
> the people are gentle, they are also alive; they are
> intelligent & kind.
>
> when i talk of the people i am talking of the fishermen
> & their families. the people who live in ayios stefanos.

others are derived from them; they have the same qualities,
but seldom to the same degree of perfection.

perfection may not be it; but these people demonstrate
their qualities in high degree.

These impressions, set down so soon after he settled on the island, are
not surprising. Travel literature is filled with the raptures of people ideal-
izing the native inhabitants of wherever they found happiness. What is
surprising is how long and how deeply he held these feelings, this vision:
for a decade or more, before events intervened. More surprising still is
that they persisted through one of the darkest periods in the turbulent
history of modern Greece.

On July 15, 1965, Greece's young king, Constantine II, forced Prime
Minister George Papandreou, the left-leaning leader whose son the
Kalymnians had cheered so exuberantly in the spring of 1964, to resign.
Papandreou was the first centrist to be elected in Greece after years of
conservative governments, and the forced resignation was viewed as a
coup d'état. The result was two tumultuous years of political wrangling
and indecision before a group of colonels from the Greek Army took
power in a real coup on April 21, 1967, just weeks before an election Pa-
pandreou was predicted to win. Conservative and staunchly anticommu-
nist, the junta, led by Colonels George Papadopoulos and Nikolaos
Makarezos and Brigadier Stylianos Pattakos, quickly consolidated power
by arresting opponents. For the next seven years Greece was a highly
militarized state and, although tourism was encouraged, foreigners were
viewed with suspicion.

In the Dodecanese this suspicion was heightened by the islands' close
proximity to Turkey and a history of invasion—by pirates and foreign
armies—going back centuries. Lax was circumspect in his writing about
the darker aspects of Greek island life during this time, but his journals
and letters contain occasional hints at how it affected him.

Four days after the coup, for example, he sent a short, cryptic message
to Merton. "Well, we have finally heard from Aunt," it began. "Sandor &
Vashti have been giving her a lot of trouble & she has finally decided to
lock them both in a closet & to sit outside with Grandpa's (you remember
Grandpa)'s slingshot to more or less keep them both in place. it is only

understandable. Aunt's nerves had been strained to the breaking point, & that is what happened." The passage sounds like more of the playful gibberish Lax and Merton often exchanged, the people and situations made up, but it is unrelated to anything before or after it in their correspondence and most likely refers to what happened in the coup. This interpretation is borne out by the lines that immediately follow it: "Everything else is quite all right. There is something wrong with the radio now—it is down to one station and only plays music all day long." Martial music blared from the radio in the days just after the coup, when opponents of the new regime were arrested and a curfew imposed. Lax, it seems, was letting his friend know that trouble had come but he was okay.

Immediately after this, in the same letter, Lax announces that he is "going to Patmos, the isle of the saints for a week or so, & then right back to Kalymnos, where I know my way around." The lines are simple and yet, given the tenuous situation in Greece at the time, they seem fraught with meaning. He needed a break from Kalymnos, where, as a foreigner, he was subject to suspicion, yet he knew it was probably safest to be somewhere where he had friends and knew how things worked.

Lax stayed on Patmos for only three days on that visit, but on May 17 he told Merton he was going again, this time for two months. "cool breezes, orderly birds," he wrote. "bye-bye (for right now) kalymnos island of phonographs." The implication here is that Kalymnos had become too noisy—and, in fact, that's what Lax told the English poet Julian Mitchell when they met on Patmos later that May. According to Mitchell, Lax tried living on an even quieter, smaller island somewhere between Patmos and Samos that summer but found that there was little to eat there and it was difficult to get off the island once you were on it, so he returned to Patmos.

The smaller island might have been Lipsi, one of the three islands—along with Kalymnos and Patmos—Lax would shuttle among in later years, or it may have been Xiliamodi, an even smaller island he immortalized in a poem over a decade later. In any case, he decided that Patmos would suit him fine. The coup and the colonels' conservative ways had scared away all but a few foreigners, so his social life could be kept to a minimum. For the most part he kept to himself, writing his vertical poems.

It was probably on Patmos that summer of 1967 that Lax had his first taste of the suspicion and harassment he'd be forced to endure on whatever island he lived on in the coming years. In an article in *Modern Painters*, Mitchell wrote that the island's chief of police kept a close eye on the foreign artists who drank and laughed in the bars there that summer, convinced that they were spying for the Turks or the CIA. His suspicions seemed to be confirmed one night when Lax, startled by the sudden appearance of the chief's car, jumped into a ditch to avoid it. It became clear after that that Lax's mail was being opened.

Antonucci almost missed connecting with Lax on Kalymnos during this period because Lax's mail was held until it could be read and then released in bunches, delaying the details of Antonucci's arrival. When they did connect, it was obvious to Antonucci that Lax was being followed all the time, and when Antonucci left again, a man Lax had told him would probably be "traveling with him" ended up in his four-bed stateroom. Nothing untoward happened, but Antonucci was anxious the whole ferry ride because Lax had given him journals and photographs he wanted out of the country.

In the midst of this turmoil and suspicion, like a scientist conducting an experiment, Lax recorded the smallest details of his interactions with the Kalymnians and sent them, sometimes in edited form, to Van Doren. Van Doren passed them on to Merton or Antonucci, who had become the de facto keeper of Lax's writings. It was those small details that fascinated Lax, what they revealed about how the people lived. "there hasn't been any art (but fishing) on the island for ages," he wrote to Van Doren on January 15, 1966. "the museum, always deserted, has only got a couple of stones that seem to have been dragged in from other places (& forgotten). all they've really been doing for ages & ages is learning when & how to say 'hello.' they've got the knack of it now, i'll bet, better than the people on any other island (or continent) in the world."

He hadn't lived among them long, but he felt sure the Kalymnian fishermen came as close as any people he'd met to living his dream "of a city where all were alive & in relative agreement"—a dream he thought was God's dream too. There was a difference, he knew, between striving for perfection and achieving it, but he felt sure that the striving on the island was a striving free of striving, an innate knowledge of what choices to make in small things that would lead to the right larger choices for the individual and the society.

He carried this idea into his writing, wanting the choices he made about words on the page to be both careful and spontaneous, revealing his inner self as well as a Kalymnian's leap from boat to shore revealed his.

Whatever other difficulties hindered Lax's observations and discoveries during this time, his greatest concern was sustaining the life he was living. So in 1967 he applied for a Guggenheim grant again, and again his application was rejected. The selection committee can be forgiven, perhaps, for denying him funding after reading that he had been working on one "very long poem" for the past three years and his proposed activity was work "with just two words, black and white, and with two immediately related concepts, light and dark, attempting through them to translate a whole world of inner and outer phenomena to the terms of two contrasting non-colors."

Publications in literary journals were gratifying, of course, but they paid little or nothing, and living on Kalymnos, though incredibly cheap, was not free. Lax sustained himself mostly on the kindness of family and friends. In 1967, for example, Teddy Bergery contacted him about appearing, for a pittance, as an extra in a movie to be shot in Greece. At other times people sent gifts. When he needed shoes, his cousin Soni would buy the kind he liked in Manhattan and ship them to him, and anytime Antonucci managed to sell a book or chapbook he'd send the meager royalty. With books selling for $1.50 and chapbooks for 50 cents, though, there was little income. As for the short experimental movies Antonucci had begun to make from Lax's work—*Some Fables* (9 min., 1962), *Oedipus* (3 min., 1962), and *Thought* (3 min., 1967)—they only cost him money.

Merton tried to help out by sending a publisher an edited collection of letters he and Lax had exchanged between 1962 and 1965, but the publisher rejected them. "You look them over," Merton wrote when he sent the collection to Lax. "If you are starving that is different, we publish. If you are not getting your regular Wheaties we publish now." Lax replied that he was pleased to see the letters without commenting on their possible publication and Merton shelved the project. (He picked it up again in the last year of his life, and the collection was finally published as *A Catch of Anti-letters* in 1978.)

The need for money was one factor in Lax's decision to return to the States near the end of 1967. An old L'Eau Vive friend, Gerry Lange, had become a professor of history at South Dakota's General Beadle State College and invited him to be a writer in residence there, a paid position. The residency wouldn't begin until the following spring, but the stress of living under a dictatorship and a spate of sad news caused Lax to head home that November.

The first sadness came in a letter from Rice Lax picked up on Kalymnos in late September or early October: Ad Reinhardt, the artist who had inspired him since high school, was dead from heart failure at fifty-four. (Another from the Columbia *Jester* crowd, Bob Gerdy, who had risen to senior editor at the *New Yorker*, had died on a Manhattan street two years earlier.) Reinhardt was just two years older than Lax. In answer to a letter from Merton passing on the same news, Lax wrote:

> One could weep with out let for old Reinhardt. . . . I sit near the sea & almost fall into it from sorrow.
>
> & then I sit (as seldom enough we do) in a church & look at the black & grey squares of the tiles, till the spirit is somewhat mended.

Reinhardt would always be associated with the color black, the primary color in his most famous paintings. For Lax, the dark night of Greece may have been the best place to ponder the life and death of his friend—two years earlier he had written to Van Doren, "one night here (when I'd been reading & went for a walk) i saw it: black, black, black, in the spaces between the trees, above the houses, & over the sea: black, black (the most promising black i ever saw in the world)." But he must have felt the loneliness of being away from those he loved most at a time like that too.

Shortly after hearing of Reinhardt's death, Lax traveled to Yugoslavia to serve as a photographer at a Belgrade space conference for an old *Jubilee* friend, Jim Harford, who had become the executive director of the American Institute of Aeronautics and Astronautics. When he returned to Kalymnos, another shock awaited him: another close friend, John Slate, had died. Slate had been with him the first time he saw

Marseilles, and the two of them once understood each other so well they could communicate without words, either silently or in barks. Now Slate's bark had been silenced. His bite—that sharp wit Lax so admired—had been stifled too.

"now indeed we are all undone," Lax wrote to Merton, "it is our undoing now, everyone. with the passing of Dom John Slate is our generation all dissolved, resolved, whatever is left gentle in the world, gone up in a fume. We are only left (& in no shape, either) to tell each other the story."

In this same letter, sent on October 15, Lax told Merton that his brother-in-law Benji Marcus had died as well. Looking back over all that had happened that year, including the coup and the Six-Day War between Israel and the Arab states, which had made Merton and others concerned about his safety, Lax wrote that it had been "a bad year for us all."

Three weeks later he was on his way to Olean, where he spent the winter and the first part of spring comforting his sister while enduring the death of yet another close friend, Sy Freedgood. Freedgood had fallen asleep after drinking and taking a sleeping pill and his cigarette had set his house on fire.

"We must pray for old Freedgood," Lax wrote to Merton, ". . . and always, every minute take care."

Strong as his reasons were for leaving when he did, Lax must have left Kalymnos with great reluctance, unsure when or if he'd ever return. During the month preceding his departure, he filled his journal with loving observations about the people and their island, adding reflections on what living among them had taught him. He wrote about the one-room house Limnina and her mother and brother lived in, a place so small they cooked and even slept on the sidewalk until cold weather drove them indoors. He wrote about the unlettered fishermen he taught to read the clock on the church campanile. And he wrote about the shopkeepers who struggled to add up their sums. One day he asked a fisherman what day of the week a certain date fell on and then felt bad when the man started "counting on fingers that were used for any kind of work but that."

When he came across Paul in town one day, he told him he had an easy, peaceful way of walking. "That's because I'm one person," Paul said, "one piece—not Paulos today and Yanni tomorrow. When a shipbuilder puts a boat in the water, however he made it is how it will sail. That's how I am and how I'll die." The years Lax had spent in Greece, especially on Kalymnos, had moved him closer to feeling this way about himself.

His years on Kalymnos had been important for his development as a poet too. The freedom he felt there had helped him let go of virtually all poetic conventions, starting with narrative. In 1965, for example, he set down one of the first of what he called his "color poems," titling it "Abstract Poem"—a nod, perhaps, to the painters he'd known:

red
red

black
black

black
black

blue

red
red

black
black

black
black

blue

black
black

blue

black
black

blue

red
red

black
black

black
black

blue

The almost subconscious beauty of this combination of simplicity, rhythm, and exactness/abstractness was something Lax could have discovered only in the way he did: by living on an island where all of life seemed to have that combination. What allowed him to translate it into art was the time he had spent with Reinhardt and the other abstract painters in New York.

Lax was trying to write only about things he felt he understood without question, using only words he felt absolutely sure of. Among these were the standard names for colors. His use of them was akin to what Gertrude Stein had been doing thirty years before, most famously in her line "A rose is a rose is a rose": reclaiming the purity of words, allowing them to stand for only the thing they were meant to stand for. In this reclaiming, Lax was also reclaiming an elemental view of life, reducing it to its essence—an essence he felt Kalymnian fishermen understood with their whole being.

The playfulness that characterized Lax's experimentation is even more evident in a poem he wrote two years later. Called "Able Charlie Baker Dance" it contains only those four words broken into syllables. Arranged and rearranged over several pages, they combine in every possible way until, at the end, Charlie emerges almost magically in full dance. The first three words, of course, are only the word equivalents for the first three letters of the English alphabet when communicated over a radio: "A as in Able, B as in Baker, C as in Charlie." What makes the poem work—what turns it into a revelation—is the addition of that fourth word and the playful rhythmic variation Lax allows.

Here's how Lax explained what he was trying to do in these simple-seeming poems:

> You can take a word like "night" that's been used so often and in so many combinations that you think it's no longer usable and try to find a way of using it, in spite of that, so that its meaning becomes "night" again.
>
> One of the things you hope happens when you repeat a word rhythmically—and in a pattern that can be listened to pleasantly—is that all of its meanings will begin to reappear or re-present themselves in the mind—all the dimensions of its meanings. (This is essentially an auditory thing; the disposition of words on a page has the same relation to the sound of a poem as notes on a page of music have to the music.)
>
> The vertical arrangement of the words has two functions: to show the reader how to read it aloud—including where pauses should be— and to present the images one at a time. We are so accustomed to skimming and skipping in the traditional horizontal word arrangement that we no longer see many of the words as words; we start picking up whole phrases. The vertical arrangement restores the original value of each word and establishes the order in which the words are to be read.

Although Lax remained mostly stationary that winter of 1967–68, his writing career didn't. A young poet and friend of Van Doren named William F. Claire dedicated the second issue of his new literary journal, *Voyages*, to his work. In his introduction, Claire stated that "homage" issues (in this case, a double issue) usually come too late in a writer's career and he wanted to feature Lax's poetry while it was "just beginning to take hold in the minds of many people on both sides of the Atlantic." "Robert Lax's vision of the world," he continued, "is unspeakably beautiful and ever new, ever today or tomorrow: a continual searching, a kind of voyage that never ends, but is always just beginning."

After praising Lax's *Circus of the Sun*, Claire shifted to what most interested him, Lax's "new" poetry: "The later poetry of Robert Lax, which has undergone various linear changes, remains almost sacramental in its attempts to grasp the essence and quiddities of a few things that are by their very nature eternal. . . . It is what we all might have seen, if we but had the eyes, if we were ourselves at our best." The last line here is a particularly clear distillation of what Lax was trying to present in his poetry, expressed as simply as he might have expressed it himself.

Although *Voyages* was a new magazine with a small circulation, the devotion of an entire issue of an attractive, well-edited magazine to Lax's life and work was a kind of coming-out party. In addition to several vertical poems, Claire included excerpts from the Kalymnos journals, photographs Lax had taken of Kalymnians, an excerpt about Lax from Van Doren's autobiography, a sampling of Merton and Lax's "anti-letters," a note from Antonucci on working with Lax, poems about him from Van Doren and Packard, and Levertov's 1961 *Nation* review of *Circus of the Sun*, as well as a 1968 postscript in which Levertov wrote that Lax's more recent poems saddened her. The problem, she wrote, was that unlike earlier Lax poems, these latest ones seemed more visual than aural. She did like the more "sonic" poems such as "Sea & Sky," though, "in which the repeated words, when the poem is read aloud properly, bring about in the imagination a more profound sense of their meanings till by the end of the poem we are hot with the sun on stone and our [ears] are filled with the susurrations of the sea and our eyes with its dazzle."

Perhaps more important in establishing Lax as a poet to be studied was an appreciation of his work by Stephen Bann, a young professor of modern cultural studies at the University of Kent at Canterbury, who had included Lax in his *Concrete Poetry: An International Anthology* the previous year. In a two-page article, Bann links Lax to the Swiss Bolivian poet Eugen Gomringer, claiming that both are precursors of the concrete poetry movement because "the Concrete aesthetic—with its insistence on the values of purity in the object and reverence in the beholder—is itself implicitly related to the religious and philosophical attitudes with which Lax and Gomringer are concerned."

Here Bann puts into print for the first time one of the keys to understanding Lax's later poetry. To use Van Doren's words, Lax was attempting to "state his bliss" by reducing whatever he saw and valued to its essentials—its "purity"—and conveying his "reverence" for what he saw, a reverence akin to the mystic's ecstatic vision. If one reads his vertical poetry—whether its focus is a stone or an anecdote or an idea—as an opportunity to view "purity of the object and reverence in the beholder," the poetry (and, even more, the reading of the poetry if it is read out loud) slows and transcends time. The simple focus and singular relationship of the actual moment become all there is. (This idea is stated more succinctly in the title of a later Lax collection, *A Thing That Is*.)

The two reasons Bann gives for why Lax's poetry matters (beyond the skill with which he does what he does) are his movement in the opposite direction from the overly secular approach to poetry then in ascendance and his clear—I'd say necessary—belief that what he was writing could make "momentous statements about human existence in our times."

Bann's placing of Lax among the early practitioners of concrete poetry was an important step in establishing him as a forerunner of the late twentieth-century avant-garde.

---

Surrounded as it was by prairies in the heart of the heart of the country (to use William Gass's phrase), General Beadle State College in Madison, South Dakota, was one of the few campuses Lax might have felt comfortable on in a year as turbulent as 1968. The school probably had its share of students opposed to the Vietnam War, but it was a small, quiet teachers college far from the centers of disruption. Lax arrived in mid-April and stayed only a month, but the experience left a deep impression on him.

During his previous teaching stints he had been a lowly instructor; this time he was a respected writer in residence.

The residency couldn't have come at a better time. Not only had the *Voyages* issue just come out, but Lax had spent his years in Greece developing a strong understanding of what he was trying to do with his poetry. In other words, he'd established a conscious aesthetic from which to talk to students about writing. Not that he spent much time in the classroom. He was required to teach just two two-hour poetry-writing workshops, offer two poetry readings, and give lectures titled "How to Read a Poem" and "Contemporary Cross-currents Between Painting and Poetry." There was a vague expectation that he would work with some individual students too, but otherwise he was free to write in his room at the Hotel Park or linger at the farm owned by his host, Gerry Lange.

For his work as a writer in residence Lax received $3,000, a fortune to him, but the most gratifying part of the whole experience was the enthusiastic response to his readings, the first he'd given in front of an audience since reading parts of his *Circus* series in small Village venues a decade before.

"Out here it's a ranch," he wrote to Van Doren, "an unlikely place at least till you get here—and then so natural you'd never believe you'd been anyplace else. I haven't seen all of it yet, but you can feel miles of silence around you—& chomping grass."

For all of his travels, Lax had never spent time in the Midwest or even the West other than Hollywood, and he was pleased with the "miles of silence" that seemed to surround him. When his residency was over, he intended to drop down into Kentucky to visit Merton, but Merton was traveling, so instead he worked his way through Rapid City, Rushmore, Deadwood, and Cheyenne to the former mining town of Kremmling, Colorado, to visit Beverly Burford (now DeBerard). There he attended the ribbon-cutting for a new road, watched roping and branding, and tried his hand at fishing—all new experiences for him. He also saw the *Middle Park Times* run an article on him in which he talked about his Greek island house with its dirt floors and writing by kerosene lamp.

While in South Dakota and on the road, Lax received postcards and letters from Merton describing his own travels. "Was two days alone on the beach with consoling visions," he wrote from California in mid-May.

The Pacific Coast seemed a perfect place for a hermitage, he said, describing a scenario remarkably like Lax's life on Greece: "Live in small white haven & write small poems each one describing over & over again one small seagull."

According to Merton, Lax brought "innumerable cans of tuna fish and several pints of whiskey" when they finally got together in mid-June. Neither of them recorded what they talked about during their six days together, but after the death of so many friends, with Lax planning to return to Greece and Merton to travel to Asia, the tenderness and concern between them must have been palpable. They hadn't seen each other in nine years, and as it turned out, they'd never see each other again.

"I don't know if he should return to Greece," Merton wrote in his journal when Lax had left. "Kalymnos seems the only place he really likes anywhere. I don't blame him. But also I don't trust a police state sustained by the C.I.A."

Using Olean as his base, Lax spent the later part of that summer visiting friends up and down the East Coast and, on one of his passes through New York City, lunching with an editor from Holt, Rinehardt & Winston to talk about the possible publication of the Merton-Lax letters. Seeing several appear in *Voyages* seems to have rekindled Merton's interest, and he'd found a woman in Santa Barbara willing to print 1,500 copies, but he still hoped a bigger house might take them. The collection had made the rounds of major publishers, but only Holt had shown interest. So Lax met with its editor and, as he reported to Merton, after being "rendered drunk on vodkum martinis," was turned down. "If only I'd known you at the beginning of your correspondence," the editor said, "I could have told you what to write."

———————

Lax finally left for Europe on October 3 and stopped in Paris, Marseilles, Valence, La Salette, and Rome on his way to Greece. His happiness at being back on Kalymnos and with life in general comes through clearly in a November 27 letter to Van Doren:

Here again & it's all beautiful. Better, even, than I'd remembered.

The simplest man on the island, seeing Dorothy's picture of us, first of all asked who you were. Then said: "But he's a simple man. A very simple man. He's . . . like a spongediver! You . . . you wear a necktie. But look at him!"

Limnina (the rug girl), too, sends her love. She thinks I've forgotten my Greek, but I think she's just forgotten how little I knew.

I had dinner out one night with a young wood-carver & his wife. We had five fish, of which I managed to eat one. When I left them I said I was going for a walk 'for my digestion'—it's a thing you say. Later he said his wife had said: "He walks to digest *one* fish?"

Merton, I'm sure you know, is in Asia, with the Dalai Lama (really) & the Abominable Snowfellow (probably).

> Love,
>
> Bob

By the time Lax's letter reached Van Doren, Merton had already left the Dalai Lama and traveled on to Ceylon, where, among other sites, he visited the ruins of the old Buddhist shrine at Polonnaruwa. There, in the presence of several large smiling Buddhas, he experienced a transcendent joy like none he had ever known. A few days before this experience, he'd written to Lax that he was hoping his abbot would let him extend his journey through Asia to Greece, where they would go to Mt. Athos together. With both of them filled with such joy, what a reunion that might have been, but it was not to be. On December 11 Gladio sent her brother a telegram saying that Merton was dead. A faulty electric fan in a room he was staying in near Bangkok had electrocuted him.

That evening, as Lax was going into town, he saw a single star and a single cloud above a hill. A poem came to him and he wrote it down, not realizing until later that it was about Merton. A few days later he enclosed it with a letter to Antonucci in which he wrote, "Think somehow night & day about [his death] & him. . . . Basically feeling o.k. Glad to be here where every part of landscape makes sense." Antonucci illustrated the poem and published it under the title "A Poem for Thomas Merton":

sin
gu
lar

star

sin
gu
lar

cloud

sin
gu
lar

hill

sin
gu
lar

cloud

sin
gu
lar

star

sin
gu
lar

hill

one
cloud

one
star

one
hill

one
hill

one

cloud


one

star

In Antonucci's final drawing, the star, which had been squeezed between the hill and the cloud in the previous illustration, soars above the cloud-covered hill.

When asked in an interview about Merton's death, Lax said he felt less that he'd lost a friend than a correspondent. Never again would he receive those wonderfully playful, encouraging, and inspiring letters. He could still read Merton's books, of course, and he did, right through the end of his own life. He read the old ones again and each new one as it appeared, no doubt hearing Merton's voice as he read.

---

Anyone who's read about Merton's last days knows that he was looking for somewhere new to live—somewhere where he could be a hermit without a monastery nearby. What few know is that Merton and Lax discussed moving somewhere together. The many disturbing events of 1968, including the assassinations of Martin Luther King Jr. and Bobby Kennedy (which happened just two days before their last time together) weighed heavily on their minds. Few countries seemed safe or even quiet, least of all America or Greece.

The California coast, the New Mexico desert, and the Alaskan wilds were places in the United States that still appealed to Merton, all of them far from the centers of civilization. Among foreign possibilities, he mentioned Ceylon, Nepal, Bhutan, and the Sanctuary of La Salette. ("Lama friend knows of rock hermitage ½ way up a cliff in Bhutan & full of Tibetan paintings," he wrote in one letter from Asia. "I don't know if it is not also full of abominable snowmen. But will investigate.")

The most intriguing possibility involving Lax came in a letter Merton sent on August 22, just two weeks before leaving Gethsemani for the West Coast and Asia:

> I got one last idea just one last idea for a place for a quiet life and no dam disturbances and less police sta[t]e. The Leper Colony on Molokai. Serious. It is on a point that can only be reached by helicopter.

And all the nice lepers scare shit out of tourists, guaranteeing peace and quiet.

Think it over. It may be where I end up.

On December 8, full of joy at being back on Kalymnos and the thought that he and Merton might travel together somewhere soon, starting perhaps with Mt. Athos, Lax wrote to his friend, "learn as many breathings as possible from the meditative monks & whatever else can be done for recollection. The conditions of modern civilization, even in tree-tops, militates strongly against the aspirations of hesychast & lama. where now is recollected silence? in scotland, really? in marakesch? do you think i can still find some in a cave, on some island?"

The silence came, more quickly and awfully than Lax imagined. Before Merton could read what his friend had written, he was dead. And Lax, despite living half his life nearby, never made it to Mt. Athos.

# 20 A Galapagos of the Spirit

Lax didn't attend Merton's funeral. He had just returned to Greece and couldn't afford another trip. Besides, as he wrote to Antonucci, he felt better staying where both the landscape and the rhythms of life made sense. He was on his own now in ways he had never been before, even during his solitary travels. After thirty-five years of sharing his spiritual and intellectual journey with a friend who was closer than a brother, he would have to go on alone. He wanted to spend the start of his solo pilgrimage in the place he felt most at home.

Over the next several years—from 1969 though the summer of 1974, when he made his next trip to the United States—Lax rarely left Greece, and only the summer heat and crowds ever drove him from Kalymnos. When he went anywhere, it was only to the nearby islands of Patmos and Lipsi. These were mostly quiet years of increasing confidence and steady growth in his understanding of his inner life.

Despite his more settled existence and distance from the world's media centers, Lax's work continued to attract attention. In October 1968, the BBC's *Third Programme* broadcast a forty-minute reading of his poems with commentary by Julian Mitchell and David Kilburn called "Is Robert Lax like Thomas Chatterton, an Invention of the CIA?" Mitchell suggested that the poet Robert Lax didn't actually exist but was only the invention of Columbia classmates Thomas Merton, Ad Reinhardt, and someone called Robert Lax. This ill-conceived attempt at humor not only caused Lax concern about his return to Greece, where people still listened to the BBC despite the colonels' control, but also misled and probably confused listeners.

Whatever distress it caused, it brought Lax a little money, as did the publication of his poem "Thought" in the December 1968 issue of *Harper's Bazaar* as part of a feature article on the overlooked work of small presses such as Journeyman.

Antonucci had already made a two-and-a-half-minute film based on "Thought" and was trying to drum up interest in it and other films he'd made from Lax's work. His most ambitious (and no doubt expensive) one to date, a twenty-minute live-action interpretation of *New Poems* called *New Film*, made it to the New York Film Festival's final selection stage in 1969, the closest any of his films ever came to any kind of real recognition.

In all, Antonucci would make nine films from Lax's writings: *Twenty-Seventh & Fourth* (1960, 22 min.), *Some Fables* (1962, 9 min.), *Oedipus* (1962, 3 min.), *Thought* (1967, 3 min.), *New Film* (1969, 20 min.), *Short Films* (1969, 20 min.), *Red & Blue* (1971, 25 min.), and *Shorts* (1971, 18 min.).

While still flush with his South Dakota success, Lax encouraged Antonucci to send his poems out in all directions. Before 1968 was over, his writing had appeared in *Columbia Forum*, *London Magazine*, another issue of *Voyages*, a journal Rice was working with called *Good Work*, a new Washington-based journal called *Dryad*, the first volume of Nicholas Zurbrugg's soon-to-be-influential *Stereo Headphones*, and a book called *Thirty-one New American Poets*. Antonucci had also issued several chapbooks: *The Angel and the Old Lady*, *Three Poems*, and *A Poem for Thomas Merton*. And, after years of listening to Merton's solicitations on Lax's behalf, James Laughlin was ready to publish his poems in the New Directions magazine—but only if Lax had more "horizontal" poems that required fewer pages.

Antonucci's letters to Lax during this period are filled with reports on contacts he's made and suggestions for future books or films. (A list of "possibilities for publishing or filming" he gave Lax in June 1971 includes 226 suggestions from things Lax had written in the past three years alone!) Lax is often portrayed as being uninterested or unengaged in publication matters, but his letters to Antonucci show both marketing and business savvy.

Of course Lax couldn't afford to be inattentive; he needed money. Payments from small publications dribbled in but they were never enough, so in October 1969 he decided to try once more for a Guggenheim. To bolster his request for funds to cover the one-year period from March 1970 to March 1971, he solicited references from an impressive group: not only Van Doren and Antonucci but William Maxwell, Denise Levertov, James Laughlin, Ned O'Gorman, Padraic Colum, John Ashbery, and Marianne Moore. His description of his project this time put more emphasis on his attempts to extract the universal from the specific Greek world around him and to break language down to its essentials:

> technically my interest of recent years has been in the syllable. i have seen it as the unit of which poems are made much as, until recently, at least, the atom was seen as the unit of physical matter. i have been interested, that is, in the syllable, not the line, not in the word, but in syllables and in rhythmic groups of syllables, which perhaps should be called lines but which as i use them rather resemble chains, vertical groups of syllables (usually common words of striking and universal significance—cut into syllables and arranged in rhythmic and semantic grouping—after the manner of poets of all time, but in vertical arrangement, rather than horizontal. the reason for this verticality is to present the eye of the reader—the ear, too, with one syllable at a time—the syllables of which the word, the words, and of which the poem is made.

---

Despite the best efforts of his recommenders, the result this time was the same as before: no grant. Lax did have some luck near the year's end, however. *Columbia Forum*, edited by his old *Jubilee* colleague Oona Sullivan, published six pages from his "Kalymnos Journal" in its winter 1969 issue; the National Endowment for the Arts chose a section of his journal already published in *Voyages* for its *American Literary Anthology 3*, netting him $500; and, in the most welcome news, Antonucci secured a $5,000 small-press grant from the National Endowment for the Arts, with which he would not only publish several of Lax's works—including his next book, *Fables*—but also pay him for his writing.

None of this income would sustain Lax for long, but it was enough to keep him alive and in Greece.

In fact the year that followed Merton's death turned out to be much better than Lax could have imagined. His work was being praised by more and more critics—including Ralph J. Gleason, one of the founders of *Rolling Stone* magazine, who said that the young, aspiring poets in San Francisco all looked up to him—and he felt more comfortable than ever on Kalymnos. After renting, at one time or another, maybe twenty different houses, he'd settled on three, using each for a different activity. In one near Chora that had a well and a kerosene lamp and rented for $50 a year he wrote his poetry. In one in the noisy center of town he did his journaling and typing. And in one in the fishermen's part of town, Agios Stefanos, "high & right over the sea," he did everything else, including sleeping, eating breakfast, and doing laundry.

That summer's journals reflect an easy feeling about his life and work. He writes lovingly about the island's people, paying particular attention to those he thinks have "found their center." When he sees these people, he says, "i like to watch them walk, or sit & mend nets, or fish, or swim"— involved, in other words, in the simplest activities, those they do unconsciously. In their simplest movements he finds "a kind of perfection."

One aspect of the island's community that Lax appreciates most is its self-contained nature. It's a Galapagos of the spirit for him, a place to observe spiritual evolution in isolation, to see life as it is meant to be lived:

> as the living body, whole body, out & in, has a texture, so has the life of the town. a tone & a texture, changing from moment to moment & yet in many aspects remaining the same.
>
> this is the texture of life, a texture that is woven as closely as on a continent, and as closely on a rock (with one living man) as on an island.
>
> it is to perceive this texture that we have seeing eyes, hearing ears and feeling hands. it is not only to be warned by it of dangers, nor invited by it to desire, but to enjoy, to appreciate it from moment to moment in its life and in its passing.
>
> our contact with life, with the flow of life, is a physical contact: spiritual, too—but physical none the less.

The last line here conveys as well as anything he ever wrote why the "hermit" label never fit him. He loved the physical "texture" of life, loved being out among people—interacting with them, observing them. He never wanted to withdraw completely into a solely spiritual or even mental apprehension of existence.

The physical activity he enjoyed most was swimming. Looking at the underwater world through a diving mask made him feel peaceful, and swimming firmed up his body, making him feel "less like a disembodied soul." But it was the social side of swimming he liked best. He swam with older men who had acquired the wisdom necessary to stay healthy and alive. The "fittest" in Darwin's phrase "survival of the fittest," he decided, were not necessarily the fiercest or fastest but simply the wisest. "to live among greeks (and especially, perhaps, among kalymnians) is to live in an atmosphere of wisdom," he writes. The wisest of these wise people, he thought, were the fishermen. They were his teachers, his mentors.

———————

Although Lax had developed a strong love for the islanders and a clear sense of why he was living among them, he worried that the reverse wasn't true. Their acceptance of him was provisional, he knew, dependent on seeing him as a peaceful man. When he asked Stellio whether the islanders liked him, Stellio assured him they did but no one could figure out why he was there. A day or two after this conversation, the first men landed on the moon and the town took pride in the Americans' accomplishment, even those who had said the Lord would never allow it. "perhaps they see my being here as though this is the moon & i am an astronaut," Lax wrote afterward, "and now that i've come here & written a little & photographed a little, they wonder why i don't go back to my planet, the earth."

Lax had no desire to go anywhere else—except, on occasion, somewhere quieter. Then he would usually travel to Patmos, as he did that October. "patmos, holy patmos," he writes. "i've never come here without the feeling, at least on the first few days, that the island is holy." Part of that holiness was a peacefulness that seemed to permeate the landscape itself—except in the summer sometimes, when the tourist crowds grew. Then Lax would often look for smaller islands to stay on. That fall, for example, he tried Fourni near Ikaria, where only a thousand people lived. He liked it but worried he wouldn't be able to get off it in winter. Next he tried Lipsi, a tiny island near Patmos he had visited before. It seemed ideal in many ways—beautiful and close to a larger island, small in population but big enough to have cafés and restaurants—yet there was something about it that wasn't quite comfortable. Things were magnified there, he thought, including the suspicion of foreigners he'd sensed among some on Kalymnos.

It wasn't uncommon for Lax to jot down initial observations, then circle back later and put them in a philosophical context. This approach helped him see even troubling aspects of his surroundings in Greece as instructional, part of a larger vision. Occasionally, though, philosophizing wasn't enough. At those times he tended to turn himself into a character, transforming whatever situation was bothering him into barely disguised autobiographical fiction. That's what he did that November on Lipsi.

Writing about himself in the third person, he recalled that he had spent hours alone as a child, dancing to music or performing in an imaginary theater, enjoying the liveliness of his mind. To make his imagination come alive now, he needed solitude, but there was a catch: the more time he spent alone, the less attention he paid to how he was dressed or whether he shaved. Worse than that, his eyes took on a far-off look that made the Greeks around him uneasy. He was determined to think, as he had from the beginning, that the island people were gentle and lovable, but they, "prodded by their demons," asked, "what would a spy be doing on our island? why should he come to trouble us, we who are so poor?"

---

Lax returned to Kalymnos at the end of 1969 to weather the winter in his houses there and greet Ed Rice, whose visit brightened an otherwise bleak period of steady rain and constant wind. Since losing *Jubilee* in a legal battle two years before and then his marriage, Rice had been working as a freelance writer and photographer for publications and organizations such as the United Nations and the Red Cross. His work had taken him around the world, but now he was having dizzy spells and had fallen into a depression so deep he had tried tranquilizers. His stop on Patmos was a chance not only to rest and see his old friend but also to talk about a book he'd decided to write on Merton, one that would tell the truth about Merton's life without sanitizing it or sanctifying him as Rice thought other authors were doing.

The visit seems to have gone well, though how much they discussed Merton is uncertain. Lax told a friend they hardly mentioned him, but all of Rice's letters from around this time solicit information for his book. It may be that Lax was reluctant to comment for publication. Despite several requests, he'd written nothing about Merton himself except the one poem.

---

While Lax was moving from island to island, capturing local life in his journal and writing occasional poetry, Antonucci was using his NEA money to produce *Fables*, a collection of Lax's more narrative poems, stretching back to "The Man With the Big General Notions." The "fables" ranged from vignettes so short they were almost jokes to more elaborate stories, all commenting in some way on how we live. They read like poetry, but not the poetry Lax had come to write. The lines are longer and the line breaks are intended to serve the story rather than focus a reader's attention on individual words or syllables. Perhaps the most popular piece in the book is a poem called "Alley Violinist," which has been reprinted several times:

if you were an alley violinist

and they threw you money
from three windows

and the first note contained
a nickel and said:
when you play, we dance and
sing, signed
a very poor family

and the second one contained
a dime and said:
i like your playing very much,
signed
a sick old lady

and the last one contained
a dollar and said:
beat it,

would you:

stand there and play?

beat it?

walk away playing your fiddle?

Another Antonucci publication that year was a poem called "Homage to Wittgenstein" that Lax had written after reading only part of the introduction to a collection of Wittgenstein's works. After reading the rest of the introduction, he realized the poem wasn't really about Wittgenstein's thought at all but the vague ideas he had gleaned about the philosopher's life. He told Antonucci to change the title if he wanted to, but Antonucci left it alone.

---

On a single day in the fall of 1970, Lax set down a number of revealing statements about how he had come to view life and its relationship to writing. Central to this was the idea that both life and writing—or art in general—must be dynamic, rising from one's true self and never rigidly restricted by laws or rules or even an overly earnest striving for perfection. "the perfectly right becomes the perfectly wrong; the imperfectly right leaves a door for the winds of change," he wrote. Here are some other thoughts from that long entry:

> the words were like precipitate that rose from a stream which flowed with remarkable consistency within him. he took them as they came, often ungrammatical, often incorrect, and not infrequently of a character not to be used in gentle society. he wrote them as they came, feeling often that the errors, the incorrect and the gross expressions were the ones which told the most, conformed to the contours, the flow of the stream. for it was the stream, the nature of the stream, he had set himself now to reveal.
>
> once he had charted its course, or had even well begun to chart it, others could follow; they could learn to distinguish, as he was now learning to distinguish, the living words from the dead, the tone of truth from that of useless falsehood. of creative truth, he meant, of a living truth; not a truth that stood like a rock against all changes of life, all appeals of mercy: a truth that could live, a truth that could act.
>
> . . . what was to be kept going in life was an action: a dance, a song, an act of love. there were not "values" to be remembered; there were not "laws" to be remembered: there was a tone, a way, a kind of action. there were ways of doing things which people (having certain gifts) could compass. there was the wise man's way and the fool's way, the fiery man's way and the slow man's way. naturally, the ways were not alike, but each man doing his action in his own way, was doing an action and was doing it in "the way". "the way" was to do it with confidence and love and truth. (and to do the thing, once decided, without hesitation).

Lax states more clearly here than elsewhere that what he has been calling "The Kalymnos Journal" is really a book of wisdom drawn from his observations of the islanders and himself. This wisdom—this "way"— comes from a combination of being careful and being relaxed. It comes from "a center of kindness, a center of love" as well. It can't be faked or merely assumed, nor can it simply be copied from others. "the way," he writes, "whatever it is, must be defined and redefined; the definitions broken and redefined (again)." The discovery of this kind of wisdom is a reason to write new books: "although there is no end of 'making books' perhaps there should not be an end; should there be an end to making songs? to having dreams? to making love?"

It all comes back, he believes, to one's desire for meaning, a desire that should be nurtured above all:

> what a writer writes should have some relation (though not necessarily a discoverable relation) to the meaning of his life.
>
> and the meaning of our lives should have some relation (to the meaning of the life of the world)
>
> but the meaning of our lives, and what we write, and what we do, is somehow in us from the beginning: in this sense, the child's only duty is to live and grow

Lax wrote these lines in the middle of one of the stranger episodes in a life full of odd occurrences. Sometime that summer, while visiting Athens, he'd had a twenty-minute conversation with a man named Sig Cohen, a program officer for the U.S. Information Agency in Washington, DC, who asked him to return for a reading at the U.S. consular office in Athens that fall. What began as a simple invitation to read close to home soon ballooned into plans for an extended reading tour through the Middle East. Lax would be representing American culture to people in other lands, Cohen told him, sweetening the pot by saying he'd buy every copy of Lax's Journeyman books available and sell them at the readings. Late that August Lax received a formal invitation suggesting a tour of two and a half months; a week later someone from Athens called to suggest a longer one, beginning in Pakistan on November 1 and ending in India four months later, with stops in Israel and several other places in between.

Lax seems to have been excited by the possibility at first—until everyone, beginning with Antonucci (who also received calls from Cohen), told him not to go. In his innocence, Lax thought it might be good to go on the tour, Antonucci told me, but that kind of propaganda trip for the government would have ruined his image in the United States, especially in the midst of an unpopular war.

———————

Although more people than ever were paying attention to Lax's writing, no one had bothered yet to do an in-depth analysis of what he was doing and why. That changed in the summer of 1970, when a British art critic named R. C. Kenedy started work on a "preliminary" study after hearing Lax's poems on the BBC. Over the next few months he sent Lax not one but two studies of his poetry. In response to the first, Lax wrote that Kenedy was saying "so many things that have long been needed in relation to the work that my first reaction was almost to cry." His response to the second was even more effusive: "twenty million joys & no sorrows in whole piece; and gratitude (if granted me to feel & show) forever." Reading such insightful criticism, he wrote, made him determined to write "many new & many better poems." Lax's words suggest that he was more anxious for critical recognition than people knew—that a lack of it, in fact, had lessened his energy for writing poems.

Kenedy's critique, which appeared in the *Lugano Review* in 1971, includes high praise for the *Circus* cycle, calling its "Sunset City" section (the same section Levertov thought most highly of) "one of the greatest poems in the English language," but he focuses most of his attention on Lax's later, simpler-seeming poems: "His statements are of the simplest kind in most of his verse. . . . Superficially they seem to be repetitive assertions of patently-obvious and axiomatic observations. However, in his best moments, they illuminate precisely stated possibilities—with implications of enormous depths."

One of the two poems Kenedy chooses to illustrate Lax's work is "This bread is bread," which he assumes is about the Eucharist:

this
bread

is
bread

this
wine

is
wine

this
bread

is
bread

this
wine

is
wine

these
hands

are
hands

these
hands

are
hands

this
bread

is
bread

this
wine

is
wine

"Lax's subjects are the most highly charged and symbolic units of our western experience," Kenedy writes in regard to the poem. "His choice of them is, obviously, not accidental. By treating them in one kaleidoscopically changing sequence of juxtapositions, he lists truths that hint at the religious mysteries of our still-changeless rites, performed as they are throughout Christendom's churches and cathedrals every Sunday. The wine—which is not-wine; the bread which is no-longer-bread—held in the hands: which distinguish man from beast. He cites the self-evident observation of the everyday to invoke a memory of transformations. Repeated repetitively, as it is in his poem, the quotidian commonplace becomes a chant—and itself, miraculous."

Kenedy doesn't like all of Lax's work. Some is too reductive, he feels, but he dismisses this as the danger of working with such elemental and seemingly obvious objects and concepts. Of being an experimenter too: "The miraculous balance between style and vision is rarely achieved by the experimental writer, and Lax is very much in the forefront of literary experimentation."

Lax could not have asked for a more perceptive or generous reader to be the first extensive explicator of his work. Kenedy gives careful consideration to all aspects of his poetry: content, form, look, sound, and effect. "Lax is, in a special sense and in many ways, an anti-visionary poet," he writes.

> He responds to immediacies and his innocence has overwhelming qualities. He attempts to glimpse things as if for the first time and the poetic labour, which he must know well, discovers hidden implications by fixing his gaze on whatever is close to his eyes. He does not depart from accuracy. His is a scheme which allots to him the honest reporter's part (hence the interest of his journals and letters). . . . He is prepared to do honest work and his thought has the clarity of logical exercises. The drunkenness his language transmits is the true poetic inspiration's which comes from rhythmic sources—like the Negro's drumbeat: which records muscular energies spent on creating an idea, and not merely the untamed forces resident in artificial banes.

It is the "verbal magic of the rhythm" of Lax's poetry that keeps him from being "a mere concrete poet," Kenedy writes. "His insistence on minimal typographic blocks, floated as these are into the airy and skylike spaces of near-blank paper, convey optical impressions of a deliberate character—but Lax's is a poetry which has aural traits strong enough to overcome its self-imposed (concrete?) limitations, or—to combine with them, in order to create a much more total impression."

In Kenedy's view, Lax's thin vertical columns "stress, if anything, the ultimate solitude of the voice which pierces a categorical emptiness. Whether the emptiness belongs to silence or to a yearning for some sort of communication." And the "light" of his best poems "is an inner light which bursts through the print in order to illuminate the understanding of the solitary creature."

Ultimately it is the person—and the humility of that person— observing his world so carefully and crafting poetry from his observation that gives the poems their power: "These compositions have the force to imply that everything is capable of being transformed into symbolic meaning by coming into contact with a passionate human being. Nothing is too small and nothing is too great to be comprehended—or to transmit the meaning which is behind meanings and which defines itself by remaining incomprehensible. Lax has chosen to write about the common experience in order to avoid seeming to be an elected person. Sanctity is meaningful to him only if it belongs to everything; to sea, sky, minnow and god."

The simple yet profound beauty of Lax's best work, including *The Circus of the Sun*, leads Kenedy to confess, "One has a guilty moment and searches the mind for a block which may have prevented one from following his gaze into the eternities revealed to this most upright man."

Appearing as it did in a small, Switzerland-based journal, Kenedy's critique didn't make much of an impact, but it did establish a theoretical framework for future considerations of Lax's work, and it may have contributed significantly to interest in Lax among European poets.

# 21　All Thoughts as They Come

Lax spent much of the summer of 1970 writing one-paragraph stories and concentrated strings of thought he called "histories." By the spring of 1971, however, he had switched to longer, free-flowing works, calling each a "tractatus," the Latin word for *treatise*, which he had borrowed from Wittgenstein. He never explained why he chose it, but he may have felt ready to set down, in his own inimitable way, the conclusions he'd come to about writing and life. Over the next three years—years that in many ways were the high point of his life—he filled his journals with thoughts on these two subjects. He had written about them before, of course, but his writing during this period was more assured, as if the questions he had long asked had been answered.

What distinguishes his *tractatus* writings from those that read more like traditional treatises is their complete freedom from divisions and definitions. They go where they go, flowing from one form of writing into another without concern for the expectations of others. "Tractatus I," for example, is a long block of prose in which he speaks of himself in the third person, interrupted by a simple poem about confrontations between "red" and "blue." It begins:

> he was determined this time not to write about anything, to keep as far away from any possible subject as he could and just to keep going, to include or to exclude whatever came to mind, not necessarily to leave it in, not necessarily to leave it out: to let things rise to his consciousness, to be examined briefly, and let fall again or invited to enter. he knew these places well, these ups and downs, these ins and outs, he saw them as he'd see a building, an old and quite familiar building. he ran round it through the day, and all through the night, in dreams, he was mounting and descending its well-worn stairs. as a watcher, he would watch things rise, or as an actor, he himself would climb, and fall. (one memory jarred with another: one would collide with another.) no, he would not approach a single subject: not one of the many that played through his mind through the day. (there was a

process of knitting going on: the form of the stitches was more impor-
tant than the color of the yarn.) to keep going: to turn one wheel after
another: a large one after a small one, a small one after a large one,
until all wheels were spinning, innumerable wheels spinning, and
spinning, perhaps, within the circumference of a single, very large
wheel; a single globe.

What seems clear in this passage is that he has moved far beyond the
seemingly arbitrary division of inspiration and writing into poetry or
prose, even fiction or nonfiction. He has given up editing his work as
well—at any level. He has turned Kerouac's idea of "first thought, best
thought" into "all thoughts as they come." If a later thought impinges on
an earlier one, each is left as it is for the reader to sort out. This is journal
and not-journal, treatise and not-treatise, thoughts that are private and
not-private at the same time.

"Tractatus II," which appeared with "I" in *Dryad* in 1972, shifts from
prose interrupted by poetry to a series of statements that move together
yet stand apart like the sea and its waves, made from the same substance
yet rising alone, each in its turn, each distinct. All of the types of writing
he has done in his life—dreamlike prose, concrete and abstract poetry,
philosophical statements, pithy stories, fables, and lyrical sequences—
appear in one tractatus or another. He would return to writing poems
that were clearly poems, fables that were clearly fables, and journal en-
tries that were clearly journal entries, but the tractatus pieces (all written
on Kalymnos or Lipsi between March and September 1971) are the best
evidence I've found that he had transcended traditional concerns in his
writing, including the question of whether anything he wrote was "good"
or "bad."

While continuing to work on his tractatus pieces, Lax began crafting
abstract color poems again. "the more i read of everybody else's meaty
poetry, the righter i feel about cool and abstract," he wrote to Antonucci.
One of the best things art did for people, he felt, was give them a sense of
relief—the kind of relief that comes "when you've heard the word red so
many times you could scream & suddenly you hear the word blue." His
return to the color poems was more than that, though, he wrote. Words
such as *red* and *blue* had what he called an "invariable value"—"cooler
and cleaner than sea and sky"—that made people feel good.

By that September Lax had begun to live more in his mind than any-
where physical, and the waking world was merging more and more
with the world of sleep, of dreams, of half-awake states in which ques-
tions came to him with their answers in tow before both disappeared.
The color poems came from this state. They weren't intended to please
the eye, but to give a deeper satisfaction, "a sense of order, a sense of
harmony, a questioning. can any tie be found between two so unlike
elements?" He was trying to draw from the wells of his subconscious
those elements that were truer to life than life itself. "deeper than all
the things he saw, was the watcher," he wrote. "deeper than all the
things he heard, the listener."

———————

From the spring of 1971 through the spring of 1974, when he left Greece
again to return to the States for the summer, Lax had little desire to go
anywhere beyond his three islands: Kalymnos, Patmos, and Lipsi. These
three specks of land in the middle of a vast sea were his home. Although
each had a different spirit and brought out something different in him,
he lived a similar life in all of them, observing the people around him
and diving deeper into himself. After decades of restless searching for
his place in the world, he had found it among an insular population that
responded to him with a combination of welcome, bemusement, and
suspicion. That he was in love with these islands and their people there
can be no question. They taught him and drew from him the dreams,
thoughts, and beliefs formed in the deepest parts of his being. He was
more than content; he was happy. And he might have gone on living this
way for years if a cruel coincidence, like an errant match, hadn't ignited
a conflagration.

Many of Lax's writings that summer were about the islands he was
moving among, as if he were trying to choose one to stay on once and for
all. He saved his most loving lines for Lipsi, the coolest and quietest of
the three. There he spent his mornings reading, his afternoons journal-
ing, and the time in between walking and talking to everyone he met. He
had come to know almost everyone on the island and many of the fisher-
men who stopped there on their way past. His contentment on Lipsi
shows in the following lines:

days absolutely golden now: classical, the
kind that must have been praised in the
ancient poems

Most of Lax's journal entries during this time—made on long strips of paper reminiscent of the endless paper rolls Kerouac fed through his typewriter—are a series of short observations and reflections on the meaning of what he observes, such as this one, set down on Lipsi on July 19: "life here is played against itself, against a background of its own making. whatever fine thing is done is done with a view to adding to fine things done already, to continuing a process begun in past ages of doing fine things as a matter of course." Other entries are less dense and focused than this: "I've never been blacker in my life, but a man comes up to me at swim today (darker than i, i'll have to admit) & says: you don't tan do you?" One entry records the major activities of a typical morning and early afternoon on Kalymnos. He begins with reading: Psalms and Isaiah, the *Paris Review* and Ashbery poems. Next comes breakfast: milk and cheese and a crust of bread he shares with cats, birds, and ants. He goes to the bathroom and examines his beard before washing it along with his hair. More reading follows, Waugh this time, which makes him laugh, and then he heads to the post office to pick up letters. Retreating to his room, he sits writing answers in colored pencil before walking back into town to drink lemonade and talk with fishermen. A short while later, on his way to swim, he takes a picture of a girl in a doorway while her mother works at a loom in the dark room behind her.

He swims from rocks filled with people of all ages, the children running and diving or skimming stones. After swimming he sits in the sun before eating a lunch offered by fishermen: salad and a stew of tomatoes, garlic, and eggplant. The fishermen drink retsina while he drinks water and then he goes home for a nap. When he wakes up, he gazes at the sea in the shadow of a bell tower near his house and then walks with a friend past locals talking in the shade or mending nets to drink coffee in a seaside café. An hour or so later he follows a low road along the water's edge alone to see where another friend wants to build a new house. On his way home afterward, he stops at a series of stores for canned milk, alcohol for his cook stove, matches (from a man who sells only matches), and a small plastic funnel. "lots of other things really happened," he writes after setting down these events, "but i was determined not to exhaust myself in recording them."

That September a man on Lipsi told him he couldn't live in America now because he had learned to live by the rhythm of the islands. Lax agreed, but even as he was agreeing he knew that the rhythm he had learned to live by wouldn't remain the same. "the world isn't planning to leave many islands like this unbreathed on," he wrote in his journal, "(the vox of america's here to assure us of that)."

Lax spent the winter of 1972–73 as he did every winter during this period of his life: holed up on Kalymnos. He was renting the upper floor of a house where a couple and their child lived downstairs. From his writing room he could hear the wind and the sea between the clicks of his typewriter keys. When he went to bed, he slept under several blankets in a cold room, his thoughts drifting to earlier times or, as they often did, to the way the islanders lived. One night he realized that the voice of his conscience was his mother's voice and that it was not a memory but "an ever present often-admonishing reality." This realization led to thoughts about his own inner voice, which he longed to hear and understand as easily and clearly as that of his mother. He believed that each person has an inner voice that is entirely his own and that God communicates with us somehow through it rather than dictating our actions and beliefs from outside. "taking dictation from an angel is meaningless as a human activity," he wrote. "(it could be done by a robot.) listening to one's inner voice is different: when the inner voice is heard, it is recognized as the speaker's own."

In seeking to hear his inner voice, he was seeking as well to be a center of calm in the world. In making decisions or answering questions, he wanted to take his time, to let the answer rise quietly and naturally from his inner being—not a partial answer but a full one he could agree with completely. "each movement should have the power of an instinctive movement," he wrote, "but should be fully informed by thought/a combination of reflection & spontaneity; a response, an immediate response to stimulus: immediate but total & mature." *Pure act.*

One of Lax's first entries in 1973 hints at how far he had moved beyond a doctrine-based approach to God since being baptized a Catholic thirty years before:

has the church
become an
old bottle
(into which
new wine
cannot be
poured)?

It wouldn't be much of a stretch to say that he had traded the Catholic Church for a new Greek church. Not the official Greek Orthodox Church but the church of the Greek islanders' daily life. Every day it preached a sermon to him. Every day it taught him how to live, how to pray, and how to act toward neighbors. Every day it showed him how to praise God with his whole being. It's hard to know how aware he was that much of what he observed was a projection of his own ideals.

As far back as his early days in New York City he had been thinking and writing about the city of God as if it were possible to find it or create it on earth. He had thought for a while that he'd found it in Marseilles, but the grubbier side of Marseilles was hard to ignore, as were the more nefarious activities of even the men he had gathered around him there. The fishing communities on Kalymnos, and then Lipsi, were different. First, each community was composed of individuals who all (at least to his knowledge) believed in, and were aware of living under, the Christian God. Second, the community was stable and had been stable for as long as anyone knew. Third, the life of the community was a simple, traditional life that stretched back to biblical times—a life of fishing, farming, and taking care of animals. Fourth, the community was self-governing, obeying not written laws so much as cultural and societal laws so well known they seemed written on each individual heart. Fifth, within the restrictions by which it lived, the community was dynamic. Each day brought not only new wine but renewed vessels into which it was poured.

Lax's church was changing, however, and besides, it had never been quite what he imagined it to be. The city of God was also a city of men.

The national troubles he chose to think had no effect on the islanders did have an effect, and the confidence he saw in them was also pride in their ethnic identity. One of his enduring traits was an avoidance of unpleasant things. He hated confrontation of the mildest kind. He believed, sometimes naïvely, that if one did everything possible to live in peace, peace would come. And so, although a policeman on Kalymnos kept a constant eye on him, his letters were read, and his rooms were occasionally searched, he preferred to think that the colonels' reign and the dangerously difficult relationships between the Greeks and the Turks weren't of real concern to his neighbors.

He preferred to believe as well that the islanders were so virtuous and traditional in their way of life that, though some were smitten with the movies, television wouldn't catch on. But catch on it did, as it would everywhere around the world, and even he couldn't ignore it.

"the island is being asphyxiated by television," he wrote in early February 1973. "it's only taken a year for it to happen, but now almost every house has its aerial, and the sound of stupidities floats like a purple mist over hills and valleys . . . where greek music used to be heard from radios & discs, now fragmented strains of ravel & debussey, watered down to the strength of incidental music for essentially dramaless teledramas, watched and wondered at by the islanders, less impressed by what they see than by the marvel of the medium itself."

Other changes were coming too, other evidence that the islands were losing their isolation, succumbing to the imperatives of the modern world. That same month he wrote about changes to the waterfront area, so many coming so fast that soon it would be unrecognizable. New cafés had opened on the ground floors of two new two-story buildings with glass façades and protective gates. Concrete had been laid over the dirt in front of them, and the shade trees under which fishermen had drunk their coffee for decades had been cut down, replaced by a different species.

"The old cafeneions [cafés] still have charm," he wrote, "but kalymnians, unsentimental, have moved, even the fishermen in great numbers, to the new." The lament in this passage is unmistakable, as is the romance. He was in love with an image of the islanders, especially the fishermen, that he was being forced to revise. While he was idealizing the old, they were embracing the new.

He went on in the same passage to mourn the way television had emptied the nighttime streets, the cafés, and even the movie theaters. The pastry shops were so quiet in the evenings now that the owners of two of the largest ones were thinking of emigrating to America. An island that once survived proudly on sponges and tangerines would soon live on tourism and money sent by those who had moved overseas.

What Lax perhaps failed to appreciate was that Kalymnos had always been changing. The islanders knew that while change might bring worse, it might bring better too.

# 22   The Flaw in the Ideal

In October 2004, while staying in Germany's Black Forest, I drove to Zurich to interview Gladys Weigner, who, with her business partner Bernhard Moosbrugger, had talked to Lax in 1955 about starting a newspaper. The newspaper never materialized, but sixteen years later they founded a publishing company, Pendo Verlag, that, over time, became the main publisher for Lax's works. They were more than his publishers, though. Lax made yearly excursions to Switzerland to stay with them, and Weigner's house became the primary depository for his journals and other papers. Moosbrugger had died two months before my visit, so Weigner was the only one left who could tell me about those sojourns.

The morning I headed to Switzerland was bright with sun, and I took the smaller roads, crossing ridge after ridge brilliant with color. When I reached Zurich, its maze-like streets slowed me down, but I soon found the lake and then the Kunst Haus, Zurich's famous art museum. Weigner's house was a block away, a freestanding four-story building with large vertical windows and elaborate wrought-iron balconies bellying out from the second floor. I had barely pulled up when a short woman with a bent back bustled out a side door. Weigner must have been eighty by then, but her voice was strong and her face alive, the kind of face Lax would have liked. She showed me where to park before leading me into what she called the Pendo Gallery, a mostly bare space on the first floor where she would be hosting a celebration of Moosbrugger's life later that month.

I talked with Weigner at a table where Lax had given readings to the musical accompaniment of her daughter, Tessa, an accomplished jazz composer. After seeing Tessa perform, a critic wrote that he was a stationmaster and she was a rare bird with a ticket to somewhere other than where the other passengers were going. She should keep doing what she was doing, he said, rather than following fads. If Lax had been reading with her that day, the critic might have said the same about him.

Although some have said they started their press to publish Lax, Weigner told me, they actually published several prose writers first. It was Weigner's husband, Fritz, who suggested they add Lax to their list. It would be odd, they thought, to publish only a single poet, so they added a poetry line and, in the fall of 1972, invited Lax to Zurich to talk about putting him on it. The book that came out of that visit was a three-language edition of a single Lax poem called *wasser/water/l'eau*, with photographs by Moosbrugger. The book was a mishmash—with alternating couplets in English, German, and French in some sections and long passages in English followed by equally long translations in German (with no French) in others—but it was attractive, thanks primarily to Moosbrugger's photographs of water in tumult or at peace, and was named one the most beautiful books to be published in Switzerland in 1973.

Pendo's second Lax book—a four-language version of the *Circus* cycle called *Circus-Zirkus-Cirque-Circo* (again with photographs by Moosbrugger)—didn't appear until 1981, but after that the Lax books came regularly: *Episodes-Episoden* in 1983, *21 Pages/21 Seiten* in 1984, and one more each year from 1986 through 1997, each the same four-by-eight-inch size with a brown-paper cover.

---

Lax's yearly visits to Zurich are emblematic of a split in his life that was probably inevitable. Much as he loved and learned from the Greek islanders, he was too different from them to meld fully or easily into their world. He wasn't a diver or fisherman, nor did he do any other kind of work they recognized. He admired their traditions and rituals but he was outside them. And the truth is, he wanted to be. He was a writer, a poet, and, for better or worse, the people who would recognize his abilities and listen to what he had to say—the people he was writing for—lived elsewhere.

When he was in Zurich or, later, traveling to other European countries at the invitation of people who had begun to appreciate his work, Lax lived in a different—and differently desirable—world. In Zurich he stayed in a quiet, comfortable third-floor room in Weigner's home or, increasingly as the years went on, in equally pleasing accommodations nearby. In the summer of 1973, for example, he spent a month in a well-furnished house overlooking Lucerne while the owners were on vacation. At other times he stayed in a seminary called Ingleterre run by Moosbrugger's younger brother, Otto, a seminary in Lucerne called Romano House, or the Hauterive Abbey near Fribourg. He enjoyed talking to the monks and particularly the young seminarians about issues of faith, theology, and philosophy. When he was at Pendo or traveling to readings or festivals, he liked talking to writers and readers too, sharing approaches to writing and literature. These were all things he couldn't do, not at the same level, on Kalymnos or the other islands, except perhaps in summer when visitors came. As his writing became known to more and more people, especially in Europe, he began to see these literary interactions as not only enjoyable but also necessary, an important reputation-building part of being an author.

Despite his yearly trips north, the gap between Lax's two realms might not have widened quite so severely or quickly if, on December 10, 1972—four years to the day after Merton died—he hadn't lost the man who had been his ideal reader: Mark Van Doren. Pleasing Van Doren with his writing had always been enough, or nearly enough, for him. Now the two men he had written for were both gone, leaving him with a more diffuse audience, as well as a greater need for recognition elsewhere.

---

Greece's relations with Turkey continued to deteriorate in 1973, the last full year Lax lived on Kalymnos, and as they did he became more conscious of how people perceived him. Early in the year, for example, while talking to a group of Turkish and Arab fishermen, he felt a need to move on rather than lingering "because they were foreigners, & even the local fish would wonder what good thing i might have in common with them." He believed he was viewed as more of a local than a foreigner, but the colonels were stoking antiforeigner feeling and it wouldn't take much, he knew, to fall into the other camp. The locals indulged him, but, as the saying goes, blood is thicker than water. And the antipathies bred by history are thicker still.

After staying on Kalymnos through the spring and Patmos (where he came to know the poet C. K. Williams and his wife, Catherine Mauger) part of the summer, Lax spent most of August in Switzerland before moving to Lipsi late that month. As he lingered there into autumn, he began to write about this smaller island the way he had once written about Kalymnos, praising its people for knowing the confines of their lives and existing within them, playing within their circle "like wise & innocent children." He wouldn't idealize the land or the people, he wrote, but of course he was idealizing them, viewing them much as the Europeans once viewed the New World natives. His writing reveals no awareness that staying "within their circle" meant leaving others out.

He does admit, however, to a certain misgiving or melancholy—a suspicion that this "dream of what a little pastoral community should be" is only a lie. As he works this suspicion through his mind, he wonders whether the falseness lies in the dream or the dreamer or, as he tentatively concludes, in the world beyond them. It is the pervasive ugliness of the world's industrial cities that makes the insular beauty of an island like this seem unreal, he writes, the lack of relationship between them.

By this point in his life Lax had spent most of his time looking for two things. One was a way for human beings to live harmoniously together. The other was his own role in the world. His own way of being. He knew the two were linked, but except for his few years in college and those summers with his college friends at the Marcus cottage, he had always seen himself as an observer rather than an active participant in whatever group seemed to be working together, whether it was jazz musicians or acrobats or Greek fishermen. As he lingered on Lipsi that fall, he began to see that his vision hadn't been capacious enough. He had been looking at parts rather than the whole, searching for models rather than an understanding of the greater scheme of things. The oneness of humanity—of all of life—wasn't something to be sought, he realized, but something to be recognized and embraced. The life flowing in his veins had been flowing in veins since the beginning of time or longer. The enduring nature of life was the important thing to understand:

> the continuity of life is
> its meaning: it begins from
> eternity & flows to eternity

there is no right way of
singing a given song: but
all ways are more or less
right

the variations of tone we
bring to our roles give life
its color: whether we will (to)
or not, we add variations

there is no one character in
whom the Lord would dwell &
not in others

he who dances in the middle
of the room, dances for me;
he who sits in the corner
watching, watches for me

. . . it is not that our lives
should so radically change,
but rather our understanding
of them

The thoughts expressed here must have been terribly freeing. He no longer had to find the *right* way to live; he just had to *live*—fully and openly—and let others live according to their understanding. The goal, if there was a goal, wasn't to see something we don't see but simply to understand and appreciate the beauty and inherent meaning of what we see all around us.

Lax's belief in the oneness of humanity and his acceptance of people's choices would be severely tested in the days ahead, but his awareness and appreciation of the fullness of life would also allow him to weather the coming storm. The hardship itself would free him from his fixation on the behaviors and beliefs of one small group to live more freely in the world at large, living fully in every moment.

---

When Lax submitted what would be his last Guggenheim application that September, Kenedy's recommendation letter made clear that perceptive critics were already appreciating in his work the awareness he was just recognizing himself. After calling *The Circus of the Sun* "in all probability, the finest volume of poems published by an English-speaking poet of the generation which comes in T. S. Eliot's wake," Kenedy praised Lax's sense of rhythm and music, his generosity to younger poets and other artists, and his blending of experimentation with poetic traditions. Then he wrote, "No one has moved further ahead than Lax, and yet Lax is almost alone in basing his advance on the heritage of poetry. His matter is the miracle of existence and he represents it in true song—which has an unequalled and unrivalled modernity."

Unfortunately appreciation for the miracle of existence doesn't seem to have been what the Guggenheim people were looking for. They turned down his application again and he stopped applying.

A poem Lax wrote one week after submitting his Guggenheim application suggests that there was still a struggle within him between awareness of the need to live every moment as it came and a desire to exist in an idealized state—even to be an idealized figure himself. Titled "Byzantine Faces," it recalls his statement to Merton thirty-five years before that he should want to be a saint.

> i won't believe
> i'm really
> alive
>
> until i'm gladder
> to be alive
> here now
> than to have
> been alive
> there then
>
> living in greece
> i may be
> thinking
> i am, was,
> alive there
> then

some byzantine
time
some classical
time

why think
that good?

i should
know better

i think good
any time except
the eighteenth
century

(not too bad)

the nineteenth
century

(bad enough)

or the twentieth

really, i'm
glad to be
alive in the
twentieth

not only glad
to be just
alive

but even to
be alive
just now
right now

—

yes but i keep
remembering

a light in the
eyes of certain
figures in
frescoes

certain figures
in mosaics

that made
me wish
i was living
then

as though
living then

were to
live

forever

some life
some liveliness
in the eye
that seemed
eternal

eternally
alive
eternally
infinitely
joyous
& penetrating

(warm with
the warmth
of life
exploding,
even, with
the joy
of life)

yet there
forever

——

is it
that see
ing them
in some
mu
se
um

seeing
them still
preserved
still
living

made me
envy
their
state

?

not
sure

am
not
sure,
either,
that it
was envy
they gave
me, but
rather a
life

a spark
of living

to keep
alive

—

"Byzantine Faces" bears a certain relation to Lax's idealizing of the landscape and people he lived among. His life had settled into such peacefulness he could imagine himself as a figure in a fresco on a church wall, a being blessed by God, an icon. While there may be a hint of pride in this, it stems more, I think, from his belief that he'd found a place where people lived as he'd long imagined people could live. He wanted the bliss he felt to last forever—as it seemed to in the faces of those ancient figures. If this condition had persisted, he might indeed have drifted further and further from living a recognizably human life—a life in which struggles rather than beatific states lead to growth. In other words, his active life might have been over, which would eventually have damaged his poetry, making it less and less about a world he was actively participating in and therefore less relevant to readers.

But as he so rightly perceived, the idyll he lived was a lie. He didn't know yet in what way this was true, but he would soon learn—and while his learning would be painful, it would revitalize his life, freeing him to live each moment fully no matter where he was.

In November 1973 Lax made one last trip for the year. He was hoping to visit Limnos, the only other island where sponge diving was still important, but it was too difficult to get there, so instead he visited a young friend and admirer, Moschos Lagouvardos. The two had met on Kalymnos the year before and now Lagouvardos, a devout Orthodox Christian, had moved to the coastal town of Volos to become a judge. Drawn especially to Lax's love for the beauty of God and his unwillingness to ever criticize anyone, he was the first of many young people who would learn from Lax in the years ahead.

After stopping in Larissa, Trikala, and Athens on his way home, Lax was happy to settle in for the winter. "it was good to get back to kalymnos," he wrote on November 15, "which, the way I live in it, is not just my island, it's myself." Two weeks later, on his fifty-eighth birthday, the winter rains began and he nestled in to wait for spring, not knowing this would be his last peaceful time on the island he loved.

———————

Antonucci wrote to Lax on the third day of 1974 with exciting news: a man named Dale McConathy, who'd published Lax's poems in *Harper's Bazaar*, was working with Reinhardt's widow, Rita, to find artists for a new project he was overseeing—an "art park" to be located seven miles north of Niagara Falls—and he wanted Lax and Antonucci to be in residence there for a month that summer. Lax would write poetry that Antonucci would print on the spot, and they'd work with local children and adults to promote the reading and writing of poetry. The best part was they'd be well paid.

The news was an answer to prayer for Lax, who had written to a friend a few months before that he was getting close to hunger and had to borrow "a thousand dollars at, really, seven hundred dollars interest," to keep him in Greece until spring. Now he had the promise of some income at least. The only unfortunate part was having to travel to the States rather than staying on Kalymnos.

It's clear from a journal entry made around the time Antonucci's letter arrived that Lax was more in love with Kalymnos than ever before. He was Pygmalion staring at his statue, having created a vision he longed to hold onto forever. In a letter to Kenedy written on the eve of an exhibition of his works Kenedy was curating at London's Victoria and Albert Museum, he expressed a quiet confidence in his position on the island as well as the beliefs he'd been working out over the past several years. Among these beliefs was that all good comes from within, where the kingdom of God is located. The good—and even the bad—that seems to come from without has more to do with our personal choices than anything external. Life is a personal, self-refining process. The important thing is to focus on one point and move slowly toward it rather than being pulled in a dozen directions.

He expressed his belief in a personally directed life of reliance on God more poetically a few days later:

life is a river
& we the streams
that feed it

each stream should
empty itself
completely

into the
river &
not hold back

our way of talking
our way of being
is what we have
to contribute
to the stream

why keep it
all dammed
up
?

————————

why should a slow
moving river try to
move fast

why should a meander
ing stream pretend
to be straight?

————————

the civilizers
build high dams
but water flows
wherever it can

————————

are you afraid
that if you're a
cow
some mouse will
get ahead of you

some bright-eyed
rodent do you
in ?

fear not

(God watches
mice & cows)

———

the animal
most to fear
is man

He had finally found the place, the beliefs, and the approach to life he had long sought. He had finally put everything together. In the days ahead, however, those last seven words would come to seem an eerie oracle.

———

Lax left Greece for his first residency at ArtPark in mid-June 1974. In the days before his departure, his mind, no doubt, was on his upcoming travels. He wasn't thinking about politics or how his leaving might look to the islanders who had accepted him into their community. His departure must have seemed routine to him—after all, he had left many times before and always returned—but it wasn't routine, not this time, to those he left behind. Coming when it did, on the eve of a political crisis, it led them to thoughts and then judgments that deeply affected his standing in their world—thoughts and judgments that not only saddened him when he heard about them but shook the foundations of his faith, shattering the worldview he had so carefully crafted.

# 23 Hell Hath No Fury

On July 15, 1974—less than a month after Lax left Greece—a military group called the EOKA-B staged a coup on the island of Cyprus, overthrowing the Cypriot government of Archbishop Makarios III. Turkey responded by invading and occupying the island's northern sector, where most of the Cypriots of Turkish descent resided. The invasion put Turkish troops into direct conflict with Greek and Greek Cypriot soldiers. Although Greece and Turkey were NATO allies, people in both countries thought the war they had long feared was about to begin.

The Greeks were especially fearful. Turkey's population was ten times as large as theirs, and Kemal Atatürk's violent expulsion of ethnic Greeks from the Turkish mainland at the end of World War I was still fresh in their collective memory. On the island of Kalymnos, lying just a few miles off the Turkish coast, fear and a compensating Greek pride became all-consuming. Soldiers flooded the main town and nightly blackouts were ordered. Rocks were used to barricade the church. A local man proclaimed later that all on the island were ready to die for their homeland.

Lax had no idea what was happening in his absence. When he left Greece in mid-June he traveled to Zurich to visit Moosbrugger and Weigner, then crossed into France. The day the Cyprus coup took place, he was probably in Rouen, where he spent a rainy five days staring at—and being bewitched by—Rouen Cathedral. While the Kalymnians were barricading their church, he was visiting friends in New York and Olean before moving on to ArtPark. He jotted impressions along the way, sending them to those he felt closest to on Lipsi and Kalymnos, but life in the islands was a long way away—until he received a letter from Limnina.

Don't come back to the island, she warned without explaining why.

---

Lax was aware, of course, that the police and others on Kalymnos had long suspected him of being a spy. A plainclothes policeman named

Spiros had followed him for years, and his mail had been opened. He didn't understand, however, that his sudden departure just days before Turkey's invasion of Cyprus made even his friends think he'd been working for the enemy. He was an American, after all, and in the minds of most Greeks, the Americans favored the Turks. He had often been seen with fishermen of Turkish descent. And, most damning of all, he was always asking questions, writing things down, and taking pictures. No one had ever come to live among them as he had. Now they knew why.

----

When ArtPark opened on July 23, 1974, it was called the "first park in the world to be dedicated to arts." Built at a cost of $7.2 million and covering 172 acres, it included a 2,400-seat theater with a stage larger than the one in New York City's Metropolitan Opera House. Among the performers scheduled to appear that first year were Van Cliburn, Don McLean, Harry Chapin, and Bonnie Raitt. Near the theater, in an L-shaped building called the ArtEl, Lax and Antonucci set up shop. The artists in residence around them included a woman who made massive designs with a bulldozer and construction pipe, one who made sculptures out of hemp and branches, and the composer Philip Glass. Since the ArtPark idea was to make art accessible, Lax wrote poetry while people watched and Antonucci printed it in booklets or on postcards.

Altogether Lax spent parts of three summers at ArtPark with Antonucci, who paid his passage from Europe on the *Queen Elizabeth 2* each time. Over the years they expanded their offerings from writing, printing, and reading they did themselves to workshops for children, a poetry wall for people to post their own work, and readings by area poets. By the end Antonucci had published approximately twenty-five small books or broadsides of Lax's poems. He'd made short films and a number of small, painted-wood sculptures based on Lax's poetry too.

(Antonucci was the first to recognize the artistic possibilities offered by Lax's poetry, but eventually others saw them. The simplicity of the later, sparer poems made them especially attractive to artists and designers of small books. The first person other than Antonucci to publish freestanding versions of his poems was Ian Hamilton Finlay of Wild Hawthorn Press who, in 1965 and 1966, combined them with Antonucci's illustrations. In 1969 David Kilburn paired the poem "Shower Girl Song" with his own photographs, and Moosbrugger followed suit in *wasser/water/l'eau* four years later. Titled *Two Contemporary Presses: An Exhibition of the Work of the Wild Hawthorn Press and the Journeyman Press*, Kenedy's display of Lax's work at the Victoria and Albert Museum in April 1974, was really a celebration of this kind of collaboration.)

When his month at ArtPark ended on September 2, 1974, Lax went back to Olean, where he earned a little money visiting two English classes on the Olean campus of Alfred State College. "Writing for a living—as a vocation—is a very difficult existence; I wouldn't wish it on my children," he told the students. "But writing for the need and enjoyment of seeing an interior thought reach completion on paper is something different. It is a talent given as a gift from God." He went on to say without irony, "In Kalymnos I have a sense of oneness with the people, the land, the universe I could not attain in the vastness of the U.S. I need the perspective of my location on the island."

Maybe he hadn't received Limnina's letter yet, or maybe his desire to feel a oneness with the islanders was so strong he considered her warning temporary. In any case, he didn't return to Greece, though he did return to Europe. The end of the year found him living on Gomera, an unusually hilly island in the Canary Islands. How he ended up there is unclear, but he often visited places because someone he met in his travels invited him. The someone this time may have been Jose Ramon Chinea Hernandez, the farmer who was his main contact there.

Lax lived with Hernandez and his fellow islanders much as he'd lived in Greece, observing and socializing at times but spending most of his days alone. The villagers he lived among were mostly potato farmers, and during the harvest they gave him the job of bagging the potatoes they had dug up. As he'd done in Greece, he idealized those around him.

Lax stayed on Gomera into the summer of 1975 and returned again in October after another month at ArtPark and travels through France, Switzerland, and Italy. Before crossing to Gomera this time, he lingered near the famous bullfighting town of Ronda, where he'd made other friends. Although he'd been away from Greece for over a year at this point, Kalymnos was never far from his mind. He longed to return but didn't dare, and the combination of longing and fear—the irreconcilable difference between what he imagined the Kalymnos community to be and the reality of Limnina's warning—depressed him. Although he told several people he was still writing poetry, he wasn't writing much. He had lost his inspiration, it seemed. His will.

Lax had taken some of his papers with him when he left Greece, but his few other possessions were still there. He'd paid a year's rent in advance so he hadn't worried about them, but now Limnina sent a second warning: his landlady wanted her house back. He considered returning and facing his fears, but he still wasn't ready, so he asked his friend Lagouvardos to clear out his things. Lagouvardos took his books and papers and left everything else to the neighbors. Lax's presence on the island he loved was only a memory.

Meanwhile Lax did his best to convince himself he might settle in Agulo, the town he was living in at the foot of a precipitous hill on Gomera. In addition to growing potatoes, the farmers harvested grapes and bananas and kept some livestock, including a cow Lax took care of for several months. In his journal he described the work and the seasons, including the planting and replanting of the banana trees and the rain and island wind that destroyed the crop before it could be harvested.

"i think life is their religion," Lax wrote, idealizing the Gomerans as he had once idealized the Kalymnians. "they take it seriously in all its visible, tangible aspects. and in as much of the intangible as they are able to respond to. (they talk of clouds coming over the sea as though they were edicts from the vatican.)"

Although he was content in a way, embraced by the people around him, his thoughts still wandered to his first love, Kalymnos. He thought about going there in the spring of 1976 but traveled to Zurich and France instead. After his final stay at ArtPark that summer, he returned to Zurich once more, and this time, overcoming his fears, headed south to Greece. It took him most of October to muster the courage to visit the islands, but near the end of the month he stopped on Lipsi and, on the 29th, after more than two years away, finally set foot on Kalymnos.

---

When Lax descended the ferry stairs that day, he didn't know how he'd be greeted. He had lived in Greece long enough to know that memories there ran long and tempers hot. The chance that someone would try to harm him or even kill him was real. The first thing he heard, though, was a baggage handler's shout of "Robertos!," followed by a chorus of welcoming calls from others.

In those days the Dodecanese islands were a tariff-free zone, a remnant of the treaty that transferred them from Italy to Greece, and everyone who arrived had to go through customs. When Lax emerged on the other side, he heard someone say, "Can I believe my eyes?" It was Dimitri, the travel agent who had always booked his excursions. Dimitri asked him to come for coffee, and after Lax had checked into the Crystal Hotel, he started down the street to meet him.

Everything had gone well so far, he thought, until he passed a café and the men outside shouted for him to have coffee with them. Wary, he used Dimitri's invitation as an excuse to keep walking. Before he was out of earshot one of them said, "Now he'll get what he deserves."

His coffee with Dimitri was joyful and led to the sharing of lunch at a restaurant. Lax recorded the meal in his journal as if to savor it: roast lamb, fried potatoes, and a salad of peppers, tomatoes, and onions topped by a slice of feta cheese. It was a classic Greek meal, the kind he'd enjoyed many times, and he was full of good feeling after it, but then came dessert: a plate of grapes that had been spoiled by the rain and a comment from a woman in the kitchen not meant for his ears: "As long as Robertos is here, I know there won't be war." He would hear the same comment over and over, and much as he wanted to believe it meant he was seen as a man of peace, he knew it meant he was thought a spy.

After lunch he headed toward the post office, where the workers had forwarded his mail the whole time he was gone. Before he could reach it, though, an old friend named Yanni came up and kissed him on both cheeks. A few moments later a tailor named Costa called out a greeting and others approached to shake his hand. Heartened, he left the post office for another day and turned toward the place he cared most about: the fishermen's quarter. His first stop was Limnina's house, but Limnina wasn't there. Her mother, whom Lax called Old Sea, told him Limnina was at her sister's, so Lax headed there. "It's good you're back for a while," a baker's wife said as he passed, "loving the island as you do." Having praised the islanders for their ability to cut to the quick with a few innocuous-seeming words, Lax knew the line could be taken two ways.

When he found Limnina, he waited until they had returned to her house together and she had put a plate of grapes in his lap to speak. "Now," he said, "tell me, why did you warn me not to come back to the island?"

"Eat your grapes," she replied, as if wanting him to have something else to think about while she told him. "The reason is, everyone here—all those who smile and say hello—they all hate you."

"Why?" he asked, feeling too sick to eat anything.

"They say," she said finally, "that twice when there was trouble you suddenly disappeared. They say that proves that you knew ahead of time what would happen. They say that proves you're a spy."

He tried to speak, to refute the notion, but couldn't find the words.

"Eat your grapes," she said at last, ending the silence. She suggested he stay on the island a couple of weeks to see who remained friendly. "Today of course it's all warm greetings, but give it a week or ten days. Watch how things change. You're not dumb. You've been around. You'll be able to tell what they're thinking."

She told him then what it was like after his departure. When his first letter from overseas arrived, the police soon followed. They wanted to know his address and what she knew about where he'd gone. Others stopped by as well, breathing threats. "They all wanted to have it out with you," she said.

He tried to eat a grape but couldn't.

"I've scared him," she said to her mother before fixing her eyes on him again. "First I gave it to you straight," she told him. "Now I'll try to make it sweeter. I gave it straight because I'm your friend. I love you. All of us love you. I'd take off my head and put it on the ground for you."

"But who is it doesn't like me?" he asked.

"Everyone."

"The police? The neighbors? Who?"

"Everyone. All those people who are smiling and shaking your hand."

---

That afternoon, after trying to calm himself with meditation, he walked through the town again. When he passed the restaurant where he and Dimitri had eaten lunch, one of the owners repeated the comment the woman in the kitchen had made about not fearing war with Robertos around. He made it sound like a joke, but Lax was distrustful until an old swimming buddy sitting at one of the tables asked him to sit down. "Do you know what good company this man can be?" the man proclaimed. By the time Lax left the restaurant he was much happier—Limnina must have exaggerated the animosity, he thought—but as he passed a group of fishermen, one of them said, "The spy is back."

The next day was much the same. At the bank the assistant manager, who had family on Cyprus, greeted him coolly. When he asked a teller if his check was made out correctly, however, the teller said, "Even if it was written on a brown paper bag, we'd take it. We trust you." The man went on to make a distinction between good and bad Americans, which prompted the woman beside him to say, "White dog, black dog—a dog's a dog."

Things went better at the post office, where the man who had forwarded his mail while he was away greeted him in three languages and workers came out of the back to shake his hand. After a stop at a cobbler's to deliver two watches the man had asked him for in a letter two years before, he stopped by Limnina's house again, feeling good. He was looking forward to giving her a box of chocolates he'd purchased for her in Switzerland, but when he arrived, Old Sea was the only one there. "How have things gone in town?" she asked. When he said they'd been going well, she crossed herself, thanking heaven.

As he walked his old routes along the water that afternoon, people kept calling to him. If he'd kept a tally, he thought, he'd been greeted enthusiastically far more often than he'd been spurned, but Limnina's words, no doubt, colored everything. When he accepted a ride to the telephone exchange (the only place to place a call in those days) on the back of an old friend's motorbike, he saw the plainclothes policeman, Spiros, on the bike just behind them.

Lax wasted little time after that buying a ticket for the midnight boat to Lipsi, where he hoped he'd be better off. As if to confirm his decision, a laborer called out to him, "Come in here and I'll fix you," slapping his hand back and forth as if frying a fish. The rest of the greetings that day were friendly, but Lax was understandably jumpy when he went out for one last walk and a man emerged from the dark. It turned out to be an older friend named Yorgos who had recently opened a fruit store. "The funny thing is," Yorgos said, "my wife just said two days ago, 'It's too bad Robertos isn't here to take our picture in it.'"

Later that night Lax returned to the restaurant where he and Dimitri had had lunch, and the owner invited him to share a beer. "To your health," the man said before adding, "Just one thing—don't ever leave." When their laugher had subsided, the man detailed what it was like on the island during the Cyprus crisis.

"I hadn't realized," Lax wrote later, "how terrible it might have been."

As the time approached for Lax to board his boat, Dimitri gave him a discount on the ferry ticket, the hotel manager charged him less than he expected for his room, and a laborer named Lefteri insisted on carrying the heaviest of his two suitcases and his typewriter down to the pier in his three-wheeled wagon. His old love, it seemed, was not going to let him go easily.

---

Lax had once called Lipsi "a dream of what a little pastoral community should be." Despite his experiences on Kalymnos, he must have hoped the smaller island would still be the haven it had seemed before politics intervened. Yet that hope could never be as strong as it had once been. When the boat docked at 4 a.m., everyone at the pier greeted him with delight, but he feared that a silhouette he saw in a doorway was a police-man. Suspicions clung to him like cobwebs.

Before long Lax had moved into a house he'd rented before and ar-ranged to have his meals at a neighbor's, but soon the problems that had plagued him on Kalymnos reappeared. A local man asked him repeatedly how long he had been away, and another asked if there'd be a war. A third had a wary look in his eye when he greeted him. At night Lax paced alone across an empty church terrace, juggling and gazing out at the sea.

One old friend who still welcomed him was a fishing boat captain named Yorgos who used to love to drink and dance but had grown glum. "The people on this island don't like a man to be *happy*," he said, using the English word. "As soon as you dance, or drink or laugh, they want to put you down. If they see you happy, they say, 'He's happy because he has money' and they come around with their hands out. It's just a small is-land, there aren't many people, but let me tell you it's not a good crowd."

Although he might once have countered Yorgos's contention, Lax was in no position to argue. The questionable incidents continued. A man at the post office stuck his finger into his ribs like a gun and laughed when he jumped. "Right to the heart," the man said. Lax tried to take it in stride. "I feel I'm being reappraised after my long absence," he wrote. "Feeling solider myself (about many things) than when I left, this doesn't make me particularly uneasy."

Whether he honestly felt comfortable there or was simply trying to convince himself that he did, he stuck around, and for a while things seemed better. A shepherd he'd known in the old days greeted him with a smile, and his old barber pretended to be angry with him for not stopping in. Lax went on juggling, literally and figuratively.

One of the things that kept him grounded during this time was a book he would read from time to time for the rest of his life, *The History of Chinese Philosophy* by Wing-tsit Chan. He found Chinese philosophy to be particularly wise and practical, especially in the situation he was facing.

As on Kalymnos, positive incidents balanced the negatives. Fishermen called out their welcome to him and postal workers asked him to stop by when he didn't have a letter to mail. These were signs, it seemed, that if he just stuck around, things might return to how they had been. But then a man told him he might have been strung from a tree if he'd been there during the crisis. The man claimed to be joking, but Lax didn't believe him.

"Does it make sense to stay here?" he wrote afterward. The man represented the viewpoint of one segment of the island, he thought, but the friends who had welcomed him back represented another. The matter would never come to a vote, he assured himself, but did it make sense to "stay in a place where people (and not unvaryingly tame ones) resent your presence for reasons that seem to have more to do with the history of the times than with your personal qualities?" He pondered the pros and cons before writing, "I've spent so much money getting here, that to get away again might in itself be difficult. And where would I go?"

It was a question he had asked much of his life, a question he thought he'd finally answered when he settled in Greece. He could go to the seminary run by Moosbrugger's brother, he thought, or the village near Ronda where he'd spent a few days. Gomera was a possibility too, of course, and Paris and Morocco. In Greece he could go to Veria, where Lagouvardos lived now, or maybe a different island. But wouldn't the attitudes be similar there?

While he was pondering what to do, the mother of Mikali, one of his friends on the island, came to see him. His landlord had spoken to her, she said. The police had asked him why the American was staying at his house rather than in a hotel. This was fine in summer, when the hotels were full, but not in winter. The landlord told them Lax was a friend of the family who had stayed with them for six years, but the police wouldn't listen. When Lax saw his landlord's wife a while later, she told him the same story. "They've asked for your passport," she said.

"What do I do?" Lax wrote in his journal. He was afraid to return to Kalymnos. Afraid the same thing might happen there. "Paranoia: I'm being pursued," he wrote. "Run out of town or off the islands." Patmos was still a possibility, but why cling to something that wasn't quite right?

Mikali went to the authorities to see what he could do. Lax could stay in a hotel for ten thousand years, they told him, but in a private house? Not even for a second.

"'Not even for a second' was enough to help me make up my mind," Lax wrote later, "pack, pay my rent & get to the boat on time."

On his way back to Kalymnos that afternoon, Lax pondered Heraclitus's statement that you can't put your foot in the same river twice. "Always believed, and now more clearly see the truth of it," he wrote. "Maybe you can live in one stream a long time. But how hop out, & hop back in & find it still one stream, same stream?"

---

Lax had not been back on Kalymnos long when a man he had known for many years greeted him pleasantly and told him what others had told him before: that when he left suddenly, everyone took it as proof that he had accumulated piles of information and sold it to whoever would pay the most for it. Something about the way the man said it made Lax understand in ways he hadn't understood before just how deep the suspicion and anger were. He could see now how "a thousand small details" might add up to his being a spy, even among his friends. But what could he do about it? He couldn't imagine changing their minds—or even trying to.

Even though they think you're a spy, the man said, they still love you. Old Sea had said the same thing.

"If the sun never shone here, or if the sea were less beautiful, I think I'd just leave," Lax wrote. "But there's more to it than that. It may be the only place in the world where I'm hated. But (may be) also the only one where I'm so generally (and in such a lively manner) understood."

---

By the time he sat down to write on the evening of November 12, two weeks after his return to Kalymnos, Lax was ready to make an effort to stay. "So much about the place feels like part of me," he wrote, "and I can see that I, too, am part, if only a small part, of many who live here. When people ask me where I've been it's as though I were a long lost, long wandering member of the family." He showed then how clearly he understood and how deeply he sympathized with the attitudes of those in the local community he loved most:

> I have a feeling that my friends in the fishing neighborhood, those who are upset or antipathetic are so because they feel the most deceived by what they now consider the facts.
>
> Deceived (they'd feel) because no one, no foreigner, had ever come to live with them before, to obviously like them and to like all the things they were doing: the boats, the nets, the fish-traps they made, their families, their children. (Why should anyone pick us out to admire?) Why should anyone gratuitously like us, and our island?
>
> After 15 years they had had to believe that I must, that I did, that I do.
>
> And then (what seemed to them) my sudden disappearance at the time of crisis. Desertion, abandonment, and just possibly perfidy as well. Anger & resentment, not from all, but clearly in the hearts of some. And it isn't hard to understand why.

As he suggested a few lines later, the island was a lover he had wooed and wed—the love of his life—but now their relationship had been damaged, perhaps irreparably: "I often said I was married to the island, and I believed I was. Then I left, from the island's point of view, abruptly. And trouble followed for the island. How can I be reconciled with her after that?"

In his journal the next day he expressed his feelings even more candidly, showing how entwined his view of Kalymnos had become with his view of life. He had found a personal paradise, a place where his truest ideals, his deepest beliefs, and even his wildest fantasies were being lived out. Losing that paradise meant losing not only a place or a people but also the ideals, beliefs, and fantasies themselves.

How do you go on when reality has shattered your most closely held illusions? Lax had dealt with this question before, at the *New Yorker*, when he was much younger and less grounded in the one thing that could help him weather this kind of crisis: his faith in God and love. He began making a list of "dogmas, false & true" he had tried to live by. Among those he still found true were these:

> Love conquers all.
> Grace conquers all.
> God is love.

The welcoming and threatening continued until both seemed part of some strangely woven fabric. A man heckled him in a bar, then a baggage handler carried his bags to his hotel for free. People brought up the Cyprus crisis to him again and again, and when he told them he had left on business of his own, they seemed to believe him but he could never be sure. One night he heard someone with a "loud bossy voice," possibly a policeman, talking to the hotel manager on the street below his room. "Passes for an American," the man said. "Talks with everyone, looks here, looks there. Ask him for his passport and we'll take care of him."

Not wanting to believe the man was talking about him, Lax told himself he'd wait to see if the landlord asked for his passport. He calmed himself with twenty minutes of meditation, then descended the stairs. "Here he comes," a maid whispered and the manager appeared.

"Please, Mr. Lax," he said, "may I have your passport." The man had never called him *Mr. Lax* before.

As Lax watched, the manager copied down the information required for the hotel registry and then information that wasn't required: his address in America and who to contact in case of accident or death.

Why stay in such an atmosphere? he wondered. For his friends, maybe, but even they would rather have him elsewhere than "nowhere," which staying might lead to.

But leaving wasn't as easy as he might have hoped. He had already agreed to rent an apartment from his friend Yanni, and his attempts to back out led to hurt feelings and then elaborate negotiations. He asked men he considered wise for advice on how to break the agreement. Tell him you've measured your line again and found yourself unable to afford it, one old man suggested. Thinking this might be a "magic phrase," Lax tried it. "You should have measured it earlier," Yanni replied. Others suggested he go to the police or simply stick with the agreement for a month at least. Everything he tried only made the situation worse. He finally decided to just pay a month's rent, figuring he'd be leaving soon in any case.

The real problem was, of course, that even after all of his years on the island he didn't really understand how things worked or trust that he was in a position to assert himself. The resulting uncertainty caused him constant anxiety, reminding him again and again that things on the island were not as he'd imagined them to be.

He finally moved into the apartment and had the first good night's sleep he'd had since leaving Lipsi. An hour of yoga and twenty minutes of meditation and he was walking into town feeling good. He felt again that he belonged there and that many others thought so too. "One day at a time," he told himself. "If I try to think in terms of months, I get baffled. I'd like to think of staying for the winter, but can I? Should I?"

The business with the apartment continued to bother him, as did the threatening comments he still heard. The sages would say to forget these things, he thought, and move slowly. Patiently. He tried, but the various interactions kept wheeling through his mind. What cheered him were small things: a kitten that followed him and, when he stopped, sat down on his shoe; a gypsy he spoke to in Romany, the gypsy language, who flattered him by saying he was a gypsy himself; and the book of Chinese philosophy he'd started reading regularly. He had long thought that faith was the inability to not believe and courage the inability to fear, but this was wrong, he wrote: "faith is in spite of doubt, courage in spite of fear."

When he saw the beauty of the winter sea or a silhouette of fishermen against the light, he longed to take his camera out, but he didn't dare. He was reluctant too to write down his interactions. He felt that even the rocks there knew him, and he could point to fishermen with thick moustaches he had known as children, yet Kalymnos had changed and he had to change with it.

"Every situation is a changing one," he wrote, "and the most important element in a situation's change is the change that takes place—consciously or unconsciously, voluntarily or involuntarily—in the observer, the active and passive observer, himself."

Two days after writing this, despite hearing that Spiros, the plainclothes policeman, had told someone to let him know if Lax was planning to go anywhere, he wrote, "The rocks, the clouds, the sky, the sea all talk to me. / (They seem to be telling me to stay.)" He wrote several poems that same day. In one he expressed the existential nature of his life and what it was based on. The threat of losing Kalymnos had helped him see that nothing that can be lost is necessary, that only God's love—from which nothing can separate us—is indispensable.

The next day, it seems, he'd made a decision—or as close to a decision as he ever made. According to everyone he talked to, the apartment he'd tried to unrent was a good one for winter—with a wooden floor, a central location, and good sun in the morning—and so he would stay. When he told Dimitri, Dimitri brought him more blankets, singing a happy tune.

———————

Lax had many fears in his life—of motorbikes and airplanes, of giving offense and making a wrong decision—but the fear he felt when he returned to Kalymnos in the fall of 1976 was the most substantial, a visceral response to a clear and present danger. His decision to stay on Kalymnos and ride things out, whether it came from actually making a decision or from not deciding and simply remaining in place, reveals both courage and conviction. He believed that what he had experienced on the island was real, and he believed that the people there were good people. He believed too that the vision he'd seen had come from God and that God was leading him. He was willing to wait in an uncomfortable position until he felt sure he should move.

By all indications he remained on Kalymnos through Easter 1977. On January 30 of that year he wrote to Soni, "You're right about my belonging here (& every letter I get from anywhere says so.) The hills, the sky, the sea speak to me (lots of people do, too: more every day)." Even so, when Easter came around, he decided to go elsewhere. He asked an old man in an Athens bus station where he might find a small, quiet village to spend the two weeks around Easter, and when the man named a village far in the north, Lax went there.

"It turned out to be even better than I'd hoped for," he wrote to his St. Bonaventure friend Griff:

> very small town, with very friendly people, quite high in the mountains. Everyone acted as though they'd been waiting for years & years for a visitor to come to town so they could treat him exactly right. And that's what they did: the local mailman took me for a hike of five hours up through the hills (then back to his home for dinner); a shoemaker had me to his house on Easter day, and each of the others did some good thing (they loaded me with gifts, too, when I went away: colored Easter eggs, home-made cookies, mountain tea I could brew at home) and yet they left me plenty of time by myself to read or write or do whatever I wanted. (so I have quite a glowing memory of the place.)

With only a few small changes, he might have been describing his first visit to Kalymnos. He had always loved the Greeks' hospitality and openness to visitors. In his years on Kalymnos he had come to love their vitality and understanding of life too. He was able to idealize them for an impressively long time, rationalizing their foibles. But Greeks are human beings, and, however admirable their traits, human beings will always disappoint—simply by being human.

# 24  Finding a Common Language

Although he remained on Kalymnos after his return there in the fall of 1976, Lax never truly settled back in. He still admired the Kalymnians and considered many of them close friends, but his confidence in his neighbors' goodwill had been replaced by wariness and uncertainty. At the same time, he was feeling a greater desire for quiet and solitude. He was in his sixties now, and after a lifetime of searching for an atmosphere in which he could be only and completely who he was, he had found it, not in a place or people but in himself. Hard as what happened on Kalymnos was, it freed him from attachment to a particular society or situation.

"all parts are parts of one whole," he wrote in the summer of 1978, "and all keep changing, part into part, according to its time. many parts, but none really separate; many parts but none really separable." He understood now that being part of the whole meant participating fully in every aspect of life, whether pleasant or painful, "not to be outside, above, or off to the side," as he'd been on Kalymnos, but "to be a part that shares in the whole . . . that takes and gives, and is hardly aware of either taking or giving."

---

Over the five years that followed his return to Kalymnos, Lax moved regularly between islands and sometimes countries. After living on Kalymnos through the winter of 1976–77 and traveling north for Easter, he stopped on Patmos for a while before spending the summer on Lipsi (with a short trip to Zurich and Lucerne that August). He intended to settle again on Kalymnos the following winter but ended up going to Spain instead, staying briefly in the village of Jimera de Líbar near Rondo before moving back to Gomera. His inability to make decisions, especially one as important as choosing where to live for what might be the last years of his life, was on clear display during this period, but when he returned to Greece in the spring of 1978, he seemed to be leaning toward Lipsi. His preference for the smaller, quieter island deepened in 1979, when his good friend Mikali was elected mayor. Suspicion of him had lessened, and he was able to live in the house he'd lived in before, without the police insisting he move. Lipsi was "a fine quiet island," he wrote to Antonucci that December, the kind of place he needed "after months in hong kong kalymnos."

Kalymnos had begun to seem like Hong Kong mostly because of the noise, which bothered him more than before: radios and recorded music, loud conversations, and even the shouts of children. He couldn't write or read or even think, he lamented, but his discomfort came from more than that. He couldn't be entirely himself, not in the way he'd been before, or the way he could on Lipsi.

He continued to vacillate for two more years—staying on Kalymnos in winter, shifting to Lipsi for spring and summer, and traveling each fall (with occasional trips to Patmos thrown in)—but by the fall of 1981 he was spending most of his time on Lipsi. He worried about living there in winter because it wasn't on the main ferry route and it lacked medical facilities, but he was prepared to do it—until he returned from a two-month trip to mainland Europe that October and found he'd lost his house. His landlady's absent daughter had returned.

Unable to find another suitable place, he resigned himself to spending one more winter on Kalymnos, but the house he rented there was damp and dark and there were fresh indications of danger: warnings that he might be murdered and high school children carrying signs that read "No Americans." (Andreas Papandreou, the prime minister's Harvard-educated son who'd visited Kalymnos during Lax's first year there, had just become prime minister himself, running on an anti-NATO and, by extension, anti-American platform.) Just when things looked bleakest, a Patmian friend offered him a quiet house with wooden floors and good light next to people he liked. From that point on, until the last few months of his life, not only Patmos but that particular house would be his home.

------

While Lax was trying to decide where to settle, Merton was becoming a cottage industry back in the United States, with books by and about him appearing regularly. One of them was the long-delayed collection of his correspondence with Lax he'd prepared before he died. When it was published as *A Catch of Anti-letters* in 1978, the advance of $3,500 was split equally between Lax and the Merton Legacy Trust. It wasn't much, but it was far more than Lax had made from any of his other books and the publication linked him inextricably to Merton.

Sales were modest, as Merton had foreseen, but it did receive a handful of reviews. *Publisher's Weekly* called it "a playful exchange of letters" between "two solitary friends" that would appeal mainly to "Merton enthusiasts." *Commonweal's* reviewer, Michael True, also focused on the value to Merton fans: "Although the private nature of their language makes these letters between Merton and Lax relatively inaccessible to the general reader, they cast some light on previously neglected aspects of Merton's personality: his wit, his gregariousness, his diverse friends."

Not everyone who looked at their friendship that year left Lax in the shadows, however. In a review of *The Collected Poems of Thomas Merton* in the February 5, 1978, issue of the *New York Times Book Review*, the critic Richard Kostelanetz used Merton's dedication of one of his poetry collections to Lax to introduce him to readers. Having stated that "Merton's true medium was not poetry at all, but *prose*," Kostelanetz showed his preference for Lax's poetic works by calling him one of "America's greatest experimental poets, a true minimalist who can weave awesome poems from remarkably few words."

Kostelanetz's praise has been cited frequently in recent years, but it's doubtful it made much impact back then. Anne McCormick, a Merton Legacy Trust trustee who worked for Knopf at the time, touted Lax's work to magazines and publishers but nothing came of her efforts either. Still, little by little, Lax the poet was becoming better known, at least among those who paid attention to experimental poetry. The same year Kostelanetz's review appeared, the founder of *Stereo Headphones*, Nicholas Zurbrugg, included a short section on Lax in an essay called "Towards the End of the Line: Dada and Experimental Poetry Today." And in 1981 Moosbrugger and Weigner reissued *The Circus of the Sun* in a four-language version that gave many European readers and writers their first look at his work. Pendo Verlag didn't sell its books in the United States, but Lax's nephew Michael Blate volunteered to be his U.S. distributor. (Although Antonucci was still applying for grants to make films from Lax's poems, he was mostly a background figure now.)

Lax's growing importance to Merton scholars was reflected in an invitation to attend a symposium on Merton and Jacques Maritain (who had inspired Merton in his younger years and become his correspondent later) in Louisville on September 25 and 26, 1980. As he had when traveling to ArtPark, Lax crossed the Atlantic on the *Queen Elizabeth 2*, his passage paid by the conference organizers. Expecting to make a presentation, he put together the only extended appreciation of his friend he ever wrote, calling it "Harpo's Progress: Notes Toward an Understanding of Merton's Ways." For some reason he never presented it, but the symposium gave him a chance to meet Daniel Berrigan and Jim Forest, important figures in the Christian peace movement. (The presentation was finally published in the *Merton Annual* eight years later.)

On his way to Olean after the conference, Lax stopped in Iowa City to see his niece Connie. After the visit, while he was catching a night bus in Columbus, Ohio, a man accosted him, demanding his wallet and threatening to kill him. "Please, friend, don't do this to me," Lax pleaded, and for some reason the man let him go. When Lax talked to Connie afterward, she told him she'd been praying for him when the incident happened.

---

Midway through this last unsettled period of his life, Lax wrote a long, vertical journal entry, almost a poem, that included a section about how different people—St. Augustine and Merton, Kerouac and Burroughs, Mario Puzo and Henry Miller—viewed writing, especially whether or not to revise. He told me several years later that the only kind of revision he believed in was writing about the same subject again and again until you produced a version that was closer to what you meant. Even then, he believed, each version had its own value. The important thing was just to write, letting the world and maybe God decide whether your writing was good or bad.

He was still reading his history of Chinese philosophy at the time and would soon return to studying Judaism—Gershom Scholem's commentary on the Kabbalah and excerpts from Maimonides. "monotheism is only one feature of the religion of israel," he wrote. "the important feature is the idea of a personal relationship (unfolding in history) of the (one) Living God with his Chosen People. the idea that the relationship continues from moment to moment, from day to day (from ritualized moment to ritualized moment) (sacred moment to sacred moment) throughout (the history of the world, of creation) and into eternity."

Around this time he expressed a desire to live in the middle, between what we call the real and the unreal, between eternal being and nonbeing:

to live in our dreams as though they were real, and through the waking day, as though we were dreaming

———————

to treat all beings, in dream and waking, with reverence due the numinous

and yet to be wide awake, both in sleeping and waking

———————

to what good end? to no good end: only to a continuation in being; to a clarification through being of what it means to be

One day, when he was back in Greece, a man he knew from Columbia stopped to see him with his son and his son's friend, twenty-four-year-olds on their way to Israel. Lax wanted to talk to the boys but wasn't able to, so he contemplated what he might have said. The advice he wrote down was reminiscent of things Brahmachari had told him when he was a young man and his own admonition to Merton that he should want to be a saint. But his thinking since then had led to a new view of the relationship between religion and spirituality, a view Merton held near the end of his own life:

finding the right culture, finding the 'right' religion, is important, as a personal choice; but more important is the progress you make—the progress you find you can make—once you have found it.

it's enough, but not quite enough, to wish to be a good jew
it's enough, but not quite enough, to wish to be a good catholic

to be a good jew, or to be a good catholic, is really just a start toward what you may (& really should wish, with G-d's grace) to become

(to be a saint, yes; to be a contemplative, yes, to be a mystic, yes)

but at the point where one is living a fully spiritual life, a contemplative and mystical life, he is out beyond the delimiting terms of any particular religion

"Everything that rises must converge," he said to me more than once, quoting Teilhard de Chardin. He had come to a place in his life, his thinking, his search, where boundaries and definitions meant little. His God was One God, the world one world, waking and sleeping part of one collective consciousness. The essence of all of these was love, and his desire—the desire he thought all children of God should have—was to become so full of God and the world and the collective consciousness that he became pure love.

The close connection between the way he was trying to live and his vision for his poetry comes through in the following description of how he viewed his seemingly enigmatic color poems:

the red blue color
poems in colored
crayon

(do a lot of
things at
once)

they're poems
but look like
paintings

yet (being
neither poems
nor paintings)

are something
beyond both

——

and are meant to

be
(that) thing
beyond both
that includes
both

———

not a matter
of mélange
des genres

a reaching
beyond known
genres

for a new one

a direction of
the discovery
of new ones

(from thesis
antithesis
to synthesis)

a reaching beyond
what is
to what
(may become)

———

is there a sense
in which all that
may ever become

already *is*?

yes, *is*
in potentia

Shortly before he moved to Patmos for good, Lax made an inventory of
his life, including not only his possessions but also his tendencies, diet,

and moods. Everything physical—most of it readable—fit in or on "10 cardboard boxes, three suitcases, a table full of papers and books." Among his tendencies he listed a "disinclination" to write, a "tendency to draw colored pictures," and "foot and leg exercises, mostly of my invention." (He walked and swam and did yoga too.) His diet consisted mostly of milk, fruit, vegetables, and some meat and fish, most of the last two items given to him by neighbors. He napped for an hour in the afternoon and went to bed at ten or eleven, only to listen to the news at midnight (the BBC on a radio a friend had given him) and then lie restlessly until 4 a.m., when he slept for two or three hours. His biggest cause of anxiety was "great stacks of (often beautiful, but) unanswered letters."

As for his mental and emotional state:

moods: range from high, to generally contented, to mildly depressed (about things like correspondence.)

neurotic symptoms: various so far mild and often changing forms of hypochondria

nocturnal restlessness: hardly enough to qualify as insomnia

feelings of accomplishment: slight, rare; frequently non-existent

of discontentment: rare, and not apparently profound

Robert Lax had just turned sixty-six when he moved to Patmos. He would live another eighteen years and go on many more trips, including a valedictory journey to the United States in 1990, but from that time on his primary residence would be that little house above the port town of Skala. Whatever his feelings about living on Patmos, he felt at home in the house right away. His only real neighbors were a pleasant couple next door he had known for years and the only possessions in the house belonged to him. In fact the house had all the essentials he'd never been able to find in a single dwelling on Kalymnos: wooden floors, electricity, indoor plumbing, a view of the sea and the port—and quiet.

That winter of 1981–82, after C. K. Williams suggested he write an autobiography, Lax spent nine days composing twenty-one pages of prose he didn't know what to do with. He tried adding to it but felt it was complete as it was. Titling it "Searching," he finally sent it to Antonucci and several others to see what they thought. All who read it agreed that it was not only finished but one of the most profound things he'd ever written—all, that is, except an editor at W. W. Norton who asked to see the completed manuscript when it was done.

As his temporary title suggests (the title was changed to 21 Pages when Pendo published it in 1983), the piece was about his search through the years for some kind of permanent meaning. Although the seemingly biographical details in the piece were invented, the contours of the search the imaginary narrator describes match Lax's. It isn't a completed search but ongoing, driven by a need to know and experience that transcends disappointment and the lack of a definitive discovery:

> I continue to watch, and that's what counts. What counts, if anything does. Something does, but the question I more often ask myself is who counts it? Do I? I do. But does anyone else? Does anyone else in the universe count what happens? Does anyone else in the universe know what matters? Does anyone care, I mean, personally care? Ah, well, why get into that, as long as I do.
>
> And I do. Seem to. Seem to want to know what's going on. From moment to moment. Why it's going on. What counts, from moment to moment. I want to know. Seem to. Seem to want to know. Seem to want to know what it's all, or even, what any small part of it's about.

Even while living on other islands, Lax had often met visitors on Patmos. It was easier to reach than Lipsi, and there were things for them to do beyond seeing him. He liked to keep a distance too between the outside world visitors often represented and the local world he had come to inhabit. When he settled on Patmos, that distance shrank, but he still managed to maintain it by allowing only certain people up to his house and meeting others down in town.

One of the first people to visit him in his new home was the one person he'd never kept any distance from: Gladio. She arrived with her daughter Marcia and a fellow schoolteacher named Gay Sheahan just before Easter, and Lax, being the gentleman he was, traveled to Athens to pick them up. They stayed on Patmos for only three or four days but he did his best to give his sister a full experience of his world, including introducing her to the man who had become his best friend, Damianos. When the three women were ready to go, he traveled with them to Athens and took them to Delphi before they flew home. It would be the last time he'd ever see his sister.

When Lax told his other sister, Sal, about the visit, she said it was good Marcia had been there to keep them on track. Lax was already aware, however, of his niece's practical bent. A smart, energetic New Yorker, Marcia was already becoming a second Antonucci, promoting her uncle's writing in every way she could. Lax's increasingly frequent letters to her were full of instructions about where to send his work or who to contact. He was willing to follow any lead, expressing doubt only about mainstream outlets—the *New Yorker*, the *Paris Review*, even *New Directions*—as if unable to believe they would ever accept his new work.

A few years later Marcia would help him in an even bigger way, by arranging to buy his house for him, freeing him at last from the need to pay rent.

---

In June 1982 Lax began what would become a valuable association with a playful German of Turkish descent named Hartmut Geerken. A poet, percussionist (with avant-garde artists such as Sun Ra), organizer, and, later, radio producer, Geerken was a tireless advocate for new poetry, and concrete poetry in particular. That year he was working for the Goethe-Institut in Athens, and on June 26, on Patmos, he recorded forty minutes of Lax reading his poetry. Later in the year he presented shows about Lax in Linz (Austria) and Berlin. In the years ahead he and his partner Sigrid Hauff would introduce Lax to thousands of listeners and readers in Germany and Austria.

On September 19, after spending much of the summer on Lipsi, Lax left for his yearly pilgrimage to Zurich, taking the train up through Yugoslavia, as had become his habit. From there he continued on to Paris where, from September 26 to October 2, he served once again as the official photographer for Harford's magazine at the annual Congress of the International Astronautical Federation. As at earlier congresses, he "had trouble fighting other photographers for position during ceremonial events," writes Harford, but then he wasn't paid much for his work ($150, out of which he had to pay his own transportation and lodging). He saved money this time by staying with his friend Jacques Vattaire, happy just to be back in Paris.

Before leaving on his trip to the north, Lax had received an invitation from Maurizio Nannucci, one of the leaders of the experimental poetry movement in Italy, to participate in a "sound-poetry" festival in Florence. Nannucci had already used some of Lax's work in a radio program in Florence the previous year. The festival, officially titled Fonè, la voce e la traccia, would go on through the winter, but Lax was involved in only one activity, a reading with four other poets—Brion Gysin, Bernard Heidsieck, Emmett Williams, and Nannucci himself—on October 23. He had no idea how much of his reading the Italians in the audience understood, but their enthusiastic applause gave him hope that something meaningful had come across. He felt more confident when he did a follow-up reading in Zurich, where a small crowd with a greater understanding of English responded just as enthusiastically.

It isn't always easy to track Lax's income and expenditures, but an "annual report" he sent to a tax accountant on February 8, 1983, gives some idea of his inflow and outflow in 1982. Most of his expenses were related to his travels, each trip to Athens costing him $350 to $400 alone. His longer journeys to mainland Europe were covered by those who invited him. They occasionally provided a small honorarium besides but not much. He lists costs of $150 for a checkup and dental visits in Zurich and $100 for small contributions to "various causes" throughout the year, but his biggest ongoing expenditure is for mail. "Writing letters, keeping in touch with readers, editors, anthologists and other writers is an inescapable part of being a writer," he writes. "Try as I may to cut down and economize, I spend about $10 a day, five days a week, on postage. . . . If I don't, I don't get invited to read in Florence, or have things published in Australia (or have my cassettes played on listener-sponsored radio in California.) Even when these performances don't pay, they're a necessary part of the game." According to a sales sheet from Antonucci, Lax's sales total for 1981–82 from all Journeyman books was $184.

The following year, 1983, was much calmer and slightly more lucrative. He received a little money early in the year when a section of his "Histories" manuscript, edited by his North Carolina friend Bob Butman, was published in New Directions #45. Before the year was out, Pendo had published a larger chunk of the manuscript under the title Episodes/Episoden and a mix of published and unpublished poems called

*Fables/Fablen.* From then on, except in 1985 and 1987, Pendo would publish a new Lax book every year through 1997.

Established U.S. publishers still ignored Lax's work, but in 1983 a man named Michael Lastnite from Passumpsic, Vermont, began putting out cheap versions of some of his unpublished poems, producing over two dozen in the next three years. He branched into sound recordings and then videos before filming interviews with Lax and many who knew him for a planned documentary. (The documentary, made with the help of longtime Lax friend Judy Emery, was completed in 1988 but never distributed.)

Lax was interviewed for another documentary that year, *Merton: A Film Biography*, which aired on PBS in 1984 and was followed by a companion book, *Merton By Those Who Knew Him Best*, that included a transcript of the Lax interview. It was the largest sign yet that the Merton machine had discovered him.

---

As Lax noted often in letters during this period, the number of foreigners visiting the islands in summer, especially Patmos, could be crushing. But he liked meeting new people and the foreigners he met were often younger men and women like me, trying to figure out how to live. He was in his late sixties by this time and seems to have slipped comfortably into the role of genial uncle or experienced advisor or even mentor, though he was careful to tell the young to find their own paths. In the years ahead, as more and more young people gravitated to him, he introduced them to one another, hoping they'd help and support each other.

Of course the foreigners he met, American or otherwise, usually went home after their time on the island, and from home they wrote him letters. Caring for people as he did, Lax felt compelled to answer each one, increasing his already voluminous correspondence. Most of the questions he received were about writing or Merton, but he dispensed gentle advice on living too. For example, to a woman named Winnie he wrote:

> i think learning to send stuff out and get it back is as important as learning to type: it's part of the business and is worth no emotional expense: it's something you just do and forget about until you find a publisher who goes for them. i think it's always a matter of being dis-

covered. but that can't happen unless you keep sending things out. is it worth while doing? yep. because then your stories get read and begin to make a difference.

it hasn't anything to do with money or prestige: it's more like trying to get a hearing for your own view of the world, and that's a pure motive and a good one.

To the poet Michael Mott, who had interviewed him several times for his forthcoming biography of Merton, he wrote, "No, no, reject slips are not supposed to build humility. They're supposed to work like toxin-antitoxin: build up your resistance and strengthen your determination to make them eat their words. I'm glad you consulted me about this. Humility is truth: humility is recognizing your gifts as a poet and using them." And in a long, encouraging letter to a young man named Don, who was struggling with many issues as he tried to find his way in life, he wrote:

just ran into your questions: 1) loneliness: i *like* it. knowing the language here does help, i'll admit. when i want to, i can talk to fisher men (& other basically peaceful, natural types), and more than talk, listen. it relaxes (& feeds) me. i used to sit with arab fishermen (at tables outside a closed cafe) in kalymnos. could sit for an hour, not understanding a word, but feeling (enough) accepted by them as just another human being, and even that relaxed me. 2) anonymity. wonderful, too. you seldom can get enough of it anywhere. i think if you were sitting at the north pole, the seals on other blocks of ice nearby would want to know your name and all about you. i've liked it though (the idea of being mostly alone and anonymous) since i was three. didn't keep me from wanting to be an actor sometimes. the idea of being one person out on the stage, and another (much quieter) back home & alone in the room. i guess you know this doesn't mean i don't like people. i do; but in sort of small doses. one human encounter gives me enough to think about for weeks.

saint: i may have gotten myself into trouble with that one. i was telling *him* [Merton] to be one. (& i think he may have gone right out & done it.) what i'd mean by it now is be, hope to be, hope to get to be, the person you were created to be.

Harford's space congress was held in Budapest in October 1983, and once again Lax worked as a photographer, his pay bumped to $200. He passed through Vienna on the way, no doubt wondering, as he had on other occasions, if his father's family had really come from there. On his way back to Greece he lingered in Zurich longer than usual, and while he was there, Thomas Kellein, curator for the Sohm Archive at the Staatsgalerie in Stuttgart, which was planning a Reinhardt retrospective, called Moosbrugger to order some of Lax's books.

"The author is right here," Moosbrugger told him and put Lax on the phone. Kellein was mainly interested in Lax as Reinhardt's friend, but after their phone conversation he traveled to Zurich to meet him in person and found himself wanting to know everything about him. What he learned made him decide to mount an exhibition of Lax's work too, including his drawings and photographs, the art books people had made from his poetry, and Antonucci's films. His interest in Lax's work would eventually result in 33 *Poems*, the first book of Lax's writings to be issued by an established U.S. publisher and still the best introduction to his work.

It was mid-December before Lax took the train down through Yugoslavia and almost Christmas when he arrived on Patmos. "I've been sort of dragging around since I got back, don't know just why," he wrote to Antonucci a few days later.

> Walked into Santa's Workshop, found all the gnomes asleep and none of this pile of Christmas mail answered. Don't know where to start. Just walk up and down.
>
> The trip took about three months and was all pretty good, but I think the best part was Budapest. Felt like the old Europe. Like Paris in 1937.

Despite the humor in the letter, a strong sense of melancholy comes through. After three months of stimulating travel and interactions with friends, editors, and other writers, he had returned to the wind, rain, and cold of deep Patmian winter. Memories of earlier times, like his first visit to Paris with Slate in 1937 and his days in New York with Antonucci, might have contributed to his pensiveness too. He ends his letter "Hope you can get to Europe this year. . . . Or that we can meet on a raft in mid-Atlantic." Again the humor and the wistfulness.

Lax and Antonucci had spent many happy years talking and exchanging letters about their work together—what they would publish and where they would send poems—but Pendo had taken over the publishing of Lax's books and Antonucci was too busy with his own career to do much for Lax's anymore. Antonucci would continue to fade from his life, until an unfortunate mistake with a book a decade later would make him disappear altogether.

When he returned to Patmos that Christmas, Lax had just turned sixty-eight. His work had been published in many places and Pendo was committed to releasing a steady stream of all-new material in future years. Still, he hadn't really broken through as a writer, hadn't received the kind of renown many thought he should have, and he was living in a rented house on an island that wasn't his first choice of where to live. It's possible some of his melancholy came from wondering about the choices he'd made in his life, the things he'd pursued—the kind of wondering at the heart of 21 Pages, in which he wrote, "How would I not know what I was looking for? But I don't. But I do. I've been doing it for so long I must know something. Not much. Not enough to hold onto. A vague idea."

He didn't know it then, but the next two years—the period during which I met him—would bring not only validation and increased recognition but also a home that wasn't rented for the first time since his long-ago days in Olean.

# 25    Pure Act Becomes Pure Love

When I dropped into Lax's world in 1985, I landed in the midst of an unusually fertile period for him as a poet and friend of Merton. Although he'd been living on obscure islands for most of the past twenty years, people across Europe and the United States had begun to seek him out. In Europe most of the attention came from avant-garde poets and other artists. In the United States it came mainly from people who knew him only as Merton's closest friend.

The previous year had been a busy one for him. In February, at Geerken's invitation, he'd met and attended a concert by the inventive musician and poet Sun Ra, a meeting that led to a collaborative venture. "Best band I can think of since Ellington," Lax wrote to his niece Marcia when he was back on Patmos, where he didn't stay long. In April he traveled to Germany to view the room where Kellein's exhibition of his work would appear the following year and to give several readings: at the seventh annual Colloquium Neue Poesie in Bielefeld (a Geerken creation) and in Saarbrucken, Nuremberg, Hannover, Heidelberg, Berlin, and Hamburg. September found him in Lausanne at another space congress, and he closed out the year as a writer in residence at Anatolia College in Thessaloniki.

"Another no-pay job," Lax wrote about the Anatolia gig to his accountant. "They gave me a place to live and I ate with the students. No pay, but no duties either. I sat at my place and wrote and just one evening gave a reading at college president's home, for 15 people, sitting in front of an open fire."

In fact he received little remuneration for any of the year's activities, but his goal wasn't income so much as making his writing better known. As a feature story on him in Zurich's *Tages-Anzeiger* newspaper suggests, he was succeeding. The poet Emmett Williams, who read with him at Bielefeld, knew him from his connection to Merton, but most of the other Europeans who praised his work had discovered it through the writings and efforts of people like Geerken, Kenedy, and Finlay. They weren't interested in him as

Merton's friend or even a spiritual person. They were interested in him as an artist.

One of Lax's European admirers, Nicholas Zurbrugg, a professor of English and cultural studies who would eventually serve as director of England's Centre for Contemporary Art, had just left Patmos when I arrived in January 1985. He had spent several days there interviewing Lax for a collection of conversations with the most influential avant-garde artists of the twentieth century, including John Cage, Philip Glass, William S. Burroughs, and Laurie Anderson. Sadly, though slated for earlier publication, Zurbrugg's book, *Art, Performance, Media: 31 Interviews*, wouldn't appear until 2004, well after Lax's death and even his own.

While Zurbrugg's interview didn't bring Lax immediate satisfaction beyond the conversation itself, a request Zurbrugg made before he left the island did. Zurbrugg had done his dissertation on Proust and Beckett and was going to be seeing Beckett soon. Would Lax autograph a copy of *21 Pages* for him? Lax was more than happy to oblige, writing:

for
Samuel
Beckett
with
all
good
wishes.

According to Lax, when Zurbrugg presented the book to Beckett, Beckett looked through it and said, "This is good, isn't it?" Then he gave Zurbrugg a book of his own to give Lax. "I'll inscribe it his way," he said and wrote:

with
all
good
wishes

When the story made it back to the States, Gladio's friend Mary Davis, who knew of Beckett's connection to and Lax's love for the author of *Finnegans Wake*, said, "It's almost like shaking hands with James Joyce."

_____

While Lax was becoming better known as a poet in Europe, American interest in Merton continued to grow, creating greater interest in Lax too. First came the PBS documentary and the book based on it. Then came the publication that would bring Lax's name to the widest audience: Michael Mott's official biography, _The Seven Mountains of Thomas Merton_. A bestseller and finalist for the Pulitzer Prize, it was based in part on extensive interviews with Lax, who appears in the text almost one hundred times.

A sizable portion of Lax's correspondence in future years would deal with Merton questions from writers and readers alike. Occasionally someone would ask him to write about Merton for publication. In the summer of 1985, for example, a St. Bonaventure history professor named Thomas Schaeper requested a 750-word review of _The Hidden Ground of Love: The Letters of Thomas Merton on Religious Experience and Social Concerns_ for a small university journal called _Cithara_. Although he turned down most requests, Lax accepted this one, spending more time on it than even he thought reasonable. One large box in his St. Bonaventure archives is filled with his many versions, a testament to the great love and respect he felt for his absent friend. It was the only review of a Merton book he ever wrote.

_____

Throughout the week I spent with Lax in March 1985 we packed boxes for the Stuttgart show. The show's sponsor, the Sohm Archive, already had a sizable collection of his published works, but Kellein wanted a wider display of his achievements and talents. To supplement the museum's holdings, he asked Lax to send him whatever he had in his island home and foster communications with people who had their own collections of his letters, drawings, and writings. He read through everything that had been written about Lax as well and put the final touches on the first complete bibliography of his work, most of which Lax's longtime friend Judy Emery had assembled.

_Robert Lax: Abstract Poetry_ was on display in the Stuttgart Staatsgalerie's Studiensaal from April 20 to May 26, a few yards from where a larger exhibition of Reinhardt's work appeared. The room was filled with many kinds of Lax materials, including all of the books issued by his two main publishers, Pendo Verlag and Journeyman Books. In addition to chapbooks from Michael Lastnite's Furthermore Press, Ian Hamilton Finlay's Wild Hawthorn Press, and David Kilburn's Green Island Press, there were smaller publications (sometimes no more than stapled booklets or single sheets) and banners with blown-up versions of Lax's color poems in his own handwriting—a combination of poetry and art. Because Lax gave each person who asked to print his poetry complete freedom in design, the display revealed a rich variety of interpretations. Other items in the show included drawings by Lax that one critic compared to work by Joseph Beuys and Willem de Kooning, photographs taken in the Greek islands, and a complete collection of the eighteen issues of *Pax*.

Friends and acquaintances came from across Europe and the United States to honor Lax, who was in residence during the first third of the run. On April 21 he read several poems to a small audience in the morning and attended a showing of Antonucci's films in the afternoon. His reading of "Black & White" was an "exercise in meditation," a reviewer for the *Stuttgarter Nachtrichten* wrote. "Whoever hears it wakes up, suddenly hearing things differently."

For his participation in the show Lax received no more than a train ticket, living expenses in Stuttgart, and $150 for reading, but the exposure and satisfaction it gave him were priceless.

---

With the busyness of the previous year and the exhibition behind him, Lax spent a quiet summer on Patmos, writing in his journal, entertaining the occasional visitor, and swimming. He caught up on his correspondence too, including a brisk back-and-forth with Rice. They had been writing to each other more frequently since the year before, when Rice had proposed making a film about Merton that showed him as he was known to his closest friends. Lax had encouraged the project until Rice insisted he write the script.

"How's a type-Z like me going to write about a type-A like Merton," Lax wrote to Jim Harford about Rice's idea. "It's like having a turtle write about Halley's comet."

The project died eventually from lack of funding as Rice turned his attention to what would become a best-selling biography of the explorer Richard Burton, but it produced letters full of reminiscences and commentary on the flood of Merton-related materials coming out.

"Mr. Moto got me surrounded," Lax wrote, using a Merton nickname. Among the many Merton publications people had sent him were Mott's biography, copies of the *Merton Annual*, an article in *Commonweal*, and Paul Wilkes's *Merton By Those Who Knew Him Best*.

After doing so much reading and thinking about Merton, Lax wrote in his journal, "m took seriously every decision he had to make. went well-informed into every arena that seemed to be his to enter. won the battles to which he was challenged. won them for many of us. (won them with all of us in mind.) & set an example for us on how to take on (inevitable) challenges, how to struggle, how to win."

A calmness pervades the journal entries Lax wrote that summer, perhaps because he felt settled in a way he never had. His reputation as a writer was well established, Patmos (unlike Kalymnos) was a peaceful haven, and, for the first time in his adult life, he lived in a house he'd never have to move from.

Shortly before his departure for Thessaloniki the previous November, his landlady had offered to sell him the house he was living in for $10,000. He didn't have that kind of money, of course, but Marcia and her husband, Jack, were willing to make the purchase. It was illegal in Greece at the time for foreigners to buy property, but a purchase could be made in the name of a Greek citizen who served then as legal guardian. In his letters to Marcia during the winter of 1984-85, Lax had suggested and, for various reasons, rejected several Greeks he knew before landing on a Patmian postal clerk named Dimitri Ypsilantis who had held and forwarded his mail for years. That summer of 1985 Marcia and Jack signed papers that, according to Lax's translation, gave them a ninety-nine-year lease on the place for the low rent of 2,500 drachmas a month (equivalent to the $10,000 they'd already paid). They could do anything with the house they wanted to, Lax wrote, but they'd need Ypsilantis's "very friendly cooperation." On the other hand, if Ypsilantis were to die, his heirs would be obliged to honor the agreement.

In a long entry that June Lax wrote about living now as an observer, looking for meaning only in those scenes that made an impression on him, whether they came from daily life or from dreams. He knew little about the world he moved through, he wrote, so he focused on those things that were constant: "up was up, down was down, for example: no question about that. right was right, left was left. black was black, white was white. grass, for whatever reason continued to be green, and the sea was blue." These were the things he wrote his poetry about: the things he knew to be constants. They didn't answer his questions or tell him where he was, but they gave him fixed points by which to navigate.

———————

As his seventieth birthday approached, there was no denying that Lax had entered his twilight years. His letters to Gladio, Marcia, and others are sprinkled with talk of ailments, medicines, and insurance claims. He took vitamins and garlic pills with his meals, ate oatmeal or organic Wheatena for breakfast, and fixed large batches of peppermint tea to drink throughout the day because someone had told him it was good for him. His only other meal most days was a cooked dinner supplied by his neighbor Katina or a former landlady, Kalliope Kleoudi, whose husband, Pandelis, ran his favorite grocery.

"My new thing—but I run through a hundred new things a day—has a lot to do with going *very* slowly," he wrote to Gladio. "Especially about waking up in the morning. Between waking up and actually getting out of bed my new thing is just to sit there—lie there for a while—but then sit up in bed for 10, 15 or 20 minutes. I wouldn't call it meditating, I'd just call it coming-to, very, very slowly. Let all the day's thoughts settle comfortably into your mind before you get out of bed and start doing things. I don't know what it does but it seems to keep the whole day in better focus than the one I'm accustomed to."

Moving slowly was just one of several precautions he took to keep his blood pressure down and protect his heart. Others were swimming, cutting down on salt, and taking that garlic pill with his main meal each day.

Patmos, it seemed, was the perfect place to grow older, filled as it was with serene and loving people. When Damianos asked Lax to douse his dry-docked boat each day while he was away, for example, Lax didn't know how to do it. Rather than ribbing him as they might have on Kalymnos, the fishermen gave him advice, "each one with a different theory and brief demonstration." Even a twelve-year-old boy tried to help out. Seeing Lax scooping water from a pier and hauling it a long way to the boat, the boy said, "Don't take it from here. That's too much work." When Lax asked where he should take it from, the boy left the octopus he'd been tenderizing and took the bucket and rope from Lax's hands. Throwing the bucket out from the beach, he pulled it back quickly and splashed the brimming water over the boat. He did this five times in order to make sure Lax understood, then handed the bucket back. When Lax tried to do what the boy had done, however, he did it too slowly, ending up with a bucket of pebbles from the bottom of the sea. "he smiled, understandingly," Lax wrote, "as i went back to my place at the pier to draw up water slowly as i had before, from a vertical position, at a deeper spot."

Reminders of how fortunate he was to be where he was, in the health he was in, came in a couple of letters from a woman who had once been very important to him, Teddy Bergery. Her life hadn't been anywhere near as satisfying or peaceful of late. Over the previous year she'd had a physical and emotional breakdown, she told him. She'd lost her business, her home, her health, many friends, and almost all of her money. She had hypoglycemia and hyperthyroid problems, for which she took iodine that made her feel like hell. And she'd had to admit that she was an alcoholic. She was going to AA meetings, though, and taking lots of vitamins. And, although she still had a place on Greenwich Avenue in New York, she'd started spending most of her time on Mykonos, just a short stretch of sea away from her old friend. She was hoping to come to Patmos, she said, but doesn't seem to have made it.

———————

However old he might have been feeling, Lax was on the road again that September, headed to Stockholm to attend another space congress. On his way home he picked up some cash doing readings in Stuttgart and Zurich. For once, when he boarded the train to Greece, he had money in his pocket—1,000 Swiss francs in travelers checks—but somewhere along the way it was lost or stolen. Once again he returned to the islands with only the clothes on his back, and once again the kindness of friends was more than equal compensation. During his time away Katina's husband,

Yannis, had patched his leaky roof and started taking down his windows and shutters. By the end of September Yannis had scorched and sanded them all to bare wood, repaired the wood, and painted them again—a soft Greek blue for the windows and shutters and a greenish-blue for the door he said would hold up better in bright sun. While her husband had worked on the roof, Katina had scrubbed the interior. Before the year was out, Yannis had arranged for a contractor to put on a more durable concrete roof—at a good price, of course.

As usual, when the wind and rain came, Lax hunkered down for the winter. "i am trying to organize my thoughts," he wrote to Emery on January 26, 1986. "they are non-union types. wild-cat operators. everyone for himself." To another friend he wrote, "In summer I schwim. In winter I raise my feet in the air, & pump an imaginary bike while lying in bed but not like I was training for the tour de france."

Around this time he started corresponding with some friends by tape rather than letter. The reasons, he explained, were that recording was less expensive than a telephone conversation and a tape captured the voice of the one recording. It also allowed the receiver to listen at his leisure and even replay what was said, paying closer attention to the meaning in words and intonations. Another reason may have been that he was tired of writing to people. His house was full of unanswered letters.

Later that year William Packard published an excellent in-depth interview with Lax in his *New York Quarterly*, one of the "craft interviews" with important poets the magazine became known for. It too was done by tape, with Packard sending him questions and Lax recording his answers.

---

Lax returned to Bielefeld, Zurich, and Lucerne for readings and visits that April, then headed north again in October for a space congress in Innsbruck. Having no pressing reason to go home right away, he lingered at the Romero House in Lucerne after having a hernia operation in Zurich. Room and board at the seminary cost only 40 Swiss francs a day (which Moosbrugger paid, with the expectation that Lax would pay him back over time), so he stayed into March, talking theology with the young seminarians and walking the shores of Lake Lucerne for hours each day. He jotted poems and jokes into notebooks and went to the doctor and dentist. After the lonely winter the year before, it must have cheered him to be in more comfortable surroundings with intelligent, spiritual company.

That summer, an issue of the *Review of Contemporary Fiction* edited by Zurbrugg and dedicated to Beckett carried a piece by Lax titled "Beckett and Deep Sleep." After quoting a line about deep sleep from a Beckett play, Lax wrote. "It is down there in deep sleep that Beckett lives, and where all of us live, but few in our time have been so expert in visiting that region, in staying there and in bringing back a living report. It isn't just a matter of visiting—one needs a specially made, specially trimmed vocabulary to bring back true reports. One must understand the rhythms of the realm. One must bring back words and images, its particular music too."

Lax stayed on Patmos from mid-March through the end of September 1987, catching up on correspondence and entertaining visitors. As would be common for the rest of his life, his letters that summer were filled with gentle advice, usually in response to questions from family members, friends, and strangers. To someone seeking a spiritual guide, for example, he recommended trusting the light that is already inside each of us; thinking of life as an ongoing conversation with God, who will guide us gently in the right way.

One of Lax's most frequent correspondents that year was Kellein, who was attempting to write an introduction, in English, for what would be the first collection of Lax's work to be published by a mainstream American publisher. Kellein was editing the book, to be called *33 Poems*, for New Directions and felt, understandably, that it should include information about Lax's life and art. Unfortunately his written English was irredeemably bad and what he wrote was often filled with errors and questionable interpretations. In one gentle attempt to guide him, Lax wrote:

> i'm not too fond of this pitch about poor old man good poet who's been neglected.
>     my feeling is if i'd had any more attention than i've had i'd probably be out of my mind with unanswered letters.

Of all the visitors Lax had that year, the one he probably looked forward to most was his cousin Soni, who had never visited him in Greece before. She came in September with her daughter and, after touring other parts of the country, landed on Patmos near the end of the month. One day, while staying at the Rex Hotel, which Lax had booked for her, she struck up a conversation with the British woman in the room next door. The next day she ran into the woman on the beach and they fell into conversation again. When the woman found out Soni was Jewish and therefore not a pilgrim, she wondered why she had chosen to vacation on Patmos.

"I'm visiting my cousin who lives here," Soni said.

"What in the world does he do here?" the woman asked.

Soni told her he was a poet and the woman looked at her strangely.

"What is his name?" she asked.

"Robert Lax."

The woman stared at her for a long time before saying, "You mean that saintly man is *your* cousin?"

Lax ended the year by traveling north once more, all the way to England this time for a space congress in Brighton and a reading in London. When he returned, he must have felt particularly good about the attention his work was receiving. Displays of his books had appeared or were about to appear in England, Finland, and Germany, with others planned for Brisbane and New York. Unfortunately the year ended badly. In mid-December he learned that a fire at a Vermont barn where Lastnite was preparing his photographs of Greek island faces for use in a book had destroyed them all, negatives as well as prints.

----

Despite the growing interest in his work and the usual invitations to give readings, for the first time since moving there permanently Lax spent most of 1988 on Patmos. That March he wrote to Jim Harford and his wife, Millie, "I spend most of my time alone: reading, writing, walking. think i'd like to do it for about 1000 years." Around the same time he wrote to another friend, "If you need any lessons in how not to work at a bank, come here for a couple of weeks and I'll show you all there is to know. You take long walks (no motor-cycle rides) write little notes, or long papers. Read the most serious book you ever heard of and never got around to till now. Memorize Lao Tzu." Before long he'd be writing to Rice, "I've started in the past couple of weeks to feel sort of like a hermit.

First time in my life. Not trying to, not trying not to. But I'm getting some idea of how the real ones in caves must have spent their days. So far I like it. If your health stayed good I think you could do it for a thousand years, and only have time to think of about half of the things you'd want to get straightened out about."

———————

Lax was slowing down, and travel had lost some of its appeal, but he was far from becoming a hermit. The number of visitors who sought him out each summer continued to grow and he did his best to accommodate each one. What had changed was his perception of himself and his life. In March 1988 he wrote to his niece Connie, "This just occurred to me: my idea of a good contemplative is something more like a cow than it is like a dancing master." In another letter to her a year later he gave both physical and social, even metaphysical reasons for slowing down and taking care of oneself. Among them was that being "healthy, calm and eventually peaceful in spirit" was the best gift you could give to those you love. "if you're calm and peaceful and healthy and see things clearly, you're there to help whoever needs you, and you're able to do whatever has to be done."

Lax spent 1989 much as he'd spent 1988, remaining on Patmos except for a short trip to Athens for dental work in the spring and his annual excursion to Zurich in the fall, this time with a side trip to Paris. At seventy-three his physical life had slowed down just as his literary life was heating up. That year New Directions published *33 Poems*, without a foreword but with carefully researched notes that gave the year each poem or journal entry was written as well as where and when it was first published. On the cover was a photograph of a willowy Lax riding a bicycle, taken by Rice on the island of Kos.

A laudatory review in the December issue of *Poetry Flash* focused on "Sea & Sky" as an example of the delights awaiting a reader unaware of Lax's work: "It's impossible to convey in a short selection the shimmering alpha wave state this columnar, sixty three page poem induces. In fact, even more than most volumes of selected poems, 33 Poems must be carefully read, digested slowly, to get some sense of Lax's work concentrating on his vision."

The *American Library Association Booklist* reviewer wrote, "Depending upon the reader, it is all either baffling or beatific."

And the *New Yorker*, in its "Books: Briefly Noted" review, said, "The author, a lifelong friend and sometimes collaborator of Thomas Merton, writes throughout with the wry surprise of humor and self-knowledge. The other common denominator here is rhythm: even the minimal-looking 'Sea & Sky' falls into a rolling ballad swing."

When he sent a copy of the *New Yorker* review to Lax, New Directions' James Laughlin, who had dragged his heels for years before agreeing to put out a Lax collection, told him the sales were good enough to contemplate a reprint and maybe a paperback version.

While praise from institutions that had long ignored his work must have been gratifying to Lax, he had always placed greater value on his friends' opinions. Nothing could have pleased him more than the response from his Columbia classmate Leonard Robinson, whose assignment to interview the Cristianis for the *New Yorker* had led to Lax writing his best-known work, *The Circus of the Sun*. Robinson praised everything in the new book, calling *21 Pages* the best poem of the century.

The letters Lax exchanged with friends like Robinson had always been an important part of his life, but as he slowed down they took on increased significance, as did the time he spent with visitors like me. The great variety of people drawn to him for different reasons might have made it tricky to respond to each of them truthfully, but he had been dealing with different kinds of people and situations all his life and had learned how to adapt himself to whatever situation he found himself in. He understood that St. Paul's instructions to be all things to all people didn't mean changing your basic beliefs or principles but rather meeting people wherever they were.

"I guess I talk one way to one person, and another to another, but I'm always saying the same thing," he wrote to his niece Connie. In letters too his approach, and even his style, would change, reflecting the approach and style of whomever he was writing to. With some he seemed reticent, with others aggressive (for him, anyway); with some humorous and even trivial, with others ponderous; with some devout, using what might be called Christian language, with others secular. Never, however, did any of his letters seem false. Nor did his conversation. In all situations he tried to see how the person he wrote or spoke to perceived the world, then started the conversation there. His talent, to put it in Martin Buber's terms, was finding the right "I" in himself to match the "thou" in another. The right form for his love.

---

Near the end of 1989 Lax received a letter that should have removed any remaining doubts about his stature as a poet. It came from the celebrity photographer Richard Avedon, who reminded him that they'd met on Patmos fifteen years earlier. Avedon had taken a snapshot of Lax then and never forgotten his writing or his face. Now he wanted to stop on Patmos between a Christmas shoot in the Holy Land and a New Year's Eve session at Berlin's Brandenburg Gate to capture that face on film. The portrait would be part of a series of portraits of poets for the high-quality French magazine *Egoiste*, where Avedon had just published his photographs of Beckett, Borges, and Francis Bacon.

Lax, of course, agreed, and Avedon arrived a few days after Christmas with two assistants and an array of lighting equipment. Positioning Lax beside the dry brush on a hill near his house, with dark hills and a swirl of winter clouds behind him, he snapped away—taking close to two hundred photographs—then left the island again after just a few hours.

The photograph appeared in *Egoiste* (a lush black-and-white production almost two feet square) in 1992, along with portraits of W. H. Auden, Peter Handke, Joseph Brodsky, and Elie Wiesel. Lax's enthusiastic letter to Gladio about the shoot was the last she'd ever read. Two days before Easter Sunday in 1990, in the middle of Passover, she died at eighty-five.

Lax spent that spring and summer at home on Patmos, saving his strength for what would be his last trip to the United States before the end of his life. St. Bonaventure University had invited him to spend three weeks on campus in late September and early October as the university's first Reginald A. Lenna Visiting Professor of English. Pleased as he was to have his hometown university honor him, he didn't relish the long trip back to the States and he didn't want the fuss to be too great. Never having shaken his fear of flying, he requested passage on the *Queen Elizabeth 2*, as he had when traveling to ArtPark, and he made his niece Marcia, who was negotiating the details for him, promise he wouldn't have to attend a gala.

By the time Lax arrived, St. Bonaventure's celebration of him and his writing had already begun. Selections of his work were on display in the university library and several public events had been arranged. From September 23 through October 12 his only duties were weekly visits to Professor Richard Simpson's creative writing class, but on October 4 he gave a well-publicized reading in the university's Dresser Auditorium. Just before the reading he attended the banquet he had tried to avoid and received an honorary doctorate.

Five days later he gave a reading at the Olean Public Library that drew a hundred people. In a review in the next day's *Olean Times Herald*, City Editor Patrick Vecchio wrote, "Mr. Lax clearly takes reading his work seriously, speaking in a slow, deliberate, inflective voice and making it clear that each word serves a purpose." Vecchio was especially impressed with Lax's supple and varied use of repetition: "The repetition in a poem about a port in a faraway place, for instance, evoked the rhythm of a moored ship rising and falling on the swell of gentle waves."

One final reading took place on October 14 at the Burchfield Art Center in Buffalo, which opened an exhibition of his work six weeks later, cosponsored by the Poetry/Rare Book Collection of the State University of New York in Buffalo. Called *Robert Lax and Concrete Poetry*, the show featured not only Lax's books and papers but also his drawings, his photographs, and his color poems, in his handwriting, printed on huge banners.

Before he returned to Europe, Lax stopped briefly in New York City, where Soni threw a party attended by many of his old friends from *Jubilee* and even Columbia days. It was the last time he would see most of them.

----

Shortly after the long, tiring time away, Lax turned seventy-five. He spent his birthday, November 30, quietly on Patmos, while hundreds of miles away in Munich, the radio broadcaster Bayerischer Rundfunk was dedicating two hours of its fourth annual *Munchner Hörspielabend* to him and his work. The rest of the winter was quiet too, broken only by a trip to Athens for free dental work and renewal of his visitor's permit. (He had been renewing it every three months for years, but this time the authorities granted him a longer stay, through December of that year.) In a February letter to Soni, he wrote that he'd thrown a bedspread over the pile of unanswered letters in his main room "& whole room sings."

Although Lax delighted in correspondence, the growing number of letters that came each month from friends and family, writers and editors, readers and Merton fans had become a psychological and even physical burden. His to-do list for November 22, 1996, for example, lists sixty-five people to write to, most with a notation beside the name of items to send or subjects to mention. It's no wonder that even a temporary break from letters made his environment cheerier.

War was in the air in early 1991, and peace, which had always been one of Lax's main concerns, was on his mind. As usual he saw the problem and the solution as interpersonal rather than international. In May, after the Gulf War had begun and ended, he sent Soni this simple poem:

peace
be
gins

when
an
y
two
be
ings

in
the
un
i
verse

at
tempt

(&
per
se
vere

in
try
ing)

to
un
der
stand

each
oth
er

—

Lax's autumn trip that year took him to Geneva, Verona, and Zurich. In 1990 Pendo had released the third of his journal books, *Journal C*, and in 1991 it published *Psalm & Homage to Wittgenstein*. (Another publisher, Stride Publications of Exeter, England, issued its first small Lax books that year as well, a second printing of *Psalm* and one called *The Rooster Poems*.) In a letter to Soni sent shortly after his return to Patmos in mid-October, Lax wrote, "even in the room, I'm on an island: sitting in bed." In the days and years ahead he would spend more and more time on his bed, using it not only for sleep but also for reading and writing and even conversations with guests.

That December, while Lax was perched on his island, Geerken pulled off his most audacious presentation yet: a ten-hour production of Lax's *The Bomb*, a "Scenario for Auditorium," as Lax labeled it, using just two nonsense words, *jabba* and *wook*, repeated in an unspecified number of voices until an explosion at the end. In *33 Poems* it runs just four pages, but the playful Geerken twisted it this way and that, using a wide variety of approaches, including a live reading by Lax done in the lobby of an Athens hotel.

Before the fierce winter winds had subsided, 1992 was already looking to be a busy year, not for Lax going elsewhere but for others coming to him. In March, Merton's former secretary, Brother Patrick Hart, arrived for a short visit, and then, in early May, a man named Arthur Biddle came to conduct an important series of interviews.

Biddle's visit was connected to Merton—and even to Hart—as well. At an International Thomas Merton Society conference the year before, Hart had told him about the many letters Lax and Merton exchanged during their lives and asked if Biddle might be interested in editing them for publication. Biddle, who had met Lax twice and liked his poetry, said he was. He secured approval from the Merton Legacy Trust, Marcia Kelly, and Lax himself, and headed to Patmos.

Biddle's two previous meetings with Lax had also taken place on Patmos, the first time without either man knowing who the other one was. As Biddle tells the story, he had gone to Patmos for vacation one hot July and, while descending from Chora by footpath, stopped to rest beneath an olive tree. "Making his way easily up the trail was a tall, white-haired and bearded figure with a staff," he wrote, "looking more like an athletic desert father than a tourist or townsman. He stopped to exchange a few words, and perhaps to assure himself that I wasn't in need of CPR. If we introduced ourselves by name, I soon forgot his. Besides I hadn't discovered Merton yet, so the name Lax wouldn't have meant anything to me."

Several years later, after he *had* discovered Merton, Biddle was on a retreat at Gethsemani and mentioned that he was returning to Patmos. Hearing of his plans, Hart asked him to take a manuscript to Lax. By this time Biddle knew who Lax was but not that he'd ever met him or how he might find him. Hart told him simply to ask at the post office, but on the day Biddle arrived on the island the post office was closed.

That night, while dining at an outdoor café, he saw a man walking across the square whose "stature alone made him stand out from everyone else." Although the only photographs he'd seen of Lax were years old, he recognized him right away and the two began to talk. When Biddle told Lax he'd been to Patmos before, Lax asked if he'd visited the monastery at Chora and walked down the footpath afterward.

"As he asked that question," Biddle wrote, "I looked into his eyes and recalled with great clarity that earlier encounter. This remarkable man had remembered me, apparently with no trouble."

Their third encounter, in May 1992, must have been a much more emotional one for Lax. Over five days Biddle took him through the letters he had exchanged with Merton throughout their friendship, asking him to clarify subjects, identify individuals they had mentioned, and talk generally about his life with and without Merton over those thirty years. The interviews produced over a hundred transcript pages.

Biddle wasn't Lax's only visitor that May. For the second time in just a few years, Soni traveled to Greece to see him. His note to her after the visit shows how aware he was that the end of his life was approaching and that every visit with someone he loved might be the last. "I had a great time too, every minute you were here, & love you, love you," he wrote. "Come back as soon as you can."

Lax's days were full of memories that year. Later in the year Soni sent him the recently published collection of old Joseph Mitchell *New Yorker* pieces, *Up in the Old Hotel*, and reminisced about the now-vanished fish market area Mitchell wrote about, an area she and Lax knew well. She mentioned that she was still trying to get to a temporary display of Lax's writings and drawings at his alma mater. Around the same time, the *Merton Annual* featured his long poem about his early days in the city,

"Remembering Merton and New York." And after traveling to Patmos to record a series of interviews, the Swiss journalist Peter P. Schneider published a long article in Zurich's *Tages-Anzeiger* newspaper looking back over his life. "Wir sind alle Wanderer auf diesem Planeten," it was titled— "We are all wanderers on this planet"—a quote from Lax.

---

Except for his yearly trips to Switzerland, Lax never left Patmos anymore. For most of his life he had gone out to see the world; now the world came to him, through visits or letters. He even heard from Brahmachari, who was living in India and seemed to Lax to be the same person who had impressed him so many years before.

With his small house paid for and neighbors supplying most of his evening meals, he had few needs and therefore few expenses. He rarely ate lunch, and for breakfast he fixed himself a simple mix of oatmeal and bran he soaked overnight, topping it with yogurt, honey, and sliced bananas, if he had them. He didn't have a refrigerator—he disliked the noise they made—but he had an ice box for his yogurt and the fish for his cats a fisherman gave him for free. Each day he would walk into town and buy a small block of ice for it. He didn't have a telephone either. He gave those few who had a real need to call him his neighbor Katina's number; when someone phoned, she came to get him. When he needed clothes, someone in his circle of doting family and friends supplied them, usually unbidden.

That February 1993, for example, he wrote to Gary Bauer, a young American living on Patmos who had gone to England, to ask him to bring back a pair of pants and a sports coat. Before he'd mailed the letter, though, his nephew's daughter had sent him two blazers. Just days later a sweater arrived from Marcia. She offered gloves, hats, scarves, and anything else he might need to keep warm. He told her not to bother with any of them: he never wore gloves, he had hats, and Geerken had just given him a "blue angora long underwear or jogging suit." She offered him a shawl too, but he already had "a wool blanket with tassels from Moschos" he thought might actually be a shawl. He had a small space heater as well, and Bauer had put plastic over his windows for insulation.

Lax's simple lifestyle became part of a movie in February 1993, when Geerken brought two German filmmakers, Nicolas Humbert and Werner Penzel, to Patmos to film him reading and eating and going about his life. They combined these shots with footage of a small French circus and Tuareg nomads who live in the mountainous areas north of the Sahara to create what they called a "cine-poem" and a *Variety* reviewer, Joe Leydon, called "an impressionistic hodgepodge." *Middle of the Moment* opened in Europe in 1995 and played to enthusiastic crowds there before making a limited appearance in the United States. No doubt Lax was pleased to see himself placed among circus people and the Tuaregs he had researched for *The Siren of Atlantis*.

Soni offered to pay Lax's way to appear at an exhibit of his books and poems in Brno, Czechoslovakia, that summer, but Lax said no. Too many visitors were coming to see him and he was content to stay where he was. He spent as much time as he could alone now, writing and reading.

Over the next couple of years little in his life would change except the stops on his annual trips. In 1993 he went to Paris to visit Jean Vanier at L'Arche and Munich to do a radio show for Geerken. The following year he stopped in Stuttgart. His only regular stop was Zurich to visit his Pendo friends, who continued to publish his books—*Journal D* in 1993 and *Dialogues* in 1994. (The entries in *Journal D* came from 1973, the last full year he lived contentedly on Kalymnos. *Dialogues*, as its title implies, was quite different. Rather than dialogues per se, it was filled mostly with one-page pairings of a question from "A" and an often witty answer from "B," with calligraphy by Lax as illustrations.) Stride issued another slender Lax book in 1994, *27th & 4th*, a poetic evocation of the people he had watched (and Antonucci had filmed) passing his *Jubilee* window forty years before. And Sheed & Ward reissued *A Catch of Anti-letters*.

Lax turned eighty in 1995, and although the year started quietly, it turned out to be quite busy, both on Patmos and in terms of publications and productions by and about him. Pendo issued a book called *Notes* as well as a comprehensive bibliography compiled by Gerhard van den Bergh and a recording of Lax reading his poetry. Tiny Trombone Press out of Exeter, England, published a chapbook, *Xiliamodi*, about a small island lying just off the coast of Patmos. And a group of young people who had invited Lax to read once in Baden, Switzerland, published two of his poems, "A shorter rooster poem" and "dr. glockenspiel's invention," in their small publication *Seiten* #1. Finally, *Columbia College Today* included his tribute in a special section commemorating the centennial of Mark Van Doren's birth.

That June the International Thomas Merton Society held its biannual conference at St. Bonaventure University. One of the highlights for attendees was a shuttle trip up into the hills to see the cottage where Merton, Lax, and their friends spent two idyllic summers while the world tilted toward war. The trip was a fulfillment of a dream Gladio had had years before, in which people from around the world converged on the cottage.

A few weeks before the conference took place, I recorded five hours of interviews with Lax on Patmos and used what he told me in an article for *Poets & Writers* magazine that appeared in 1997. Around the same time, a BBC journalist named Peter France, who had a house on Patmos, interviewed him for inclusion in a book called *Hermits*.

"i'm a hermit?" Lax wrote with puckish amusement in a letter explaining the book's focus. He wasn't really, not in the way France intended, putting him in the company of the Desert Fathers and the Russian *startsy*, but he was, at eighty, much less active than he'd been just a few years before. He still went down into town each day to shop and collect his mail, but he spent most of his time sitting on his bed reading and writing or working on a computer given to him by Nicholas Negroponte, the renowned director of MIT's Media Lab, who owned a house in Chora. He still entertained guests and answered those who wrote him letters, but his replies had grown shorter and more whimsical.

A couple of Lax's letters to Marcia that year dealt with potential projects, including making a great books list. "So what are our criteria?" Lax asked rhetorically. "Good, well-written text, of lasting value. Clearly nonviolent. socially well-oriented. unambiguously human, humane and well-balanced." Marcia and her husband, Jack, had just published *One Hundred Graces*, a collection of "mealtime blessings," including one by Lax, and he encouraged them to compile a similar collection of aphorisms. His own writing was tending more and more toward the aphoristic, although he never called his pithy vertical sayings aphorisms. "Every so many years I think it's time to have new collections of wise sayings," he wrote, "eliminating some of the old ones, like 'pound your neighbor to a pulp' and replacing them with good, sensible, nonviolent ones, like 'have him arrested.'"

Around this same time he sent an aphorism to his friend the artist Nancy Goldring that beautifully summarized how he had come to see his—and maybe everyone's—task in life:

not
so
much
find
ing

a
path
in
the
woods

as
find
ing

a
rhythm

to
walk
in

Lax's reading that winter and spring included a retrospective short-story collection from his old friend William Maxwell called *All the Days and Nights* (a title Lax would adopt in slightly altered form for the 2000 publication of his three circus cycles, *Circus Days & Nights*) and a variety of religious books, including *Eastern Definitions*, *Ten Eastern Religions*, *The Wisdom of Chuang Tzu*, and sometimes the Philokalia or bits of a book on the Kabbalah. He continued to read Buber and was working his way through Brahmachari's dissertation, submitted to the University of Chicago in 1939 and published in book form in India years later.

In answer to a question from Soni about how he spent his time, he said, "what do i do: read write eat sleep, take walks and say hello to people. some old friends stop by to see me, and the neighbors say, when they do, they can always hear us laughing." His writing consisted primarily of jotting brief poems and jokes into a small notebook with the hope of transcribing them one day. On his daily outings he would pick up his mail or fish for his cats, knowing that his neighbor Katina would bring over something, usually a vegetarian dish, for his own evening meal.

Another question from Soni asked which parts of his life he wished had gone on longer. His answer:

> well, i can name times i liked very much (& i will) but as i thought about your question i felt that most of them probably ended or trailed off just about when they should have so i could get onto some other good things. most of the first ones that come to mind were in europe or in greece beginning in the fifties, but one of the best to start them all off was in n y, florida, & canada when i met and travelled with the Cristianis (out in Saskatchewan). great times in europe: living in (around) marseille, on & off for about 4 years. a book about the first part (written long ago) should be out pretty soon & I'll send you a copy. later, travelling with a french circus in italy, from rome to pescara was great too (& just about long enough); i've written about that too. then greece, specially kalymnos (which reminded me of marseille), & i think it too went on just long enough. (town got too noisy & busy.) when i moved up here i was ready to. (though keep in touch with my friends there and dash down to see them when they come here) and now really, i'm loving it here. would be glad if these days, and the way i spend them, could go on just as long as they can.

The celebration of the 1900th anniversary of St. John's Revelation flooded the island with visitors that summer, including a man Lax had last seen at L'Eau Vive forty-five years before and several priests he'd known in France, who served him the one essential his life on Patmos lacked: the Eucharist.

Although he made a conscious effort to be a loving presence and a model for how to live a peaceful life, Lax couldn't have known just how important visits with him were to those who came to see him. Jen Harford, who spent five weeks on Patmos that June, tells of accompanying him to Pandelis's tiny grocery store, a place "stocked with lots of little bits of everything: steel wool, bleach, ammonia, canned food, maybe even olives in barrels" that was "more closet than store." When he saw that others were in the store, Lax suggested they wait outside.

"It was clear," Harford wrote about the incident, "that we waited outside not because Lax avoided crowds, which he largely did, but out of kindness and respect to others and particularly to the shop owners. They were a kind couple, they could not possibly serve everyone at once, and why rush and put our needs in front of them when they couldn't help us anyway? What possible good would be accomplished by our rushing? Lax got all this across to me without words."

When the store had cleared, Lax moved "with a gentle hesitant intentionality" inside, where the two of them were greeted warmly. Before they left, Lax handed several clean plastic containers to Pandelis's wife, who replaced them with similar containers filled with food for him.

Having observed Lax's behavior, Harford thought she'd try something similar when she went shopping on her own at a larger store later. Since the store clerks were busy when she arrived, she waited patiently at the meat counter in the rear of the store, but no one noticed her. Finally a French woman came in, and when she called out for help, someone came to help her. A man came in after her, and he too was served. Then the clerk who had helped them helped Harford.

The next day she returned to the same store and waited as before. The same thing happened: another customer came in and asked for help, and Harford was served after him.

The third day she did the same. This time a clerk served her right away.

When she went back the fourth day, the clerk greeted her with a warm "Yassou" and headed straight to the meat counter to help her.

"I felt that as I showed Lax's patience . . . I was rewarded with a kind of love," she wrote.

Years later, having returned to the United States and fallen back into old patterns, she remembered the lesson learned on Patmos and decided to try Lax's approach again. In a crowded Kinko's where people were scrambling to claim a computer or get their print order done, she stood to the side waiting for things to settle down. "I was worried that no one would ever notice me," she wrote. "But eventually a very harried gentleman smiled at me and said that he wished all customers were like me and he helped me right away."

A couple of months earlier Lax had sent the following Merton quote to Marcia:

> If you are yourself at peace, then there is at least some peace in the world. Then share your peace with everyone and everyone will be at peace.

———————

Lax made his usual trip to Zurich in October 1995 but kept it short, returning to Patmos in mid-November, grateful, no doubt, for the quiet of the island winter. Gary Bauer usually spent his winters elsewhere, but that winter he stayed on Patmos, too, helping Lax celebrate his eightieth birthday. Family called and congratulatory letters arrived from many friends—including Mogador, who wrote that he'd hoped to attend the celebratory birthday reading Lax's Pendo friends were holding in Zurich (assuming perhaps that Lax would be there) but couldn't because of prostate and colon problems. He sent a video and posters of the Cristianis instead. Lax was happy to spend the day quietly in his little island home. "I'm loving it right here," he wrote to Soni. "Love the light that comes into the hall through the mottled glass window in the front door. Stand in front of it every morning as though it was the Mona Lisa."

———————

It's clear now, looking back, that Lax's life changed greatly in 1996—that the life he'd led for decades, the life he'd long thought of as his life, was ending. During her visit the year before, Jen Harford had perceived that what had once been simple and easy was more complicated and difficult for him now. Answering letters, for example, and taking care of his house and himself. When she returned to the United States she suggested to his family that he might need an assistant of some kind. Marcia and Connie liked the idea, and Connie found John Beer, a young University of Iowa Writers Workshop grad who seemed perfect. That summer he moved to Patmos to help Lax in any way Lax needed.

Beer was an ideal choice. Although Lax was wary of having someone so intimately involved in his life, he took to Beer right away. Beer was a poet with a passing knowledge of philosophy, an intellect with a sense of humor that matched Lax's well. He was hardworking and efficient, and before long Lax had come to depend on him for many things.

Beer lived in a room nearby and came up every afternoon to cook a meal they ate together and work on bringing order to the papers that had piled up over many years. Together they packed bundles that Beer mailed to the Lax archives at St. Bonaventure and Columbia. At first Lax continued to answer letters himself, but eventually he let Beer write many letters for him, especially those to strangers or editors.

"Were you right about sending John here!" Lax wrote to Jen Harford. "100% angelic assistant: calm, quiet, orderly, & great to have around— not bad at catching flies, either. . . . He's copied at least 3000 pages of little poems from notebooks (& still has boxes of notebooks to go on with) & has sorted notes, poems, drawings & letters that were in piles on the shelves. You'd cheer if you saw how it's going."

Although no one realized it yet, Beer's coming signaled a shift for Lax into the last years of his life—years of increasing dependence on others. Ironically, that same year Peter France's *Hermits* book appeared.

---

The poet Lax was honored in book form that year too. Thanks to the efforts of a young man named James Uebbing, a graduate student in Columbia University's MFA program in poetry who entered and then swiftly left Lax's life, a top-tier U.S. publisher finally published a collection of his work. The book, *Love Had a Compass: Journals and Poetry*, was published by Grove Press as part of its ongoing poetry series. It included an introduction by Uebbing and Avedon's *Egoiste* photograph on its dust jacket.

Unfortunately this was Uebbing's first attempt at editing a book and, although *Compass* is a reasonably good introduction to Lax's work— including, among fragments from other periods, the first publication of his Marseilles writings—it lacks some of the strengths of *33 Poems*— when the works were written and published, for example, and any mention of Emil Antonucci, the man who published many of the poems and almost single-handedly kept Lax in print for years.

In a letter that November, Lax, who hadn't been associated with a particular church for decades, explained what had attracted him to Catholicism in his youth: "Being by temperament disorganized myself, I rather appreciate organized religion, if only for keeping (& passing from generation to generation) a catalogue of the essentials of belief, & of 'the way.'" Immediately after this, however, he wrote, "Though I do think the essentials are 'simple': Love God & love your neighbor as yourself. And spend your life as earnestly (& joyously) as you can in learning whatever you're able to learn about the meaning, in your own life, your own experience, of such words as 'God,' 'love,' 'neighbor' and 'self.' For me, at least, keeping an informal journal (of jottings, if you like) about such thoughts as these seems to help."

"Jottings" is a good description of what his journals had become by this time: short vertical thoughts or brief amusing vignettes about whatever aspect of life ran through his mind, jotted into pocket notebooks. Some were whimsical ideas or simple metaphors. Others dealt with Greek expressions or things to tell people. Occasionally the jottings were followed by abstract drawings or sketches of faces or fish. By the time he reached the last year of his life, his notes were as simple as this:

one
well-
chos
en

step
at
a
time

The physical decline Harford had noticed in the summer of 1995 continued throughout 1996 and 1997. "I've been in bed a lot of the time since mid-November," Lax wrote to Rice in early February 1997.

irregular heart-beat & lately, swollen legs associated with it. Weather's often cold & windy but on calm days I walk into town (with a stick) & climb back up the hill very slowly—then back to the horizontal position.

No complaint in all this. Woman next door brings food (completely non-salt diet), friends come to visit & I get more mail than I can handle. Also a friend from upstate N.Y. [Beer] comes here for several hours a day, helps me straighten papers (still the same mess) & copy all my unpublished note-books (I keep writing them) on the computer & helps me edit them for (mostly small-press) publication.

So the days are plenty busy and I enjoy them. Even in the old days at the cottage in Olean, I used to spend plenty of time in bed. So that's not very new either.

. . . What I'm interested in these days: the evolution of consciousness. Not the world's consciousness, so much—just my own. Have I really learned anything since I was born? What does it mean to me if I have? And what's it all supposed to be evolving toward. Pretty vague statement of what I have in mind. But it's what I keep coming back to.

He ended the letter with this: "Keep taking good care of yourself. They ain't too many of us left."

Rice's reply, written on Ash Wednesday, is in a script so small and labored it is difficult to read. The lines slant upward as they cross the page. He hadn't written anything in months, he said, not even a letter. Parkinson's was destroying his body.

———————————

As Lax grew frailer, Beer wrote more and more of his letters and, along with his girlfriend, Paula Diaz, who had moved to Patmos to help, urged him to eat and exercise better. Beer led him down into town to walk, and he and Paula steamed whatever vegetables were available. Beer continued to pack and send boxes too. One box included an unpublished manuscript Lax had written about traveling with the circus in Italy, "Voyage to Pescara," which Pendo was slated to publish but never did. It was finally published in 1999—almost fifty years after it had been written—with The Circus of the Sun and Mogador's Book in Overlook Press's Circus Days and Nights.

Lax and Beer collaborated on more pleasant labor too. Beer edited Pendo's Journal F and a selection called Sleeping Waking for a tiny press out of Charleston, Illinois, called tel-net, both published in 1997. And he worked with Lax for weeks on a radio play they called A Room Full of Voices. Assembled from "Bob's dialogues, one-liners and fables," the play was filled with jokes that "would probably be lost on a non-American audience," Beer wrote to Connie, so they were looking for someone in the United States to perform it. (It was never performed during Lax's lifetime, but recent performances have received good reviews. Another show they collaborated on, *Black/White Oratorio*, was performed at the 1997 Festival la Bâtie in Geneva and has been performed elsewhere since.)

Lax had long been a curiosity to many on Patmos. When he went into town now he carried a walking stick he often held horizontally across his chest as he walked back and forth under an arbor, lifting his legs as high as he could to stretch the muscles. On these walks he wore a straw hat and large dark glasses that kept out every ray of sunlight. He usually wore a thick coat too. "Being exactly the kind of nut you were meant to be: do you think that's a good thing?" he wrote to Soni on August 20, 1998. "(People on the street seem to treat me as though I was coming along pretty well.) When I wear my overcoat into town in the middle of summer, they laugh indulgently."

# Epilogue: The Singer and the Song

The last time I saw Lax was in the spring of 1999, a year and a half before he died. I didn't know how soon he would die, of course, but I could see the decline in him. He'd lost a couple of teeth in front, and although his mind was still sharp, he had trouble finding some words. He told me two or three stories about his life I hadn't heard before, but the telling seemed rote, as if he'd been telling those stories to visitors for weeks. He could still engage in lively discussion, but sometimes he got a joke wrong or started a story he'd already told me the day before. Another young couple, Michael and Rebecca Daugherty, had taken over for John and Paula, and when I saw Rebecca down by the sea, she told me he no longer walked into town without help or ate anything that wasn't puréed.

I spent two weeks on Patmos that spring. The first night I saw Lax, he gave me the news on mutual friends, showed me the books people had sent, and told me a film crew had filmed him for a museum piece to be called *Three Windows*. There were gaps in our conversation, times when we lapsed into silence, and I wondered if he was tapped out, depleted from too many visitors, until I remembered that gaps had always been part of our talks. Others have mentioned the same experience. It was discomforting until you let go. Let yourself rest. Let the quiet become a soothing bubble you sat in together.

It took a few days for me to realize that others were visiting him in the morning and that there was tension with his caregivers, impatience sometimes on both sides. I found that if I stayed after dinner, waiting until whoever had served him that night had gone, he became his old self again. By the time I'd been there a week we were sitting up late each night, talking like the longtime friends we were. Not because we had urgent things to say but because we enjoyed the companionship, those hours at the end of a day that allow a writer to be solitary the rest of the time. I had just finished my second year of teaching full time and I needed the spirit being with Lax gave me. It was a spirit of love but not laxity, peace but not passivity, assurance but not arrogance, hope but not selfish ambition, wisdom but not condescension, and faith but not a rigid belief about how things should or will be.

One night he showed me a quote he'd just taped to his wall. It was from Nelson Mandela:

> Our deepest fear is not that we are inadequate. Our deepest fear is that we are powerful beyond measure. It is our light, not our darkness that most frightens us. We ask ourselves, Who am I to be brilliant, gorgeous, talented, fabulous? Actually, who are you *not* to be? You are a child of God. Your playing small does not serve the world. There is nothing enlightened about shrinking so that others won't feel insecure around you. We are all meant to shine, as children do. We were born to make manifest the glory of God that is within us. It's not just in some of us; it's in everyone. And as we let our own light shine, we unconsciously give other people permission to do the same. As we are liberated from our own fear, our presence automatically liberates others.

It was a night or two after he showed me this quote that he told me he'd had the dream in which I assured him peace *is* a good thing to seek and love *does* conquer all. A couple nights later—my last night on the island—Gary Bauer, who had been living on Patmos off and on for close to two decades, joined us for dinner. In those early years when I would visit in early spring or late fall, before or after leading my tours, Bauer would often spend the evening with us, the three of us talking, debating, and laughing. The two of them hadn't spent much time together lately, but that night seemed like old times, all of us laughing so hard we had tears in our eyes. It seemed for those hours as if we were back in those earlier days, all with plenty of time ahead. When Bauer left, I lingered a while, talking to Lax about Aristotle and Bakhtin. He told me my visit had been good for him, in part because it produced that dream. When I finally left that night, I felt unusually whole and satisfied. I didn't know those final few minutes were the last I would ever spend alone with him.

I saw Lax again the next day, but there were people around. When he hugged me goodbye, he held me longer than ever before, squeezing more tightly than I thought possible. He couldn't walk me down to the ferry but others did, and when I had dropped my things in my cabin I came out to wave to them. As the boat left the quay, I glanced toward the hill behind the harbor. There, in the midst of those whitewashed houses, a light blinked once and then twice before going dark. Goodbye, my friend, I said to the night, knowing that in his way he could hear me. I stayed on the deck until the glow from Skala and the lights along the harbor road had disappeared. My last view of the Holy Isle was the lights of Chora, gleamings from the celestial city floating through the night.

———————

Back in the States after my trip, I told Marcia about her uncle's condition, and we agreed the time had come for him to leave the islands he loved. I don't know how she convinced him to go but she did, and when she had, she asked if I would help him move. I was teaching again but told her I would if I could. When the call finally came, it came from him, his voice so meek and fragile it hurt my heart. I wanted to drop everything and rush to Patmos, devote myself to helping however I could. But I had a hundred students spread over four classes and we were only halfway through the term. I couldn't leave them.

Years have passed since that dark night, but I remember it clearly: The look of the light in the room I was in. The weight of the phone. The feeling of wanting to say anything but what I was saying. I pictured him hearing my words as he sat on his bed, his swollen legs under him. I imagined the cold in the room, the wind rattling the window. He understood why I couldn't come, of course, as he understood everything. Someone else would take my place, some other plan work out.

In the end Marcia and her husband, Jack, went themselves. Lax had made arrangements to live in the seminary he liked in Lucerne, but there were problems with his stomach and his legs and he ended up in the Deux Alice Clinic in Brussels instead. The trip began with local friends carrying him in a wheelchair down to a cruise ship for a four-day journey to Civitavecchia in Italy. From there he rode a train to Rome and on to Belgium through Switzerland and France, as if on a farewell tour through his favorite countries. The decision on where to go and how to get him there took time—so long, in fact, that he was still on Patmos when my school year ended. By then my wife and I had made arrangements to travel to Turkey. We might just make it to Greece in time to see him, we thought, so I called him from a Turkish town.

Since allowing a phone to be installed in his house a few years before, Lax had established a ritual, answering only after the third ring. The rings on his phone were drawn-out *brrrrrrs* and as I listened to each one I thought of sitting in that room with him, watching as he turned a simple call into an expectant act. When the third ring came, the line clicked and there it was, that pleasing voice, stronger and nearer. I told him I was on my way. But seeing him again was not to be. He was almost out the door, he said. The men were there to carry him. He thanked me for calling, though— pleased, it seemed, that mine would be his final call on Patmos.

---

Lax spent a month in Brussels, although doctors there found little wrong except some swelling in his knees. His blood pressure was a consistent 120/80 and various tests revealed no clear problems. He had little energy or will to move, however. Meanwhile those in charge at the Swiss seminary were having doubts about his living with them in his weakened condition, and Marcia was having a hard time finding another place for him. So one day she raised the possibility of his moving back to Olean, where he could live in his sister's old house, where he'd stayed with Merton when young and while recovering from the *New Yorker*. It was the house his father and sister had both lived in just before they died, a place where family and the memory of family would be all around him. As she feared, his answer was no, but when she asked why, his reason surprised her: he didn't want to fly.

"If you didn't have to fly, would you consider it?" she asked.

"Yes," he said, "I'd like that."

And so he crossed the ocean one last time on a luxury liner, sailing from Southampton and spending his last night in Europe at Winchester Cathedral, in the bed British kings once slept in on the night before their wedding.

---

Lax died on September 26, 2000, the feast day of St. John (Orthodox). I was at school when the call came. It was late afternoon and I had a class that night, so all I could do was turn off the light to hide my tears. My office was a concrete box with a view of an indoor atrium and, if I craned my neck, a patch of sky through a skylight. When I looked that afternoon, the sky was a deep Greek blue. "Go teach them," it seemed Lax was saying, "and give them all A's."

---

Several people who knew Lax have said he found what Merton was looking for: a kind of solitude, simplicity, and peace that passes human understanding. Some have even said he was the one who became a saint. None of this would have meant much to him except perhaps as inspiration to others. What he—and Merton—found, he thought, was his own way of walking. His own way of singing the song. His own way of being *pure act*. For, as he once wrote,

> there are not many songs
> there is only one song
>
> the animals lope to it
> the fish swim to it
> the sun circles to it
> the stars rise
> the snow falls
> the grass grows
>
> there is no end to the song and no beginning
> the singer may die
> but the song is forever
>
> truth is the name of the song
> and the song is truth.

# Notes

Some of Lax's journals are archived in the Robert Lax Collection at Columbia University and some in the Robert Lax Papers at St. Bonaventure University; selections were published by Pendo Verlag between 1986 and 1997. Most of the personal information not cited comes from my conversations with Robert Lax and those who knew him.

## Epigraph

"I think it's a metaphysical concept": Merton and Lax, *When Prophecy Still Had a Voice*, 438.

## Prologue: Going Back

1, "Acquire the spirit": St. Seraphim.

4, The scene is familiar: Merton, *The Seven Storey Mountain*, 260–61.

## 1. A Mutual Wonder-field

10, "voluntary exile": William Packard, "Craft Interview: Robert Lax," *New York Quarterly* 30 (Summer 1986): 17–35.

10, "He'd take me to a field": Robert Lax to William Maxwell, March 3, 1995, Robert Lax Papers, St. Bonaventure University.

11, "combination of Hamlet and Elias": Merton, *The Seven Storey Mountain*, 198.

12, Stuttgart exhibition: *Robert Lax: Abstract Poetry*, April 20–May 26, 1985, Studiensaal, Alten Staatsgalerie, Stuttgart, advertising flyer, Soni Holman Fink private collection.

15, "An old friend": Wilfrid Sheed, "The Beat Movement, Concluded," *New York Times Book Review*, February 13, 1973, 2, 32.

15, "some incomprehensible woe": Merton, *The Seven Storey Mountain*, 197.

15, "state his bliss": Van Doren, *The Autobiography of Mark Van Doren*, 212.

15, "laughing Buddha": Jack Kerouac to Philip Whalen, February 2, 1961, in Kerouac, *Selected Letters 1957–1969*, 321.

16, "Merton looked up": Wilkes, *Merton By Those Who Knew Him*, 65.

18, "created a mutual wonder-field": Seitz, *Song for Nobody*, 59–60.

19, The most intimate record: Robert Lax, "Remembering Merton and New York," *Merton Annual* 5 (1992): 39–61.

19, "I can understand": Thomas Merton to Henry Miller, May 12, 1963, in Merton, *The Courage for Truth*, 279.

20, "It's not fair": Nancy Flagg, "The Beats in the Jungle," *Art International*, September 1977, 56–59.

20, the poet who fell off the map: James Uebbing, introduction to Lax, *Love Had a Compass*, x.


## 2. Ends and Means

22, "The man who fears": Merton, *No Man Is an Island*, 228.

24, "A real jam session": Robert Lax, in Merton and Lax, *When Prophecy Still Had a Voice*, 435.

25, Although he'd done well: Lax journal, February 2, 1941, Columbia University.

26, "associated with bilious attacks": Lax journal, June 8, 1939, Columbia University.

27, The yearbook for Lax's senior year: *The Columbian*, 1938.

27, "leader of the more establishment-oriented part": Geir Lundestad, "The Nobel Peace Prize, 1901–2000," www.nobelprize.org/nobel_prizes/themes/peace/lundestad-review/, accessed August 4, 2014.

28, When Lax, a Jew: Merton, *The Seven Storey Mountain*, 447.

28, As late as 1938: Leonard Dinnerstein, *Anti-Semitism in America* (New York: Oxford University Press, 1994), 127.

28, from 40 to 20 percent: Marcia G. Synnott, "*Numerus Clausus* (United States)," in *Antisemitism: A Historical Encyclopedia of Prejudice and Persecution*, vol. 1, edited by Richard S. Levy (Santa Barbara, CA: ABC-CLIO, 2005), 514.

29, "It was the noisiest": Merton, *The Seven Storey Mountain*, 170.

29, Subway Mysticism: Mott, *The Seven Mountains of Thomas Merton*, 115.

29, "so uncommunicative": Van Doren, *The Autobiography of Mark Van Doren*, 212.

30, "a horse, Count Orgaz": Lax journal, May 1, 1939, Columbia University.

30, "love of the world": Van Doren, *The Autobiography of Mark Van Doren*, 212.

30, "Characteristically he conceived": Merton, *The Seven Storey Mountain*, 259.

30, "The daily life": Alex Eliot, "A Fax Re Robert Lax," in Miller and Zurbrugg, *The ABCs of Robert Lax*, 205.

31, I think a writer should be immersed: William Packard, "Craft Interview: Robert Lax," *New York Quarterly* 30 (Summer 1986): 29.

31, In 1970, while working: Ed Rice to Robert Lax, January 13, 1970, Robert Lax Papers, St. Bonaventure University.

32, "When I was in college": Lax journal, November 24, 1973, Columbia University.

32, Although he took no notes: Robert Lax to Rev. Father Thomas, September 2, 1938, Robert Lax Papers, St. Bonaventure University.

33, funniest college humor magazine: The commendation was printed on subsequent *Jester* covers.

33, That same year Lax won: *The Columbian*, 1938.

34, Their itinerary: Robert Lax to Marcia Kelly and Jack Kelly, July 30, 1995, Robert Lax Papers, St. Bonaventure University.

35, "All one's views": Eliot, *Essays Ancient and Modern*, 118.

36, Huxley was too sharp: Merton, *The Seven Storey Mountain*, 202.

36, "Not only that": Ibid., 203.

37, he was a musician: Robert Lax, "Mark the Teacher," undated poem, Robert Lax Collection, Columbia University.

38, "All that year": Merton, *The Seven Storey Mountain*, 197.

39, According to Merton, Brahmachari: Ibid., 209ff.

39, "I feel sure," Lex said: "III. Robert Lax's Recollections of Dr. Brahmachari," in Buchanan, *Dr. Mahanambrato Brahmachari*, 32.

39, "It was easy": Ibid., 27.

40, "He didn't make a fuss": Ibid.


## 3. Portals to a Land of Dusk

42, The book is dedicated: Markowski, *Kazimierz*.

42, "Every moment is a gift": Georgiou, *The Way of the Dreamcatcher*, 75.

43, Maurice was a sickly baby: Email from Soni Holman Fink to Marcia Kelly, July 7, 2007; Betty Lax, "Autobiography," February 19, 1934, Soni Holman

Fink private collection. All information in this section is from this collection.

45, forebears had been rabbinical scholars: Robert Lax to Richard Kostelanetz, January 24, 1996, Robert Lax Papers, St. Bonaventure University.

45, Siggie lived with his uncle: Most of the Sigmund Lax information in this section comes from Gladys Marcus, quoted in Bicentennial Book Committee, *Enchanted Land* (unpaginated).

46, Harris Wolfe Marcus: Details are from Robin Conwit, "The Marcus Story," *Sandpumpings* 2.1 (Oct.–Nov. 1976); Bicentennial Book Committee, *Enchanted Land* (both unpaginated). The magazine *Sandpumpings* was written and produced by the students of Olean High School.

47, Olean House Hotel: Conwit, "The Marcus Story"; Bicentennial Book Committee, *Enchanted Land* (both unpaginated).

48, The college's first building: All St. Bonaventure and Francis Griffin details are from Terry Smith, "Griff Recalls Old Bonas," *The Bona Venture*, Dec. 11, 1970; Marsha Ducey, "Spirit of St. Francis Seen in Griff's Life," *The Bona Venture*, Nov. 16, 1990. *The Bona Venture* is the St. Bonaventure College (now University) student newspaper.

49, The best description of Betty: Celia Holman, unpublished and undated reminiscence, Soni Holman Fink private collection.

50, "dull, blinding": Betty Lax, "Autobiography," Soni Holman Fink private collection.

51, "depiction of human relations": Jeannine Mizingou, "Robert Lax [1915–2000]: The Circus of the Sun," in Reichardt, *Encyclopedia of Catholic Literature*, 416.

52, The importance and impact of the circus: Information in this paragraph comes from circusinamerica.org, accessed April 2, 2007, and Chindahl, *A History of the Circus in America*.

53, "1009 zoological rarities": *Olean Evening Times*, June 27 and 30, 1927.

53, They are with me now: Lax, *The Circus of the Sun*, unpaginated.

54, St. Louis Chamber of Commerce: Lax journal, Feb. 17, 1940, Columbia University.

55, It happened on a fair May night: Harford, *Merton and Friends*, 5.

55, Betty wrote Polonius's advice: Robert Lax to Marcia Kelly, March 27, 1995, Robert Lax Papers, St. Bonaventure University.

55, Lax's Oleanders: Robert Lax to Gladys Marcus, March 23, 1986, Robert Lax Papers, St. Bonaventure University.

55, Gladio told an Olean historian: Bicentennial Book Committee, *Enchanted Land* (unpaginated).

56, In a 1939 journal entry: Lax journal, December 18, Columbia University.

56, "served as secretary to Daniel Guggenheim": Fowler, *Good Night, Sweet Prince*, 184.

57, And stand out he did: Details of Lax's high school honors and activities are from a packet of photocopied articles from the Newtown High School *X-Ray*, Robert Lax Papers, St. Bonaventure University.

58, In a long, unsent letter: Robert Lax to "Mr. Griffin," May 30, 1939, Robert Lax Collection, Columbia University.

## 4. The Cottage

61, "a complete dry run": Wilfrid Sheed, "The Beat Movement, Concluded," *New York Times Book Review*, February 13, 1973, 2, 32.

62, "The last year of school": Robert Lax to "Mr. Griffin," May 30, 1939, Robert Lax Collection, Columbia University.

62, In pastoral song a city dies: Robert Lax, "The Last Days of a City," *Columbia Poetry 1938*, 37.

63, "Those deep valleys": Merton, *The Seven Storey Mountain*, 219.

63, "one of the voices": Ibid., 260.

63, "I don't know what was the matter": Ibid., 220.

64, "Merton saw the need": Mott, *The Seven Mountains of Thomas Merton*, 115.

65, The more I failed: Merton, *The Seven Storey Mountain*, 258–59.

65, "The only criterion": Lax journal, November 27, 1939, Columbia University.

66, "torpor, stupor": Robert Lax, undated, in Merton and Lax, *When Prophecy Still Had a Voice*, 9.

68, "I know that the things": Lax journal, August 4, 1938, Columbia University.

68, The spider's innermost dream: Lax journal, August 20, 1938, Columbia University.

69, At that point: Robert Lax to Arthur Biddle, May 16, 1992, Robert Lax Papers, St. Bonaventure University.

69, "strong-featured rather than pretty": Lewis, *Hotel Kid*, 26.

69, "The first Saturday night": Lax journal, October 16, 1940, Columbia University.

69, Stephen Lewis gives a different version: Lewis, *Hotel Kid*, 118–20.

70, "Mother never fully registered": Ibid., 119.

71, I walked around: Lax journal, May 29, 1939, Columbia University.

71, "Don't say excrement": Lax journal, October 15, 1938, Columbia University.

72, It had the six tallest buildings: All New York City statistics are from Gelernter, *1939*.

73, "The brilliance of New York": Ibid., 19.

73, "That spring we sat": Lax journal, October 20, 1940, Columbia University.

75, The guide was never published: Robert Lax, "How to Read *Finnegans Wake*," Robert Lax Papers, St. Bonaventure University.

75, "Dull pain in side": Lax journal, May 2, 1939, Columbia University.

75, "reasons to cry": Lax journal, May 20, 1939, Columbia University.

76, I go to Minette's: Lax journal, April 23, 1939, Columbia University.

76, "I used to think": Lax journal, April 24, 1939, Columbia University.

77, The book [i.e., the journal]: Robert Lax to Mark Van Doren, undated (May 3, 1939), Mark Van Doren Collection, Columbia University.

79, a man named Bill Griffin: Merton and Lax, *When Prophecy Still Had a Voice*, 433.

80, "Mornings, though": Lax journal, January 18, 1982, St. Bonaventure University.

80, "have three novels": Lax journal, June 14, 1939, Columbia University.

80, "glowering at each other": Rice, *The Man in the Sycamore Tree*, 19.

82, "five days of fast": Lax journal, June 12, 1939, Columbia University.

83, "Doing it is no worse": Lax journal, July 17, 1939, Columbia University.

83, "Desires can not be killed": Ibid.

84, "weak with hunger": Robert Lax, "Where I've worked," undated paper, Robert Lax Collection, Columbia University.

84, "a young man": Ibid.

84, Sitting in the office: Ibid.


5. *Lo, the Sun Walks Forth!*

86, On September 17: The entire scene is from Lax journal, September 17, 1939, Columbia University.

87, "Speech to draft officers": Lax journal, October 2, 1939, Columbia University.

88, "It is difficult to live": Lax journal, October 20, 1939, Columbia University.

89, Rabbi David Lefkowitz: Letter to Robert Lax, November 20, 1939, Robert Lax Papers, St. Bonaventure University.

89, "I really believe": Lax journal, December 6, 1939, Columbia University.

90, Corwin called Lax's scripts "brilliant": Undated Lax transcription of letter from Norman Corwin to Robert Lax dated February 13, 1940, Robert Lax Collection, Columbia University.

90, I didn't like the looks: Undated Lax transcription of letter from E. B. White to Robert Lax dated February 5, 1940, Robert Lax Collection, Columbia University.

92, "Poem came out": Lax journal, May 5, 1940, Columbia University.

92, earned him $26: Lax journal, April 6, 1940 , Columbia University.

93, "I'm not trying to give": Lax journal, March 15, 1940, Columbia University.

93, "quick unaffected judgments": Lax journal, March 12, 1940, Columbia University.

94, "Keep wanting as I have": Lax journal, April 15, 1940, Columbia University.

95, Everywhere is the happy: Lax journal, June 16, 1940, Columbia University.

96, Merton left today: Lax journal, July 19, 1940, Columbia University.

96, cottage conversation: Lax journal, August 5, 1940, Columbia University.

96, World War I posters: Lax journal, August 25, 1940, Columbia University.

97, Last night it was pretty: ibid.


## 6. Suicide Notes

99, "Now what you say": Lax journal, August 29, 1940, Columbia University.

101, Despite Benji's wishes: Lax journal, October 16, 1940, Columbia University.

101, True to his nature: Lax journal, December 3, 1940, Columbia University.

101, Driving through a snowstorm: Lax journal, December 3, 1940, Columbia University.

101, This time Lobrano: Lax journal, December 16, 1940, Columbia University.

102, Having to see one more guy: Lax journal, January 8, 1941, Columbia University.

103, "The letters i write": Lax journal, January 18, 1941, Columbia University.

103, "such raptures": Lax journal, January 18, 1941, Columbia University.

103, "sometimes i think if i write": Ibid.

104, "Now that I've got": Lax journal, January 19, 1941, Columbia University.

105, "Short, serious": Lax journal, January 25, 1941, Columbia University.

105, "They seem a little tight": Lax journal, February 18, 1941, Columbia University.

106, "move the buildings": Lax journal, undated paper (possibly February 26, 1941), , Columbia University.

107, "In any number of ways": Yagoda, *About Town*, 168–69.

108, "City of the Lord": Lax journal, undated, Columbia University.

108, "After a number of years": Lax journal, March 18, 1941, Columbia University.

109, If I have an inner argument: Lax journal, undated, Columbia University.

110, "I'd have felt like a fish": Robert Lax to Leonard Robinson, undated, Robert Lax Papers, St. Bonaventure University.

110, "For, she said": Merton, *The Seven Storey Mountain*, 373.

111, "luny": Lax journal, July 15, 1942, Columbia University.

111, The room was small: Robert Lax to Felice Valen, May 31, 1975, Robert Lax Collection, Columbia University.

112, "All the world is wasting": Lax journal, undated (1941), Columbia University.

112, The first thing Perelman did: Perelman story is from Felice Valen letter to Robert Lax, May 13, 1975, and Robert Lax letter to Valen, May 31, 1975, both in Robert Lax Collection, Columbia University.

113, "Sitting in a dark": Robert Lax, "Where I've worked," undated paper, Robert Lax Collection, Columbia University.

114, In an undated entry: Lax journal, Columbia University.


## 7. The Scream

115, "Day went to Harlem": Lax journal, undated, Columbia University.

116, "This is how it feels": Lax journal, undated, Columbia University.

117, I am sick: Lax journal, undated (late 1941 or early 1942), Columbia University.

117, "Singing a good song": Lax journal, undated, Columbia University.

118, "a hand to administer charity": Lax journal, January 20, 1943, St. Bonaventure University.

118, "He is one of the Persons": Robert Lax, "Jack the Cat," undated manuscript, probably from 1958, Robert Lax Collection, Columbia University.

119, "One walks up the hill": Lax journal, April 21, 1942, Columbia University.

119, "one hand at one corner": Lax journal, undated (1942), Columbia University.

120, "tomorrow goes gerdy": Lax journal, May 15, 1942, Columbia University.

120, "grants that you": Lax journal, April 18, 1942, Columbia University.

120, "the light of the sun": Lax journal, April 20, 1942, Columbia University.

120, "If those in whom": Book 1, *The Dark Night*, in Kavanaugh and Rodriquez, *The Collected Works of St. John of the Cross*, 315.

121, "There is no more or less": Lax journal, April 22, 1942, Columbia University.

122, "Whatever work it is": Robert Lax to Thomas Merton, undated (1942), in Merton and Lax, *When Prophecy Still Had a Voice*, 93.

123, "here i am folks": Lax journal, July 15, 1942, Columbia University.

123, "Gibney has just been discharged": Lax journal, undated (August 1942), Columbia University.

124, "The people who say": Lax journal, January 20, 1943, Columbia University.

124, "He would look": Lax journal, undated (1943), Columbia University.

124, "sweetness and depth": Lax journal, January 20, 1943, Columbia University.

## 8. Aquinas and the Circus Beckon

126, They had performed in New York: Hubler, *The Cristianis*, 251.

126, Around the table: Ibid., 252–53.

126, Being an acrobat: The Cristiani history here is from Robert Lax, "The Incomparable Cristianis," *Jubilee*, May 1953, 53–55; Cristiani Rossi, *Spangles, Elephants, Violets and Me*.

128, "At that point, Lucio": Leonard Robinson, "Waiting for Lucio," *New Yorker*, June 5, 1943.

128, "such warm, alive": Robert Lax to author, in interview March 12, 1996.

128, I still haven't gotten to say: Lax, *Mogador's Book*, in *Circus Days and Nights*, 107.

130, "I guess I've been fired": Robert Lax, undated letter from Chapel Hill, Mark Van Doren Collection, Columbia University.

130, Kuhn told Lax: Ibid.

130, Kenan fellowship: Helmut Kuhn to Robert Lax, May 26, 1944, Robert Lax Papers, St. Bonaventure University.

131, "I guess you could say": Ed Rice, interview with Michael Lastnite and Judy Emergy, 1983, Robert Lax Papers, St. Bonaventure University.

131, "Man who first said": Lax journal, November 3, 1943, St. Bonaventure University.

131, In trying to explain his conversion: Robert Lax interview with Peter Schneider, April 1994, Robert Lax Papers, St. Bonaventure University.

131, His sister Gladio: Gladys Marcus interview with Judy Emery and Michael Lastnite, September 1983, Robert Lax Papers, St. Bonaventure University.

132, "I am glad that you have found": Siggie Lax to Robert Lax, January 8, 1944, Robert Lax Collection, Columbia University.

132, Dear Dad: Robert Lax to Siggie Lax, undated, Robert Lax Collection, Columbia University.

133, "Of all the monks": Robert Lax to Gladys Marcus, December 28, 1943, Mark Van Doren Collection, Columbia University.

133, Merton remembers: Merton, *The Seven Storey Mountain*, 446.

133, "Then a bell rings": Robert Lax to Gladys Marcus, December 28, 1943, Mark Van Doren Collection.

134, "Get thee behind me": Lax, *Journal E*, February 24, 1944, 14.

134, "Probably an apostle": Lax journal, February 8, 1944, Columbia University.

134, "I want to write a book": Lax journal, October 30, 1944, Columbia University.

134, Concerned for Lax's spiritual life: Thomas Merton to Robert Lax, November 30, 1944, in Merton and Lax, *When Prophecy Still Had a Voice*, 95–97.

135, "The newspapers say": Copy in Lax journal, August 4, 1944, Columbia University.

135, "This is the day after": Lax journal, August 7, 1944, Columbia University.

136, Alex Eliot: From unpublished Eliot memoir, Robert Lax Papers, St. Bonaventure University.

137, "We were just making up": Harford, *Merton and Friends*, 64.

137, according to Eliot: Alex Eliot, "A Fax Re Robert Lax," in Miller and Zurbrugg, *The ABCs of Robert Lax*, 204.

## 9. The Siren Call of Hollywood

139, "nosey, tight-fisted": Lax, *Journal E*, July 13, 1947, 36.

140, According to its entry: All *Siren of Atlantis* production details and quotes are from www.afi.com/members/catalog, accessed February 2, 2004. My plot summary is a paraphrase of the one on the AFI site.

140, "[German producer] Seymour Nebenzal's picture": Ibid.

142, But despite the fact: *New York Times*, August 22, 1949, accessed online October 20, 2007.

142, His first movie: Robert Lax to Thomas Merton, November 29, 1947, in Merton and Lax, *When Prophecy Still Had a Voice*, 103–4.

142, He was still absorbing: Lax, *Journal E*, September 1, 1947, 40–42.

143, He knew he was not alone: Ibid., 42.

144, He ran the stream: Lax, *Journal E*, September 20, 1947, 48–50.

144, "called variously Monte Carlo": Lax journal, April 10, 1948, St. Bonaventure University.

145, The light of afternoon: Lax, *Journal E*, November 12, 1947, 66.

## 10. On the Road with the Cristianis

147, $500 for research: Robert Lax to "Sweetums" (Bob Butman), undated (1991), Robert Lax Papers, St. Bonaventure University.

147, A bad performer: Lax journal, December 24, 1948, St. Bonaventure University.

147, Holding on the invisible wires: Ibid.

148, "is fuller of joy": Robert Lax to Mark Van Doren, undated, Mark Van Doren Collection, Columbia University.

149, "the blond dirt road": Lax, *Mogador's Book*, in *Circus Days & Nights*, 92.

149, "from the center": Ibid., 100.

149, It was, I think: Ibid., 100.

149, We talked about the fact: Ibid., 104.

150, "You gotta like him": Harford, *Merton and Friends*, 74.

150, "I walked around the ring": *Circus Days & Nights*, 12.

151, "sober as a judge": Robert Lax to Bill Buchanan, July 25, 1996, Robert Lax Papers, St. Bonaventure University.

151, "unearthly sweetness": Robert Lax quoted in Van Doren, *The Autobiography of Mark Van Doren*, 300.

153, A "semi-drunk lady": Lax, *Journal E*, July 6, 1949, 74.

153, Sat around living room: Ibid., 76.

154, "I've got quite a few words": Robert Lax to Thomas Merton, undated, in Merton and Lax, *When Prophecy Still Had a Voice*, 114.

## 11. Being a Presence in Postwar Marseilles

155, *The Little Mandate*: Madonna House, www.madonnahouse.org/mandate/, accessed on August 8, 2014.

155, the baroness's dream: Robert Lax to Thomas Merton, September 23, 1950, in Merton and Lax, *When Prophecy Still Had a Voice*, 114.

156, Money might have been a concern: Ibid.

156, "Europe is an aging Roquefort cheese": Robert Lax, "Acey-Ducey," unpublished manuscript, Robert Lax Collection, Columbia University. Sometimes called "Reflections of a Temple Dancer." Various versions are in Columbia University and St. Bonaventure University. Unless otherwise indicated, all quotes and details in the rest of this chapter are from versions of this manuscript in Columbia University, including one set down in Lax journal entries between November 7, 1959, and March 7, 1960.

157, "dope, whores": Fisher, quoting an unnamed newspaper, in Fisher, "A Considerable Town," in *Two Towns in Provence*, 3.

158, A lifetime has prepared me: Lax journal, July 29, 1959, transcription of a November 1950 journal entry, Columbia University.

159, "If there were a beautiful poverty": Saul Bellow, *Herzog* (New York: Viking Press, 1964), 47.

161, "a minor gangster": Bob Butman to Paul Spaeth, March 6, 1991, Robert Lax Papers, St. Bonaventure University.

162, "Okay, but nothing fragmentary": Robert Lax to Bob Butman, March or May 1951, Robert Lax Papers, St. Bonaventure University.

162, As Lax tapped his way: Lax, "Acey-Ducey."

162, "hangdog and belligerent": Ibid.

163, "this is my home": Ibid.

164, Lax became friends with the man's son: Robert Lax told me the parenthetical anecdotes here.

167, "like a Warner Brothers movie": Robert Lax to Thomas Merton, April 7, 1951, in Merton and Lax, *When Prophecy Still Had a Voice*, 115.

173, I have seen love: Robert Lax, "A Song for Our Lady: Notre Dame de la Garde, Marseilles," in Miller and Zurbrugg, *The ABCs of Robert Lax*, 237.

## 12. Entering the Lion's Mouth

175, Surrounded by other pilgrims . . . started back up the steps: All quotes and details in this section are from long journal entries Lax wrote on March 9 and 18, 1960. Lax journals, Columbia University.

179, With his passport and camera held hostage . . . with his hand / and smile: Except where noted, all details and quotes in this section are from a black notebook titled "Fritz" and a blue notebook with "Georgetown University" on the cover and individual page dates stretching from October 16, 1958, through January 28, 1959; these seem to be early versions of *Voyage to Pescara*. Robert Lax Collection, Columbia University.

180, The circus is here: Lax, *Voyage to Pescara* in *Circus Days and Nights*, 119.

181, "One of the central metaphors": Paul J. Spaeth, introduction to Lax, *Circus Days and Nights*, 19.

181"I lay still": Lax, *Voyage to Pescara* in *Circus Days and Nights*, 161.

183, I felt melancholy: Ibid., 179.

183, "As I crossed the road": Ibid., 188.


## 13. Paris, *Jubilee*, and Kerouac

185, while Marcus headed to Scotland: Lax journal, March 6, 1960, Columbia University.

185, he'd call his generation the Beat Generation: Robert Lax to Gerald Nicosia, July 27, 1978, Robert Lax Papers, St. Bonaventure University.

186, "You listen": Robert Lax to Mark Van Doren, undated (probably 1951), Mark Van Doren Collection, Columbia University.

187, An unpublished manuscript: Black notebook titled "Fritz," Robert Lax Collection, Columbia University.

187, "More and more I become": Robert Lax to Thomas Merton, undated, in Merton and Lax, *When Prophecy Still Had a Voice*, 120.

188, "made him sad": Robert Lax to Thomas Merton, undated, in Merton and Lax, *When Prophecy Still Had a Voice*, 119.

188, "I wondered whether": Robert Lax to Thomas Merton, undated, in Merton and Lax, *When Prophecy Still Had a Voice*, 120.

188, Rice laid out his approach: Harford, *Merton and Friends*, 83–84.

189, In a plan inspired by the Social Encyclicals: Untitled, *Jubilee*, May 1953, 1.

189, receiving $75 a month: Robert Lax to "R," undated, Robert Lax Papers, St. Bonaventure University.

190, I told Lax which stories: Harford, *Merton and Friends*, 97.

191, "O no, Bob": Kerouac, *Selected Letters 1940–56*, 447.

191, "Kerouac had been corresponding": Christy, *The Long Slow Death of Jack Kerouac*, 28.

192, Dear Jack: Robert Lax to Jack Kerouac, undated (probably 1955 or 1956), Soni Holman Fink private collection.

192, "in a large secular monastery": Ginsberg, *Journals*, 78–79.

193, I called from a neighboring town: Van Doren, *The Selected Letters*, 210.

195, "He was tall and thin": Gilman, *Faith, Sex, Mystery*, 145.

196, "Lax's idea of a perfect editing job": Sheed, *Frank and Maisie*, 269.

196, "If you worked with Lax": Harford, *Merton and Friends*, 104.

196, "Our artists and writers": Harford, *Merton and Friends*, 98.

196, "At *Jubilee*, we strove": Sheed, *Frank and Maisie*, 268–69.

## 14. Inspiration in a Greek Diner

200, Thanks to Burford: Robert Lax to Sigrid Hauff and Hartmut Geerken, March 4, 1985, Robert Lax Papers, St. Bonaventure University.

201, According to Tom Cornell: Tom Cornell, "A Winter with Robert Lax," *Catholic Worker*, January–February 2001, 7.

202, a story she tells: Email from Soni Holman Fink to author, September 30, 2003.

202, According to Rice: Ed Rice interview with Judy Emery and Michael Lastnite, 1983, Robert Lax Papers, St. Bonaventure University.

202, To lower his sedimentation rates: Robert Lax to "Madame Vanier," November 3, 1957, Robert Lax Papers, St. Bonaventure University.

203, "So many haven't found themselves": Henry Hotchener to Robert Lax, February 16, 1956, Robert Lax Papers, St. Bonaventure University

203, calmest and "most legitimate": Robert Lax to Thomas Merton August 12, 1957, and Thomas Merton to Robert Lax August 21, 1957, in Merton and Lax, *When Prophecy Still Had a Voice*, 132, 137.

204, "the long abandoned circus book": Robert Lax to Thomas Merton, April 23, 1958, in Merton and Lax, *When Prophecy Still Had a Voice*, 147.

205, "Most beautiful": Lax journal, page titled "from earlier in August" in "Sep. '59" notebook, Columbia University.

205, "dreamlike and vivid": Denise Levertov, "On Robert Lax's *The Circus of the Sun*," in Miller and Zurbrugg, *The ABCs of Robert Lax*, 181.

205, "The effect of 'Circus of the Sun'": William Packard, "*The Circus of the Sun by Robert Lax*," in Miller and Zurbrugg, *The ABCs of Robert Lax*, 178.

205, "evoking the wonder": Review cited in letter from William Claire to Robert Lax, April 4, 1960, Robert Lax Papers, Columbia University.

205, e. e. cummings, who chatted: Robert Lax to "Ron," January 2, 1994, Robert Lax Papers, St. Bonaventure University.

205, "It is one very fine book": Thomas Merton to Robert Lax, December 29, 1959, in Merton and Lax, *When Prophecy Still Had a Voice*, 182.

207, Deprived of *being*: Robert Lax, "Jack the Cat," undated manuscript (probably 1958), Robert Lax Collection, Columbia University.

208, set yrself a time: Lax journal, May 17, 1959, Columbia University.

208, a new translation of *The Midrash on Psalms*: Lax journal, May 25, 1959, Columbia University.

208, "carbuncles": Ibid.

208, "filled with probably smouldering": Lax journal, June 8, 1959, Columbia University.

208, He liked Indian music: Lax journal, July 5, 1959, Columbia University.

209, you never: Lax journal, June 28, 1959, Columbia University.

210, "As soon as I heard": Robert Lax to Mark Van Doren, undated, Mark Van Doren Collection, Columbia University.

210, "just like Gulliver": Robert Lax to Mark Van Doren, October 29, 1959, Mark Van Doren Collection, Columbia University.

210, If by some crazy miracle: Robert Lax to Charlie Van Doren, November 2, 1959, Charles Van Doren private collection.

## 15. A New Poetics

214, "I'd usually find him": Robert Lax to Gerald Nicosia, July 27, 1978, Robert Lax Papers, St. Bonaventure University.

214, "Lax," Ginsberg said: Robert Lax to Marcia Kelly and Jack Kelly, July 30, 1995, Robert Lax Papers, St. Bonaventure University.

214, POEM: journal book dated "winter '57–'58," Columbia University.

215, "Robert Lax, simply a Pilgrim": Jack Kerouac quoted in Miller and Zurbrugg, *The ABCs of Robert Lax*, 13.

215, As Lax told the story: Robert Lax to Marcia Kelly and Jack Kelly, July 30, 1995, Robert Lax Papers, St. Bonaventure University; Robert Lax to Gerald Nicosia, July 27, 1978, Robert Lax Papers, St. Bonaventure University.

216, In a letter to Don Allen: Kerouac, *Selected Letters 1957–1969*, 115.

216, the big thing, says j ker: Lax journal, September 2, 1973, Columbia University.

216, the reckless writers: Lax journal, October 26, 1973, Columbia University

217, "another village brawl": Lax journal, May 21, 1958, Columbia University.

218, has big blue calm: Ibid.

218, "was best known for enormous horizontal canvases": Roberta Smith, Dave Budd obituary, *New York Times*, October 10, 1991.

219, "If Reinhardt repeated himself": Barbara Rose, introduction to Reinhardt, *Art-as-Art*, xv.

220, "He was a serious artist": Robert Lax interview with Judy Emery and Michael Lastnite, 1984, Robert Lax Papers, St. Bonaventure University.

220, "I think he really liked looking": Robert Lax to David Miller, August 22, 1984, Robert Lax Papers, St. Bonaventure University.

221, The one thing to say about art: Reinhardt, *Art-as-Art*, 53–56.

223, "laconic"—and "dogmatic"—"slumber": Lax journal, June 8, 1959, Columbia University.

223, what i want to say: Lax journal, March 22, 1958, Columbia University.

228, why did they: Lax journal, December 6, 1958, Columbia University.

229, "I prefer the long speculation": Lax journal, December 12, 1958, Columbia University.

230, "No more inching along": Lax journal, March 22, 1959, Columbia University.

231, "What I like about Beckett": Lax journal, May 19, 1959, Columbia University.

231, "my language, our language": Lax journal, June 6, 1959, Columbia University.

231, "had a good knowledge": Ibid.

231, "i am hard at work": Robert Lax to Thomas Merton, February 14, 1960, in Merton and Lax, *When Prophecy Still Had a Voice*, 184.

232, an ancient look: Lax journal, March 7, 1959, Columbia University.

233, kerouac, salinger, beckett: Lax journal, November 15, 1960, Columbia University.

234, "One stone": Lax journal, December 4, 1960, Columbia University; published in Lax, *New Poems* (1962).

## 16. "Original Child Bomb" and an Island Home

238, The miracle of the desert fathers: Merton, *The Solitary Life*, 2–3.

238, "It fits my present needs": Robert Lax to Thomas Merton, undated, in Merton and Lax, *When Prophecy Still Had a Voice*, 200.

238, *Portrait of the Poet Robert Lax*: Larry Pointer and Donald Goddard, *Harry Jackson* (New York: Harry N. Abrams, 1981), 109.

239, Years later a Carmelite priest: in Harford, *Merton and Friends*, 109.

239, "Say prayers plenty": Robert Lax to Thomas Merton, undated, in Merton and Lax, *When Prophecy Still Had a Voice*, 216.

239, "owl-haunted Delphi": Robert Lax to Mark Van Doren, April 13, 1961, Mark Van Doren Collection, Columbia University.

240, "In a minute I write a solemn": Thomas Merton to Robert Lax, January 14, 1962, in Merton and Lax, *When Prophecy Still Had a Voice*, 216.

240, "It comes to mind": Thomas Merton to Robert Lax, October 17, 1960, in Merton and Lax, *When Prophecy Still Had a Voice*, 209.

240, "Original child is come down": Robert Lax to Thomas Merton, undated, in Merton and Lax, *When Prophecy Still Had a Voice*, 218.

240, "the minute I get back": Robert Lax to Thomas Merton, undated, in Merton and Lax, *When Prophecy Still Had a Voice*, 220.

241, "cryptic and poetic": Thomas Merton to Dona Luisa Coomaraswamy, September 24, 1961, in Merton, *The Hidden Ground of Love*, 132.

241, "That Atom Bomb I sent": Thomas Merton to Robert Lax, June 17, 1961, in Merton and Lax, *When Prophecy Still Had a Voice*, 222.

241, "[Laughlin] say Ferlinghetti wants": Thomas Merton to Robert Lax, June 30, 1961, in Merton and Lax, *When Prophecy Still Had a Voice*, 223.

242, "the final revised adapted": Thomas Merton to Robert Lax, July 7, 1961, in Merton and Lax, *When Prophecy Still Had a Voice*, 224.

242, "this latest version": Robert Lax to Thomas Merton, undated, in Merton and Lax, *When Prophecy Still Had a Voice*, 225.

242, "a loophole": Shannon et al., *The Thomas Merton Encyclopedia*, 48.

242, "New censor regulation": Thomas Merton to Robert Lax, August 16, 1961, in Merton and Lax, *When Prophecy Still Had a Voice*, 226.

244, "feeling," he wrote later: Robert Lax to "Rocco" (Ed Rice), August 12, 1987, Robert Lax Papers, St. Bonaventure University.

245, His proposed project: Robert Lax to Mark Van Doren, undated, Mark Van Doren Collection, Columbia University.

245, "what he /was really": Lax journal, October 7, 1962, Columbia University.

245, "Here is absolutely capital": Robert Lax to Thomas Merton, September 1962, in Merton and Lax, *When Prophecy Still Had a Voice*, 240.

245, The idea of traveling to Mytilene: Most of the details in the section from this point through Lax's arrival on Kos are from Lax journals in the Robert Lax Collection, Columbia University.

247, His visit corresponded: Robert Lax to "Matt," July 23, 1982, Robert Lax Papers, St. Bonaventure University.

248, He arrived on Kos at 6 a.m.: All details and quotes from here through the end of the chapter are from an unpublished manuscript by Lax titled "March in the Dodekanese: A Kind of Novel by Albert Waltz," Robert Lax Papers, St. Bonaventure University.

254, "reconciled to my presence": Lax journal, March 17, 1964, Columbia University.

254, "having all the words": Ibid.

## 17. The Sorrow of the Sponge Diver

256, Unless otherwise noted, the details and quotes in this chapter are from Lax's journal entries in April 1964, most consolidated in an unpublished manuscript titled "Pserimu," Robert Lax Papers, St. Bonaventure University.

257, "stellio's attitude": Lax journal, March 26, 1964, Columbia University.

259, "she sat at the loom": Lax journal, April 2, 1964, Columbia University.

260, "as though he wanted to be a movie heavy": Lax journal, April 6, 1964, St. Bonaventure University.

262, "an ancient attitude": Ibid.

262, "I don't know": Lax journal, April 8, 1964, St. Bonaventure University.

263, "barefooted": Lax journal, April 6, 1964, St. Bonaventure University.

263, "They only have": Lax journal, April 13, 1964, St. Bonaventure University.

263, "there is no such thing": Lax journal, April 14, 1964, St. Bonaventure University.

264, "they are at the bottom rung": Ibid.

264, "the real aristocracy": Lax journal, April 16, 1964, St. Bonaventure University.

265, "he came to sit": Lax journal, April 20, 1964, St. Bonaventure University.

266, "the captain threw back his head": Ibid. You can hear Pandelis singing this song, "Dirlada Kai Tez Oloi," online at: http://www.gtc-music1.com/pro_uploads/kalogeros/DIRLADA_PandelisGIANNHS.mp3.

267, "now the captain started to sing": Lax journal, April 20, 1964, St. Bonaventure University.

269, "solemn and merry": Ibid.

270, "as clowns do": Lax journal, April 25, 1964, St. Bonaventure University.

270, "it was more as though": Lax journal, April 27, 1964, St. Bonaventure University.

270, "squatting around a low chest": Ibid.

271, "it looked like a trappist": Lax journal, April 30, 1964, St. Bonaventure University.

## 18. A Saint of the Avant-Garde

273, "A grand poem": Mark Van Doren to Robert Lax, October 31, 1965, Robert Lax Collection, Columbia University.

273, "Your summer chronicle": Mark Van Doren to Robert Lax, September 29, 1963, Robert Lax Collection, Columbia University.

273, "About coming home": Robert Lax to Mark Van Doren, October 12 (no year but probably 1964), Mark Van Doren Collection, Columbia University.

274, The invitation came from a friend: Robert Lax undated (June 1965) to Soni Holman Fink, Soni Holman Fink private collection.

274, One typical page: Robert Lax, "Sea & Sky," *Lugano Review* 1.3–4 (1965): 15–132.

274, "I'm not sure": Robert Lax to Father Irenaeus, Ascension Day 1966, Robert Lax Papers, St. Bonaventure University.

275, "the new 'saints'": Zurbrugg, *Art, Performance, Media*, 233.

275, In a letter to Solt: Robert Lax to Mary Ellen Solt undated (1966), Robert Lax Papers, St. Bonaventure University.

277, "solitude and writing": Robert Lax to "captain," undated, Robert Lax Papers, St. Bonaventure University.

277, "little smoke-blackened shed": Lax journal, February 17, 1966, Columbia University.

277, the (town): Lax journal, August 16, 1965, St. Bonaventure University.

278, though it's obviously: Lax journal, July 23, 1965, Columbia University.

279, "Well, we have finally": Robert Lax to Thomas Merton, April 25, 1967, in Merton and Lax, *When Prophecy Still Had a Voice*, 364.

280, "cool breezes": Robert Lax to Thomas Merton, May 17, 1967, in Merton and Lax, *When Prophecy Still Had a Voice*, 364.

281, In an article in *Modern Painters*: Reprinted as Julian Mitchell, "The Poet of Patmos," in Miller and Zurbrugg, *The ABCs of Robert Lax*, 207–11.

281, "there hasn't been any art": Robert Lax to Mark Van Doren, January 15, 1966, Mark Van Doren Collection, Columbia University.

281, "of a city where all were alive": Lax journal, July 24, 1965, Columbia University.

282, "very long poem": Robert Lax Guggenheim application, July 7, 1967, Robert Lax Papers, St. Bonaventure University.

282, "You look them over": Thomas Merton to Robert Lax, July 17, 1965, in Merton and Lax, *When Prophecy Still Had a Voice*, 307.

283, One could weep: Robert Lax to Thomas Merton, September 13, 1967, in Merton and Lax, *When Prophecy Still Had a Voice*, 370.

283, "one night here": Robert Lax to Mark Van Doren, January 15, 1966, Mark Van Doren Collection, Columbia University.

284, "now indeed": Robert Lax to Thomas Merton, October 15, 1967, in Merton and Lax, *When Prophecy Still Had a Voice*, 372.

284, "We must pray": Robert Lax to Thomas Merton, January 21, 1968, in Merton and Lax, *When Prophecy Still Had a Voice*, 379.


19. Alone in the World

285, he filled his journal: Lax journal, October 18, 1967, St. Bonaventure University.

285, "counting on fingers": Ibid.

285, "That's because I'm one person": Lax journal, October 30, 1967, St. Bonaventure University.

285, "Abstract Poem": Published as one of "Three Concrete Poems" in Lax, *Love Had a Compass*, 17

287, You can take a word: Robert Lax to Soni Holman Fink, September 1988, Robert Lax Papers, St. Bonaventure University.

288, "homage" issues: William F. Claire, introduction to Robert Lax Special Issue, *Voyages* 2.1–2 (1968): 4–5.

288, the more "sonic" poems: Denise Levertov, "Denise Levertov on Robert Lax's CIRCUS OF THE SUN," Robert Lax Special Issue, *Voyages* 2.1–2 (1968): 94.

289, Bann links Lax: Stephen Bann, "Concrete Poetry and the Recent Work of Robert Lax," in Miller and Zurbrugg, *The ABCs of Robert Lax*, 64–65.

289, "momentous statements": Bann, quoting Eugen Gomringer, "Concrete Poetry and the Recent Work of Robert Lax," 65.

290, "Out here it's a ranch": Robert Lax to Mark Van Doren, May 26, 1968, Mark Van Doren Collection, Columbia University.

290, an article on him: "Fay DeBerards Have Writer Friend Visiting at Ranch," *Middle Park Times* (Kremmling, CO), May 30, 1968.

290, "Was two days alone": Thomas Merton to Robert Lax, May 14, 1968, in Merton and Lax, *When Prophecy Still Had a Voice*, 398.

291, "innumerable cans": Thomas Merton to Mark Van Doren, July 23, 1968, in Merton, *The Road to Joy*, 54.

291, "I don't know if he should return": Thomas Merton journal, June 13, 1968, in Harford, *Merton and Friends*, 184.

291, "rendered drunk": Robert Lax to Thomas Merton, August 12, 1968, in Merton and Lax, *When Prophecy Still Had a Voice*, 409.

291, "Here again": Robert Lax to Mark Van Doren, November 27, 1968, Mark Van Doren Collection, Columbia University.

292, "Think somehow": Robert Lax to Emil Antonucci, December 29, 1968, Robert Lax Collection, Columbia University.

294, When asked in an interview: Robert Lax interview with Arthur Biddle, May 19, 1992, Robert Lax Papers, St. Bonaventure University.

294, "Lama friend": Thomas Merton to Robert Lax, October 21, 1968, in Merton and Lax, *When Prophecy Still Had a Voice*, 416.

294, I got one last idea: Thomas Merton to Robert Lax, August 22, 1968, in Merton and Lax, *When Prophecy Still Had a Voice*, 412.

295, "learn as many breathings": Robert Lax to Thomas Merton, December 8, 1968, in Merton and Lax, *When Prophecy Still Had a Voice*, 420.


## 20. A Galapagos of the Spirit

297, And, after years of listening: James Laughlin to Robert Lax, July 2, 1969, Robert Lax Collection, Columbia University.

297, A list of "possibilities": Emil Antonucci to Robert Lax, June 1971, Robert Lax Papers, St. Bonaventure University.

298, technically my interest: Robert Lax Guggenheim application, October 1969, Robert Lax Collection, Columbia University.

298, the young, aspiring poets: Quoted by Ed Rice in letter to Robert Lax, October 7, 1969, Robert Lax Papers, St. Bonaventure University.

299, "high & right": Lax, *Journal C*, July 21, 1969, 36.

299, "i like to watch": Lax, *Journal C*, July 29, 1969, 48.

299, as the living body: Lax, *Journal C*, August 21, 1969, 54–56.

299, "less like a disembodied soul": Ibid., 58.

300, "to live among greeks": Ibid., 62.

300, "perhaps they see":, Lax, *Journal C*, July 21, 1969, 34.

300, "patmos, holy patmos": Lax journal, October 6, 1969, St. Bonaventure University.

301, "prodded by their demons": Lax, *Journal C*, November 22, 1969, 140.

302, "Alley Violinist": Lax, *Love Had a Compass*, 38.

303, "the perfectly right": Lax journal, October 27, 1970, Columbia University.

305, "so many things": Robert Lax to R. C. Kenedy, December 6, 1970, Robert Lax Collection, Columbia University.

305, "twenty million joys": Robert Lax to R.C. Kenedy, December 8, 1970, Robert Lax Collection, Columbia University.

305, Kenedy's critique: R. C. Kenedy, "Robert Lax," reprinted in Miller and Zurbrugg, *The ABCs of Robert Lax*, 66–79.

## 21. All Thoughts as They Come

309, he was determined: Lax, "Tractatus I-II," in *33 Poems*, 160–63.

310, "the more i read": Robert Lax to Emil Antonucci, July 5, 1971, Robert Lax Collection, Columbia University.

311, "a sense of order": Lax journal, September 7, 1971, Columbia University.

312, days absolutely golden: Lax journal, July 19, 1972, Columbia University.

312, "life here is played": Ibid.

312, "I've never been blacker": Lax journal, July 21, 1972, Columbia University.

312, One entry records the major activities: Ibid.

313, "the world isn't planning": Lax journal, September 19, 1972, Columbia University.

313, "an ever present": Lax journal, December 21, 1972, Columbia University.

313, "each movement": Ibid.

314, has the church: Lax journal, titled "Jan./Feb. '73," Columbia University.

315, "the island is being asphyxiated": Lax journal, February 7, 1973, Columbia University.

315, "The old cafeneions": Lax journal, February 22, 1973, Columbia University.

## 22. The Flaw in the Ideal

319, "because they were foreigners": Lax journal, February 14, 1973, Columbia University.

320, "like wise & innocent children": Lax journal, August 30, 1973, Columbia University.

320, "dream of what": Ibid.

320, "the continuity of life": Lax journal, September 1, 1973, Columbia University.

322, "in all probability": R. C. Kenedy, quoted in Lax journal, November 26, 1973, St. Bonaventure University.

322, "Byzantine Faces": Lax journal, September 22, 1973, Columbia University; Lax, *A Thing That Is*, 50–52.

326, "it was good": Lax journal, November 15, 1973, Columbia University.

327, Antonucci wrote: Emil Antonucci to Robert Lax, January 3, 1974, Robert Lax Papers, St. Bonaventure University.

327, "a thousand dollars": Robert Lax to "Gris," September 19 (1973), Robert Lax Papers, St. Bonaventure University.

327, Lax was more in love: Lax journal, January 4, 1974, Columbia University.

327, In a letter to Kenedy: Robert Lax to R. C. Kenedy, February 1, 1974, Robert Lax Papers, St. Bonaventure University.

327, life is a river: Lax journal, May 19, 1974, St. Bonaventure University.

## 23. Hell Hath No Fury

331, When ArtPark opened: Robert Schnettler, "ArtPark: Latest Culture Addition," *Times Herald Weekender*, August 3, 1974, 4–5.

332, "Writing for a living": *Olean Times Herald*, September 17, 1974.

333, "i think life": Lax journal, December 30, 1977, St. Bonaventure University.

333, When Lax descended: Except where otherwise noted, the details and quotes in the rest of this chapter are from journal entries made between October 31 and November 27, 1976, published as Lax, *Journal F*.

343, "You're right about my belonging": Robert Lax to Soni Holman Fink, January 30, 1977, Soni Holman Fink private collection.

344, "It turned out to be": Quoted in Lax journal, May 6, 1977, St. Bonaventure University.

## 24. Finding a Common Language

345, "all parts": Lax journal, August 22, 1978, St. Bonaventure University.

345, His preference for the smaller: Robert Lax to Emil Antonucci, December 11, 1979, Robert Lax Papers, St. Bonaventure University.

346, Just when things looked bleakest: Robert Lax to Gladys Weigner and Bernhard Moosbrugger, undated (1982), Robert Lax Papers, St. Bonaventure University.

347, *Publisher's Weekly* called it: October 9, 1978, 71, Robert Lax Papers, St. Bonaventure University.

347, *Commonweal's* reviewer: Michael True, "In Brief," undated clipping, Robert Lax Papers, St. Bonaventure University.

347, In a review of *The Collected Poems*: Richard Kostelanetz, "The Sounds of Silence: The Collected Poems of Thomas Merton," *New York Times Book Review*, February 5, 1978, 20.

347, "Towards the End of the Line": Nicholas Zurbrugg, "Towards the End of the Line: Dada and Experimental Poetry Today," in *Dada Spectrum: The Dialectics of Revolt*, ed. Stephen C. Foster and Rudolf E. Kuenzli (Iowa City: University of Iowa Press, 1978), 240–41.

348, "Harpo's Progress": Robert Lax, "Harpo's Progress: Notes Toward an Understanding of Merton's Ways," *Merton Annual* 1 (1988): 35–54.

348, Midway through this last unsettled period: Lax journal, October 25, 1978, St. Bonaventure University.

348, "monotheism is only one feature": Lax journal, March 28, 1981, St. Bonaventure University.

349, to live in our dreams: Lax journal, March 28, 1979, St. Bonaventure University.

349, finding the right culture: Lax journal, June 21, 1979, St. Bonaventure University.

350, the red blue color: Lax journal, June 17, 1981, St. Bonaventure University.

352, "10 cardboard boxes": Lax journal, June 15, 1981, St. Bonaventure University.

353, an editor at W. W. Norton: Kathy Anderson to Robert Lax, May 31, 1983, Robert Lax Papers, St. Bonaventure University.

353, I continue to watch: Lax, *33 Poems*, 195

354, As at earlier congresses: Harford, *Merton and Friends*, 232.

355, "annual report": Robert Lax to Irving Block, February 8, 1983, Robert Lax Papers, St. Bonaventure University.

355, According to a sales sheet: Emil Antonucci, 1981–82 Journeyman Press sales, Robert Lax Papers, St. Bonaventure University.

356, i think learning: Robert Lax to "Winnie," June 23, 1982, Robert Lax Papers, St. Bonaventure University.

357, "No, no, reject slips": Robert Lax to Michael Mott, January 28, 1983, Robert Lax Papers, St. Bonaventure University.

357, just ran into your questions: Robert Lax to Don McCoy, June 17, 1983, Robert Lax Papers, St. Bonaventure University.

358, "The author is right here": Thomas Kellein to Marcia Kelly and Jack Kelly, December 27, 2000, Robert Lax Papers, St. Bonaventure University.

358, "I've been sort of dragging": Robert Lax to Emil Antonucci, January 3, 1984, Robert Lax Papers, St. Bonaventure University.

359, "How would I not know": Lax, *33 Poems*, 188.

## 25. Pure Act Becomes Pure Love

360, "Best band": Robert Lax to Marcia Kelly, March 1, 1984, Robert Lax Papers, St. Bonaventure University.

360, "Another no-pay job": Robert Lax to Irving Block, January 29, 1985, Robert Lax Papers, St. Bonaventure University.

361, According to Lax, when Zurbrugg: Robert Lax to Soni Holman Fink, February 25, 1985, Soni Holman Fink private collection.

361, "It's almost like shaking hands": Gladys Marcus to Robert Lax, undated (1984), Robert Lax Papers, St. Bonaventure University.

363, "exercise in meditation": Jurgen Holwein, "Der Witz steckt im Schwebezustand," *Stuttgarter Nachtrichten*, April 23, 1985, 13.

363, "How's a type-Z": Robert Lax to Jim Harford, July 19, 1985, in Harford, *Merton and Friends*, 236.

364, "Mr. Moto got me surrounded": Robert Lax to Ed Rice, December 7, 1984, in Harford, *Merton and Friends*, 236.

364, "m took seriously": Lax journal, June 10, 1985, St. Bonaventure University.

364, "very friendly cooperation": Robert Lax to Marcia Kelly, July 29, 1985, Robert Lax Papers, St. Bonaventure University.

365, "up was up": Lax journal, June 3, 1985, St. Bonaventure University.

365, He took vitamins: Robert Lax to Gladys Marcus, January 8, 1986, Robert Lax Papers, St. Bonaventure University.

365, "My new thing": Robert Lax to Gladys Marcus, September 16, 1985, Robert Lax Papers, St. Bonaventure University.

365, When Damianos asked Lax: Lax journal, July 17, 1985, St. Bonaventure University.

366, a woman who had once: Teddy Bergery to Robert Lax, August 3, 1985, Robert Lax Papers, St. Bonaventure University. On a brighter note, Bergery became a fine painter in her later years, turning out colorful portraits of her life in New York and Greece. Some of her work can be viewed at http://theodorabergery.free.fr/bio/bio.htm.

367, By the end of September: Robert Lax to Gladys Marcus, November 27, 1985, and to Marcia Kelly and Jack Kelly, November 30, 1985, both in Robert Lax Papers, St. Bonaventure University.

367, "i am trying to organize": Robert Lax to Judy Emery, January 26, 1986, Robert Lax Papers, St. Bonaventure University.

367, "In summer I schwim": Robert Lax to "Cher Pi't" (Peter Walsh, from L'Eau Vive and *Jubilee*), January 29, 1986, Robert Lax Papers, St. Bonaventure University.

367, Around this time he started corresponding: Lax journal, February 28, 1986, St. Bonaventure University.

368, "It is down there": Robert Lax, "Beckett and Deep Sleep," *Review of Contemporary Fiction*, Summer 1987, 34.

368, i'm not too fond: Robert Lax to Thomas Kellein, February 16, 1988, Robert Lax Papers, St. Bonaventure University.

369, One day, while staying: Soni Holman Fink, "1987: A Visit to Patmos," Soni Holman Fink private collection.

369, In mid-December he learned that a fire: Robert Lax to Monique Kenedy, February 10, 1988, Robert Lax Papers, St. Bonaventure University.

369, "I spend most of my time": Robert Lax to Jim & Millie Harford, March 7, 1988, Robert Lax Papers, St. Bonaventure University.

369, "If you need any lessons": Robert Lax letter to "Adam," February 26, 1988, Robert Lax Papers, St. Bonaventure University.

369, "I've started in the past couple": Robert Lax to Ed Rice, January 31, 1990, Robert Lax Papers, St. Bonaventure University.

370, "This just occurred to me": Robert Lax to Connie Brothers, March 4, 1988, Robert Lax Papers, St. Bonaventure University.

370, In another letter to her: Robert Lax to Connie Brothers, February 10, 1989, Robert Lax Papers, St. Bonaventure University.


26. The Peacemaker's Handbook

371, "It's impossible to convey": *Poetry Flash*, December 1988, clipping in Robert Lax Papers, St. Bonaventure University.

371, "Depending upon the reader": *American Library Association Booklist*, 1988, clipping in Robert Lax Papers, St. Bonaventure University.

371, "The author, a lifelong friend": "Books: Briefly Noted," *New Yorker*, October 31, 1988, 105.

371, When he sent a copy: James Laughlin to Robert Lax, October 28, 1988, Robert Lax Papers, St. Bonaventure University.

372, Robinson praised everything: Leonard Robinson to Robert Lax, October 15, 1988, Robert Lax Papers, St. Bonaventure University.

372, "I guess I talk": Robert Lax to Connie Brothers, March 4, 1988, Robert Lax Papers, St. Bonaventure University.

372, Near the end of 1989: Richard Avedon to Robert Lax, December 19, 1989, Robert Lax Papers, St. Bonaventure University.

373, The photograph appeared: *Egoiste* 12 (1992): 140–41.

373, Lax's enthusiastic letter: Robert Lax to Gladys Marcus, March 23, 1990, Robert Lax Papers, St. Bonaventure University.

373, "Mr. Lax clearly": Patrick Vecchio, "Poet Lax Entrances Listeners," *Olean Times Herald*, October 10, 1990, Robert Lax Papers, St. Bonaventure University.

374, "& whole room sings": Robert Lax to Soni Holman Fink, February 24, 1991, Soni Holman Fink private collection.

374, His to-do list: Robert Lax, to-do list, November 22, 1996, Robert Lax Collection, Columbia University.

374, "In May, after the Gulf War": Robert Lax to Soni Holman Fink, May 26, 1991, Soni Holman Fink private collection.

376, "even in the room": Robert Lax to Soni Holman Fink, "first Sunday in November" (1990), Soni Holman Fink private collection.

376, That December, while Lax: Robert Lax to Marcia Kelly, undated (November 1991), Soni Holman Fink private collection.

376, Biddle's visit: This section is taken from Merton and Lax, *When Prophecy Still Had a Voice*, 421–22.

377, "I had a great time too": Robert Lax to Soni Holman Fink, June 23, 1992, Soni Holman Fink private collection.

377, Soni sent him the recently published collection: Soni Holman Fink to Robert Lax, October 13, 1992, Soni Holman Fink private collection.

377, the *Merton Annual* featured: Robert Lax, "Remembering Merton and New York," *Merton Annual* 5 (1992): 39–61.

378, the Swiss journalist: Peter P. Schneider, "Wir sind alle Wanderer auf diesem Planeten: Ein Gesprach mit dem amerikanischen Dichter Robert Lax," *Tages-Anzeiger* (Zurich), November 13, 1992.

378, He even heard from Brahmachari: Robert Lax to Ed Rice, February 7, 1993, Robert Lax Papers, St. Bonaventure University.

378, he had an ice box: Robert Lax to Soni Holman Fink, June 23, 1992, Soni Holman Fink private collection.

378, That February 1993: Robert Lax to Gary Bauer, February 8, 1993, and to Soni Holman Fink February 23, 1993, both in Soni Holman Fink private collection.

378, He told her not to bother: Robert Lax to Marcia Kelly, February 19, 1993, Robert Lax Papers, St. Bonaventure University.

379, Lax's simple lifestyle: Ibid.

379, "an impressionistic hodgepodge": Joe Leydon, "Middle of the Moment," *Variety*, May 15–21, 1995, 104.

379, *Middle of the Moment*: Directed by Nicolas Humbert and Werner Penzel, Cine Nomad, 1995.

380, The trip was a fulfillment: Robert Lax to Gladys Marcus, undated (April 1988), Soni Holman Fink private collection.

380, I recorded five hours: Michael McGregor, "Turning the Jungle into a Garden," *Poets & Writers*, March/April 1997, 78–87.

380, "i'm a hermit?": Robert Lax to Marcia Kelly, May 9, 1995, Robert Lax Papers, St. Bonaventure University.

380, "So what are our criteria?": Robert Lax to Marcia Kelly and Jack Kelly, March 27, 1995, Robert Lax Papers, St. Bonaventure University.

380, "Every so many years": Robert Lax to Marcia Kelly, March 2, 1995, Robert Lax Papers, St. Bonaventure University.

381, he sent an aphorism: Robert Lax to Nancy Goldring, April 12, 1995, Nancy Goldring private collection.

382, "what do i do": Robert Lax to Soni Holman Fink, March 20, 1995, Soni Holman Fink private collection.

382, well, i can name times: Ibid.

383, "stocked with lots of little bits": Jen Harford email to author, November 26, 2000, published in *Merton Seasonal*, Spring 2001, 24–25.

384, If you are: Merton, *Conjectures of a Guilty Bystander*, 198.

384, including Mogador, who wrote: Mogador Cristiani to Robert Lax, November 6, 1995, Robert Lax Papers, St. Bonaventure University.

384, "I'm loving it right here": Robert Lax to Soni Holman Fink, January 23, 1996, Soni Holman Fink private collection.

385, "Were you right": Robert Lax to Jen Harford, November 27, 1996, Robert Lax Papers, St. Bonaventure University.

386, "Being by temperament": Robert Lax to Pamela Hodgson, November 27, 1996, Robert Lax Papers, St. Bonaventure University.

386, By the time he reached: Lax journal, March 21, 2000, St. Bonaventure University.

386, "I've been in bed": Robert Lax to Ed Rice, February 3, 1997, Robert Lax Papers, St. Bonaventure University.

387, Rice's reply: Ed Rice to Robert Lax, "Ash Wed/97," Robert Lax Papers, St. Bonaventure University.

387, Assembled from "Bob's dialogues": John Beer to Connie Brothers, January 8, 1998, Robert Lax Papers, St. Bonaventure University.

388, "Being exactly the kind of nut": Robert Lax to Soni Holman Fink, August 20, 1998, Soni Holman Fink private collection.


## Epilogue: The Singer and the Song

391, In the end: The details of Lax's move from Patmos to Olean are from Jack Kelly, "Robert Lax—Coming Home," *Merton Seasonal*, Spring 2001, 3–6.

393, there are not many songs: Lax journal, November 16, 1959, Columbia University.

# Bibliography

## Archives

Lax, Robert, Collection. Rare Book and Manuscript Library, Columbia University.
———, Papers. Friedsam Library, St. Bonaventure University.
Merton, Thomas, Collection. Rare Book and Manuscript Library, Columbia University.
———, Papers. Friedsam Library, St. Bonaventure University.
Mott, Michael, Collection. Northwestern University Library Archival and Manuscript Collections.
Van Doren, Mark, Collection. Rare Book and Manuscript Library, Columbia University.
*New Yorker* archives online.

## Books

Bair, Deirdre. *Samuel Beckett, a Biography*. New York: Harcourt Brace Jovanovich, 1978.
Bicentennial Book Committee. *Enchanted Land, 1776–1976: The Story of Olean*. Olean, NY: Foster Advertising, 1976.
Blake, William. *The Portable Blake*. Edited by Alfred Kazin. New York: Penguin/Viking Press, 1976.
Buchanan, William. *Dr. Mahanambrato Brahmachari: My Impressions*. Ganges, MN: Vivekananda Monastery and Retreat, n.d.
Charters, Ann. *Kerouac, a Biography*. New York: St. Martin's Press, 1994.
Chindahl, George L. *A History of the Circus in America*. Caldwell, ID: Caxton Printers, 1959.
Christy, Jim. *The Long, Slow Death of Jack Kerouac*. Toronto: ECW Press, 1998.
Cocteau, Jean. *Opium: The Diary of a Cure*. London: P. Owen, 1957.
*Columbia Poetry 1938*. New York: Columbia University Press, 1938.
Costik, Sally Ryan, and Harvey L. Golubock. *The Bradford Oil Refinery*. Mount Pleasant, SC: Arcadia, 2006.

Cristiani Rossi, Victoria B. *Spangles, Elephants, Violets and Me: The Circus Inside and Out*. New York: iUniverse, 2009.

de Hueck, Catherine. *Friendship House*. New York: Sheed and Ward, 1947.

Eliot, T. S. *Essays Ancient and Modern*. New York: Harcourt, Brace, 1936.

Ellmann, Richard. *James Joyce*. Oxford: Oxford University Press, 1982.

Feininger, Andreas, and John von Hartz. *New York in the Forties*. New York: Dover, 1978.

Fettke, Charles R. *The Bradford Oil Field, Pennsylvania and New York*. Harrisburg, PA: Department of Internal Affairs, 1938.

Fisher, M. F. K. *Two Towns in Provence*. New York: Vintage, 1983.

Fowler, Gene. *Good Night, Sweet Prince: The Life and Times of John Barrymore*. New York: Viking Press, 1944.

France, Peter. *Hermits: The Insights of Solitude*. New York: St. Martin's Press, 1996.

Furlong, Monica. *Merton: A Biography*. San Francisco: Harper & Row, 1980.

Gelernter, David. *1939: The Lost World of the Fair*. New York: Free Press, 1995.

Georgiou, S. T. *The Way of the Dreamcatcher. Spirit Lessons with Robert Lax: Poet, Peacemaker, Sage*. Ottawa: Novalis, 2002.

Gill, Brendan. *Here at the New Yorker*. New York: Random House, 1975.

Gilman, Richard. *Faith, Sex, Mystery: A Memoir*. New York: Simon and Schuster, 1986.

Gilson, Etienne. *The Philosophy of St. Thomas Aquinas*. New York: Barnes & Noble Books, 1993.

Ginsberg, Allen. *Journals: Early Fifties, Early Sixties*. Edited by Gordon Ball. New York: Grove Press, 1994.

Harford, James. *Merton and Friends: A Joint Biography of Thomas Merton, Robert Lax, and Edward Rice*. New York: Continuum, 2006.

Hari, Albert. *A Short Guide to Notre-Dame de La Salette*. Strasbourg: Editions du Signe, 2002.

Hauff, Sigrid. *A Line in Three Circles: The Inner Biography of Robert Lax*. Munich: Belleville Verlag, 1999.

Hubler, Richard. *The Cristianis*. Boston: Little, Brown, 1966.

Huxley, Aldous. *Ends and Means: An Inquiry into the Nature of Ideals and into the Methods Employed for Their Realization*. London: Chatto & Windus, 1938.

Johnston, Mary Ann. *A Pocket of Peace: A History of Bradford 1879–1979*. Bradford: Pennsylvania Bank and Trust Company, 1979

Joyce, James. *Finnegans Wake*. New York: Penguin, 1999.

———. *Ulysses*. Middlesex, UK: Penguin, 1986.

Kalafatas, Michael N. *The Bellstone: The Greek Sponge Divers of the Aegean*. Waltham, MA: Brandeis University Press, 2003.

Kavanaugh, Kieran, and Otilio Rodriguez, trans. *The Collected Works of St. John of the Cross*. Washington, DC: Institute of Carmelite Studies, 1979.

Kerouac, Jack. *Jack Kerouac: Selected Letters 1940–1956*. Edited by Ann Charters. New York: Penguin, 1996.

———. *Jack Kerouac: Selected Letters 1957–1969*. Edited by Ann Charters. New York: Penguin, 2000.

———. *On the Road*. New York: Penguin, 1999.

Kerouac, Jack, and Joyce Johnson. *Door Wide Open: A Beat Love Affair in Letters, 1957–1958*. New York: Viking, 2000.

Lax, Robert. *Circus Days and Nights*. Woodstock, NY: Overlook Press, 2000.

———. *The Circus of the Sun*. New York: Journeyman Press, 1959.

———. *Circus Zirkus Cirque Circo*. Zurich: Pendo Verlag, 1981.

———. *Dialogues*. Zurich: Pendo Verlag, 1994.

———. *Journal A*. Zurich: Pendo Verlag, 1986.

———. *Journal B*. Zurich: Pendo Verlag, 1988.

———. *Journal C*. Zurich: Pendo Verlag, 1990.

———. *Journal D*. Zurich: Pendo Verlag, 1993.

———. *Journal E*. Zurich: Pendo Verlag, 1996.

———. *Journal F*. Zurich: Pendo Verlag, 1997.

———. *Love Had a Compass: Journals and Poetry*. Edited by James J. Uebbing. New York: Grove Press, 1996.

———. *New Poems*. New York: Journeyman Press, 1962.

———. *Notes*. Zurich: Pendo Verlag, 1995.

———. *Peacemaker's Handbook*. Zurich: Pendo Verlag, 2001.

———. *A Poem for Thomas Merton*. New York: Journeyman Press, 1969.

———. *Psalm & Homage to Wittgenstein*. Zurich: Pendo Verlag, 1991.

———. *Tertium Quid*. Devon, UK: Stride, 2005.

———. *A Thing That Is*. Woodstock, NY: Overlook Press, 1997.

———. *33 Poems*. Edited by Thomas Kellein. New York: New Directions, 1988.

———. *21 Pages*. Zurich: Pendo Verlag, 1984.

———. *27th & 4th*. Devon, UK: Stride, 1994.

Lewis, Stephen. *Hotel Kid: A Times Square Childhood*. Philadelphia: Paul Dry Books, 2002.

Markowski, Stanislaw. *Kazimierz: The Jewish Quarter of Crakow 1870–1988*. Krakow: Wydawnictwo Arka, 1992.

Maxwell, William. *All the Days and Nights: The Collected Stories*. New York: Vintage, 1995.

McDarrah, Fred W. *Greenwich Village*. New York: Corinth Books, 1963.

Merton, Thomas. *The Asian Journal of Thomas Merton*. New York: New Directions, 1975.

———. *Conjectures of a Guilty Bystander*. New York: Image Books, 2009.

———. *The Courage for Truth: Letters to Writers*. Edited by Christine M. Bochen. New York: Farrar, Straus and Giroux, 1993.

———. *The Hidden Ground of Love: The Letters of Thomas Merton on Religious Experience and Social Concerns.* Edited by William H. Shannon. New York: Harcourt Brace Jovanovich, 1993.

———. *New Seeds of Contemplation.* New York: New Directions, 1961.

———. *No Man Is an Island.* New York: Harcourt Brace Jovanovich, 1955.

———. *The Road to Joy: Letters to New and Old Friends.* Edited by Robert E. Daggy. New York: HarperCollins, 1990.

———. *Run to the Mountain: The Story of a Vocation. The Journals of Thomas Merton, Volume One 1939–1941.* Edited by Patrick Hart. San Francisco: Harper, 1995.

———. *The Seven Storey Mountain.* 50th anniversary edition. New York: Harcourt Brace, 1998.

———. *The Solitary Life.* Lexington, KY: Stamperia del Santuccio, 1960.

———. *Thomas Merton: A Vow of Conversation. Journals 1964–65.* Edited by Naomi Burton Stone. New York: Farrar, Straus and Giroux, 1988.

———. *Zen and the Birds of Appetite.* New York: New Directions, 1968.

Merton, Thomas, and Robert Lax. *A Catch of Anti-letters.* New York: Sheed and Ward, 1994.

Merton, Thomas, and Robert Lax. *When Prophecy Still Had a Voice: The Letters of Thomas Merton and Robert Lax.* Edited by Arthur W. Biddle. Lexington: University Press of Kentucky, 2001.

Miller, David, and Nicholas Zurbrugg, eds. *The ABCs of Robert Lax.* Devon, UK: Stride, 1999.

Miller, William, D. *Dorothy Day: A Biography.* San Francisco: Harper & Row, 1982.

Moosbrugger, Bernhard. *Bernhard Moosbrugger: Fotograf und Verleger.* Zurich: Pendo Verlag, 2005.

Mott, Michael. *The Seven Mountains of Thomas Merton.* Boston: Houghton Mifflin, 1984.

Museum Tinguely. *Robert Lax.* Exhibit catalogue. Bern: Benteli Verlag, 2004.

Olean City School District. *A Study of Olean, Past and Present.* Olean, NY: Olean City School District, 1987.

Rabelais, François. *Gargantua and Pantagruel.* Translated by J. M. Cohen. London: Penguin, 1955.

Reichardt, Mary, ed. *Encyclopedia of Catholic Literature.* Vol. 1. Westport, CT: Greenwood Press, 2004.

Reinhardt, Ad. *Art-as-Art: The Selected Writings of Ad Reinhardt.* Edited by Barbara Rose. New York: Viking Press, 1975.

Rice, Edward. *The Man in the Sycamore Tree: The Good Times and Hard Life of Thomas Merton.* San Diego: Harvest/Harcourt Brace Jovanovich, 1979.

Ross, Joseph E. *Krotona of Old Hollywood. Volume 1.* Montecito, CA: El Montecito Oaks Press, 1989.

Sawyer-Laucanno, Christopher. *The Continual Pilgrimage: American Writers in Paris, 1944–1960.* New York: Grove Press, 1992.

Seigel, Jerrold. *Bohemian Paris.* New York: Viking Press, 1986.

Seitz, Ron. *Song for Nobody: A Memory Vision of Thomas Merton.* Ligouri, MO: Triumph Books, 1993.

Shannon, William H. *Silent Lamp: The Thomas Merton Story.* New York: Crossroad, 1992.

Shannon, William H., Christine M. Bochen, and Patrick F. O'Connell, eds. *The Thomas Merton Encyclopedia.* Maryknoll, NY: Orbis Books, 2002.

Sheed, Wilfrid. *Frank and Maisie: A Memoir with Parents.* New York: Simon and Schuster, 1985.

Stone, Tom. *Patmos.* Athens: Lycabettus Press, 1981.

Sutton, David E. *Memories Cast in Stone: The Relevance of the Past in Everyday Life.* Oxford: Berg, 1998.

Tolstoy, Leo. *The Kingdom of God Is within You.* Lincoln: University of Nebraska Press, 1984.

Van Doren, Mark. *The Autobiography of Mark Van Doren.* New York: Harcourt, Brace, 1958.

———. *New Poems.* New York: William Slone, 1948.

———. *The Selected Letters of Mark Van Doren.* Edited by George Hendrick. Baton Rouge: Louisiana State University Press, 1987.

———. *Selected Poems.* New York: Henry Holt, 1954.

Warn, Faith. *The Bitter Sea: The Real Story of Greek Sponge Diving.* South Woodham Ferrers, UK: Guardian Angel Press, 2001.

Wetzsteon, Ross. *Republic of Dreams: Greenwich Village. The American Bohemia, 1910–1960.* New York: Simon and Schuster, 2002.

Wilkes, Paul, ed. *Merton By Those Who Knew Him Best.* San Francisco: Harper & Row, 1984.

Yagoda, Ben. *About Town: The* New Yorker *and the World It Made.* New York: Da Capo/Perseus, 2000.

Zurbrugg, Nicholas, ed. *Art, Performance, Media: 31 Interviews.* Minneapolis: University of Minnesota Press, 2004.

# Index

Agee, James, 136
Alfred Court Zoo Circus, 180–83, 187, 382
Alfred State College (Pennsylvania), 332
*American Library Association Booklist*, 371
*American Literary Anthology 3* (National Endowment for the Arts), 298
Anatolia College (Thessaloniki), 360
Anglican Church, 35
anti-Semitism, 27, 28, 41, 132–33
Antonucci, Emil, 197–200, 202, 204–6, 208, 210–11, 212–13, 241, 243, 244, 245, 276, 281, 282, 288, 292, 294, 296–98, 301–5, 310, 327, 331–32, 346, 347, 353,-55, 358–59, 363, 379, 385; *New Film* (film), 297; *Oedipus* (film), 282, 297; *Red & Blue* (film), 297; *Short Films* (film), 297; *Shorts* (film), 297; *Some Fables* (film), 282, 297; *Thought* (film), 282, 297; *Twenty-Seventh & Fourth* (film), 297, 379
*Approaches* (journal), 243
Aquinas, Thomas (Saint), 25, 35, 63, 84, 130–31, 152, 154; *Summa Theologica*, 130
Aristotle's *Delta Metaphysics*, 88
Armstrong, Louis, 19, 81, 217, 228–29
*Art International*, 221
ArtPark, 327, 329–30, 331–33, 348
Ashbery, John, 275, 297, 312
Athenagoras I, 247
*Atlantis* (film). *See Siren of Atlantis* (film)
Augustine, Saint, 31, 81, 84, 88, 89, 130, 131, 348
Aumont, Jean-Pierre, 139, 140
Auslander, Joseph, 58

Avedon, Richard, 372–73, 385

Bann, Stephen, 275, 288–89; *Concrete Poetry: An International Anthology* (ed.), 275, 289
Barrymore, John, 56, 138
Barzun, Jacques, 33
Bauer, Gary, 378, 384, 390
Bayerischer Rundfunk, 374
Beam, Mike, 135, 138, 139, 161
Beats, 48, 61, 77–78, 95, 185, 216
Beckett, Samuel, 218, 223, 231, 233, 361, 368; *The Unnamable*, 231
Beer, John, 384–85, 387
Bellow, Saul, 159
Bergerys, Jean François and Teddy (Flynn), 156, 162, 164, 175, 176, 184, 185–86, 194, 282, 366
Berrigan, Daniel, 348
Berryman, John, 33–34, 77
Besant, Annie, 57
Bible, 10, 84, 87, 88, 99, 101, 113, 126, 157–58, 176, 179, 180–81, 196, 208, 314; Book of Isaiah, 312; Book of Job, 231; Psalms, 16, 100, 208, 312; Revelation, 5, 382
Biddle, Arthur W., 17, 24, 376–77
Billiris, Harilaos, 272
*Black & White* (film), 137
Blake, William, 19, 81, 88, 124, 131
Blate, Michael (nephew), 347
Blumenthal, Joe, 204, 205
Boar's Head Society, 33–34
Boehner, Philotheus (priest), 153–54, 156, 162
Brahmachari, Mahanambrata, 38–40, 62, 63, 78, 79, 106, 192, 349, 378, 381
Breen, Joseph I., 140

British Broadcasting Corporation (BBC), 276, 296, 305, 352, 380
Brothers, Connie Marcus (niece), 51, 247–48, 348, 370, 372, 384, 387
Brussels, 391, 392
Buber, Martin, 372, 381
Buck, Pearl, 82
Budd, Dave and Corky, 218–19, 248
Buddhism, 63, 191–92
Buffalo exhibition, 374
Burford, Bob, 185, 190, 200
Burke, Robert, 27
Burroughs, William, 184, 216, 248, 348, 361
Burton, Ginny, 102
Burton, Robert: *The Anatomy of Melancholy*, 90
Butler, Nicholas Murray, 27
Butman, Bob, 161, 185, 355

Canary Islands, 20, 332
Cardenal, Ernesto, 14, 125
Catholicism, 4, 5, 28, 31, 35, 40, 48, 51, 63, 72, 78, 79, 84, 110, 118, 120, 130, 131, 133, 135, 151, 153, 156, 186, 188, 189, 190, 191, 192, 196, 197, 201, 207, 209, 214, 215, 242, 274, 349–50, 386; and Kerouac, 190–92; Lax moving beyond traditional form of, 314–15; publications, 188, 196. *See also Lax and Merton headings for conversion and faith-related activities*
*Catholic Worker* newspaper, 201, 241, 242
censorship, 31, 241, 242
Chan, Wing-tsit: *The History of Chinese Philosophy*, 338
Chaplin, Charlie, 19, 96, 138–39
Charles (sponge specialist), 260–61
Charters, Ann, 191
Chinese philosophy, 338, 342, 348
Christy, Jim: *The Long Slow Death of Jack Kerouac*, 191–92
circus, 1, 10, 20, 25, 51, 52–53, 55, 125–37, 148, 180–83, 190, 193–94, 382. *See also Cristiani circus family*
Circus Roberto, 7
*Cithara* (journal), 362
Claire, William, 205, 288

Cocteau, Jean: *Les Enfants Terribles*, 88, 91; *Opium*, 88
Cohen, Sig, 304
collectibles market, 199
*Columbia College Today*, 380
*Columbia Forum*, 297, 298
Columbia University: anti-Semitism at, 27, 28; humor magazine, *Jester*, 16, 26, 29, 33, 68, 79, 104, 188; Kerouac at, 78; Lax archives at, 60, 115, 385; literary magazine, *Columbia Review*, 33; Mark Van Doren Award, 37; Merton and Lax at, 16, 25–26, 28–29, 31–34, 35, 37–38, 62, 221; outsider status at, 27; Scholastic philosophy class at, 35; student newspaper, *Spectator*, 28
commercialism, 11, 211, 219, 256
commercial writing, 79, 84–85, 188. *See also specific magazines and newspapers*
concrete poets, 221, 243, 275, 289, 307, 354, 374
Connecticut College, 135, 145–46, 148, 156
conscientious objector status, 61, 87, 100–101, 110–11, 197
Constantine II (King of Greece), 279
Cornell, Tom, 201, 203
Corps seminary, 188, 191, 193–94, 197, 207
Corwin, Norman, 90, 91
Crider, Jim, 136
Cristiani, Paul (Mogador), 127–29, 146, 147–50, 153, 158, 164, 187, 253, 384
Cristiani circus family, 53, 125–29, 138, 146–53, 159, 180, 181, 189, 210, 219, 251, 253, 278, 371, 382
cummings, e. e., 57, 199–200, 205
Cyprus crisis, 250–51, 330–31, 337, 341

Dalai Lama, 14, 16, 98, 292
Dante, 19, 74, 88, 101, 112, 124, 131, 158, 178, 179, 192
Daugherty, Michael and Rebecca, 389
Davis, Mary, 361
Day, Dorothy, 18, 201, 241
DeBerard, Beverly (Burford), 190, 290
decision making, 24–25, 36, 42, 66, 99, 100, 155, 202, 252, 343, 345, 364

de Hueck, Catherine, 110, 119, 154, 155–56, 157
Deiches, Saul, 45
de Kooning, Willem, 219, 363
Deux Alice Clinic (Brussels), 391
Diaz, Paula, 387
Dimitri (travel agent), 334, 337, 343
Divine Love. *See* God and Divine Love
Dodecanese islands. *See* Kalymnos; Lipsi; Patmos
Doherty, Eddie, 154
Donne, John, 88
dreams, 5, 98–99, 155–56, 192–93, 309, 311, 349, 380, 390
*Dryad* (journal), 297, 310
Duell, Sloan & Pearce (publishing company), 146

Eastern religious and philosophical texts, 36–37, 338, 342, 348
Edman, Irwin, 221
*Egoiste* (French magazine), 372–73, 385
Eisenhower, Dwight, 98
Eliot, Alex, 30–31, 136, 137, 142, 161, 211, 237, 239, 244, 274
Eliot, T. S., 35, 88, 185, 322; *Essays Ancient and Modern*, 35
Ellington, Duke, 19, 96, 102, 142, 360
Emery, Judy, 15, 356, 362
European travel: (1937), 34–35, 157; (1950–53), 157–90; (1954–55), 193–95; (1963), 247–48

Ferlinghetti, Lawrence, 16, 241
films. *See specific titles or directors*
Finlay, Ian Hamilton, 275, 276, 332, 360, 363
Fisher, M. F. K.: *Two Towns in Provence*, 158
Fitzsimmons, James, 273, 274, 275
Flagg, Nancy, 20, 66, 67, 91, 94, 96, 97, 138, 151–52, 209
Flynn, Teddy. *See* Bergery, Teddy Flynn
Forest, Jim, 242, 348
Fowler, Gene, 56–57
France, Peter: *Hermits*, 380, 385
Freedgood, Seymour (Sy), 26, 37, 38, 66, 77, 94, 95, 97, 148, 284
Friede, Donald, 139

Friendship House (Harlem), 110–11, 116–17, 119, 122–23, 134, 188, 201
Furthermore Press, 363

Geerken, Hartmut, 354, 360, 376, 378, 379
Gelernter, David, 73
General Beadle State College (South Dakota), 283, 289–90
Gerdy, Robert, 27, 35, 120, 283
Germany, introduction of Lax's works to, 354, 360, 362, 374, 379
Gethsemani monastery (Kentucky), 111, 114, 118, 132–34, 148, 240, 294, 377
Ghenis, Pandelis (Greek captain), 265–68
Gibney, Nancy. *See* Flagg, Nancy
Gibney, Robert, 20, 27, 28, 35, 77, 94, 95, 96–97, 100, 101, 102, 110–11, 123, 129, 131, 137, 138, 151–53, 209
Gilman, Richard, 195
Ginsberg, Allen, 184, 192–93, 214, 216, 242
Giroux, Robert, 148, 188
Glass, Philip, 331, 361
Gleason, Ralph J., 298
God and Divine Love, 25, 36, 82–84, 89, 106, 109, 117, 124, 178, 196, 206–8, 314–15, 327–29, 341, 343, 348–49, 386
Goldring, Nancy, 381
Gomera, 332–33, 338, 345
Gomringer, Eugen, 289
*Good Work* (journal), 297
Greece, 211, 239, 244–55, 273, 279. *See also* Kalymnos; Lipsi; Patmos
Greek history and politics, 10, 250, 251, 263, 266
Greene, Graham, 81
Green Island Press, 363
Griffin, Bill, 79
Griffin, Francis "Griff," 49, 344
Grove Press, 216, 385
Guggenheim, Daniel, 56
Gysin, Brion, 248, 355

Harbutt, Charles, 196, 204
Harford, Jen, 382–84, 385, 386
Harford, Jim, 283, 354, 357, 363, 369

Harlem, 19, 31, 102, 110–11, 115, 116, 117–23, 135
*Harper's Bazaar,* 296, 327
Hart, Patrick, 376–77
Hauff, Sigrid, 354
Hernandez, Jose Ramon Chinea, 332
Herscher, Irenaeus (priest), 81, 274
Hinduism, 63
Hiroshima bombing, 135–36, 240
Holiday, Billie, 19, 31, 102
Hollywood, 138–45
Holman, Soni (cousin), 161, 202, 282, 343, 368–69, 374–77, 379, 382, 384, 388
Holt, Rinehart & Winston, 291
homosexuality, 67, 164
Hopkins, Gerard Manley, 19, 66, 74, 88, 131
Hotchner, Rebecca (Betty). *See* Lax, Rebecca (Betty) Hotchner
Hotchner family of Lax's mother (Betty), 43–45, 49–50, 56, 203
Humbert, Nicolas, 379
humor, 15, 17, 18, 29, 33, 41, 66, 70, 195, 296, 387
Huston, John: *The Dead* (movie), 74
Huxley, Aldous, 33, 63, 144–45; *Ends and Means,* 33, 35, 36–37
H. W. Marcus Department Store, 47

International Astronautical Federation congresses, 283, 354, 357, 360, 366, 367, 369
International Thomas Merton Society, 376, 380

Jackson, Harry, 238, 274
Jackson Heights, Queens, 55, 56, 207, 208, 209
Jacobson, Herb, 16
James, William, 23
jazz musicians, 18, 24–25, 27, 159, 216, 223–28
Jesus, 86, 87, 112, 118, 124, 157, 165, 249
Jews and Judaism, 28, 40, 42–43, 45, 47, 52, 56, 84, 86–87, 131–33, 181, 348–50. *See also* anti-Semitism
Jimera de Líbar (Spain), 345
John, Saint, 171, 247, 382, 392
John of the Cross, Saint, 81, 83, 101, 120, 131, 188; *The Ascent of Mt.*

*Carmel,* 88, 89; *The Dark Night of the Soul,* 19, 88, 89
Johnson, Benjamin W., 27
Johnston, Mary Ann: *A Pocket of Peace: A History of Bradford 1879–1979,* 46
*Journal for the Protection of All Beings,* 241
Journeyman Press, 205, 276, 296, 304, 332, 355, 363
Joyce, James, 88, 89, 96, 101, 122, 131, 184; and Beckett, 231, 361; *Dubliners,* 74; *Finnegans Wake,* 17, 74–75, 81, 93, 215, 361; *Ulysses,* 74, 162, 185, 199
*Jubilee* magazine, 15, 77, 188–90, 194–98, 201, 203, 204, 206, 210, 218, 220, 237, 244, 301, 374

Kalymnos, 1, 20, 51, 122, 247, 248, 256–73, 277–81, 285, 291–94, 296–301, 310, 311, 313–16, 320, 326–27, 332–34, 339–46, 379
Katina and Yannis (Greek neighbors), 22, 365, 366–67, 378, 382
Kazimierz (Krakow Jewish ghetto), 7, 42, 43
Kellein, Thomas, 358, 360, 362–63, 368
Kelly, Marcia Marcus (niece), 60, 353–54, 360, 364, 373, 376, 378, 380, 384, 391, 392; *One Hundred Graces,* 380
Kenan Fellowship, 130
Kenedy, R. C., 305–8, 321–22, 327, 332, 360
Kerouac, Jack, 14, 15, 20, 72, 78, 185, 190–93, 199–200, 209, 233, 312, 348; "Gerard," 218; "Hymn," 218; influence on Lax, 213–18, 223, 228, 248, 310; *Jack Kerouac: Selected Letters 1940–1956* (Charters, ed.), 191; prose style of, 223–28; *On the Road,* 78, 143, 185
Kilburn, David, 296, 332, 363
Kos, 1, 248–55, 265
Kostelanetz, Richard, 347
Krishnamurti, J., 57
Kuhn, Helmut, 130, 154

Labre, Benedict Joseph, Saint, 156–57, 160, 164, 167, 175, 178, 188
Lagouvardos, Moschos, 326, 333, 339

Lambert, Marcel, 160, 163–65
Lange, Gerry, 283, 290
La Salette. *See* Sanctuary of Notre
Dame de la Salette
Lastnite, Michael, 356, 363, 369
Laughlin, James, 133–34, 148, 206, 241,
297, 371
Laughlin, Pat, 138, 139, 161–62
Lawrence, D. H.: *Lady Chatterley's
Lover*, 80
Lax, Gladio (sister). *See* Marcus, Gladio
(Gladys) Lax
Lax, Joseph (uncle), 45, 53–54
Lax, Rebecca (Betty) Hotchner
(mother), 11, 25, 41–45, 48–51, 54,
55–56, 72, 76, 313
Lax, Robert: abstinence of, 32, 67;
advice to author from, 40; Bible
reading by, 84, 87, 113; as celebrity,
372–73; and circus, 125–30, 146–51,
180–83, 382; clowning technique of,
150–51; conscientious objector
status, 100–101; conversion to
Catholicism, 28, 35, 130–35, 386;
correspondence as regular part of
life, 355, 356, 367, 368, 372, 374;
death of, 392–93; dislike of
confrontation, 315; documentary on,
356; and Eastern religion, 39;
embracing the world, 30–31, 350;
family and childhood of, 41–43,
50–57; and father's death, 148;
fearful, anxious nature of, 343, 352,
373; as film critic, 136; Guggenheim
application of, 204, 206, 244–45,
248, 282, 297–98, 321–22; Harlem
charity work and life of, 111, 116,
117–20; health problems and
appearance of, 6, 62, 69, 111, 118,
123, 152, 195–96, 202–3, 207, 231,
238–39, 244, 365, 386, 388; high
school years of, 57–59; on his father
(Siggie), 52, 131–32; humor of, 15, 17,
18, 33, 41, 66, 70, 195, 387;
idealization by, 322–26; income and
accounting of, 355; interviews of,
146, 361, 367, 376–77, 380; Jewish
immigrant background of, 25, 41,
43–45; journals of, 26, 32, 67–68, 70,
72, 73, 75, 76, 82, 86–87, 93, 97, 102,
105–8, 115, 131, 142–43, 158, 172, 203,
216, 222, 233, 277, 309, 312, 340–41,
348, 386; on Kellys' book of mealtime
blessings, 380–81; as mentor to the
young, 356–57; and mother's death,
72, 76; and mother's voice, 313;
moviemaking by, 137, 138–45; naïveté
of, 24, 87, 171, 315; nonconventional
thinking of, 20, 85; obscurity of, 20,
360; personality of, 15, 25, 352;
Petros as nickname of, 12; as
photographer, 135, 142, 185, 189, 193,
283, 288, 300, 354, 357, 358, 363,
369, 374; on poet-suicide, 116–17;
portrait of (by Jackson), 238–39;
post-college employment, 68–70; on
poverty, 118–119, 159, 207; purchase
of home on Patmos, 364; readings by,
242, 276, 290, 304, 317, 354, 355,
360, 363, 366, 373–74, 376;
recordings instead of letters, use of,
367; reflecting on favorite times in
his life, 382; relationships with
strangers and friends, 12–13, 15;
sadness of, 103–4, 111–12, 148, 238;
self-awareness of, 32, 158–60, 206,
313, 320, 353; sensitivity of, 187,
206–7, 383; spy status, suspected of,
1, 281, 301, 330–31, 334–36, 339–40;
on success, 106, 117, 124, 209; torpor
of, 66, 67, 123; wandering life of, 117,
151, 154, 276, 345; on women and sex,
32, 67; and World War II, 96–97, 111,
119–22; on writing, 31, 65–66, 68, 71,
76–77, 83, 134, 146. *See also* Merton
and Lax relationship; *specific
employers, publishers, colleagues, and
locations of travel and residence*
Lax, Robert, works by, 75, 204; "Able
Charlie Baker Dance," 287; "Abstract
Poem," 285–86; "Acey-Ducey" or
"Reflections of a Temple Dancer,"
163, 166; "Ah! The Nature Poets,"
243; "Alley Violinist," 302; *The Angel
and the Old Lady*, 297; aphorisms,
380–81; "Beckett and Deep Sleep,"
368; "Black & White," 142, 275, 276,
363; *Black/White Oratorio* (Lax &
Beer), 388; *The Bomb*, 376; Buffalo
exhibition, 374; "Byzantine Faces,"

322–26; *A Catch of Anti-letters* (Merton & Lax), 17, 283, 288, 347, 379; "CHERUBIM & PALM-TREES," 223–28; "Circus," 148, 188; *Circus Days and Nights*, 381, 387; "Circus of the Sun," 184, 276; *The Circus of the Sun*, 14, 51, 53, 125, 128, 145, 154, 161–62, 181, 200, 201, 203, 204–6, 209–10, 213, 215, 288, 305, 308, 318, 322, 347, 372, 387; *Circus-Zirkus-Cirque-Circo*, 318; *Dialogues*, 379; "dr. glockenspiel's invention," 380; *Drama: An Abstract Verse Play*, 276; *Episodes-Episoden*, 318, 355; *Fables/Fablen*, 298, 302, 356; "Greeting to Spring (Not Without Trepidation)," 92; "The Groundhog Poem," 104; "Harpo's Progress: Notes Toward an Understanding of Merton's Ways," 348; "histories"/"Histories," 309, 355; "Homage to Wittgenstein," 302–3; "The Incomparable Cristianis," 189; "Invitation," 58; *Journal C*, 375; *Journal D*, 379; *Journal F*, 387; "Juggler," 204; "Kalymnos Journal," 297–98, 304; "The Last Days of a City," 33, 62; "The Last Syllable," 93; "Light Dark, Dark Light," 142; *Love Had a Compass: Journals and Poetry*, 385; "The Man With the Big General Notions," 92, 302; *Mogador's Book*, 128–29, 149–50, 387; *New Poems*, 243, 276, 297; *The Night Sea Journey*, 245; *Notes*, 379; "Oedipus," 204; *The Peacemaker's Handbook*, 61; "The Plague Full Swift Goes By," 82; "Poem (for Jack Kerouac and Allen Ginsburg)," 214; "A Poem for Thomas Merton," 292–94; *A Poem for Thomas Merton*, 297; "Poem of Gratuitous Invective Against New Jersey," 93; "The Poppy," 58; "The Prologue," 104; *Psalm & Homage to Wittgenstein*, 376; "Question," 204; "A Radio Masque for My Girl Coming Down from Northampton," 91–92; "Remembering Merton and New York," 19, 24, 377–78; reviews and studies of, 305–8, 347; *Robert Lax: Abstract Poetry* (Stuttgart exhibit), 12, 13, 362–63; *Robert Lax and Concrete Poetry* (exhibit), 374; *A Room Full of Voices* (Lax & Beer), 387; *The Rooster Poems*, 376; *Sea Poem*, 276; "Searching" (autobiography), 352–53; "Sea & Sky," 273, 274–75, 276, 288, 371; "A shorter rooster poem," 380; "Shower Girl Song," 332; *Sleeping Waking* (Beer, ed.), 387; "Solomon's High Dive," 188, 275–76; "The Spangled Palace," 82; "Speech to draft officers," 87–88; *Subway to Camelot*, 58; "Sun Poem," 188; *A Thing That Is*, 289; *33 Poems*, 13, 358, 368, 371, 376, 385; "This bread is bread," 305–6; *Thought*, 276; "Thought," 296; *3 or 4 Poems about the Sea*, 276; *Three Poems*, 297; "Tractatus I" and "Tractatus II," 309–10; "Tree," 204; *21 Pages/21 Seiten*, 318, 353, 359, 361, 372; *27th & 4th*, 379; "Two Thieves and the Master of Krove," 58; *Voyage to Pescara*, 180–83, 387; "Wages of Convalescence," 59; *wasser/water/l'eau*, 318, 332; *Xiliamodi*, 379; X-Ray articles (high school newspaper), 58. *See also* Antonucci, Emil *for films made from Lax's writings*; writing style

Lax, Sigmund (Siggie) (father), 10–11, 41, 45–52, 53–54, 56, 131–32, 148
Lax, Sylvia (Sal) (sister), 41, 48, 56, 354
Leadbeater, C.W., 57
Lefkowitz, David, 89
Levertov, Denise, 205, 213, 288, 297, 305
Lewis, Peter (Lax pen name), 199
Lewis, Stephen, 69, 70; *Hotel Kid*, 69
Leydon, Joe, 379
Liebling, A. J., 107
*Life* magazine, 136
Limnina (rug-maker on Kalymnos), 258–59, 277, 285, 292, 330, 332, 333, 334–36
Lindbergh, Charles, 28, 54–55
Lipsi (Greek island), 280, 296, 300, 310–14, 320, 333, 337, 345–46, 354
Lobrano, Gus, 90–91, 92–93, 101–5, 113, 114

*Locus Solus* (journal), 275, 276
*London Magazine*, 297
love and reconciliation, 30, 61, 86–87, 89, 117, 134, 157, 372. *See also* God and Divine Love; pure love
Lowe, Jacques, 189–90
Lowell, Robert, 134–35, 233
*Lugano Review*, 273, 276, 305

Mack, Bob, 95, 101, 116, 129, 132, 135, 145–47, 160, 163, 183, 184–85, 203
Madonna House (Ontario), 154, 155
Mahoney, Mary, 146–47, 162
Maimonides, 348
Makarios III, 330
Malraux, André, 221
Mamere (Kerouac's mother), 215
Mandela, Nelson, 390
Marcus, Benjamin (Benji) (brother-in-law), 47, 48, 55, 61, 62, 80, 86, 90, 100–101, 123, 284
Marcus, Dick (nephew), 183, 184–85
Marcus, Gladio (Gladys) Lax (sister), 41, 45, 47, 48, 54, 55–56, 60, 72, 84, 86–87, 90, 123, 131, 133, 247, 292, 353–54, 361, 365, 373, 380
Marcus, Harris Wolfe, 46–47
Maritain, Jacques, 131, 186, 348
Marseilles, 34, 35, 157–60, 162–75, 232, 247, 278, 284, 291, 314, 382
Maxwell, William, 7, 10, 109–10, 199–200, 243, 297, 381
McConathy, Dale, 327
McCormick, Anne, 347
McGlynn, Père, 274
McGregor, Michael N.: 1985 visit with Lax, 6, 7, 11, 13–14, 15–16, 20–21, 125, 360, 362; 1987 visit with Lax, 23; 1989 visit with Lax, 98; 1999 visit with Lax, 389–91; Antonucci interview and help with research, 212–213; call to Lax as Lax was leaving Patmos for last time, 392; choice of Greece as place to write, 237; and collectibles market of publications, 199; interview recording, 146, 380; and Paris, 184; research at Columbia University's Lax's archives, 115; and Sanctuary of Notre Dame de la Salette, 174;

Weigner interview and help with research, 317–18
Mehmedi (Turkish diver), 260–62, 271
*Merton: A Film Biography* (PBS documentary), 356
Merton, Thomas: background of, 27–28; and Beat lifestyle, 77–78; behavior of, 15, 276; books about, 346, 357; Brahmachari's influence on, 38–40; "Chant to Be Used in Processions around a Site with Furnaces," 241; *The Collected Poems of Thomas Merton*, 347; collectibles of work, 199; at Columbia University, 28–29, 33–34, 188; conversion to Catholicism, 31, 36, 63, 95; and Dalai Lama, 14, 292; *Figures for an Apocalypse*, 144–45; at Gethsemani Trappist monastery, 111, 114, 118; Harlem charity work of, 110–11; introduction of author to Lax, 1; journals of, 74; and *Jubilee* magazine, 188–89; Kerouac's admiration of, 190, 215; last days and death of, 292–95; letters of, 18; literary influences on, 88–89; *New Seeds of Contemplation*, 89; in New York City, 72–77; "The Night Before the Battle," 81; ordination of, 148; "Original Child Bomb," 240–42; *Pax* writings of, 199–200, 241; poetry in *New Yorker* by, 123; Rice's interest in writing about, 301; and St. Bonaventure, 63–64, 95, 110, 111; *The Seven Storey Mountain* (autobiography), 3–4, 16, 31, 63, 74, 79, 88, 99, 133, 142, 188, 189; *The Solitary Life*, 237–38; spiritual development of, 35–40, 63–64; *Thirty Poems*, 133–34, 135; travels of, 290–92; and World War II, 110–11
Merton and Lax relationship, 4–5, 11–12, 66; *A Catch of Anti-letters* (Merton & Lax correspondence), 17, 283, 288, 347, 379; *Circus of the Sun* (Lax) praised by Merton, 205–6; college friendship, 16–17, 27–28, 31, 62; comparison of Merton and Lax, 32, 64–65, 94–95; and conversion to Catholicism, 36, 94–95, 130–31;

correspondence, 16–18, 40, 66, 75, 123, 167, 187–88, 220, 231–32, 239–40, 245, 279–80, 282–84, 290–91, 294–95, 346–47; description of, 18–19; encouragement of Lax, 142, 203, 282; and *Ends and Means* (Huxley), 36; first meeting, 16; and Gethsemani ordination of Merton, 148; Gethsemani visits of Lax to Merton, 133–34, 201, 208; Harlem Friendship House time together, 111; and Hollywood work of Lax, 138; importance to Merton scholars, 348, 356, 364; intimacy of, 67; and jazz musicians, 24–25; and Kerouac, 215; Lax on Merton's death, 294; Lax writing about Merton, 292–94, 301, 348, 362, 363; literary influences on, 17, 74–75, 88–89; Merton on Lax's writing, 77; mortification of the flesh, discussions on, 64, 83; and mysticism, 29; New York City time together (1939), 72–74; Olean cottage visits, 62–66, 67, 77, 78, 79–84, 94–97, 380; publication of their correspondence, 282–83, 291, 346–47, 376–77; reaction of Lax to Merton's *The Solitary Life*, 238; reunion (1968), 291; on woe of Lax, 15

*Merton Annual*, 348, 364, 377
Middle East reading tour, rejection of (1970), 304–5
*Middle of the Moment* (film), 379
*Middle Park Times*, 290
*The Midrash on Psalms*, 208
Mikali (Greek friend), 339, 346
Miller, Henry, 19, 216, 217, 348; *Tropic of Cancer*, 71, 80
minimalism, 218, 219, 221, 222–23, 275, 305, 307, 347, 371
Mitchell, Joseph: *Up in the Old Hotel*, 377
Mitchell, Julian, 280–81, 296
Mizingou, Jeannine, 51
Montez, Maria, 139, 140, 141
Moosbrugger, Bernhard, 194, 201, 317–18, 330, 332, 347, 358, 367
Mott, Michael, 64, 80, 357, 362; *The Seven Mountains of Thomas Merton*, 362, 364

moviemaking, 137, 138–45. *See also specific directors*
Munch, Edvard: *The Scream*, 116
mysticism, 29, 36, 63, 78
Mytilene/Lesbos, 245–48, 273

Nannucci, Maurizio, 355
National Endowment for the Arts, 298, 301–2
Nebenzal, Seymour, 140–41
*New Directions*, 354, 355
New Directions press, 133–34, 241, 297, 368, 371
*New-Story* magazine, 20, 175, 184–87, 200
*Newtown Lantern*, 58, 59
New York City, 45, 49, 50–51, 72–73, 113, 135, 146, 190–93, 195, 200–201, 209–10, 213, 219–20, 231, 278, 283, 291, 374
*New Yorker*: change in editorial direction of, 107; and Cristianis article, 146–47; as inspiration for *Jester*, 26; Lax's first subscription to, 57; Lax's submissions to, 89–94, 134, 148, 161, 188, 275, 354; Lax working for, 20, 68, 85, 101–14, 124, 129, 341; Merton's poetry in, 123; review of *33 Poems* (Lax), 371; and Robinson, 125, 127
*New York Herald Tribune*, 23, 75
*New York Quarterly*, 205, 243, 367
*New York Times*, 75, 140, 141, 218
*New York Times Book Review*, 15, 77, 347
Nicos (Greek captain), 261, 267–68

Olean, New York, 25, 45–56, 60–67, 67, 77, 78, 79–85, 94–97, 101, 153–54, 156, 202–04, 214, 217, 223, 284, 291, 332, 348, 373, 380, 392; moving between New York City and, 51, 54, 123–24, 125, 135
oneness of humanity, 30–31, 320–21, 332, 340, 345. *See also* peace
Overlook Press, 387

pacifism. *See* conscientious objector status
Packard, William, 205, 242–43, 367
Padre Pio, 274

Papandreou, Andreas, 266, 346
Papandreou, George, 251, 266, 279
*Parade* magazine, 136–37, 139
Paris, 34, 50, 157, 172, 175, 184–87, 193, 198, 199, 248, 291, 339, 354, 371, 379
*Paris Review*, 184, 312, 354
Pasternak, Boris, 18, 206
Patmos, 1–2, 4, 5–7, 9–10, 14, 21, 22, 23, 171, 247, 260, 262, 269, 280, 281, 296, 298, 300, 301, 311, 320, 345, 346, 352–53, 358, 363, 365, 368–71, 374, 382, 388–90
Paul (Kalymnos friend), 259, 261, 264, 266–70, 285
Paul, Saint, 124, 131, 246, 372
*Pax* (journal), 61, 175, 199–200, 203, 210, 218, 239–42, 363
peace, 1, 22, 23, 34, 61, 98, 116, 155, 162, 165, 167, 255, 315, 348, 374, 375, 382, 384
Pearce, Cap, 146–47
Pendo Verlag (publisher), 12–13, 128, 195, 317–18, 347, 353, 355–56, 359, 363, 375–76, 379, 384, 387
Penzel, Werner, 379
Perelman, S. J., 112–13, 233
Petrakis, Carlos, 246–47
Philolexian Society, 33
Picasso's *Guernica*, 34
Pietrasanta, Italy, 273–74
Pius XII (pope), 74, 125, 185
Plato, 78, 141
poetry, style of. *See* writing style
*Poetry Flash* (journal), 371
*Poets & Writers* (magazine), 380
Pollock, Jackson, 217, 219
*Poor. Old. Tired. Horse.* (journal), 275
poverty, 2–3, 110–12, 117–19, 122, 156, 159, 178, 207
*Publisher's Weekly*, 347
pure act, 24, 25, 130, 149, 159, 228, 278, 313, 360–70, 393
pure love, 25, 350, 360–70

Rabelais, François, 19, 75, 81, 101, 124, 217
radio station job (Olean), 84–85
Reef, Arthur, 139
Reinhardt, Ad, 25–26, 27, 33, 37, 94, 97, 152–53, 188, 208, 213, 219–23, 228,

263, 283, 358, 362; "Art-as-Art," 221–22
Reinhardt, Rita, 327
religion: conversion to Catholicism, 14, 28, 35, 63, 130–35, 386; Eastern thought, 36–37, 39, 78, 89, 338, 348; and Lax, 5, 109, 342; living in non-Catholic country, 14–15; religious imagery in poetry, 306–7; spiritual maturing of Lax vs. Merton, 64–65. *See also specific faith*
*Review of Contemporary Fiction* (Zurbrugg, ed.), 368
Rice, Ed, 77–84, 94, 95, 97, 131, 136, 146, 148, 188–90, 193–96, 202, 203, 207, 209–210, 240, 283, 297, 301, 363, 369, 371, 386–87; "The Blue Horse," 81; *The Man in the Sycamore Tree*, 31, 77, 79
Ringling Brothers and Barnum & Bailey Circus, 52–53, 126
Ripley, Arthur, Jr., 139
Ripley, Arthur, Sr., 139, 140
Robinson, Leonard, 110, 125–26, 127–28, 136–37, 371–72
Rome, 153, 156, 160–61, 165, 172, 175–78, 183, 187, 291
Rose, Barbara, 219
Ross, Harold, 57, 90, 105, 107
Rusak, Marie, 57, 138–39
Rush, Joe, 201–2

St. Bonaventure University (formerly College), 48–49, 60, 63, 68, 81, 95, 110, 111, 153, 373, 380; Lax archives at, 181, 362, 385
St. John visit to Gibney, 151–53
Sainte-Marie, François de, 193–94
Salinger, J. D., 218, 223, 231, 233
Sanctuary of Notre Dame de la Salette, 118, 172, 174, 175, 194, 291, 294
Saroyan, Aram, 275
Saroyan, William, 80, 112
Schaeper, Thomas, 362
Schneider, Peter P., 378
Scholastic philosophy, 35, 63
Scholem, Gershom, 348
Seitz, Ron, 18–19
Selective Service draft. *See* World War II and draft board

September 11, 2001, terrorist attacks, 61–62
Shakespeare, William, 37–38, 101, 124
Shapiro, Meyer, 37, 221
Shawn, William, 107
Sheed, Wilfrid, 15, 196; "The Beat Movement, Concluded" (Sheed), 77–78
Sheed & Ward, 197, 379
Shuman, Ik, 102, 105
Simpson, Richard, 373
Siren of Atlantis (film), 139–42, 379
Slate, John, 26, 28, 34–35, 66, 68–69, 129, 157, 283–84
Smith, Pete, 127
Smith, Roberta, 218
Socrates, 124
Soisy-sur-Seine, 186–87
solitude, 22–23, 26, 67, 85, 100, 111, 114, 193, 208, 237–38, 277, 301, 308, 345, 389, 393
Solt, Mary Ellen: Concrete Poetry: A World View: United States, 275
Spaeth, Paul J., 60, 181
Spencer Collection, 198
Spielberg, Stephen, 42
Spiros (Greek policeman), 330–31, 336, 343
sponge diving and divers, 257–64, 266–71
Staatsgalerie exhibition (Stuttgart), 12, 13, 358, 362–63
State University of New York in Buffalo, 374
Stein, Gertrude, 221, 228, 286–87
Stellio (Turkish friend), 256–58, 300
Stereo Headphones, 275, 297
Steves, Rick, 21, 22, 98
Stride Publications, 376, 379
Stuttgarter Nachtrichten (newspaper), 363
Subway Mysticism, 29
Sullivan, Frank, 107
Sullivan, Oona, 196, 201, 298
Sun Ra, 354, 360
Swift, Jonathan: Gulliver's Travels, 210, 231
Switzerland, 317–20, 332, 345, 367, 375, 378

Tabernacle, 181

Tages-Anzeiger (newspaper), 360, 378
Tallas, Gregg, 140
Teilhard de Chardin, Pierre, 278, 350
television in Greece, 315–16
tel-net (publisher), 387
Theodosiou, Damianos, 15, 353, 365–66
Theophilous (Greek captain), 270
Theosophy, 50, 56, 57, 138
Thich Nhat Hanh, 16
Third Programme (BBC), 296
Thirty-one New American Poets, 297
Thomas, Dylan, 14
Thomas Aquinas. See Aquinas, Saint Thomas
Three Windows (video), 6, 389
Thurber, James, 26, 104, 107
Tiananmen Square (1989), 98
Time-Life, 136–37
Tolstoy, Leo: The Kingdom of God Is within You, 24
Trappists, 111, 114, 118, 160, 172, 175–76
Trilling, Lionel, 37
Trombone Press, 379
True, Michael, 347
Turks vs. Greeks, 250–51, 263, 319, 330–31
Twenty-One (quiz show), 209–10
Two Contemporary Presses: An Exhibition of the Work of the Wild Hawthorn Press and the Journeyman Press, 332

Uebbing, James, 385
University of North Carolina, 129–30, 131, 135, 136
University Press of Kentucky, 17

van den Bergh, Gerhard, 379
Van Doren, Charlie, 186, 209–10
Van Doren, Mark: centennial commemoration of birth of, 380; Collected Poems, 1922–1938, 37; on Columbia University years of Lax, 29–30, 33; death of, 319; giving advice to Lax, 82; and Greece, 273; on Lax at Friendship House, 122; Lax correspondence with, 130, 151, 186, 210, 239, 245, 259, 273, 281, 283, 290, 291–92; Lax on teaching prowess of, 37–38; Merton giving his poetry to, 133; Pax writings, 199;

reading and reviewing Lax's writing, 76–77, 104, 148, 205, 273, 289; as reference for Lax's Guggenheim application, 297; visit to Lax in Corps seminary, 193; on woe of Lax, 15

Vanier, Jean, 186, 379

Vecchio, Patrick, 373

Victoria and Albert Museum (London), 327, 332

*Voyages* (literary journal), 205, 288, 290, 297, 298

Weigner, Fritz, 194, 318

Weigner, Gladys, 194, 201, 317–19, 330, 347

*When Prophecy Still Had a Voice* (Biddle, ed.), 17

White, E. B., 26, 89–90, 104–5

White, Katherine, 89–90, 104–5

Whitman, Walt, 97, 124

Wild Hawthorn Press, 276, 332, 363

Wilkes, Paul: *Merton By Those Who Knew Him Best,* 14, 356, 364

Williams, C. K., 320, 352

Williams, Emmett, 275, 355, 360

Wittgenstein, Ludwig, 302–3, 309, 376

Wolcott, Alexander, 141–42

women and sex, 32, 67, 171

World Congress of Religions, 39

World Exposition (Paris 1937), 34

World's Fair (NYC 1939), 73

World War II and draft board, 85–86, 96–97, 99, 107, 119–22

writing process, 303, 348

writing style, 11, 17–18, 19–20, 29; abstract poetry, 221, 286; color poems, 285, 310–11, 350; concrete poetry, 221, 243, 275, 289, 307, 354; evolution of, 213, 223, 288; hash marks to break lines, 230; horizontal style, 297; Joyce's influence, 74–75; Kerouac's influence, 213–18, 248; little, common words, use of, 134; minimalism, 222–23, 275, 305, 347; pure poetry, 120; repetition, 373–74; and rhythm, 287; Van Doren's influence, 37–38; vertical style, 58, 115–16, 213, 230, 275, 287, 308

xenophobia, 258, 279, 281, 300–301, 319

Xiliamodi (Greek island), 280, 379

Yagga (housemaid), 44

Yagoda, Ben: *About Town: The New Yorker and the World It Made,* 107

Yanni (Greek friend), 334, 342

Zahn, Gordon, 240

Zurbrugg, Nicholas, 275, 297, 347, 361; *Art, Performance, Media: 31 Interviews,* 361

Zurich, 194–95, 244, 317, 318, 330, 333, 345, 354, 355, 358, 366, 367, 371, 375, 379, 384

# Acknowledgments

My deepest thanks to all who aided and sustained me during the many years I worked on this book. To the staff and my fellow scholars at the Collegeville Institute for encouragement and friendship during my months in residency there, especially Don Ottenhoff and Carla Durand. To Portland State University for financial support and time away from teaching. To Oregon Literary Arts for the Leslie Bradshaw Fellowship. To *Image*, *Portland Magazine* and *Poets & Writers* for publishing parts of this book in different form. To the Merton Legacy Trust and Houghton Mifflin Harcourt for permission to quote from Thomas Merton's writings. To Marcia Kelly for too many graces to name, starting long before I considered writing about her uncle. To Connie Brothers, Jack Kelly, Dick Marcus, and particularly Soni Holman Fink for hours of informative and enjoyable conversation as well as the warmest hospitality. To Paul Spaeth and the staff at St. Bonaventure University's Friedsam Library for helping me in countless ways. To the staff of the Columbia Rare Book and Manuscript Library for both in-person and remote assistance (including all of those photocopies!). To Paul Pearson at the Merton Center at Bellarmine University for a prompt and courteous response to every question. To Judy Emery and Nancy Goldring for enthusiasm through the years. To the International Thomas Merton Society, Professor Lauren Matz, and the English and Visiting Writers Programs at St. Bonaventure University for opportunities to test (and correct) my writing in front of knowledgeable audiences. To Angela Alaimo O'Donnell for championing my work at Fordham University Press. To Fred Nachbaur, Will Cerbone, and the rest of the Press's staff for taking things from there. To the many I met on Patmos who helped me discover facets of Lax's personality and story—especially Gary, Eva, Ulf, Don, Steve, John, Dave, Linda, Niko, Ritsa, Katina, and Pandelis. To the people of Greece who welcomed me, tested me, and taught me so many things I needed to know. To all who so affably sat with me for interviews or answered questions by phone, letter, or email. To the students who helped me see writing and the art of biography more clearly. To Gene Openshaw and Mel Conner for years of companionship as fellow miners of light. To Mr. Moak for giving me faith in the future. And to Sylvia, who has made it all possible—and worthwhile.

CATHOLIC PRACTICE IN NORTH AMERICA

SERIES CO-EDITORS

Angela Alaimo O'Donnell, Associate Director of the Francis and Ann
    Curran Center for American Catholic Studies, Fordham
    University
John C. Seitz, Assistant Professor, Theology Department, Fordham University

James T. Fisher and Margaret M. McGuinness (eds.), *The Catholic Studies Reader*
Jeremy Bonner, Christopher D. Denny, and Mary Beth Fraser Connolly (eds.),
    *Empowering the People of God: Catholic Action before and after Vatican II*
Christine Firer Hinze and J. Patrick Hornbeck II (eds.), *More than a Monologue: Sexual
    Diversity and the Catholic Church. Volume I: Voices of Our Times*
J. Patrick Hornbeck II and Michael A. Norko (eds.), *More than a Monologue: Sexual
    Diversity and the Catholic Church. Volume II: Inquiry, Thought, and Expression*
Jack Lee Downey, *The Bread of the Strong: Lacouturisme and the Folly of the Cross,
    1910–1985*
Mary Dunn, *The Cruelest of All Mothers: Marie de l'Incarnation, Motherhood, and
    Christian Tradition*
Michael N. McGregor, *Pure Act: The Uncommon Life of Robert Lax*